THE BIBLE IN EARLY TRANSATLANTIC
PIETISM AND EVANGELICALISM

 PIETIST, MORAVIAN, AND ANABAPTIST STUDIES

EDITOR

Craig D. Atwood
Director of the Center for Moravian Studies, Moravian Seminary

Volumes in the Pietist, Moravian, and Anabaptist Studies Series take multidisciplinary approaches to the history and theology of these groups and their religious and cultural influence around the globe. The series seeks to enrich the dynamic international study of post-Reformation Protestantism through original works of scholarship.

ADVISORY BOARD

Bill Leonard, *Wake Forest University*
Katherine Faull, *Bucknell University*
A. G. Roeber, *Penn State University*
Jonathan Strom, *Emory University*
Rachel Wheeler, *Indiana University–Purdue University Indianapolis*

EDITED BY RYAN P. HOSELTON,
JAN STIEVERMANN, DOUGLAS A.
SWEENEY, MICHAEL A. G. HAYKIN

THE BIBLE IN EARLY TRANSATLANTIC PIETISM AND EVANGELICALISM

The Pennsylvania State University Press
University Park, Pennsylvania

Library of Congress Cataloging-in-Publication Data

Names: Hoselton, Ryan P. (Ryan Patrick), 1987– editor. | Stievermann, Jan, editor. | Sweeney, Douglas A., editor. | Haykin, Michael A. G., editor.
Title: The Bible in early transatlantic Pietism and Evangelicalism / edited by Ryan P. Hoselton, Jan Stievermann, Douglas A. Sweeney, Michael A. G. Haykin.
Other titles: Pietist, Moravian, and Anabaptist studies.
Description: University Park, Pennsylvania : The Pennsylvania State University Press, [2022] | Series: Pietist, Moravian, and Anabaptist studies | Includes bibliographical references and index.
Summary: "A collection of essays exploring the variety and complexity of biblical interpretation and practice among early awakened Protestants, providing insight into the history of the Bible and the entangled religious cultures of the eighteenth-century North Atlantic world"—Provided by publisher.
Identifiers: LCCN 2022005959 | ISBN 9780271092867 (pb)
Subjects: LCSH: Evangelicalism—Europe—History—18th century. | Evangelicalism—North America—History—18th century. | Pietism—Europe—History—18th century. | Pietism—North America—History—18th century. | Bible—Criticism, interpretation, etc.—History—18th century. | Bible—Commentaries—History and criticism. | LCGFT: Essays.
Classification: LCC BR1640 .B49 2022 | DDC 270.8/2—dc23/eng/20220329
LC record available at https://lccn.loc.gov/2022005959

Copyright © 2022 The Pennsylvania State University Press
All rights reserved
Printed in the United States of America
Published by The Pennsylvania State University Press,
University Park, PA 16802–1003

The Pennsylvania State University Press is a member of the Association of University Presses.

It is the policy of The Pennsylvania State University Press to use acid-free paper. Publications on uncoated stock satisfy the minimum requirements of American National Standard for Information Sciences—Permanence of Paper for Printed Library Material, ANSI Z39.48–1992.

CONTENTS

Acknowledgments vii
List of Abbreviations ix

Introduction 1
RYAN P. HOSELTON

Part 1 Commentators and Commentaries

1 Bible Editions, Translations, and Commentaries
   in German Pietism 17
   DOUGLAS H. SHANTZ

2 Biblical Aids, Editions, Translations, and Commentaries
   by Dissenters, Methodists, and Church of England
   Evangelicals in Eighteenth-Century England 36
   ISABEL RIVERS

Part 2 Historical Trajectories and Transitions

3 Early Modern Dutch Reformed Exegesis and Its
   Pietist-Evangelical Reception 55
   ADRIAAN C. NEELE

4 Reading the Bible: John Owen and Early
   Evangelical "Biblicism" 73
   CRAWFORD GRIBBEN

5 Bible Politics and Early Evangelicalism:
   Scriptural Submission and Resistance
   in Nonconformist Commentary 91
   ROBERT E. BROWN

6 The Bible in Early Pietist and Evangelical Missions 109
   RYAN P. HOSELTON

Part 3 Interpretive Approaches, Issues, and Debates

7 The Evangelical Supernatural in Early Modern British Protestantism: Cotton Mather and Jonathan Edwards on the Miracles of Jesus 131
DOUGLAS A. SWEENEY

8 Lay Appropriations and Female Interpretations of the Bible in German Pietism 148
RUTH ALBRECHT

9 "My Beloved Is White and Ruddy": Particular Baptist Readings of the Song of Songs in the Long Eighteenth Century 166
MICHAEL A. G. HAYKIN

10 Cotton Mather, Jonathan Edwards, and the Relationship Between Historical and Spiritual Exegesis in Early Evangelicalism 182
KENNETH P. MINKEMA

11 Reading Revelation and Revelatory Readings in Early Awakened Protestantism: A Transatlantic Comparison 200
JAN STIEVERMANN

Part 4 The Bible and Lived Religion

12 "At Any Price Give Me the Book of God!": Devotional Intent and Bible Reading for the Early Evangelicals 223
BRUCE HINDMARSH

13 Spirit of the Word: Scripture in the Lives of Evangelical and Moravian Women in the New World, 1730–1830 242
BENJAMIN M. PIETRENKA AND MARILYN J. WESTERKAMP

14 Moravians and the Bible in the Atlantic World: The Case of the Daily Watchwords in Bethlehem, PA, 1742–1745 261
PETER VOGT

Conclusion 280
DOUGLAS A. SWEENEY, JAN STIEVERMANN, AND RYAN P. HOSELTON

List of Contributors 285
Index of Scripture 289
General Index 293

ACKNOWLEDGMENTS

Some of the chapters in this volume have their origin in contributions to a conference held in September 2018 at the Southern Baptist Theological Seminary in Louisville, Kentucky. The conference was co-organized by the Andrew Fuller Center for Baptist Studies at Southern Seminary and the Jonathan Edwards Center Germany at Heidelberg University. We want to thank both of these institutions for their support, and the Fuller Center and its director, Michael Haykin, for their gracious hospitality. The other chapters were commissioned to further develop the comparative perspective of the volume. We are very grateful to both groups of authors for their hard work, expertise, and excellent contributions.

We would also like to thank Craig Atwood, who gave his enthusiastic support for including this volume in the Pietist, Moravian, and Anabaptist Studies series with Penn State University Press, and to Kathryn Yahner for guiding the editorial process with professionalism and attentiveness. The anonymous readers also deserve our gratitude for their positive and constructive feedback. Many thanks to Layla Koch for assistance with the translation of chapter 8, and to Samuel Hagos and Colby Brandt for compiling the index. Finally, we wish to thank our families for their love and companionship.

ABBREVIATIONS

BA   Cotton Mather. *Biblia Americana*. Edited by Reiner Smolinski et al.
          Vols. 1-5, 9. Tübingen: Mohr Siebeck, 2010-.
Biblia   Cotton Mather. "Biblia Americana" (holograph manuscript).
          6 vols. Folio. The Massachusetts Historical Society, Boston.
          The Papers of Cotton Mather. Part 1. Reels 10-13.
CH   *Church History*
GdP   *Geschichte des Pietismus*. Edited by Martin Brecht et al. 4 vols.
          Göttingen: Vandenhoeck & Ruprecht, 1993-2004.
JMH   *Journal of Moravian History*
KJV   King James Version
PRRD   Richard A. Muller, *Post-Reformation Reformed Dogmatics*. 4 vols.
          Grand Rapids: Baker Academic, 2003.
PuN   *Pietismus und Neuzeit: Ein Jahrbuch zur Geschichte des neueren
          Protestantismus*
WJE   Jonathan Edwards. *The Works of Jonathan Edwards*. 26 vols. New
          Haven: Yale University Press, 1957-2008.
WJEO   Jonathan Edwards. *The Works of Jonathan Edwards Online*.
          Jonathan Edwards Center, Yale University, New Haven.
          Online at http://edwards.yale.edu.
WMQ   *William and Mary Quarterly*

INTRODUCTION

RYAN P. HOSELTON

"What do we wish to become, my brothers and sisters?" asked Nikolaus Ludwig von Zinzendorf, the founder and leader of the Moravians: "Bibelfest."[1] This question absorbed Pietists and evangelicals throughout the early modern Atlantic world in their quest for true religion. Their yearning to obtain from the Word a spiritual knowledge of God that was at once experiential and practical greatly shaped the courses and legacies of their movements. The myriad ways they read, preached, interpreted, translated, and practiced the Bible are inextricable from how they pursued religious and social reform, fashioned new forms of devotion, founded new institutions, engaged the early Enlightenment, and made sense of their world. The essays in this collection showcase the prevalence, variety, and complexity of Pietist and early evangelical biblical practices in the context of the long eighteenth century. At the same time, they highlight the many parallels, networks, exchanges, and common impulses that connected these traditions on both sides of the Atlantic in their engagement with the Bible.

This book expands and bridges three vibrant areas of study: Pietism, early evangelicalism, and the history of the Bible.[2] Surprisingly enough, there is relatively little overlap between these scholarly fields. Most authors continue to approach Pietism and evangelicalism as separate phenomena, viewing the former chiefly through the lens of German church history or as an indirect forerunner to the Anglophone evangelical awakenings of the 1740s. Important interventions have challenged these perceptions, but many studies remain at the survey level or absorb one movement into the other and thus blur important distinctions.[3]

The recent historiographical turn to viewing the early modern Atlantic world as a shared context has opened up new vistas for historians of religion beyond ethnocentric or nation-centric church histories.[4] This lens can help us better perceive the interrelationship between Pietism and early evangelicalism since both movements took shape amidst widespread transatlantic religious and social transformations. In highlighting the many affinities, however, it is also important not to diminish the national, cultural, ethnic, regional, confessional, and ecclesial diversity both between and within the movements.

Pietism emerged in the late seventeenth century as a movement of Christian renewal in German-speaking lands.[5] Inspired by the writings of post-Reformation Protestants such as Johann Arndt, the Puritans, proponents of the *Nadere Reformatie*, and various esoteric traditions, Pietists pursued widespread reform of church and society by promoting spiritual rebirth, personal experiential piety, biblicism over theological dogmatism, greater lay participation, small-group conventicles for Bible study and Christian fellowship, charitable activism, and zeal for the millennial kingdom—an agenda outlined most famously in Philip Jakob Spener's influential manifesto *Pia Desideria* (1675). From the beginning, the movement encompassed Reformed and Lutheran Pietists, "churchly" Pietists working within the established churches and creedal traditions yet also separatists who found these churches too corrupt and the traditions too restricting, and various mystical and chiliastic teachings. It also contained diverse regional cultures with hotspots throughout the Holy Roman Empire, other parts of Europe (esp. the Netherlands, Switzerland, Scandinavia, the Baltic, and various parts of Britain), and European colonies abroad (esp. British North America, the Caribbean, and southeast India). The missions-minded and nomadic Moravians were especially ubiquitous. This branch of Pietism formed in the 1720s when descendants of the *Unitas Fratrum* (mostly from Moravia) arrived as refugees on the estate of the Halle-educated Count Zinzendorf and founded the Herrnhut settlement near Berthelsdorf. After the settlers experienced a communal revival, Zinzendorf became the patron of the renewed Brethren and transformed them into a global missionary force committed to spreading the joyful message of instant salvation and sensible assurance flowing from the "blood and wounds" of Christ.[6]

Many trace the origins of the evangelical movement to the revivals of the 1730s and 1740s in Britain and its North American colonies, though W. R. Ward has made a strong case for widening the scope and dating it back to the 1670s to include European Pietist roots.[7] Definitional and genealogical complexities aside, numerous Anglophone Protestants networked and collaborated with awakened Protestants in continental Europe and promoted similar means of reform and pious renewal in the late seventeenth and early eighteenth centuries. These efforts reached a peak in the 1730s and 1740s when spiritual awakenings erupted throughout the British Empire. Revival-minded ministers and itinerants promoted the new birth and experiential piety with a heightened fervor, confident that they were partaking in a unified and extraordinary work of the Spirit in anticipation of the millennial kingdom. However, like Pietism, the evangelical movement contained significant diversity. It included those within the respective established churches (i.e., members of the Church of England, Church of Scotland Presbyterians, and New England Congregationalists) as well as Dissenters; various theological traditions (Calvinist and Arminian, diverse ecclesiologies, liturgies, sacramental practices, etc.); moderates who advocated a more "orderly" and clergy-led revivalism as opposed to the "enthusiasm" and separatism of radical evangelicals; and various ethnonational and regional cultures (English, Welsh, Scottish, Scots-Irish, colonials, Blacks, and Native Americans). Two particularly influential evangelical networks and trajectories emerged in the 1740s. One was international Calvinism, which linked evangelicals who embraced the doctrine of predestination together in transdenominational collaborations and global exchanges. The other was the Methodist movement, which arose in the late 1730s within the Church of England and initially encompassed Calvinist and Arminian wings, associated respectively with George Whitefield and John Wesley. The Methodists pioneered innovative revival practices such as open-air preaching, itinerancy, and religious societies. By the late eighteenth century the first Methodist churches in America were founded, the Wesleyan Methodists had separated from the Church of England, and the Welsh Calvinistic Methodists were soon to separate from the Anglican Church in Wales.[8]

While key differences between early German-speaking Pietism and Anglophone evangelicalism existed and persisted, the relationship went much deeper than parallel characteristics and sporadic points of contact. The movements became closely intertwined in the wider contexts of eighteenth-century transatlantic migration, revivals, missions, new media and print exchanges, intellectual transformations of the early Enlightenment, and political developments. Pietists and evangelicals shared a common Protestant Reformation heritage, a zeal to complete the Reformation in doctrine with a reformation in practice, close interaction with Enlightenment-era philosophies, a vitalistic cosmology manifested in a heightened experimental occupation with pneumatology and apocalypticism, and common sources of piety such as the *devotio moderna*, Puritan practical divinity, Christian mysticism, and even esoteric traditions such as Paracelsianism, hermeticism, and Christian Kabbalism.[9] Their shared concerns and collaborations contributed to the construction of a new "Protestant international" religious identity around the turn of the eighteenth century through their efforts to advance the "Protestant interest" against Catholic powers, revitalize the Protestant world, and expand Christian missions abroad. In the process, they became less invested in projects of confessionalization and instead came to promote a more ecumenically minded, doctrinally minimalistic, Christocentric, new birth–oriented, biblicist, and experiential religion as the basis for true global Christianity.[10] Pietists and early evangelicals perceived these marks of true Christianity in each other and saw themselves as participants in the same redemptive work of the Spirit to advance the kingdom of God in the world. The Bible was central in all of these respects. Thus, by examining their biblical practices side by side, this volume contributes valuable texture to our understanding of Pietism's and evangelicalism's entangled religious cultures and histories.

Scholars of Pietism have long recognized the importance of the Bible to the movement,[11] and scholars of evangelicalism regularly identify "biblicism," or a high view of Scripture's authority, as one of its core pillars.[12] Despite this fact, there have been few detailed studies of the Bible in early evangelicalism, and little attempt has been made to draw connections with Pietist biblical practices. Moreover, most histories of biblical interpretation have given meager attention to the contributions of early evangelicals (Pietism has fared slightly better), thus overlooking the emergence of their unique ways of engaging with Scripture, which have influenced millions around the world over the past three centuries.[13] Typically these works have also disregarded British North America, perhaps due in part to a prevalent misconception that colonial American engagement in European intellectual currents and Enlightenment discourses was predominantly political (culminating in the Revolution) rather than religious. The new interest in the exegesis of colonial American evangelicals such as Cotton Mather and Jonathan Edwards has helped reverse these trends. The recent critical editions of Mather's massive yet heretofore unpublished Bible commentary, the "Biblia Americana," and the editions of Edwards's exegetical notebooks have facilitated pioneering studies, yielding fresh insights into their life, thought, and times.[14] One important contribution of this collection is to set the exegesis of awakened colonial Protestants such as Mather, Edwards, and others in transatlantic perspective and thereby underscore early America's participation and embeddedness in wider currents of early modern European religion and ideas.

The essays in this volume examine the diverse biblical practices of a wide range of late seventeenth- and eighteenth-century awakened Protestants from various confessional, linguistic, national, and regional traditions. They include awakened Lutherans, Reformed, Moravians, Anglicans, Presbyterians, Congregationalists, Baptists, and Methodists. Readers will encounter familiar names such as the German Pietists Philip Jakob Spener, August Hermann Francke, Anton Wilhelm Böhme, Bartholomäus Ziegenbalg, and Johann Albrecht Bengel; the Dutch Reformed Johannes Cocceius and Theodorus Jacobus Frelinghuysen; English evangelicals Philip Doddridge, John and Charles Wesley, George Whitefield, John Newton, and Andrew Fuller; and colonial American evangelicals such as Cotton Mather, Jonathan Edwards, and David Brainerd. These names represent well-known, educated, European male leaders categorized often in the literature as "churchly" or "moderate" as opposed to "radical"—though these designations are sometimes contested and blurry.[15] Expanding beyond this traditional frame, the volume also features lay believers, women such as Anne Dutton and Hannah Heaton, Africans such as Rebecca Protten and Native Americans such as Samson Occom, and proponents of the more "radical" wings, including immigrant Moravian communities and separatist Pietists such as Heinrich Horch and Johanna Eleonora Petersen. Furthermore, in order to reflect the variety of their engagement with the Bible, the chapters explore an assortment of primary source material, from major exegetical commentaries and theological writings to sermons, private notebooks, letters, and diaries. Some essays examine Pietists and evangelicals together, while others lay greater focus on one or the other. As a whole, they provide a broad profile of the Bible in transatlantic Pietism and evangelicalism, covering issues pertinent to both movements, such as reception history, spiritual interpretation, biblical scholarship, experiential authority, history of redemption, missions, gender, politics, piety, apocalypticism, and more.

There are four thematic parts to this volume. Part 1, "Commentators and Commentaries," introduces leading Pietist and evangelical biblical interpreters and their works. In chapter 1, Douglas Shantz surveys three forms of exegetical writings from German Pietists and Moravians: popular manuals for lay Bible reading, translations and editions, as well as commentaries. By blending new experiential pieties with the scholarly techniques and media of the early Enlightenment era, Shantz argues, Pietists adapted to shifting modern conditions with significant implications for how they engaged the Bible. In chapter 2, Isabel Rivers examines analogous forms of publications from English evangelicals. Similar to the work of the Pietist Canstein *Bibelanstalt* in Halle, English evangelicals amplified their labors over the eighteenth century to expand access to Holy Writ by producing and distributing Bibles. A flood of practical reading aids and meditative tracts accompanied this endeavor, such as *A Spiritual Treasury, for the Children of God*, an English translation of a work by the Halle Pietist author Karl Heinrich von Bogatzky. Finally, evangelicals produced widely read annotated Bibles and commentaries. Like many Pietist commentaries, notes Rivers, these works "were explicitly aimed at lay readers and encouraged their active participation in interpreting the text." It is no wonder, therefore, that the Pietist Friedrich Eberhard Rambach translated Doddridge's lengthy commentary into German.

Pietists and evangelicals not only produced and exchanged similar print material on the Bible, they also partook in overlapping "Historical Trajectories and Transitions" in the early modern Atlantic world—the theme of part 2. In chapter 3, Adriaan Neele shows how "the appreciation of piety or *praxis pietatis*" linked leading seventeenth-century Dutch Reformed exegetes of the *Nadere Reformatie* with Puritans, Pietists, and evangelicals of various stripes across the north Atlantic and beyond (including Africa, Asia, and South America). After surveying major works and themes of early modern Dutch Reformed exegesis, Neele traces both continuities and significant contextual adaptations in its Pietist and evangelical reception—including changes in theological meanings and polemical applications in the context of revivals. In chapter 4, Crawford Gribben traces the historical trajectory of "biblicist" tendencies from seventeenth-century Puritanism to eighteenth-century evangelicalism via a case study on John Owen's scriptural practices and reception. Owen relied heavily on learning and operated within his confessional and exegetical tradition, yet he also nurtured a somewhat countervailing approach that emphasized the need for simple reading, liberty of conscience, and personal dependence on the Spirit to discover the Bible's meaning. While Owen's latter orientation anticipated individualist and subjectivist biblical practices among early evangelicals, many surrendered the same degree of deference to traditions and interpretive communities—a shift that swayed the evangelical movement in new democratic and populist directions.

In chapter 5, Robert Brown investigates a key moment in the transition from seventeenth-century state-church establishment paradigms to the rising demand for freedom of religion and conscience among eighteenth-century evangelicals. Operating in new conditions of the Restoration and the revoked Massachusetts charter, marginalized nonconformists such as Richard Baxter in England and Cotton Mather in New England revisited the Bible's teachings on the relationship between Christianity and politics—especially Rom 13. Drawing on rights of conscience theory in their Calvinist tradition and on Enlightenment thinkers, notably John Locke, their interpretation of these passages anticipated later evangelical political theory by laying greater weight on individual rights and religious liberty and the proper place for political submission and resistance. In chapter 6, Ryan Hoselton demonstrates how the rise of Pietist and evangelical missions was closely intertwined with shifts in their biblical practices—developments that helped lay the foundation for the modern missionary movement and the globalization of Protestant

Christianity over the past three centuries. Joined together through transatlantic missionary networks, print exchanges, and theological constructions of an imagined global Protestant community, Pietist and evangelical conceptions of their role in the Bible's sacred redemptive history enkindled a common missionary activism to fulfill Christ's Great Commission in preparation for his imminent Second Coming. Furthermore, their heightened emphasis on the Word as the Spirit's chief means of renewal and redemption engendered more active measures to propagate the Word in the world through preaching, Bible translation and distribution, and education. Finally, innovations in piety greatly shaped their missionary methods on the ground as they labored to instill an experiential and Christocentric knowledge of the Word among non-Christian populations.

The five chapters in part 3 explore "Interpretive Approaches, Issues, and Debates." Whether addressing challenges to traditional beliefs or emboldened by new conceptions of lay and experiential interpretive authority, Pietists and evangelicals engaged the Word with confidence in its truthfulness, its sacredness, and the Spirit's illumination to understand it. A number of scholars have argued that eighteenth-century Protestant apologists of Scripture inadvertently contributed to secularization by adopting the rationalist and empirical paradigms of the Bible's critics. In chapter 7, however, Douglas Sweeney finds this assessment uneven and urges a fuller consideration of the "resilience of their modern supernaturalism." As he demonstrates in his study on Cotton Mather's and Jonathan Edwards's reading of Jesus's miracles, evangelicals no doubt utilized reason and evidence to defend the veracity of the Bible's accounts of supernatural phenomena. But they were far more invested in explicating and defending the reality of these miracles in order to engender vital faith in God's active presence in the world and Christ's work of spiritual renewal.

From the beginning, the Pietist movement combined an emphasis on the priesthood of all believers with the charge for every Christian to read and interpret the Bible. In chapter 8, Ruth Albrecht offers three illustrations of lay German Pietists—all steeped in transatlantic radical religious networks—who felt emboldened by this principle to interpret the Word in ways that bolstered their religious aims and challenged traditional stances and customs of Lutheran Orthodoxy. Her case studies examine the biblical primitivism of layman and separatist Johann Jakob Schütz, the biblical mysticism of Anna Catharina Scharschmidt, and the quasi-prophetic millennialism of Johanna Eleonora Petersen.

Chapters 9 and 10 illustrate how evangelicals approached perennial issues in the history of biblical interpretation—especially the proper domains and methods of allegorical, spiritual, and historical exegesis—in light of new challenges in their times. Christians through the centuries had interpreted the Song of Songs—an Old Testament marital poem about Solomon and his betrothed—as an allegory of the relationship between Christ and the church, but this view was increasingly challenged over the course of the eighteenth century as many questioned not only the merit of allegorical exegesis but also traditional beliefs based upon it. As Michael Haykin shows, this was a highly contested issue among English Baptists. The more evangelical-oriented Baptists, however, such as Joseph Stennett I, John Gill, Andrew Fuller, and Anne Dutton, championed an allegorical reading in continuity with the early church fathers and Puritans. When they read Song 5:10, "My beloved is white and ruddy," in contrast to the rising rationalist and historicizing exegetical approaches of their age, they perceived the beauty and divinity of Jesus Christ. In chapter 10, Kenneth Minkema brings us again to the other side of the Atlantic in his study of Cotton Mather's and Jonathan Edwards's approaches to the relationship between historical and spiritual exegesis. He compares their interpretations of four historical accounts in the Old Testament: the sun standing still in Josh 10, Jephthah's vow in Judg 11, and the books of Ruth and Esther. Letting the primary sources speak for themselves, these vignettes give rise to a variety of insights into the exegetical methods and interests of early evangelicals. While Mather and Edwards evinced differences in style and emphasis, both availed themselves of the fruits of the new learning to elucidate these texts, leaned on exegetical tradition and learning, drew from eclectic and even esoteric sources, employed reasoned arguments and scholarship to defend the historicity of the accounts, gleaned devotional reflections to spur experiential religion and application, and cast the stories in the wider framework of redemptive history.

The interplay between exegesis, experientialism, and reliance on the Spirit gave rise to unique tensions in Pietism and evangelicalism. As Jan Stievermann demonstrates in chapter 11, a spiritualistic tendency led many Pietist and evangelical exegetes to blur the "line between reading with the Spirit and having quasi-revelatory experiences that were usually rooted in Scripture but transcended it," especially when reading the Bible's apocalyptic books. Yet there was a wide spectrum in how far they were willing to go when determining matters such as the timing of Christ's return, the nature of the millennial kingdom, or the restoration of prophetic and charismatic gifts as promised in Joel 2:28. Some were curious but more guarded, while others pushed canonical boundaries and advertently or inadvertently engaged in prophetic discourses and bred new revelations.

The history of the Bible in Pietism and evangelicalism consisted not only of major texts, transformative ideas, turning points, institutions, and influential characters, but also the everyday lived religion of believers. Thus, the three essays in the final part, "The Bible and Lived Religion," are devoted to how Pietists and evangelicals practiced the Bible. In chapter 12, Bruce Hindmarsh probes the devotional habits of evangelicals. Hans Frei and others have influentially argued that the eighteenth century witnessed a loss of biblical realism as readers sought to fit the Bible into the modern world rather than fit their world into the narrative of the Bible. For Hindmarsh, the devotional practices of evangelicals challenge this claim and show that modern conditions had not eradicated vital biblical religion. Building upon Pietist antecedents, evangelical leaders and lay believers alike sought to assimilate their lives to Scripture's narrative framework. By means of what Hindmarsh calls "evangelical figuration," they labored to personalize the Bible's salvation history, participate as characters in its narratives, and adopt its language as one's own.

As Benjamin Pietrenka and Marilyn Westerkamp display in chapter 13 with a treasure of primary source material from an array of Moravians and evangelicals, women experienced and practiced the Bible differently from men. Denied the same privileges of education and social status, women approached the Word with their gendered experiences of pregnancy and birth, housewifery, motherhood, daughterhood and sisterhood, caregiving, female missions and exhortation, sexual abuse, widowhood, friendships, and enslavement and racialized oppression. Generally, their Bible reading focused less on grasping doctrinal complexities and more on their experiences. While many contented themselves with traditional gender roles, others felt empowered by the Spirit and the Word to follow their true calling to preach and lead. In the final chapter, Peter Vogt details a communal practice of reading Scripture that linked the Moravians in Bethlehem, Pennsylvania, with believers around the world. When these Moravians immigrated in the early 1740s, they brought a unique tradition that Zinzendorf called the *Losungen*, or "watchwords" (still used to this day). The *Losungen* contain a Bible passage for each day of the year designed to order and spur the global Moravian community's meditation and worship, "offering to them, as it were, a running divine commentary on the earthly realities that they encountered." Vogt examines how the *Losungen* were chosen, distributed, and devotionally practiced, and how these daily words of Scripture became meaningfully interwoven in the everyday lives of individuals and the community.

The portrait that emerges from these focused studies on the Bible in Pietism and evangelicalism is one of vitality and versatility yet also tensions and paradoxes. Pietists and evangelicals sought to learn from and uphold their Protestant exegetical tradition, yet they also employed the Bible to revive and transform that heritage. They utilized reason and empirical-evidentialist frameworks to defend the Bible's historicity and truthfulness against skeptics, yet they ultimately looked to the inner testimony of the Spirit for unassailable certainty in the Bible's authority and divine origin. They readily availed themselves of the latest intellectual developments in experimental philosophy, philology, and history to elucidate Holy Writ, yet they emphasized the need for experiential knowledge of the Word from the Spirit in order to attain a true spiritual understanding. Practitioners stressed the importance of simple and plain Bible reading while also zealously searching for spiritual mysteries and apocalyptic hints hidden beneath the surface. They applied the Word to liberate souls from the bondage of sin, unshackle true religion from the manmade traditions and hierarchies of Christendom, and unyoke civil rights and freedom of conscience from political tyranny; however, not until the Protestant antislavery movement arose in the 1770s was there a concerted effort to apply Scripture to liberate their colonized neighbors from enslavement, dispossession, and social inequity. Their emphasis on the priesthood of all believers and personally experiencing the Spirit's new birth and indwelling light empowered the marginalized and united true Christians across denominations—yet it also emboldened individuals to employ Scripture in ways that divided and damaged long-standing communities. In sum, their biblical practices were complex. Daily they read, heard, and meditated on the Word in search of truth, assurance, comfort, and wisdom for their relationships and values. Ultimately, they sought to encounter the triune God. Whether writing lengthy Bible commentaries or letters to friends, sitting at the table with family or traveling to distant lands on mission, advising magistrates or instructing orphans, Pietists and evangelicals expended extensive energy and resources to understand, apply, and propagate the Word.

Notes

I would like to thank my fellow editors and Isabel Rivers for their invaluable feedback on this introduction. Unless otherwise noted or unless quoted from another source, all Bible references in this volume are from the King James Version (KJV).

1. *Bibelfest* means to be well-versed in the Bible. Nikolaus Ludwig von Zinzendorf, *Vier und Dreyßig homiliae über die Wunden=Litaney der Brüder, Gehalten auf dem Herrnhaag in den Sommer=Monathen 1747 von dem Ordinario Fratrum* (n.p., 1747), 147.

2. For the history of the Bible, see esp. Nathan O. Hatch and Mark A. Noll, eds., *The Bible in America: Essays in Cultural History* (New York: Oxford University Press, 1982); Paul C. Gutjahr, *An American Bible: History of the Good Book in the United States, 1777–1880* (Stanford: Stanford University Press, 1999); Gutjahr, ed., *The Oxford Handbook of the Bible in America* (New York: Oxford University Press, 2017); Peter Harrison, *The Bible, Protestantism, and the Rise of Natural Science* (Cambridge: Cambridge University Press, 1998); Ian Green, *Print and Protestantism in Early Modern England* (New York: Oxford University Press, 2000), chaps. 2–3;

Lisa Gordis, *Opening Scripture: Bible Reading and Interpretive Authority in Puritan New England* (Chicago: University of Chicago Press, 2003); Jonathan Sheehan, *The Enlightenment Bible: Translation, Scholarship, Culture* (Princeton: Princeton University Press, 2007); Constance M. Furey et al., eds., *Encyclopedia of the Bible and Its Reception* (Berlin: De Gruyter, 2009–); Scott Mandelbrote and Michael Ledger-Lomas, eds., *Dissent and the Bible in Britain, c. 1650–1950* (New York: Oxford University Press, 2013); James P. Byrd, *Sacred Scripture, Sacred War: The Bible and the American Revolution* (New York: Oxford University Press, 2013); James Carlton Paget et al., *The New Cambridge History of the Bible*, 4 vols. (Cambridge: Cambridge University Press, 2012–16); Kevin Killeen, Helen Smith, and Rachel Willie, eds., *The Oxford Handbook of the Bible in Early Modern England, c. 1530–1700* (Oxford: Oxford University Press, 2015); Mark A. Noll, *In the Beginning Was the Word: The Bible in American Public Life, 1492–1783* (New York: Oxford University Press, 2015); John Fea, *The Bible Cause: A History of the American Bible Society* (New York: Oxford University Press, 2016); Philip Goff, Arthur E. Farnsley II, and Peter J. Thuesen, eds., *The Bible in American Life* (New York: Oxford University Press, 2017); and Seth Perry, *Bible Culture and Authority in the Early United States* (Princeton: Princeton University Press, 2018).

3. See F. Ernest Stoeffler, ed., *Continental Pietism and Early American Christianity* (Grand Rapids, MI: Eerdmans, 1976); Geoffrey F. Nuttall, "Continental Pietism and the Evangelical Movement in Britain," in *Pietismus und Reveil*, ed. J. Van den Berg and J. P. Van Dooren (Leiden: Brill, 1978), 207–36; J. Steven O'Malley, "Pietistic Influence on John Wesley: Wesley and Gerhard Tersteegen," *Wesleyan Theological Journal* 31 (1996): 48–70; Jonathan Strom, Hartmut Lehmann, and James Van Horm Melton, eds., *Pietism in Germany and North America, 1680–1820* (Burlington, VT: Ashgate, 2009); Oliver Scheiding, "The World as Parish: Cotton Mather, August Hermann Francke, and Transatlantic Religious Networks," in *Cotton Mather and Biblia Americana—America's First Bible Commentary: Essays in Reappraisal*, ed. Reiner Smolinski and Jan Stievermann (Grand Rapids, MI: Baker, 2011), 131–66; Scott Kisker, "Pietist Connections with English Anglicans and Evangelicals," in *A Companion to German Pietism, 1660–1800*, ed. Douglas H. Shantz (Leiden: Brill, 2015), 225–55; and J. Steven O'Malley, "Pietism and Transatlantic Revivals," in Shantz, *Companion to German Pietism*, 256–89.

For examples of otherwise excellent studies that bring Pietism under the label of evangelicalism, see W. R. Ward, *The Protestant Evangelical Awakening* (Cambridge: Cambridge University Press, 1992); Ward, *Early Evangelicalism: A Global Intellectual History, 1670–1789* (New York: Cambridge University Press, 2006). Conversely, in following a definitional approach to Pietism based primarily on characteristics and propensities (as opposed to regional or ecclesial identities), the pioneering four-volume *GdP* subsumes Puritanism, the *Nadere Reformatie*, and evangelicalism under Pietism.

For a recent assessment of the historiography on early Pietist and evangelical connections, and a case for an "entangled histories approach," see Jan Stievermann, "German Lutheran and Reformed Protestants," in *The Oxford Handbook of Early Evangelicalism*, ed. Jonathan Yeager (New York: Oxford University Press, forthcoming).

4. See, among others, Horst Pietschmann, ed., *Atlantic History: History of the Atlantic System, 1580–1830* (Göttingen: Vandenhoeck & Ruprecht, 2002); Bernard Bailyn, *Atlantic History: Concept and Contours* (Cambridge, MA: Harvard University Press, 2005); Bernard Bailyn and Patricia L. Denault, eds., *Soundings in Atlantic History: Latent Structures and Intellectual Currents, 1500–1830* (Cambridge, MA: Harvard University Press, 2009). For examples of religious histories in transatlantic perspective, see esp. the monograph series from Palgrave Macmillan, Christianities in the Trans-Atlantic World, edited by Crawford Gribben and Scott Spurlock.

5. Scholars disagree widely about the exact origins, features, and scope of Pietism. See esp. F. Ernest Stoeffler, *The Rise of Evangelical Pietism* (Leiden: Brill, 1965); the four-volume *GdP*; the yearly periodical *PuN*; Johannes Wallmann, *Der Pietismus* (Göttingen: Vandenhoeck & Ruprecht, 2005); Douglas H. Shantz, *An Introduction to German Pietism: Protestant Renewal at the Dawn*

of Modern Europe (Baltimore: Johns Hopkins University Press, 2013); and Wolfgang Breul and Thomas Hahn-Bruckart, eds., *Pietismus Handbuch* (Tübingen: Mohr Siebeck, 2021).

6. For Moravianism, see esp. Craig D. Atwood, *Community of the Cross: Moravian Piety in Colonial Bethlehem* (University Park: Penn State University Press, 2004); and Dietrich Meyer, *Zinzendorf und die Herrnhuter Brüdergemeine: 1700–2000* (Göttingen: Vandenhoeck & Ruprecht, 2009).

7. Ward, *Early Evangelicalism*, 1. For early evangelicalism in Britain and its colonies, see esp. D. W. Bebbington, *Evangelicalism in Modern Britain: A History from the 1730s to the 1980s* (Boston: Unwin Hyman, 1989); Michael J. Crawford, *Seasons of Grace: Colonial New England's Revival Tradition in Its British Context* (New York: Oxford University Press, 1991); Mark A. Noll, David. W. Bebbington, and George Rawlyk, eds., *Evangelicalism: Comparative Studies of Popular Protestantism in North America, the British Isles, and Beyond* (New York: Oxford University Press, 1994); Mark A. Noll, *The Rise of Evangelicalism: The Age of Edwards, Whitefield and the Wesleys* (Downers Grove, IL: InterVarsity Press, 2003); Thomas S. Kidd, *The Great Awakening: The Roots of Evangelical Christianity in Colonial America* (New Haven: Yale University Press, 2007); and D. Bruce Hindmarsh, *The Spirit of Early Evangelicalism: True Religion in a Modern World* (New York: Oxford University Press, 2018).

8. See esp. Richard P. Heitzenrater, *Wesley and the People Called Methodists* (Nashville: Abingdon Press, 1995); David Ceri Jones, *"A Glorious Work in the World": Welsh Methodism and the International Evangelical Revival, 1735–1750* (Cardiff: University of Wales Press, 2004); David Hempton, *Methodism: Empire of the Spirit* (New Haven: Yale University Press, 2005); Isabel Rivers, *Vanity Fair and the Celestial City: Dissenting, Methodist, and Evangelical Literary Culture in England, 1720–1800* (Oxford: Oxford University Press, 2018), 3–4.

9. See Ward, *Early Evangelicalism*, 6–23; Brett Malcolm Grainger, "Vital Nature and Vital Piety: Johann Arndt and the Evangelical Vitalism of Cotton Mather," *CH* 81, no. 4 (2012): 852–72.

10. See Thomas S. Kidd, *The Protestant Interest: New England After Puritanism* (New Haven: Yale University Press, 2004); Andrew C. Thompson, *Britain, Hanover and the Protestant Interest, 1688–1756* (Rochester, NY: Boydell, 2006); Mark A. Peterson, "Theopolis Americana: The City-State of Boston, the Republic of Letters, and the Protestant International, 1689–1739," in Bailyn and Denault, *Soundings in Atlantic History*, 329–70; A. G. Roeber, "The Waters of Rebirth: The Eighteenth Century and Transoceanic Protestant Christianity," *CH* 79, no. 1 (2010): 40–76; Edward E. Andrews, "Tranquebar: Charting the Protestant International in the British Atlantic and Beyond," *WMQ* 74, no. 1 (2017): 3–34; and Jan Stievermann, "A 'Syncretism of Piety': Imagining Global Protestantism in Early Eighteenth-Century Boston, Tranquebar, and Halle," *CH* 89 (2020): 829–56.

11. See among others Kurt Aland, ed., *Pietismus und Bibel* (Witten: Luther-Verlag, 1970); Martin Brecht, "Die Bedeutung der Bibel im deutschen Pietismus," in *GdP*, 4:102–20; Shantz, *Introduction to German Pietism*, 204–36; Johannes Wallmann, "Scriptural Understanding and Interpretation in Pietism," in *Hebrew Bible / Old Testament: The History of Its Interpretation*, vol. 2, *From the Renaissance to the Enlightenment*, ed. Magne Sæbø (Göttingen: Vandenhoeck & Ruprecht, 2008), 902–25; Fred van Lieburg, "Bible Reading and Pietism in the Dutch Reformed Tradition," in *Lay Bibles in Europe, 1450–1800*, ed. M. Lamberigts and A. A. den Hollander (Leuven: Leuven University Press, 2006), 223–44; and Susanne Luther, "Schriftverständnis im Pietismus," in Breul and Hahn-Bruckart, *Pietismus Handbuch*, 349–59; and Thomas Hahn-Bruckart, "Bibel," in Breul and Hahn-Bruckart, *Pietismus Handbuch*, 420–27.

12. Bebbington includes "biblicism" in his widely cited "quadrilateral" of evangelical identity, the other three pillars being crucicentrism, conversionism, and activism. Bebbington, *Evangelicalism in Modern Britain*, 2–17. Others who have offered a similar but modified version of Bebbington's quadrilateral also emphasize the Bible. See, among others, Kidd, *Great Awakening*, xiv; Timothy Larsen, "Defining and Locating Evangelicalism," in *The Cambridge Companion to Evangelical*

Theology, ed. Timothy Larsen and Daniel J. Treier (New York: Cambridge University Press, 2007), 1–14; and Mark A. Noll, "What Is 'Evangelical'?," in *The Oxford Handbook of Evangelical Theology*, ed. Gerald R. McDermott (New York: Oxford University Press, 2010), 19–33. See also the essays in Timothy Larsen, ed., *Every Leaf, Line, and Letter: Evangelicals and the Bible from the 1730s to the Present* (Downers Grove, IL: IVP Academic, 2021).

13. The following popular histories and readers of biblical interpretation embody the meager attention given to the early evangelical tradition: Henning Graf Reventlow, *Epochen der Bibelauslegung*, 4 vols. (Munich: C. H. Beck, 1990–2001); Gerald L. Bray, *Biblical Interpretation: Past and Present* (Downers Grove, IL: IVP Academic, 2000); Alan J. Hauser and Duane F. Watson, eds., *A History of Biblical Interpretation*, 4 vols. (Grand Rapids, MI: Eerdmans, 2003–); William Yarchin, *History of Biblical Interpretation: A Reader* (Grand Rapids, MI: Baker Academic, 2011); Darren Sarinski, *Theology, History, and Biblical Interpretation: Modern Readings* (London: Bloomsbury T&T Clark, 2015); Oda Wischmeyer, ed., *Handbuch der Bibelhermeneutiken* (Berlin: De Gruyter, 2016).

14. See Mather's *BA* (vols. 1–5 and 9 are already published, and the other four volumes are under contract) and Edwards's *WJE* 5 (*Apocalyptic Writings*), *WJE* 15 (*Notes on Scripture*), and *WJE* 24 (*The "Blank Bible"*).

Aside from the editorial introductions to the critical editions, see Smolinski and Stievermann, *Cotton Mather and "Biblia Americana"*; and Jan Stievermann, *Prophecy, Piety, and the Problem of Historicity: Interpreting the Hebrew Scriptures in Cotton Mather's "Biblia Americana,"* Beiträge zur historischen Theologie 179 (Tübingen: Mohr Siebeck, 2016). See also Reiner Smolinski, "Authority and Interpretation: Cotton Mather's Response to the European Spinozists," in *Shaping the Stuart World, 1603–1714: The Atlantic Connection*, ed. Allan I. Macinnes and Arthur H. Williamson (Leiden: Brill, 2006), 175–203; Smolinski, "How to Go to Heaven, or How Heaven Goes? Natural Science and Interpretation in Cotton Mather's 'Biblia Americana' (1693–1728)," *New England Quarterly* 81, no. 2 (2008): 278–329; Harry C. Maddux, "God's Responsibility: Narrative Choice and Providential History in Mather's *Biblia Americana* Commentary on Ezra," *Early American Literature* 42 (2007): 305–21; Jan Stievermann, "Reading Canticles in the Tradition of New England Millennialism: John Cotton and Cotton Mather's Commentaries on the Song of Songs," in *Prophecy and Eschatology in the Transatlantic World, 1550–1800*, ed. Andrew Crome (London: Palgrave Macmillan, 2016), 213–38; Stievermann, "The Debate over Prophetic Evidence for the Authority of the Bible in Cotton Mather's *Biblia Americana*," in Goff, Farnsley, and Thuesen, *Bible in American Life*, 48–62; and Grace Sarah Harwood, "'Perhaps No One General Answer Will Do': Cotton Mather's Commentary on the Synoptic Gospels in 'Biblia Americana'" (PhD diss., Georgia State University, 2018).

For Jonathan Edwards's exegesis, see esp. Stephen J. Stein, "The Quest for the Spiritual Sense: The Biblical Hermeneutics of Jonathan Edwards," *Harvard Theological Review* 70 (1977): 99–113; Robert E. Brown, *Jonathan Edwards and the Bible* (Bloomington: Indiana University Press, 2002); Stephen R. C. Nichols, *Jonathan Edwards' Bible: The Relationship of the Old and New Testaments* (Eugene, OR: Pickwick, 2013); David P. Barshinger, *Jonathan Edwards and the Psalms: A Redemptive-Historical Vision of Scripture* (New York: Oxford University Press, 2014); Douglas A. Sweeney, *Edwards the Exegete: Biblical Interpretation and Anglo-Protestant Culture on the Edge of the Enlightenment* (New York: Oxford University Press, 2015); and Barshinger and Sweeney, eds., *Jonathan Edwards and Scripture: Biblical Exegesis in British North America* (New York: Oxford University Press, 2018). For a much more extensive list, see the endnotes to chapter 1 of Sweeney, *Edwards the Exegete*, 226–37, esp. nn. 1–30.

For comparative works on Mather and Edwards, see Stephen J. Stein, "Cotton Mather and Jonathan Edwards on the Epistle of James: A Comparative Study," in Smolinski and Stievermann, *Cotton Mather and "Biblia Americana,"* 363–82; Michael P. Clark, "The Eschatology of Signs in Cotton Mather's 'Biblia Americana' and Jonathan Edwards's Case for the Legibility of Providence," in Smolinski and Stievermann, *Cotton Mather and "Biblia Americana,"* 413–38; Jan Stievermann and Ryan P. Hoselton, "Spiritual Meaning and Experimental Piety in the Exegesis of Cotton Mather and Jonathan Edwards," in Barshinger and Sweeney, *Edwards and Scripture*, 86–105; Ava Chamberlain, "A Fish Tale: Jonathan Edwards and Cotton Mather on Jonah's Whale," in Barshinger and Sweeney, *Edwards and Scripture*, 144–62; and Ryan P. Hoselton, "Spiritually Discerned: Cotton Mather, Jonathan Edwards, and Experiential Exegesis in Early Evangelicalism" (PhD diss., Ruprecht-Karls-Universität Heidelberg, 2019).

15. For the difference between churchly and radical Pietists, see Wallmann, *Pietismus*, 24. Concerning evangelicals, Kidd suggests replacing the oft-used categories of Old Light v. New Light with a continuum from conservative antirevivalists to moderate evangelicals and radical evangelicals. Kidd, *Great Awakening*, xiv. Others see the line between so-called moderates and radical enthusiasts as less clear cut; see esp. Douglas L. Winiarski, *Darkness Falls on the Land of Light: Experiencing Religious Awakenings in Eighteenth-Century New England* (Chapel Hill: University of North Carolina Press, 2017).

PART 1

COMMENTATORS AND COMMENTARIES

1

BIBLE EDITIONS, TRANSLATIONS, AND COMMENTARIES IN GERMAN PIETISM

DOUGLAS H. SHANTZ

Introduction: German Pietism and the Bible

German Pietism represents a key historical moment in Protestant engagement with Scripture. Johannes Wallmann observed that despite Luther's emphasis upon *sola Scriptura*, German Lutheranism in the sixteenth and seventeenth centuries was largely a "catechism Christianity,"[1] with Luther's catechism serving as the lay Bible. Lay Bible reading only became a reality with the arrival of German Pietism. For the Pietists, the Bible was not just a book for clergy; it was a book for born-again believers, whose "eyes of understanding" had been illumined by the Spirit of wisdom.[2] Pietist culture, language, and worldview were all shaped by the Bible.

From the beginning of the Pietist movement in the second half of the seventeenth century, informal gatherings of believers, the *collegia pietatis*, provided a communal and institutional setting for Pietist engagement with the Bible. This engagement was reflected in multiple ways: in the genre of Pietist tracts and forewords that explained the importance of lay Bible reading and some rules for doing so successfully, in Halle's publication of affordable Bibles, in Pietist editions and translations of the Bible, and in Pietist commentaries and works of interpretation.

On the Importance of Lay Bible Reading

In his study of *Evangelische Bibelvorreden* from the Reformation to the Enlightenment, Jürgen Quack devotes almost a third of his book to "Bible prefaces" in German Pietism.[3] Quack examines prefaces written by Spener in 1694 and 1699, by disciples of Spener such as Francke in 1694 and 1708, by Zinzendorf in 1755, and by the radical Pietists Johann Henrich Reitz in 1703 (*Das neue Testament*), Heinrich Horch in 1712 (*Die Marburger Bibel*), and Johann Friedrich Haug in 1726 (*Die Berleburger Bibel*). Quack rejects the idea that Bible prefaces in the period between Luther and the Enlightenment represent a formal genre with distinct characteristics.[4] However, the Bible prefaces composed by the Pietists do seem to develop into a distinct genre focused on encouraging and guiding lay Bible reading.

Philipp Jakob Spener, "Das nötige und nützliche Lesen der heiligen Schrift" (1694)

In his 1675 *Pia Desideria*, Spener discussed the lamentable state of the church in German lands and offered some remedies for this situation. Spener's chief remedy was the promotion of lay Bible reading by individuals, by fathers and mothers in homes, and in small gatherings of believers—*collegia pietatis*. "The more richly the Word dwells with us, the more we will bring faith and its fruits into being."[5] In a forty-page preface on "the necessary and profitable reading of holy Scripture," written after he arrived in Berlin in 1691, Spener reflects on God's mercy in providing a revelation of himself after humanity had lost the image and knowledge of God through the fall into sin. It is a further sign of God's grace that he used Martin Luther "to truly and clearly translate holy Scripture from the original languages" and to encourage believers to study it.[6]

Spener observed that while the Council of Trent warned of the dangers of translating the Bible into the language of the people, the early Christian church promoted popular reading of the Bible. "The ecumenical councils have never forbidden the reading of the Bible in the vernacular languages." The Bible was soon translated into Latin for the use of Christians in the Western church. Augustine reflected that in his day there was such a multitude of translations available that he could not count them. Spener cited Anselm, Thomas Aquinas, and Pico della Mirandola on the value of reading the Bible. He quoted further from Basil, Cyril, Jerome, and Chrysostom. The latter wrote, "I will not cease to admonish you not only to pay attention to what others say to you but that you in your own homes continually read the holy Scriptures." "I ask you, who are of a worldly station, purchase a Bible for yourself, for it is the medicine of the soul." German Protestant Christians should be especially grateful that they have the Bible available to them in the German language. As faithful and clear as Luther's translation may be, one cannot claim that it is without error. Spener reflected that the invention of the printing press had made it possible for ordinary Christians to obtain a Bible. "Very few fathers are so poor that they cannot afford to purchase a Bible."[7]

For Spener, the foremost reason for Christians to devote themselves to reading the Bible is that it contains truths that cannot be discovered by our natural mind. Even the Scriptures cannot be understood without divine help. The same Holy Spirit who inspired the apostolic authors to write down God's revelation must reveal to readers the truth that Scripture contains. Finally, Spener offers some rules that readers should follow in their study of God's Word. The first is the need for prayer. As Luther wrote, "Kneel down in your room and ask the Lord in all humility to give you his Holy Spirit that he may enlighten you, guide you, and give you understanding." In Ps 119, David continually asked the Lord for teaching and guidance. Second, the reader must bring to Scripture a repentant heart. There must be a heartfelt desire to know and understand God's will. Third, the reader must bring a resolve to put what he reads into practice. God will not grant light to those who do not intend to use it to his honor and glory. A godly life is no small resource in the profitable reading of Scripture. Fourth, reading must be accompanied by attentiveness. This means reading each passage with attention to the context and to the meaning of each word. One should compare the passage with other places in Scripture that teach the same point, for Scripture interprets Scripture. One should follow the natural meaning of the words and avoid preoccupation with the figurative and allegorical meanings.[8]

Fifth, the reader should take the Bible's commands and promises as if they were addressed directly and especially to them, for the Bible is a book for all times and all people. God's commands and laws are intended for us as his servants today. "Everything that was written in earlier times was written for our instruction" (Rom 15:4). Johann Arndt observed, "God did not reveal the holy Scripture to remain a dead letter on paper, but to become alive in us in spirit and faith, to make of us a completely new person." Sixth, Spener considers the order in which the biblical books should be read. He emphasizes that the New Testament should have priority and be read the most often since the articles of Christian faith are based primarily upon it. It teaches most clearly the things that are essential for salvation. The Old Testament should be read in light of the New Testament (NT). After reading the NT, one should then read the five books of Moses, followed again by the NT. One should then read the books of Job, the Psalms, and the writings of Solomon, followed again by the NT. Finally, one should read the prophets and the apocrypha, followed again by the NT. It is always better to read one chapter of Scripture with care than to read many chapters rapidly. One should always seek to find in one's reading something for personal use, either some instruction, admonition, warning, or comfort.[9]

Finally, the reader should not hesitate to profit from the godly wisdom of other Christian readers of the Bible. We should remember that other Christians also have the Holy Spirit within them and may come to understand certain things in Scripture that we have not yet come to understand. In this respect, one should avoid two opposite errors: despising other interpreters, assuming one has no need of instruction from others, or holding too firmly to a commentary or interpreter of a passage in the belief that no other view can be right.[10] Spener never wavered from his conviction that "the more richly the Word dwells with us, the more we will bring faith and its fruits into being." Spener's prioritizing of the NT for lay readers and his appreciation for the wisdom of other interpreters are emphases unique to him.

August Hermann Francke, "Einfältiger Unterricht wie man die H. Shrifft zu seiner wahren Erbauung lesen solle . . ." (Halle 1694), and A. H. Francke, "Vorrede zur Bibelausgabe" (1708)

Jürgen Quack identifies Francke's "Einfältiger Unterricht wie man die H. Shrifft zu seiner wahren Erbauung lesen solle" as the most popular and most-published of all German prefaces, along with Luther's. Francke's "Einfältiger Unterricht" was included in most of the Bibles published by the Canstein Bible Society in Halle.[11]

Francke's instruction in 1694 on how to read the Scriptures for one's edification offers seven rules for the profitable reading of Scripture. First, one must be careful not to read the Bible with the wrong reason in one's heart or an improper intention. Improper reasons and intentions include reading the Bible to pass the time or to read interesting stories, reading a chapter of the Bible morning and evening out of habit and thinking that this is pleasing to God, or reading the Bible in order to gain a reputation for being learned.[12] Second, one must read the Bible with a simple and upright heart, and with the sincere desire to be instructed so that one might believe and live according to God's Word. Third, one should begin with the prayer that God will open our eyes to understand what we read. Fourth, one should pray out of deep hunger for God's Word. When the soul hungers for God's Word, then the Spirit will not leave it unsatisfied. Fifth, to prayer one must join quiet reflection, in which we recognize our corruption and desire to model our lives according to God's teaching. Sixth, after reading, one should pray as follows: write all that I have read upon my heart with the finger of your Holy Spirit. Seventh, to prayer and reflection one should add temptations and trials as the means by which one is taught by God. When we encounter opposition, from within or without, it is God testing us to see what we have learned from Holy Scripture. "The cross is a powerful means for understanding, tasting and experiencing holy Scripture." "One should always have a supply of Scripture passages at hand, and gather together a treasure of these, so that they are available when you need them."[13] This last suggestion brings to mind the later advice of Count Zinzendorf, who encouraged the Moravians to treat the Bible as a treasure chest of gems of wisdom and comfort to be drawn upon as the occasion required.[14]

Along with his promotion of lay reading of the German Bible, Francke reflected on the suitability of Luther's translation for eighteenth-century readers. It was clear to Francke that the Luther Bible was sorely lacking in accuracy and clarity. If Luther had still been alive, insisted Francke, he would have wanted to revise the translation to make it more accessible for German readers. If the German Bible was properly updated, then "both unlearned and learned Germans would read and use the German Bible with more enthusiasm and with greater edification."[15] In response to those who objected to any tampering with Luther's translation, Francke wrote, "Only the original languages must remain as they are, because in them God's word is contained. But concerning a translation that here and there is inconsistent with the original languages and with the purity of our own spoken tongue, no one can rightly insist that the translation must be left as it is."[16] To fail to undertake such a revised translation would be to hinder the spread of God's Word throughout German lands and in German churches. In 1695, Francke began a monthly publication, *Observationes biblicae*, in which he pointed out the various shortcomings that he had found in Luther's translation of the Bible.

Nevertheless, over the years the Halle Foundations would print and sell Luther Bibles and make a good profit by doing so. The first Halle edition of the Luther Bible appeared in April 1708. Francke reflected on the great blessing that had come to German readers over the years from the many editions of Luther's translation of the Bible. He indicated that this new edition of the Luther translation was intended mainly for pastors and theology students.[17] This was apparently his justification for publishing a Bible whose language was outdated and somewhat inaccessible to ordinary Germans.

In his preface to the 1708 Bible, Francke distinguished three kinds of Bible readers: those who gain no, little, or much benefit from their reading. Francke offers six characteristics of those who derive great benefit from Bible reading, repeating some of the points he had made in 1694. First, these readers look to gain not just knowledge but how to be converted, become friends of God, and become united with God. Second, they read the Bible in fear and reverence, and view it not as the word of men but of God. Third, they read with awareness of their spiritual blindness and pray that God will open the eyes of their understanding. Fourth, they are not put off by the difficulty of the Bible but persist in their reading and gradually grow in their understanding. Fifth, they read the Bible to find nourishment for their souls. Finally, these readers find Christ in all of Scripture, for it testifies to him as the kernel and heart of the Bible.[18] Francke concludes, "I wish with all my heart that every reader of the Bible might read it repeatedly, with great and abundant benefit for the daily quickening and strengthening of his soul, and might grasp Jesus Christ, the kernel of Scripture, in true faith, and taste him sweetly in his heart, and become one heart and soul and spirit with him, and live and triumph with him eternally."[19] There is a clear continuity in Francke's guidelines with those of Spener, with his emphases on prayer, obedience, and Christ as the heart of Scripture.

Carl Hildebrand Freiherr von Canstein, "Ohnmaaßgebender Vorschlag, wie Gottes Wort den Armen zur Erbauung um einen geringen Preis in die Hände zu bringen sey" (1710)

Beate Köster suggests that the 1708 edition of the Luther Bible was an early indication of Francke's intention to publish Bibles and make them more readily available to German readers. Two years later, in 1710, the Canstein Bible Society was established in Halle. In Berlin on March 1, 1710, Carl Hildebrand von Canstein explained his vision for publishing God's Word at an affordable price for the benefit of poor people. When he first presented his plan, he was met with mockery and laughter at such an undertaking. He therefore directed his proposal (*Vorschlag*) primarily to those who confessed Jesus as Lord by the Holy Spirit. Von Canstein reflected on the importance of placing the Bible in the hands of the people.

> The holy Scripture is the one great light by which God, through his Spirit, illumines the souls of humankind. The best of human books, like stars, lose their light when the sun shines forth. And any truth that may be found in such books only exists to the degree it flows from the words of Christ. So it is best to put this book into the hands of all of humankind. . . . If then we combine and direct our energies towards such a purpose, to spread God's precious word abundantly among humanity,

then they will come to know the will of the Lord Jesus and become his obedient disciples.

Von Canstein encouraged individuals to support his plan according to their ability. He was hopeful of success in the enterprise because they were living in a time when God had brought about a great movement of awakening in people's hearts. He was also inspired by the recent publication in Holland of an English Bible at an affordable price.[20]

Von Canstein estimated that he could print over one hundred thousand copies of the New Testament for about 1,200 Reichsthaler. He would republish an earlier edition, and thus save on the costs of layout and copy editing. Each copy of the NT would sell for 2 Groschen. To publish a thousand copies of the complete Bible he would have to raise about 3,000 Reichsthaler. He would print the Bibles on good paper and in a readably sized print and sell them for 6 Groschen each. He only asked that those who purchased Bibles and New Testaments at these prices not resell them in order to make a profit.[21]

The first printing of the German New Testament by the Halle Canstein Bible Society finally appeared in June 1712. In a brief foreword, von Canstein apologized for the delay, noting that the society had spared neither time nor effort. He commented on the many difficulties they had encountered along the way, and the laborious work of pouring and cutting the type.[22] The first printing of the German New Testament sold out in a few weeks. Over the next seven years, one hundred thousand New Testaments and eighty thousand Bibles were produced. In the first hundred years of its existence, the Canstein Bible Society published almost two million Bibles in 380 editions. By comparison, the first edition of the Luther Bible appeared in 1534, and by 1626 Wittenberg printers had produced two hundred thousand copies in about one hundred editions.[23]

Count Ludwig von Zinzendorf, "Vorrede zu den Losungen" (1755)

Zinzendorf's hope was that members of the Moravian *Gemeine* would read the Bible each day and that it would find its way into their hearts, so they might become a "living Bible." Since May 1728 it had been Zinzendorf's practice to provide members with a Bible passage and a hymn text for each day of the week so that they might take these texts to heart and align their lives with the truths found in them. These *Losungen der Brüder* included passages from the books of Moses, the Prophets, the Psalms, as well as the NT. He estimated that over a period of thirty years the number of Scripture texts would exceed seven thousand. It was his prayer that these would "go directly into people's hearts and enable the personal working of the Holy Spirit upon each individual." With these small texts, Zinzendorf aimed to "serve up Scripture in small, appetizing portions for the nourishment of my people."[24]

In contrast to the Lutheran and Reformed churches, Zinzendorf was not overly concerned with principles of biblical interpretation, or hermeneutical rules, or a certain manner of preaching. He describes what it means for believers to be *Bibelfest* (dedicated to Scripture): "*Bibelfest* does not mean memorizing hundreds of Bible passages, or stringing together a hundred proof-texts, of which fifty can be set aside because they are irrelevant or out of context, and another twenty-five are lost because they are wrongly translated. That is misguided. Rather, the apostles demanded of people a true heart, so that what they read and saw before their eyes they believed and put into practice." Zinzendorf was most interested in the Moravian community becoming a "lived Bible."[25]

Pietist Bible Translations and Editions

Shortly before his death in 1752, Johann Albrecht Bengel observed, "Never have there been more conflicts on account of new translations of Holy Scripture than there are now."[26] Never before had there been so many new translations of the Bible available to German believers besides Luther's. Until the age of Pietism, no important new translations had appeared in the German Protestant world. Among Orthodox Lutherans, the Luther Bible was viewed as an inspired text. Only in 1854 would Lutherans attempt an official revision of Luther's translation.[27]

Kurt Aland identified ten new German translations in the first half of the eighteenth century, mostly of the New Testament.[28] This translation work took place mainly in radical Pietist circles. Their efforts were marked by word-for-word translation with the goal of keeping as closely as possible to the original Greek and Hebrew text. The result was often incomprehensible. Such a philosophy inspired the efforts of Ernst Triller (1703), Johann Henrich Reitz (1703), and Johann Jakob Junckherrot (1732). Concerning the latter's New Testament translation, a contemporary wrote: "It is perhaps the only book in the world for which the proverb does not hold: 'there is no book so bad that something good cannot be found in it.'"[29] It is not surprising that these efforts met with little publishing success.

The translation efforts of Johann Kayser (Timotheus Philadelphus) and Count von Zinzendorf in the 1730s followed a different philosophy. Kayser belonged to the small Philadelphian community in Stuttgart. His translation was intended to serve this community as well as aid in the evangelization of the Jews. Zinzendorf's translation was based upon the Greek text edited by Bengel in 1734. Zinzendorf realized that the German language had changed since Luther's translation appeared, so that it was no longer easily understandable for many readers. He sought to reproduce the sense and meaning of the Greek text rather than aiming at a word-for-word translation. Zinzendorf often closely followed Luther's version; he explained that he did so unconsciously, for he had virtually memorized much of the Luther Bible.[30]

The translation philosophy of the Berleburg Bible and Johann Albrecht Bengel followed a middle way, seeking to keep close to the original but aiming to be readable and understandable. The eight-volume Berleburg work came about through the oversight of Johann Friedrich Haug (1680–1753) of Strasbourg. The Berleburg Bible gained a wide readership.[31]

Bengel's German translation appeared in 1753, a year after his death. In the preface, Bengel explained his philosophy of translation: "In translating the word of God, which deals with heavenly and eternal matters, one should act with deep respect, with fear and trembling, so that one does not spoil or undermine or confuse anything." This fear of misinterpreting God's Word was the hallmark of Pietist translation efforts. Bengel offered nine rules of good translation: first, it must be based upon an accurate original text edition; second, it must impact the reader in exactly the same manner as the original; third, one must not add, withhold, or change anything; fourth, it must be as unclear or as clear as the original; fifth, it must be in good German, but not stylistically too impressive; sixth, one should avoid, if possible, introducing words from other languages; seventh, when the original uses the same word in the same context, the translator should use the same German word in the same context; eighth, it should not overemphasize or underemphasize certain meanings; finally, it should seek to follow the word order of the original.[32]

The Biblia Pentapla *(1710–1712)*

Possibly the most original and fascinating translation effort among the Pietists was the *Biblia Pentapla* of Johann Otto Glüsing (1675–1727). After studying theology in Jena from 1696 to 1700, Glüsing took a tutoring position in Copenhagen. The conventicle he established there marks the beginning of Pietism in Denmark and Norway. He denounced Lutheran clergy as false apostles; they in turn considered him a Quaker who taught "the most extreme kind of heresy."[33] He left for Oslo in October 1706 but was banished from Norway by royal decree in December 1706. Finding refuge in Altona, he joined followers of Johann Georg Gichtel, known as the society of "Angel brothers." Here he began working on the *Biblia Pentapla*, finally publishing the three volumes anonymously from 1710 to 1712.

Following the lead of Origen's *Hexapla*, Glüsing's *Pentapla* offered five German versions of the Bible in parallel columns: Catholic, Lutheran, German Reformed, Dutch Reformed, and a Yiddish translation of the Hebrew Bible in a revised edition with Latin letters. The latter was the first Jewish translation of the Hebrew Bible into German. The New Testament volume of the *Pentapla* appeared in print in 1710; the two Old Testament volumes appeared in 1711 and 1712.

It was Glüsing's judgment that the *Pentapla* contained "the five most distinguished, best known, and most useful German translations of the whole Bible."[34] The *Pentapla* would help believers to better understand the Bible; the similar or slightly varying versions would clarify the meaning for readers. It would also help Christians to appreciate the differing beliefs of the various confessions and thus encourage Christian peace and unity and promote ecumenical mindedness and tolerance.

Michael Berns, Orthodox Lutheran pastor in Wandsbek, wasted no time in publishing a denunciation of Glüsing's *Pentapla*, calling it "poison from hell."[35] The various German translations would sow confusion among people and undermine the Bible's authority. Berns was especially unhappy that Glüsing had included a Jewish translation of the Old Testament along with a New Testament translation by the Pietist separatist Johann Henrich Reitz, versions Berns judged to be "of the devil."[36] Luther's translation did not need the help of misguided Pietists and Jews.

Bengel's Edition of the Greek New Testament, Novum Testamentum Graecum *(1734), and His German New Testament (1753)*

The Württemberg Pietist Johann Albrecht Bengel (1687–1752) was an exceptionally gifted biblical scholar and commentator. After studying arts and theology in Tübingen, in December 1713 he took up a teaching position in the Denkendorf Cloister near Esslingen. For twenty-eight years he taught Latin, Greek, and Hebrew in the Denkendorf school, all the while continuing his academic work. His two great achievements were an edition of the Greek New Testament (1734) and his NT commentary, the *Gnomon* (1742). Kurt Aland called Bengel "the father of textual criticism."[37]

Bengel guided his students in reading through the entire Greek New Testament over a two-year period. In a letter dated February 24, 1721, Bengel wrote to a student who was bothered by the variant readings that turned up in the Greek texts. As a student in Tübingen in 1703, Bengel had likewise been disturbed when he discovered that there were variant readings among the New Testament Greek manuscripts passed down from ancient times. Bengel shared with the student how he came to terms with this disparity in the textual legacy.

> Concerning the various readings in the New Testament, I should really say more than I can manage in this letter. Simply eat the bread that comes to you, and don't be worried if now and then you find in it a grain of sand from the flour mill. Christ and his church present themselves to the eyes of the world in the garb of weakness and humility; it is the same with his Word. I find this entirely appropriate to the character of Christ and his word. If the holy Scriptures, which were so often copied down by error-prone human beings, should be without any defect, that would be such a great miracle that faith would no longer be needed. On the contrary, I am amazed that many more variant readings have not arisen, and that the texts available to us in no way bring the foundation of our faith into question. And so you can confidently set aside this doubt which once also disturbed me so terribly.[38]

Bengel here demonstrates his unique gifts as a textual critic and pastor to students.

In Denkendorf Bengel began collecting handwritten and published texts of the Greek New Testament, many of which he borrowed from distant libraries and universities. Having assembled over thirty different versions of the Greek NT, he proceeded to compare textual variants in order to reconstruct the best, most authentic text. He learned to sift through the multitude of scribal errors and to identify the main families of variant readings. Bengel distinguished two main families of Greek New Testament manuscripts: Asian (originating in Constantinople) and African (originating in Alexandria). He formulated a rule still used by biblical scholars today: *Lectio difficilior potior*, or, the more difficult reading is to be preferred. Ancient copyists were more likely to harmonize a text with passages they knew than to introduce a novel, more difficult alternative.[39]

On the basis of his determination of a reliable Greek text, Bengel then worked on his own German translation of the Bible. His purpose was to produce a German biblical text "upon which I might found and build my German interpretation of the New Testament and not always have to say about the Luther translation: 'In Greek it actually says such and such.'"[40] Although he completed it in 1740, he hesitated to publish his translation because of the conflicts he observed within Lutheranism over new German translations by

Reitz, Horch, Zinzendorf, and others. He also did not wish to show any disrespect for the Luther Bible. Bengel finally gave his German translation to a publisher in Stuttgart in 1752, shortly before he died.

The Ebersdorf Bible (1727) and Zinzendorf's New Testament (1739)

Dietrich Meyer has shown that Zinzendorf's preoccupation with the Bible extended far beyond his work in compiling the *Losungen*. Scholars have devoted too little attention to his efforts to make the Bible readily available and his desire to provide the Moravian community with a reliable and readable translation of the Bible. Following the lead of the Canstein Bible Society, Zinzendorf sought to publish Bibles at an affordable price and to make them available for as wide a public as possible. To this end, in 1727, he and pastor Johann Andreas Rothe produced the Ebersdorf Bible. Basing it upon the Luther text published by the Canstein Society, they retranslated some passages and added summaries of Bible books and chapters. The publication history of the Ebersdorf Bible "reads like a detective novel," writes Peter Zimmerling.[41] Its production encountered many problems, including opposition from church and secular authorities in Saxony, lack of finances, and a disgruntled printer.[42]

One must also consider Zinzendorf's efforts between 1732 and 1738 at translating various parts of the Bible in the setting of a *Collegium Biblicum* in which F. C. Oetinger and August Gottlieb Spangenberg and other theologians also participated. In 1739, Zinzendorf published a new translation of the complete New Testament in two volumes. He would publish revisions of the two volumes in 1744 and 1746. He based his translation upon Bengel's *Novum Testamentum Graecum* of 1734.[43]

Pietist Bible Commentaries

The Marburg Bible (1712)

Heinrich Horch (1652–1729) had a colorful career as a radical Pietist. He identified with the Philadelphian movement inspired by the English mystical author Jane Leade, who taught a postmillennial eschatology that looked for a new church age marked by peace and unity among Christians. From 1698 to 1708, Horch experienced "a restless and fanatical life" in which he gave up his doctor title and grew out his beard. He joined up with a Swiss chiliastic preacher, Samuel König, in organizing separatist Philadelphian communities around Herborn and Eschwege. These gatherings grew in size and attracted attention from the authorities because of their displays of prophetic enthusiasm. Horch was imprisoned in the Marburg castle for nine months.[44] After he was banished from that part of Hesse, his life during this period was that of a "homeless mind," with travels to Holland and England.[45]

Horch spent the last years of his life, from 1708 to 1729, near Marburg in Kirchhain. It was here that he devoted himself to his work on the *Mystische und Prophetische Bibel*. He was assisted in producing the Bible by Pastor Ludwig Christoph Schefer in Berleburg. The full title of the work indicates the perspective Horch and Schefer brought to their Bible commentary: *Mystische und Profetische Bibel, Das ist Die gantze Heil. Schrifft, Altes und Neues Testaments, Aufs neue nach dem Grund verbessert, Sampt Erklärung Der fürnemsten Sinnbilder und Weissagungen, Sonderlich Des H. Lieds Salomons Und der Offenbarung J.C.*[46] For them, the interpretive key to Scripture lay in the Song of Solomon and the Revelation of John. In the address to the reader, Horch lays out his purpose in publishing the Marburg Bible:

> The goal of those who have worked on this edition is this: that they might awaken a new desire for following the word of the Lord, which is represented in this book, so that in this dark world it might be a light to our feet and a lamp for our way, especially in these last times ... of which the Lord said long ago, that the hour of temptation would come upon all who dwell upon the earth, when even the elect would be in great danger Matt 24:24, Rev 3:10. Just as the founder and fulfiller of our faith [Jesus Christ] frustrated the tempter through God's word Matt 4:4, so also the sword of the Spirit, which is the word of God, is placed in our hand as the armour of God for gaining spiritual victory.[47]

He aims to serve readers who are living in the last days, and who need encouragement and guidance for living in such difficult times.

Horch explains the meaning of the words in the title, "mystical and prophetical Bible." Believers must grasp the Bible's mystical message not just with their minds but with their hearts, by faith. Under the guidance of the Holy Spirit, believers can move beyond the outward letter and symbol and pry out the hidden kernel of spiritual truth. In this way the whole of Scripture becomes a kind of pharmacy of the most precious medicines, and believers find nourishment for their souls. The editors also sought to explain the main prophecies in the Bible according to their proper chronology and characteristics. For Horch and Schefer, Scripture was an eschatological puzzle whose meaning revealed the crucial importance of the early eighteenth century to the realization of God's kingdom on earth.⁴⁸ When we come to understand the timing of Christ's return, the day of the Lord will not surprise us like a thief in the night.

The spiritual reading of the Song of Solomon would find nothing sexual in the account; rather, the book reveals, symbolically, the different periods of the Christian church from the beginning to the end of the world. Likewise, the letters to the seven churches in Rev 2 and 3 signified seven ages of the church throughout history. The church of Sardis signified the church during the period of the Reformation. This age would be superseded by the Philadelphian age, when believers would put aside confessional conflicts and be of one heart and soul.⁴⁹ Horch and Schefer observed the preparations for the Philadelphian age in their own time.

The Berleburg Bible (1726–1742)

The Berleburg Bible is the classic expression of radical Pietist biblical interpretation. While the *Biblia Pentapla* provided an archive of German Bible translations, the Berleburg Bible offered an encyclopedia of biblical interpretation. In the tolerant setting of Sayn-Wittgenstein, with the support of Count Casimir and Berleburg court preacher Ludwig Christoph Schefer, Johann Friedrich Haug (1680–1753) was invited to oversee the multiyear project. The Berleburg Bible would occupy Haug for seventeen years. He was provided with free lodging, firewood, and a garden. When the final volume appeared, Haug rejoiced that "the Bible is even better than we imagined. It is a miracle that we have reached this point."⁵⁰

The eight-volume Bible included a new German translation from the Greek, accompanied by multifaceted commentary that explained the mystical and spiritual meaning of the biblical text. Like the Marburg Bible, it reflected the expectation of the Philadelphian age of Christian peace and unity on the earth. The commentary drew upon a wide variety of radical, Spiritualist, and alchemical traditions including Johann Arndt, Jakob Böhme, Friedrich Breckling, Paracelsus, the Talmud, Gottfried Arnold, and Madame Guyon. The commentary reflected the fourfold medieval exegesis that found literal, moral, allegorical, and mystical meanings in the biblical text. A typical page would have a biblical passage at the top, with two columns of commentary beneath. The result was that the Berleburg Bible offered a confusing mass of information. An example is the commentary on Exod 32:15, when Moses received the Ten Commandments on two tablets. One finds comments by Philo, Josephus, Athanasius, Saint Augustine, and Ambrose, each offering a different interpretation of how the commandments were distributed on the two tablets.⁵¹

Johann Albrecht Bengel's Gnomon Novi Testamenti *(1742)*

The result of some twenty years of study and reflection, Bengel's *Gnomon* represents "the supreme achievement of Pietist biblical interpretation."[52] Deriving its name from the pointer on a sundial, Bengel's *Gnomon* offers comments on various aspects of the biblical text, ranging from text-critical to historical, exegetical, and practical Christian living. He intended it to serve as a resource for pastors in their sermon preparation. In this Bengel was astonishingly successful; the *Gnomon* has been used by generations of Protestant interpreters, right up to the present: the ninth German edition appeared in 1970. With its combination of piety and scholarship, Bengel's *Gnomon* is the classic theological expression of Württemberg Pietism.[53] Bengel's aphorisms on the Bible have had a timeless appeal: "Apply yourself wholly to the text; apply the text wholly to yourself."[54] "Bring nothing into the text, but take everything from it and leave behind nothing that is in it."[55]

John Wesley relied extensively upon Bengel in his *Explanatory Notes upon the New Testament* (1755), as he acknowledged in his preface: "I once designed to write down barely what occurred to my own mind, consulting none but the inspired writers. But no sooner was I acquainted with that great light of the Christian world (lately gone to his reward) Bengelius, than I entirely changed my design, being thoroughly convinced it might be of more service to the cause of religion, were I barely to translate his *Gnomon Novi Testamenti*, than to write many volumes upon it."[56] It is clear that in compiling his *Explanatory Notes* Wesley contributed very little that was original with him. According to Robert Brown, "Wesley's *Notes* were part translation, part abridgement of Bengel's *Gnomon*."[57] Bengel the Pietist thus made an essential contribution to the early Methodist Church.[58]

Conclusion

Interpretive questions around the issue of Pietism and the Bible include connections with the German Enlightenment and with early Anglophone evangelicals, especially John Wesley. Scholars such as Martin Gierl and Jonathan Sheehan are part of a new historiography that views the Enlightenment not as a movement of antireligious rationalism, but as a movement promoting new scholarly techniques, practices, and institutions such as journals, book reviews, translations, and salons. The Enlightenment movement sought not to discard religion but to remake it.[59]

Gierl and Sheehan have shown how Enlightenment techniques, practices, and institutions overlap with Pietism in interesting ways.[60] On the issue of

Pietist and Enlightenment approaches to the Bible, Sheehan suggests that "Bengel the Pietist offered the earliest version of the Enlightenment Bible," a Bible based upon philology, not theology. The *Biblia Pentapla* (1710–12), edited by Johann Otto Glüsing, offered five different German translations in parallel columns so that readers could compare the various Protestant versions. The Pietists thus helped create "an ecumenical German Bible unstained by devotion to party and doctrine."[61] Rather than serving denominational theology and theological strife within Europe, the Bible became a source document, a subject for scholarly research and for multiple translation possibilities. The new scholarly and religious landscapes brought about by the Enlightenment and Pietism helped to bring about a changed approach to the Bible.

Comparison of Pietist use of Scripture with John Wesley's reveals substantial points of agreement. This chapter began by observing how informal gatherings of believers, *collegia pietatis*, provided a communal and institutional setting for Pietist engagement with the Bible. Wesley too promoted communal Bible reading, specifically in the setting of the "band societies" that he formed for spiritual accountability among his followers.[62] This institutional promotion of lay Bible reading represents a fundamental evangelical inheritance from German Pietism.

Wesley scholar Steve Harper describes how Wesley encouraged "using the Bible formatively" and "approaching the Bible in a devotional spirit."[63] Focusing on Wesley's 1746 preface to the *Sermons on Several Occasions*, Harper identifies six aspects of Wesley's approach to Scripture: first is reading a passage of Scripture in God's presence; second is turning to God in prayer to resolve any difficulties or unclarities that arise in the reading; third is seeking out parallel passages in Scripture, comparing Scripture with Scripture and thereby allowing Scripture to interpret Scripture; fourth is attentive reflection and meditation upon the reading; fifth is consulting other Christian interpreters to whom God has granted understanding by his Spirit; and the sixth involves considering the writings of earlier Christian believers.[64] Early evangelicalism followed Wesley's emphases on lay Bible reading and approaching the Bible in a devotional way.[65] All these aspects can be found in the Bible prefaces of Spener and Francke. As with the Pietists, early evangelical culture, language, and worldview were all shaped by the Bible.

Notes

1. Johannes Wallmann, *Der Pietismus* (Göttingen: Vandenhoeck & Ruprecht, 2005), 26.
2. The quotation is from Philipp Jakob Spener, "Das nötige und nützliche Lesen der heiligen Schrift" (1694), in *Hauptschriften Philipp Jakob Speners*, ed. Paul Grünberg (Gotha: Friedrich

Andreas Perthes, 1889). See also Martin Brecht, "Die Bedeutung der Bibel im deutschen Pietismus," in *GdP*, 4:102–10.

3. Jürgen Quack, *Evangelische Bibelvorreden von der Reformation bis zur Aufklärung* (Gütersloh: Gütersloher Verlagshaus, 1975), 231–321, is devoted to Pietist prefaces to editions of the Bible.

4. Ibid., 11.

5. Philipp Jakob Spener, *Pia Desideria*, ed. Beate Köster (Giessen: Brunnen Verlag, 2005), 108, 110.

6. Spener, "Das nötige und nützliche Lesen," 232.

7. Ibid., 234–37, 239.

8. Ibid., 240–41, 247, 250.

9. Ibid., 256, 262.

10. Ibid., 265.

11. Quack, *Evangelische Bibelvorreden*, 280.

12. A. H. Francke, *Einfältiger Unterricht wie man die H. Shrifft zu seiner wahren Erbauung lesen solle* (Halle: Christoph Salfelden, 1694), Rule 1.

13. "Doch sollst du billig allezeit viele gute Sprüchlein der Heiligen Schrift in Vorrat haben und gleichsam einen Schatz davon sammeln, damit es dir niemals fehle, wenn du deren eines bedarfst." Ibid., Rule 7.

14. Douglas H. Shantz, *An Introduction to German Pietism* (Baltimore: Johns Hopkins University Press, 2013), 209.

15. Kurt Aland, "Bibel und Bibeltext bei August Hermann Francke und Johann Albrecht Bengel," in *Pietismus und Bibel*, ed. Kurt Aland (Witten: Luther-Verlag, 1970), 96.

16. Ibid., 98.

17. A. H. Francke, "Vorrede zur Bibelausgabe von 1708," in Beate Köster, "Die erste Bibelausgabe des halleschen Pietismus," *PuN* 5 (1979): 162.

18. Ibid., 156–62. See Francke, *Christus der Kern Heiliger Schrift* (1702).

19. Francke, "Vorrede zur Bibelausgabe von 1708," 163.

20. Carl Hildebrand von Canstein, "Ohnmaaßgebender Vorschlag, wie Gottes Wort den Armen zur Erbauung um einen geringen Preis in die Hände zu bringen sey," in Carl Heinrich Christian Platt, *Carl Hildebrand Freiherr v. Canstein* (Halle: Verlag der Buchhandlung des Waisenhauses, 1861), 125–27, 122–23.

21. Ibid., 123–24.

22. Carl Hildebrand von Canstein, "Vorrede zur ersten Ausgabe des Neuen Testaments, 1712," in Platt, *Carl Hildebrand*, 129.

23. Aland, "Bibel und Bibeltext," 91.

24. Nikolaus Ludwig Graf von Zinzendorf, "Vorrede zu den Losungen" (1755), in *Nikolaus Ludwig Graf von Zinzendorf: Eine Auswahl seiner Reden, Briefe und Lieder*, ed. Dietrich Meyer (Gießen: Brunnen Verlag, 2000), 266–69.

25. Zinzendorf, "Über die Bedeutung der Bibel für die Gemeinde," in Meyer, *Nikolaus Ludwig Graf von Zinzendorf*, 216–17, 211, 213.

26. Foreword to Bengel's translation of the New Testament, dated October 10, 1752. See Beate Köster, "Mit tiefem Respekt, mit Furcht und Zittern: Bibelübersetzungen im Pietismus," *PuN* 24 (1998): 95.

27. "Erst 1854 . . . wurde im Luthertum offiziell der Versuch gemacht, eine Revision der Lutherübersetzung vorzulegen." See Peter Zimmerling, review of *Nikolaus Ludwig von Zinzendorf: Bibel und Bibelgebrauch*, ed. Dietrich Meyer, vols. 1 and 2, *AfeT Rezensionen* 2 (October 18, 2017): https://rezensionen.afet.de/?p=418.

28. Aland, *Pietismus und Bibel*, 141. See also Shantz, *Introduction to German Pietism*, 206–7.

29. Köster, "Mit tiefem Respekt," 98, 102.

30. Ibid., 104.

31. Ibid., 110.
32. Ibid., 112.
33. Shantz, *Introduction to German Pietism*, 211–12.
34. Johann Otto Glüsing, "Allgemeiner Vorbericht," in *Das Alte Testament*, part 1 (Schiffbeck: Hermann Heinrich Holle, 1711).
35. Michael Berns, *Entdeckung Des Greuel Wesens, Welches Die so genandte Neue Christen Mit der biß dathin in Wandesbeck gedruckten Biblia Pentapla vorhaben* (Hamburg: Neumann Verlag, 1710); and Hermann Patsch, "Arnoldiana in der *Biblia Pentapla*," *PuN* 26 (2000): 104.
36. Michael Berns, *Das natürliche Licht des Verstandes* (Hamburg: Neumann Verlag, 1711), 22.
37. Aland, "Bibel und Bibeltext," 136.
38. Ibid., 130.
39. Wallmann, *Pietismus*, 219–20; Shantz, *Introduction to German Pietism*, 233–34.
40. Jonathan Sheehan, *The Enlightenment Bible: Translation, Scholarship, Culture* (Princeton: Princeton University Press, 2005), 111–12.
41. Zimmerling, review of *Nikolaus Ludwig von Zinzendorf*.
42. Jürgen Quack, "Einleitung," in Meyer, *Nikolaus Ludwig von Zinzendorf*, 9–16.
43. Zimmerling, review of *Nikolaus Ludwig von Zinzendorf*.
44. Max Goebel, *Geschichte des christlichen Lebens in der rheinisch-westphälischen evangelischen Kirche*, vol. 2 (Coblenz: Karl Bädeker, 1852), 744–48; Hans Schneider, "Der radikale Pietismus im 18. Jahrhundert," in *GdP*, 2:119–21.
45. Douglas H. Shantz, "'Homeless Minds': The Migration of Radical Pietists, Their Writings, and Ideas in Early Modern Europe," in *Pietism in Germany and North America, 1680–1820*, ed. Jonathan Strom, Hartmut Lehmann, and James Van Horn Melton (Farnham, UK: Routledge, 2009), 85–99.
46. In English the title reads, *The Mystical and Prophetical Bible, the Holy Scriptures of the Old and New Testaments in a revised translation according to the original languages, including an explanation of the most important metaphors and prophecies, especially of the Song of Solomon and the Revelation of Jesus Christ*.
47. *Mystische und Profetische Bibel, Das ist Die gantze Heil. Schrifft, Altes und Neues Testaments, Aufs neue nach dem Grund verbessert, Sampt Erklärung Der fürnemsten Sinnbilder und Weissagungen, Sonderlich Des H. Lieds Salomons Und der Offenbarung J.C.* (Marburg: Joh. Kürßner, 1712).
48. Douglas H. Shantz, "The Millennial Study Bible of Heinrich Horch," in *The Practical Calvinist*, ed. Peter Lillback (Fearn, UK: Christian Focus, 2002), 398–400.
49. Ibid., 404–5.
50. Hans-Jürgen Schrader, *Literaturproduktion und Büchermarkt des radikalen Pietismus* (Göttingen: Vandenhoeck & Ruprecht, 1989), 198; Martin Brecht, "Die Berleburger Bibel: Hinweise zu ihrem Verständnis," *PuN* 8 (1982): 179.
51. Shantz, *Introduction to German Pietism*, 227–28.
52. Martin Brecht, "Johann Albrecht Bengel," in *Orthodoxie und Pietismus*, ed. Martin Greschat (Stuttgart: Kohlhammer, 1982), 327.
53. Wallmann, *Pietismus*, 221.
54. "Te totum applica ad textum, Rem totam applica ad te." Bengel, *Handausgabe des griechischen Neuen Testaments* (1734), 3.9.
55. Shantz, *Introduction to German Pietism*, 235.
56. John Wesley, *Explanatory Notes upon the New Testament* (London: Charles H. Kelly, 1896), 7: preface.
57. Robert S. Brown, "Joy of Heaven to Earth Come Down: Perfection and Millennium in the Eschatology of John Wesley" (M.Phil. thesis, University of Manchester, 2011), 64. See also Bruce Roger Marino, "Through A Glass Darkly—The Eschatological Vision of John Wesley" (PhD diss., Drew University, 1994), 69–70.

58. Donald K. McKim, ed., *Historical Handbook of Major Biblical Interpreters* (Downers Grove, IL: IVP, 1998), 292.

59. Sheehan, *Enlightenment Bible*, xi, xii, 260. See also Jonathan Sheehan, "Enlightenment, Religion, and the Enigma of Secularization," *American Historical Review* 108, no. 4 (2003): 1061–80.

60. Martin Gierl, "Pietism, Enlightenment, and Modernity," in *A Companion to German Pietism, 1660–1800*, ed. Douglas H. Shantz (Leiden: Brill, 2015), 371, 72.

61. Sheehan, *Enlightenment Bible*, 112, 115, 29.

62. Jason E. Vickers, *Wesley: A Guide for the Perplexed* (London: T&T Clark International, 2009), 18.

63. Steve Harper, "Wesley's Sermons as Spiritual Formation Documents," *Methodist History* 26, no. 3 (1988): 131, 137.

64. John Wesley, Preface, *Sermons on Several Occasions* (New York: Lane and Tippett, 1845), 1:6. All these aspects can be found in the Bible prefaces of Spener and Francke.

65. Bruce Hindmarsh, "What Is Evangelicalism?," *Christianity Today*, March 14, 2018.

2

BIBLICAL AIDS, EDITIONS, TRANSLATIONS, AND COMMENTARIES BY DISSENTERS, METHODISTS, AND CHURCH OF ENGLAND EVANGELICALS IN EIGHTEENTH-CENTURY ENGLAND

ISABEL RIVERS

This chapter focuses on the following religious denominations and groups in England: Protestant Dissenters from the Church of England (who were so designated in the Toleration Act of 1689, and did not achieve full religious and political parity until the nineteenth century), especially Congregationalists and Baptists, who in the second half of the eighteenth century came to call themselves evangelical Dissenters; members of the Church of England who formed Methodist societies from the 1730s onward; evangelical members of the Church of England who disapproved of Methodist practices and of the theology of the Arminian wing of Methodism, but who shared with Methodists the view that the church should return to its sixteenth-century founding statements. It explores the following questions: How did people get hold of Bibles and from whom, and what sizes and prices of Bibles were available? What kinds of help with reading the Bible were given to readers at different educational levels, both ministerial and lay? What kinds of aids exploited Bible texts in user-friendly ways? What were the most important editions of the Bible that we would now call evangelical?[1]

Bible Distribution

Two important societies were concerned with Bible distribution. One very large society, the Society for Promoting Christian Knowledge (SPCK), founded in 1699 and still in existence, is much studied, but it was a nonevangelical Church of England society; the other, smaller one, the Society for Promoting Religious Knowledge among the Poor (SPRKP), founded in 1750 and petering out in the 1920s, is much less known, but it was in contrast an interdenominational, evangelical, moderate Calvinist society.[2] Both societies kept detailed accounts of their activities and the books they distributed—Bibles and other kinds of religious literature—and they provided lists of their members. These books and tracts were bought by the societies' subscribing members for distribution. The SPCK's catalogues began with complete Bibles, Testaments, and Books of Common Prayer, and the popular rhyming version of the Psalms by Nahum Tate and Nicholas Brady. The prices for members in the 1795 book catalogue, for example, ranged from 7s to 2s for complete Bibles in different sizes, the Testaments from 1s 7d to 7½d, and the Common Prayers from 2s 11d to 9d. In the SPRKP's account for two years later, 1797, the prices of complete Bibles ranged from 4s 6d to 2s 4d, and the Testaments from 2s 8d to 1s 1½d. The SPRKP did not distribute Common Prayers, because these were specific to the Church of England, and they distributed Isaac Watts's versions of the Psalms, not Tate and Brady's. By 1797 the total number of all sizes of Bible and Testaments distributed by the SPRKP was 152,863, from a total number of 574,760 books distributed. In the year 1797, the figure for both Bibles and Testaments was 3,240. In contrast, in the 1750s and 1760s the SPCK was distributing approximately 5,000 copies of Bibles and Testaments each year, and in the 1790s about 14,000 copies each year.[3]

The SPRKP helpfully published extracts in its annual accounts of how recipients of its books responded, as recorded by the clergy and Dissenting ministers who distributed them. In addition, the Baptist minister John Rippon published an exceptionally useful *Discourse on the Origin and Progress of the Society for Promoting Religious Knowledge Among the Poor*, in which he drew on the Society's letterbook. For example, Rippon recorded a letter of 1765 from the evangelical clergyman John Newton: the poor woman to whom he gave a Bible "received it with a joy bordering upon astonishment. . . . She had before shewn me a borrowed one, which, though greatly torn and defaced, she should have esteemed as her choicest treasure if she could have called it *her own*."[4] The importance of personal ownership was much stressed. The shortage of Bibles was often noted, and the fact that those who did have access to one usually only had a piece (reflecting the sale of Bibles in parts). Thus, Mr. Callender of

Newcastle upon Tyne is quoted in the 1763 report: "One poor widow had only a few leaves of the blessed Word of GOD, these she had read over and over again, but when a bible was given her, how did she praise GOD, and pray for those who had sent her such an acceptable present!"[5] There is a comparable account by Sampson Staniforth, one of John Wesley's preachers, who first encountered a preaching and prayer group when he served with the army in Germany in 1744. One of them asked "if I had a Bible or any good Book? I said No; I knew not that ever I had read any. He said, I have a piece of an old Bible: take it. I can do better without it than you." He sent his mother an account of his conversion, which came into the hands of a Dissenting minister; the latter then sent him a Bible, while his mother (evidently a member of the Church of England) sent him a Book of Common Prayer. He and his group then received other books from Wesley.[6] Rippon made a pessimistic deduction from his analysis of the manuscript letters received by the SPRKP from its inception: "there are two awful facts clearly perceptible—That there are certainly *thousands of families* in this land, which have not a single Bible; and that there are *many dissenting congregations* which have but a few."[7] In 1804, the interdenominational British and Foreign Bible Society was set up to address this problem.[8]

Aids to Reading the Bible

Putting the Bible into people's hands was one thing; getting them to understand and use it was another. Clergy and ministers were well aware that people needed help to interpret the Bible, and incentives to enjoy it. These ranged from works for the ignorant and young to works for educated families with time and money to spend. After the Bible, one of the most important works distributed by the SPRKP was *A Compassionate Address to the Christian World*, by the Presbyterian minister John Reynolds, a short work designed to set out the basics of Christianity for the ignorant, first published in the 1720s. Reynolds summarized the function of the Bible for this audience: "*Consider what the Bible is*. The book that God has sent you, to teach you the Way to Heaven, and Happiness, and himself: The Book that is to make you good and wise; yea, wise for Salvation: The Book that contains the Law of God and Gospel of Christ: The Law of God, and what he commands you, as your Duty, and Obedience, and Thankfulness to him: The Gospel of Christ, and the Way in which you are to be pardoned, and saved, and accepted with God. There you are told what God has done in the Creation, Preservation, Redemption, and Government of the World."[9]

Two longer and more complex works designed for younger readers were *A Short View of the Whole Scripture History*, by the Congregationalist Isaac Watts, first published in 1732, and *Sacred History Selected from the Scriptures*, by the Church of England educational writer Sarah Trimmer, first published in six volumes from 1782 to 1785. These books were designed to set out and explain the biblical narrative and the traditional Christian interpretation of the complex relationship between the Old and New Testaments as one of types, promises, prophecies, and their fulfillment.

Watts asked in his preface, "How shall Persons, whose capacity is weak, or who have little time to employ on these Subjects, be led in the shortest and easiest way to a competent Acquaintance with the sacred History? And how shall those who are young in Years be trained up in the plainest and most alluring manner to some Knowledge of these important Affairs, till their growing Age and further Advantages shall give them a more extensive and capacious View of all the Transactions between God and Men recorded in Scripture?"[10] The answer was by abridgment, and by the catechetical method of question-and-answer, which Watts thought the best method of instruction. He rearranged some of the chronology and included information from nonbiblical sources. His chapters and sections all have headings that summarize the contents, and the answers to the questions all include biblical references to enable the reader to follow them up—there is not much biblical quotation, so to use the book effectively the reader needed a Bible at hand. The SPRKP distributed this too, but it was relatively expensive: the Society's edition in 1797 cost 2s 6d, slightly more than the cheapest small Bible, at 2s 4d, whereas *A Compassionate Address* cost 4½d.

Sarah Trimmer's aims and intended audience for *Sacred History* were similar, but she went further than Watts in his *Short View*: she provided a selected version of the Bible. She explained that her abridgment consisted of "extracts from the HOLY SCRIPTURES, divided into distinct sections, with explanatory notes and practical reflections; intended to display in some degree, *the great plan of* DIVINE PROVIDENCE *in the redemption of mankind*, and to point out *the influence which the examples contained in* HOLY WRIT ought to have on our conduct."[11] *Sacred History* was extremely successful, going through eight editions by 1824. Much-abridged versions of her Old Testament and New Testament in one volume each were adopted by the SPCK, specified in their list as "for the Use of Charity Schools, Kitchens, and Cottages," with the Old Testament priced at 1s 3d and the New Testament at 11d.[12] In *An Abridgment of the New Testament*, reduced to 167 pages, she explained, "The following Work was composed with a view to render the study of the New Testament easy and pleasant to the young and ignorant, by laying before them such parts only as are the most easy to be explained to their tender capacities."[13]

A very different kind of advice about Bible reading was provided by the evangelical clergyman Henry Venn, stressing that it was a laborious process of self-examination. Venn's *The Complete Duty of Man*, a substantial practical handbook for families first published in 1763, was designed as an evangelical replacement for the very long-lived but doctrinally deficient (as Venn saw it) seventeenth-century handbook *The Whole Duty of Man*, which was one of the SPCK's staple publications. The *Complete Duty* went through five editions in the eighteenth century and was much reprinted in the nineteenth. Venn provided a very detailed and demanding set of instructions in the chapter "On Devotional Duties." Alongside prayer, the study of Scripture is a "constant and continual exercise of devotion." Some examples are given here of the italicized marginal headings of his rules for reading in order to procure "some spiritual advantage and real edification," together with some elaborations in the text:

> *The Bible must be studied with prayer, in order to understand it....Internal revelation necessary to make the external one effectual....Prejudice against this doctrine fatal to the soul....The Bible must be read with pauses and recollection....* We must by no means therefore content ourselves with having the words and expressions of God before our eyes, or in our mouths. On the contrary, we must pause and deliberate much on the things signified by the words. We must labour to fix the true import of the divine expressions deep in our minds; so that the very spirit of the Bible may be, as it were, transcribed into them.... *And with self application...* [We must] exact of ourselves correspondent affections.... Unless we thus read all Scripture with self-application, we shall do just enough to flatter and deceive ourselves that we are something, when we are nothing; enough to make us imagine we have a great regard to Scripture, when in fact it has no weight at all with us to form our judgment, or determine us in the grand object of our pursuit.[14]

Venn stresses that Bible reading, properly understood, is a strenuous inward and transformative process, which readers will initially struggle against but which will prove infinitely rewarding. These rules illustrate two general trends in evangelical engagement with the Bible: emphasis on both experiential reading and practical application.

Biblical Treasuries

A new biblical aid came to the fore in the mid-eighteenth century, in the shape of two popular little books that used biblical texts as a springboard for their authors' and hence their readers' own meditations: *A Golden Treasury for the Children of God, Whose Treasure Is in Heaven*, a translation of the enormously popular work by the Lutheran and Halle Pietist author Karl Heinrich von Bogatzky, and an imitative work, *A Spiritual Treasury, for the Children of God*, by the Church of England evangelical layman William Mason. In its passage from Germany to England, the book was taken up and modified by editors, sellers, and authors of different denominations. The first English translation of Bogatzky's *Güldenes Schatz-Kästlein der Kinder Gottes, deren Schatz im Himmel ist* was published in 1754 by the London-based German bookseller Andreas Linde, a member of the Lutheran church in the Savoy.[15] The subtitle explains the book's structure and function: *Consisting of Select Texts of the Bible, with Practical Observations in Prose and Verse, for Every Day in the Year.* Each of the daily pages has a text, or in some cases more than one, followed by a short meditation, with verses at the foot. In the English translation the German verses were replaced by extracts from Watts's hymns and psalms. Although the biblical texts are the foundation of the work, they are not presented in an immediately obvious order, and the work does not attempt to explain or analyze the Bible historically. Rather, the book is a contribution to the practice of heart religion. The translator (presumably Linde) says that it will not suit those who "*mistake mere outward Morality, for true Christianity.... But such as either have, or desire to have a real Experience of the Kingdom of God in their Souls, will find much in it to the Awakening, Comforting and Encouraging their Heart in the right Way.*"[16]

The subsequent history of this work in England shows the keenness with which it was edited and circulated, usually in small oblong format. A translation of Bogatzky's second part was published in 1764 by the Baptist Joseph Johnson and Linde's widow.[17] The first part was revised and republished in 1775 *With Some Alterations and Improvements by Various Hands* and then again in 1790 with further alterations.[18] The editor was the evangelical Church of England philanthropist John Thornton, who made extensive changes to Bogatzky's text and incorporated material from a large number of English authors. The 1775 edition included contributions from the evangelical clergy Thomas Adam, Charles de Coetlogon, Richard Conyers, John William Fletcher, Martin Madan, Newton, William Romaine, and Venn. It also included passages from, among others, the seventeenth-century nonconformists John Howe and John Owen and the New England minister Jonathan Edwards. The revised 1790 edition had further contributions by the evangelical clergyman John Berridge and the Congregational minister William Bull. Thornton's versions went through a large number of editions right through the nineteenth century, including one by the Religious Tract Society.

The revised preface to the 1775 edition, by Thornton (who is unnamed), makes several suggestions as to how the book is to be used, which involve careful searching and comparison by the reader. For example:

> In almost every page there are different portions of scripture put together, which serve to elucidate and explain each other; so that what in one is obscure, is generally opened by its parallel; which will be found very useful, if diligently compared; and serve to shew the abundance, the super-abundance of light, promises, privileges, and advantages there are in the word of GOD....
>
> In this book are several parts of scripture-history evangelized, or applied to spiritual purposes in a gospel way; which may serve as specimens for the improving of many more to the same end; hereby great advantages will arise to the intelligent reader.[19]

William Mason seems to have borrowed the idea for his *Spiritual Treasury*, first published in 1765, from Bogatzky's *Golden Treasury*, but he made no mention of it.[20] His title echoes Bogatzky's, and he used the same method of a page for each day of the year, with a Scripture text at the top followed by a prose meditation. However, Mason's meditations are much longer—the format is octavo, so there are far more words on the page than for the *Golden Treasury*—and there are fewer passages of verse. The *Spiritual Treasury* was prefaced by the evangelical clergyman Romaine (himself a contributor to the *Golden Treasury*), vouching for the value of the layman Mason's book, and it went through four editions by the end of the century. At some point Mason brought out a second part of evening meditations, with the first part now designated morning meditations. In 1828, this was amalgamated into a single substantial octavo volume of 740 pages, with each day of the year having a morning and evening meditation. The 1839 Religious Tract Society edition of part 2 includes Mason's preface, in which he saw himself as a humble hewer of wood and drawer of water, with characteristic embellishment of the biblical text (Deut 29:11): "Though not blessed with the tongue of the eloquent, nor the pen of the learned—though neither called nor qualified to preach the everlasting gospel; yet if our Lord is pleased to enable me to hew some few splinters of wood, which may kindle the fire of love in the hearts of any of his dear people; and to draw a little water from the rock Christ, which may refresh their spirits, my soul delights in being thus honourably employed."[21] Mason's *Spiritual Treasury* had evidently taken a place in family prayer, and perhaps even replaced Bible reading by making it easier.

Annotated Bibles

Annotated editions of the Bible by ministers and clergy published from the mid-eighteenth century to the beginning of the nineteenth were targeted primarily at lay audiences. Early nineteenth-century readers were well supplied with excellent up-to-date guides to Bible commentaries in the reading list the Congregational minister Edward Williams appended to his *Christian Preacher*,[22] in the preface by the Methodist minister Adam Clarke to his edition of the Bible,[23] and in the Congregational minister William Orme's *Bibliotheca Biblica*,[24] all of great use to the modern reader. Until the eighteenth century, annotated Bibles were primarily designed for clerical readers, though some lay readers used them. The most admired early eighteenth-century work was the Presbyterian minister Matthew Henry's *An Exposition of All the Books of the Old and New Testament*, published in stages from 1707 to 1721, with the commentary on the Epistles and Revelation by other hands, and then issued complete in six folio volumes. It went through many editions right through the century and well beyond.[25] Despite its size and expense, Henry did not design it only for the learned. He set out his two principal aims, to enable the reader to understand and to use the text, in the preface to his first volume. This is the second aim:

> But we are concerned not only to *understand* what we read, but to *improve* it to some good Purpose, and in order thereunto to be affected with it, and to receive the Impression of it. The Word of God is designed not only to be a Light *to our Eyes*, the entertaining Subject of our Contemplation, but a *Light* to *our Feet*, and a *Lamp to our Path*, to direct us in the Way of our Duty, and to prevent our turning aside into any By-Way: We must therefore in searching the Scriptures enquire, not only *What is this?* but *What is this to us?* What use may we make of it? How may we accommodate it to some of the Purposes of that Divine and Heavenly Life, which by the Grace of God we are resolved to live?[26]

The huge success of Henry's work in no way inhibited the production later in the century of annotated New Testaments and Bibles in a variety of formats, edited by evangelical Dissenters, Methodists, and Church of England evangelicals, that were explicitly aimed at lay readers and encouraged their active participation in interpreting the text. The most important were the Congregational minister Philip Doddridge's *The Family Expositor*, first published from 1739 to 1756; John Wesley's *Explanatory Notes upon the New Testament*, first published in 1755; and the evangelical clergyman Thomas Scott's *The Holy Bible ... with Original Notes, and Practical Observations*, first published from 1788 to 1792.

Doddridge's *Family Expositor* has a very complicated structure and is not easy to use.[27] The whole New Testament is divided into sections (usually part of a chapter, but sometimes containing parts of different chapters from different books). Each section is in four parts: the text of the King James Bible (which Doddridge refers to as the received or common translation) in the inner column or margin; his own version, in italics, interwoven with his lengthy paraphrase, as the main text in a larger font; footnotes to the text, in the same font as the KJV text; and the improvement (suggested prayer and meditation) at the end of each section in the larger font of Doddridge's version and paraphrase. Each section has a title, which also specifies which verses of which chapters are included; in addition, each page has a heading with chapter and verse.

In his lengthy preface, Doddridge explained his aims in devising this system, and how the reader should go about using it. He said his design "was chiefly to promote *Family Religion*, and to render the reading of the *New Testament* more pleasant and improving, to those that wanted [i.e., *lacked*] the Benefit of a learned Education, and had not Opportunity or Inclination to consult a Variety of *Commentators*.... In pursuit of this I have given a large *Paraphrase* on the Sacred Text, well knowing that this is the most agreeable, and useful Manner of explaining it to common Readers, who hardly know how to manage Annotations, especially when they are to be read to others." The notes, on the other hand, were principally aimed at a student, not a family, audience. His motive for providing his own version of the text was largely literary—"raising some of those Ornaments, which were before depressed; and sufficiently proving, that several Objections urged against it [the received translation] were intirely of an *English* Growth." He explained the function of the improvement thus: "The *Improvement* of each *Section* is entirely of a practical Nature, and generally consists of pressing Exhortations, and devout Meditations, grounded on the general Design, or on some particular Passages, of the *Section* to which they are annexed. They are all in an *Evangelical Strain*, and they could not with any Propriety have been otherwise."[28]

In the advertisement preceding the first section he gave clear advice about how his book should be read in families: first, the passage of Scripture should be read in the common translation in the margin, unless the family had their own Bible in front of them; then Doddridge's new version in italics should be read by itself; then the paraphrase and the improvement should be read. The person officiating should choose some of the notes of general interest to read after the relevant paragraph; other notes might be made the subject of conversation after the reading, but this would depend on "the State and Character of the Families in Question."[29] The notes were studied with great interest by some ministers and clergy: for example, Jonathan Edwards made considerable use of *The Family Expositor* (the final volume came out two years before his death), both in published works and in his "Blank Bible," the latter containing over three hundred comments on Doddridge's notes and translations.[30]

The Family Expositor was a handsome and expensive set of six volumes in quarto, with the last three volumes completed and edited after Doddridge's death by a group of former pupils and friends.[31] The Pietist Friedrich Eberhard Rambach of Magdeburg and Halle, a correspondent of Doddridge, published a four-volume translation as *Paraphrastische Erklärung Der sämtlichen Schriften Neues Testaments* (1750–56), with a foreword by Johann Adam Steinmetz.[32] The six-volume English set went through eleven editions by 1821, with some later editions in different formats up to the 1850s, but abridged cheap versions were not a success. The Congregational minister Samuel Palmer published an abridgment in 1800, not reissued in England but with an American edition in 1807. He explained in his preface that he had done this in order to carry out Doddridge's own intention, "to print a cheaper edition, without the Paraphrase, the Prefaces, or the learned notes, for the sake of extending its usefulness in the families of plain Christians."[33] Palmer's unsatisfactory attempt to make *The Family Expositor* more usable by families illustrates the problems Doddridge created by combining so many disparate approaches to the presentation and interpretation of the New Testament.

Wesley's *Explanatory Notes upon the New Testament* was in most respects a very different work from Doddridge's.[34] The first edition, published in 1755, was a substantial quarto volume, quite unlike the cheap duodecimo publications Wesley usually distributed.[35] The most important and influential edition was the third, published in three duodecimo volumes from 1760 to 1762,[36] for which the biblical text and the notes were revised and enlarged with the assistance of Charles Wesley and others; this was the version widely distributed among the Methodist Societies. From 1763 Methodist preachers were required to *"preach no other doctrine than is contained in Mr. W's Notes upon the New Testament and four Vol[umes] of Sermons,"*[37] and this definition of the *Notes* as a doctrinal standard ensured their continued reprinting in a variety of formats.[38] In 1790, Wesley produced a further edition of his New Testament with revisions but without his notes.[39] He also edited *Explanatory Notes upon the Old Testament*, published in weekly numbers and in three volumes in 1765–67; this was not a success and was not reprinted.[40]

Wesley's arrangement of the New Testament was straightforward and easy to use. Each book, headed "Notes on . . . ," is preceded by a brief account of the book and a summary of the contents by chapter and verse, in a small typeface; the main text, in a larger typeface, is divided into paragraphs with the verse numbers in the left-hand margin; the notes at the foot are in small type. At the end of the third volume is "An Index Chiefly of Words Explained in the Preceding Comment." In his preface Wesley set out his aims and methods in relation to his readers, the translation, the notes, and his sources. His edition, unlike Doddridge's, was not intended for readers of different educational levels. His notes "were not principally designed for men of learning; who are provided with many other helps: and much less for men of long and deep experience in the ways and word of God. I desire to sit at their feet, and to learn of them. But I write chiefly for plain, unlettered men, who understand only their mother-tongue, and yet reverence and love the word of God, and have a desire to save their souls." He went on to explain his principles of translation: "I design first to set down the text itself, for the most part, in the common *English* translation, which is in general (so far as I can judge) abundantly the best that I have seen. Yet I do not say, it is incapable of being brought in several places nearer to the original. Neither will I affirm, that the *Greek* copies from which this translation was made, are always the most correct. And therefore, I shall take the liberty, as occasion may require, to make here and there a small alteration."[41] The last sentence deliberately downplayed his alterations to the text.[42] Unlike Doddridge, whose format enabled the reader to see on the page the differences between the common version and his own, Wesley gave no indication of what his alterations were, or where they originated. The anonymous author of the introduction to a new edition of Wesley's translation of 1790 observed that his version was a proper medium between two kinds of biblical translation, the literal and the free.[43]

Wesley stressed that his notes were not meant to be of academic interest: "I have endeavoured to make the notes as short as possible, that the comment may not obscure or swallow up the text: and as plain as possible, in pursuance of my main design, to assist the unlearned reader: for this reason I have studiously avoided, not only all curious and critical enquiries, and all use of the learned languages, but all such methods of reasoning and modes of expression, as people in common life are unacquainted with.... I purposely decline going deep into many difficulties, lest I should leave the ordinary reader behind me."[44] He briefly identified his sources in the preface: the German Lutheran Pietist Johann Albrecht Bengel, "that great light of the Christian world"; the editions of the Congregationalists Doddridge and John Guyse; and the *Theological Lectures* of the Church of England clergyman John Heylin. He made a point of not identifying sources in the notes themselves, even when he was quoting directly, "that nothing might divert the mind of the reader from keeping close to the point in view, and receiving what was spoke, only according to its own intrinsic value." His greatest debt was to Bengel's *Gnomon Novi Testamenti* (1742) and his edition of the Greek text, *Novum Testamentum Graecum* (1737): he translated or abridged many of the notes in the *Gnomon* and incorporated many of Bengel's textual readings; following Bengel's practice he divided the text into paragraphs while retaining chapters and verses, and he took the analysis preceding each book from Bengel.[45]

Thomas Scott's annotated edition of *The Holy Bible, Containing the Old and New Testaments* probably had a wider and longer influence than either Doddridge's *Family Expositor* or Wesley's *Explanatory Notes*. It was first published in weekly parts from 1788 to 1792. The second edition was published in four quarto volumes in 1792,[46] and continued to be reprinted. Scott then revised the whole in four further editions published between 1802 and 1822. It was republished up to the 1870s, with some versions amalgamating Scott's commentary with Henry's.

A great deal can be learned about the writing and sales of Scott's Bible, together with the toll it took on him, from his son John's biography of his father. Part-publication had become an established way of selling the Bible and was increasingly important from the 1760s onward, but it proved financially disastrous for Scott and his first publisher. With hindsight, in an account written in 1812, Scott thought himself naïve; he said "I had hardly an idea of the arduousness of the work, and of the various kinds of talent and knowledge which it required; of most of which I was at that time destitute."[47] His son thought it an advantage that because of the speed at which Scott was forced to work he had little time to consult other authors for his commentary (though he did so for his later editions), and was obliged to rely on his own reflections.

At the end of volume 3, Scott provided a number of aids to the reader, including (with a separate title page) the third edition of *An Useful Concordance to the Holy Bible* by Vavasor Powell, as recommended by John Owen, first published with Owen's recommendation in 1673, thus making a clear association between late eighteenth-century Church of England evangelicalism and seventeenth-century nonconformity.[48] He also listed the names of ministers who provided letters recommending his Bible, including evangelical Dissenters such as John Ryland Sr., John Ryland Jr., and William Bull, and Church of England evangelicals such as Rowland Hill and Berridge.

Unlike Doddridge and Wesley, Scott had no interest in altering the KJV translation. The biblical text is set out in the traditional way with chapters and verses, and is confined to the upper half of the page, in a large type; the notes underneath, in double columns with a smaller type, are very full and take up a great deal of space, sometimes over three-quarters of the page, and usually cover a verse or a group of verses; at the end of each chapter is a separate essay entitled "Practical Observations." Scott's preface to the first volume set out at length the argument that the Bible was the revealed word of God, and then turned to the basic question of how to read it: "We are therein addressed as creatures endued with common sense, and expected to employ it, in deducing instruction, and forming practical conclusions from what we read, and from comparing spiritual things with spiritual.—We are expected also to have such a value for divine truth, as to be willing to bestow some pains in searching for it as for hid treasure."

Scott did not expect readers to do this unassisted, and went on to explain the rationale for his notes and observations.[49] While not wishing to undervalue critical commentary on the Bible, he thought practical expositions more useful. His own defense for adding to them was a personal one: "experiencing the utility, efficacy, and comfort of that measure of acquaintance with the word of God, with which he has been favoured, he would wish, were it possible, that all the world should enjoy the same felicity." He thought some existing commentaries were "too learned for plain people." Scott's practical observations were his equivalents of Doddridge's improvements, placed as they were at the end of each chapter; Scott gave them this name "not because doctrine and experience will be excluded; but because he would refer the whole to its practical effect upon the heart and life."[50] These observations constitute the most striking part of his Bible. Though his later revised editions contained parallel Scripture references (below the biblical text, not in the margin) and some quotations from other commentators in the notes, the essence of his edition was his own interpretation, which effectively dominates the page.

In a letter of 1795, Scott described to his son John, then an undergraduate at Cambridge, how he read the Bible: "I have found it advantageous sometimes to read the scriptures with such exactness, as to weigh every expression, and its connexions, as if I were about to preach on every verse; and then to apply the result to my own case, character, experience, and conduct, as if it had been directly addressed to me—not as a new promise or revelation, but as a message containing warning, caution, reproof, exhortation, encouragement, or direction, according to my previous or present state of mind, and my peculiar circumstances."[51] It was this personal element in his biblical commentary that impressed his contemporaries. Daniel Wilson, prominent London evangelical clergyman and later bishop of Calcutta, emphasized in his funeral sermon for Scott: "Every part of it is thought out by the author for himself, not borrowed from others. It is not a compilation, it is an original production, in which you have the deliberate judgement of a masculine and independent mind on all the parts of Holy Scripture."[52]

The similarities and differences between these three English biblical editors and commentators of the mid- to late eighteenth century are worth summarizing. All were writing for lay readers. The Dissenting minister Doddridge is the most obviously scholarly of the three, keen to provide different interpretations of the New Testament Greek for the learned, while at the same time addressing less sophisticated readers. The two Church of England clergymen took a different approach. Wesley downplayed his scholarly researches with the aim of making his edition easily accessible and of a manageable size, with succinct notes for Methodists to pore over. Scott's very full commentary is the most personal and direct of the three, which perhaps explains the great success of his edition despite its size, and it indicates the growing appetite for this kind of biblical interpretation among evangelicals on both sides of the Atlantic in the nineteenth century.[53]

Notes

This chapter draws on chapter 8, "Interpreting the Bible," and chapter 9, "Practical Works," in Isabel Rivers, *Vanity Fair and the Celestial City: Dissenting, Methodist, and Evangelical Literary Culture in England, 1720–1800* (Oxford: Oxford University Press, 2018), reproduced by permission of Oxford University Press, https://global.oup.com/academic/product/vanity-fair-and-the-celestial-city-9780198269960.

1. For the range of meanings of "evangelical" in England at this time in relation to different denominations, see the summary in Rivers, *Vanity Fair*, 3–4; and Rivers, "Writing the History of Early Evangelicalism," *History of European Ideas* 35 (2009): 105–11. For definitions of denominations and groups, see Rivers and David L. Wykes, "Historical Information," https://www.qmul.ac.uk/sed/religionandliterature/dissenting-academies/historical-information.

2. Rivers, *Vanity Fair*, 45–57.

3. Scott Mandelbrote, "The Publishing and Distribution of Religious Books by Voluntary Associations: From the Society for Promoting Christian Knowledge to the British and Foreign Bible Society," in *The Cambridge History of the Book in Britain*, vol. 5, *1695–1830*, ed. Michael F. Suarez, S. J., and Michael Turner (Cambridge: Cambridge University Press, 2009), 621.

4. John Rippon, *Discourse on the Origin and Progress of the Society for Promoting Religious Knowledge among the Poor, from it's [sic] Commencement in 1750, to the Year 1802* (London: the Bookseller to the Society, ?1803), 38.

5. *An Account of the Society for Promoting Religious Knowledge among the Poor: Begun Anno 1750* (London: Thomas Field, Bookseller to the Society, 1763), 35.

6. "A Short Account of Mr. Sampson Staniforth: In a Letter to the Rev. Mr. Wesley," *Arminian Magazine* 6 (1783): 69, 122–23.

7. Rippon, *Discourse*, 39.

8. Leslie Howsam, *Cheap Bibles: Nineteenth-Century Publishing and the British and Foreign Bible Society* (Cambridge: Cambridge University Press, 1991), chap. 1.

9. [John Reynolds], *A Compassionate Address to the Christian World* (London: T. Wilkins, 1797), 12–13.

10. Isaac Watts, *A Short View of the Whole Scripture History, with a Continuation of the Jewish Affairs, from the Old Testament, till the Time of Christ; and an Account of the Chief Prophecies that Relate to Him: Represented in a Way of Question and Answer* (London: Eman. Matthews; Richard Ford; Richard Hett, 1732), vii.

11. Sarah Trimmer, *Sacred History Selected from the Scriptures, with Annotations and Reflections, Suited to the Comprehension of Young Minds*, 6 vols. (London: J. Dodsley; T. Longman and G. Robinson; and J. Johnson, 1782–85), vol. 1, preface.

12. *An Account of the Society for Promoting Christian Knowledge* (London: Francis and Charles Rivington, 1795), 96. This audience is specified in the earliest surviving copy of *An Abridgment of Scripture History; Consisting of Lessons Selected from the Old Testament; Designed Chiefly for Charity Schools, Kitchens, and Cottages* (1792), but dropped in later editions in favor of "Schools and Families."

13. Sarah Trimmer, *An Abridgment of The New Testament; Consisting of Lessons Composed from the Writings of the Four Evangelists. For the Use of Schools and Families*, 2nd ed. (1797), Advertisement.

14. Henry Venn, *The Complete Duty of Man: Or, a System of Doctrinal and Practical Christianity. To which are added, Forms of Prayer and Offices of Devotion, for the various Circumstances of Life. Designed for the Use of Families*, 2nd ed., corrected and improved (London: J. Newbery; R. Baldwin; S. Crowder; J. Coote, 1765), 450–60.

15. See Graham Jefcoate, *Deutsche Drucker und Buchhändler in London 1680–1811* (Berlin: De Gruyter, 2015), chap. 8, on Linde; bibliography 1754.6 and 1754.7, for his editions of *A Golden Treasury*.

16. Carl Heinrich von Bogatzky, *A Golden Treasury for the Children of God, whose Treasure is in Heaven; Consisting of Select Texts of the Bible, with Practical Observations in Prose and Verse, for Every Day in the Year . . . translated from the 19th Edition of the German* (London: A. Linde and A. Millar, 1754), "To the Reader," 4 (italics in original). Bogatzky, in his autobiography, described the book's development over time: *The Life of Charles Henry V. Bogatsky written by himself*, trans. Samuel Jackson (London: Seeley, Jackson, and Halliday, 1856), 43, 49, 55, 162, 183.

17. *The Second Part of A Golden Treasury for the Children of God, whose Treasure is in Heaven* (London: J. Johnson and Mrs Linde; J. Gore, Liverpool; W. Edwards, Halifax; G. Coppurthwaite, Leeds, 1764).

18. *A Golden Treasury for the Children of God, whose Treasure is in Heaven . . . With Some Alterations and Improvements by various Hands* (London [s.n.], 1775).

19. Ibid., preface, x–xi, xiv–xv. See *Bogatzky's Golden Treasury: A Reprint of Mr. John Thornton's Edition of 1775, together with Critical Notes, hitherto Unpublished, by John Berridge*, ed. Charles P. Phinn, with introduction by H. C. G. Moule (London: Elliot Stock, 1891).

20. William Mason, *A Spiritual Treasury, for the Children of God: Consisting of a Meditation for Each Day in the Year, upon Select Texts of Scripture. Humbly Intended to Establish the Faith, Promote the Comfort, and Influence the Practice of the Followers of the Lamb* (London: M. Lewis; E. and C. Dilly, 1765).

21. William Mason, *A Spiritual Treasury, for the Children of God* [title as 1765] (London: Religious Tract Society, 1839), preface, iii–iv.

22. Edward Williams, *The Christian Preacher, or, Discourses on Preaching, by Several Eminent Divines, English and Foreign, Revised and Abridged; with an Appendix on the Choice of Books* (Halifax: for J. Fawcett, Ewood-Hall, near Halifax; sold by T. Wills, W. Button, London; J. Smith, Sheffield; T. Hannam, Leeds; P. Holden, Halifax, 1800), 425–39.

23. Adam Clarke, *The Holy Bible, Containing the Old and New Testaments . . . With a Commentary and Critical Notes; Designed as a Help to a Better Understanding of the Sacred Writings . . . A New Edition with the Author's Final Corrections*, 6 vols., vol. 1 (London: Thomas Tegg, 1836), "General Preface III: Protestant Commentators."

24. William Orme, *Bibliotheca Biblica: A Select List of Books on Sacred Literature; with Notices, Biographical, Critical, and Bibliographical* (Edinburgh: Adam Black; London: Longman, Hurst, Rees, Orme, Brown and Green, 1824).

25. See Scott Mandelbrote, "A Family Bible? The Henrys and Dissenting Readings of the Bible, 1650–1750," in *Dissent and the Bible in Britain, c. 1650–1950*, ed. Scott Mandelbrote and Michael Ledger-Lomas (Oxford: Oxford University Press, 2013), 38–56; Matthew A. Collins and Paul Middleton, eds., *Matthew Henry: The Bible, Prayer, and Piety* (London: T&T Clark, 2019), part 2.

26. Matthew Henry, *An Exposition of All the Books of the Old and New Testament . . . with Practical Remarks and Observations*, 3rd ed., 6 vols. (London: J. Clark and R. Hett; J. Knapton, J. and B. Sprint, J. Darby, D. Midwinter [and thirteen others], 1725), I, [A3v] (italics reversed).

27. See Isabel Rivers, "Philip Doddridge's New Testament: *The Family Expositor* (1739–56)," in *The King James Bible After 400 Years: Literary, Linguistic and Cultural Influences*, ed. Hannibal Hamlin and Norman Jones (Cambridge: Cambridge University Press, 2010), 124–45.

28. Philip Doddridge, *The Family Expositor: Or, a Paraphrase and Version of the New Testament; With Critical Notes; and a Practical Improvement of each Section*, vol. 1 (London: Richard Hett, 1739), preface, [i]–iii.

29. Ibid., Advertisement, xxviii.

30. See, for example, Edwards, *An Humble Inquiry into the Rules of the Word of God*, in *WJE*, 12:335–36, 343; and *The "Blank Bible,"* in *WJE*, 24:64–66, 113.

31. See Tessa Whitehouse, "*The Family Expositor*, the Doddridge Circle and the Booksellers," *Library*, 7th ser., 11, no. 3 (2010), 321–44, appendix.

32. See Geoffrey F. Nuttall, "Continental Pietism and the Evangelical Movement in Britain," in *Pietismus und Reveil*, ed. J. Van den Berg and J. P. Van Dooren (Leiden: Brill, 1978), 229–30.

33. *The Family Expositor Abridged: According to the Plan of its Author, the Rev. P. Doddridge D. D.*, by S. Palmer, 2 vols. (Hartford, CT: Lincoln & Gleason, 1807), 1:xvii.

34. See Robin Scroggs, "John Wesley as Biblical Scholar," *Journal of Biblical Religion* 28 (1960): 415–22; and Frank Baker, "John Wesley, Biblical Commentator," *Bulletin of the John Rylands University Library of Manchester* 71, no. 1 (1989): 109–20.

35. John Wesley, *Explanatory Notes upon the New Testament* (London: William Bowyer, 1755).

36. John Wesley, *Explanatory Notes upon the New Testament*, 3rd ed., corrected, 3 vols. (vol. 1: Bristol: Grabham and Pine, 1760; vols. 2 and 3: Bristol: Pine, 1761–62).

37. *The Methodist Societies: The Minutes of Conference*, ed. Henry D. Rack, vol. 10 of *The Bicentennial Edition of the Works of John Wesley* (Nashville: Abingdon Press, 2011), 869–70.

38. A new edition, *Works of John Wesley*, vols. 5 and 6, is in preparation.

39. *The New Testament with an Analysis of the Several Books and Chapters: By the Rev. J. Wesley, M. A.* (London: Printed and sold at the New-Chapel, City Road; and at the Rev. J. Wesley's Preaching-Houses in Town and Country, 1790).

40. See William M. Arnett, "A Study in John Wesley's Explanatory Notes upon the Old Testament," *Wesleyan Theological Journal* 8 (1973): 14–32; Baker, "Wesley, Biblical Commentator," 115–19.

41. Wesley, *Explanatory Notes*, 3rd ed., vol. 1, preface, [iii]–iv.

42. See George C. Cell, *John Wesley's New Testament Compared with the Authorized Version* (Philadelphia: John C. Winston, 1938), introduction, xi. Cell used Wesley's *New Testament with an Analysis* (1790) as his copy text, marking Wesley's multiple changes in italics.

43. *A New Translation and Analysis, of All the Books of the New Testament, in which the Subjects are Properly Distributed into Paragraphs, by the Rev. John Wesley, M.A.* (Dunfermline: Robert Harley, 1818), iv–vi.

44. Wesley, *Explanatory Notes*, 3rd ed., vol. 1, preface, iv–v.

45. Ibid., v–vi. See Baker, "Wesley, Biblical Commentator," 110–11.

46. *The Holy Bible, Containing the Old and New Testaments; with Original Notes, and Practical Observations, by the Rev. Thomas Scott . . . To which are added, A Concordance, General Index, and Tables*, 2nd ed., 4 vols. (London: Bellamy and Robarts, 1792).

47. John Scott, *The Life of the Rev. Thomas Scott*, 2nd ed. (London: L. B. Seeley; Hatchard and Son, 1822), chap. 10, 269–70. At least twelve thousand copies had been printed up to 1821, with a further twenty-five thousand in the United States (294–95).

48. The title page describes Powell's *Concordance* as *Designed to Accompany the Rev. T. Scott's Family Bible, or any other in Quarto*. The 1792 edition was the first in circa 90 years.

49. Scott, *Holy Bible* (1792), 1:xxi–xxii.

50. Ibid., xxiii–xxiv.

51. Scott, *Life of Thomas Scott*, 333, December 10, 1795.

52. Daniel Wilson, *The Aged Minister's Encouragement to his Younger Brethren. Two Sermons Occasioned by the Death of the Rev. Thomas Scott* (London: G. Wilson; L. B. Seeley; J. Hatchard and Son, 1821), 26, 28. Scott, *Life of Thomas Scott*, 581–97, contains a lengthy edited extract.

53. For American editions of their works, see Margaret T. Hills, ed., *The English Bible in America: A Bibliography of Editions of the Bible and the New Testament Published in America, 1777–1957* (New York: American Bible Society and New York Public Library, 1961). Items up to 1825 are listed here: Doddridge, 147 (1807–8), 148 (1807); Wesley, 35 (1791), 137 (1806), 222 (1812), 291 (1815), 356 (1818); and Scott, 113 (1804–9), 146 (1807), 175, 176 (1810–12), 189 (1811–12), 210 (1812), 232, 233 (1813), 258 (1814–16), 259 (1815), 295 (1816–18), 297 (1816–18), 298 (1816).

PART 2

HISTORICAL TRAJECTORIES AND TRANSITIONS

3

EARLY MODERN DUTCH REFORMED EXEGESIS
AND ITS PIETIST-EVANGELICAL RECEPTION

ADRIAAN C. NEELE

The early modern era of exegesis in the Dutch Republic from circa 1600 to 1750 falls within the broader context of post-Reformation Reformed biblical exegesis, but it also encompasses the *Nadere Reformatie* (Dutch Further Reformation), a Dutch movement within the Reformed church with a strong emphasis on piety.[1] Dutch exegetes produced learned commentaries from an academic context, but the *Nadere Reformatie* also gave rise to more practically oriented commentaries originating from sermons. In addition to these two contributions in biblical interpretation, the Dutch Bible with annotations (*Statenbijbel* or *Statenvertaling met aantekeningen*, 1637), as well as translated commentaries into the Dutch language, shaped the renaissance of biblical exegesis in the Dutch Republic. In fact, to a great degree, the center of Reformed biblical interpretation had shifted around the turn of the century (1600) from the Swiss Confederacy to the Dutch Republic. Reflections on Scripture by Heinrich Bullinger (1504–1575, Zürich), John Calvin (1509–1564, Geneva), Peter Martyr Vermigli (1499–1562, Zürich), and Wolfgang Musculus (1497–1563, Bern)[2] were now articulated and advanced in the Lowlands. Students of the Genevan and other academies took up positions in the newly founded universities of the Dutch Republic in Leiden (1575), Dordrecht (1579), Franeker (1585), Groningen (1612), Amsterdam (1632), and Utrecht (1636). The reception of early modern Dutch biblical exegesis, furthermore, was transatlantic, international, and interdenominational. Therefore, in what follows, I offer (1) a broad outline of early modern Reformed exegesis in the Dutch Republic of the seventeenth and early eighteenth centuries, followed by brief observations on (2) the Dutch Bible with annotations, (3) commentaries arising from sermons, (4) translated works of biblical commentary, and (5) a sketch of reception history with attention to the New World, especially the Puritan-evangelical and Pietist traditions, together with some concluding remarks.

Early Modern Dutch Exegesis

The Reformed theologians of the academy of the early modern era in the Dutch Republic were first and foremost biblical exegetes. Doctrine and practice arose primarily from the examination of and meditation on Scripture and was formulated with the words of Scripture—notwithstanding a discerning use of medieval scholasticism in the service of defining doctrines precisely, and a discriminating use of medieval Bernardine piety. Furthermore, biblical commentary arose in the academic context of disputations (*disputationes*), where students of theology were instructed on matters of exegesis with critical reflection on Scripture.[3] In other words, the biblical exegesis of the early modern era was integral to the theological enterprise. As such, it was not uncommon for theologians to spend years teaching and writing biblical commentaries before publishing a systematic theology. The Leiden professors Johannes Cocceius (1603–1669) and Johannes à Marck (1656–1731), for example, taught and published on Old and New Testament exegesis for over twenty years before each published his magnum opus of theology, the *Summa doctrinae de foedere* and *Christianae Theologiae medulla*, respectively.[4] This biblical exegetical approach to theology reigned from the period of early orthodoxy through the high orthodox period to the first part of late orthodoxy—the era from circa 1565 to circa 1725.[5] Subsequently, with the rise of the Enlightenment and biblical criticism, a stricter division between the disciplines of biblical studies and dogmatic theology occurred.

Representative early modern biblical exegetes of the Dutch Republic who worked in a university context include Johannes Leusden (1624–1699) and Campegius Vitringa Sr. (1659–1722), among many others.[6] A review of their work shows that the University of Leiden was the premier academy of the Republic for biblical exegesis, commencing with Junius (early orthodox period) and finding its summit in the high orthodox period.

Moreover, there was strong attention given to the exegesis of the Hebrew Scriptures in *Neerlands Israel* (Dutch Israel).[7] This development of so-called Christian Hebraism originated in the Dutch Republic at the University of Franeker. Drusius had laid a foundation for the philological study of the

Hebrew Bible since his arrival at the Franeker academy in 1585. For Drusius the prerequisite of theology remained philology—a view continued by his successor, Sixtinus Amama (1593–1629), who was also a noted philologist and defender of the study of Hebrew as the proper foundation for theology. Also included in the Hebraist trajectory were (the philologist-exegete and theologian) Cocceius and Vitringa, who were present at the Franeker academy.[8] The importance of the Hebrew language at the Universities of Franeker, Leiden (Gerardus Vossius), and Utrecht (Petrus van Mastricht) was based on the following considerations: Hebrew was one of the oldest languages; insight into New Testament Greek rests on knowledge of Hebrew; such knowledge is indispensable for theology, the *praxis pietatis*, and the conversion of Jews, and it offers access to rabbinic sources.[9] This extraordinary attention to Hebrew was not at the expense of the New Testament, considering the many commentaries produced in the Dutch Republic, including exegetical reflections on the book of Revelation—a biblical book on which Calvin refrained from commenting.

One of the exegetical developments in the second half of the seventeenth century in the Dutch Republic was a difference in approach between Cocceius and Voetius. Cocceius understood Scripture as a revelation of the history of redemption, and not primarily as a book of Reformed doctrines and practices.[10] History, for Cocceius, is redemptive history or covenant history, which is progressive in nature: the covenant of works is abrogated, and the covenant of grace culminates in the coming of God's kingdom. Hence, the words of Scripture must be understood in light of prophecy and redemptive history. As such, the Old Testament is foundational for the New Testament, so that the latter can only be understood through the former. For Cocceius the agreement between the two testaments is the centrality of Christ. This hermeneutical key led to two implications: on the one hand, this was a positive assessment of the Old Testament, as all the prophecies that it contains are sufficient for salvation; on the other hand, it was a negative appraisal of the Old Testament. Under the old covenant, according to Cocceius, God would not yet have given complete forgiveness (*paresis*) as he would under the new covenant through Christ's sacrifice (*áphesis*) and suretyship, due to the progressive nature of redemptive history. The distinction between redemptive history before and after Christ also implied the importance of typology, which he strongly distinguished from allegory.

A further implication for Cocceius is that exegesis becomes intensely Christological. Christ is the key to the understanding of the entirety of Scripture. Philology, the understanding of the meaning of the words of Scripture, is indispensable, as is the literary genre of each book of the Bible, as only then, according to Cocceius, can doctrine arise from exegesis—and not from an a priori confessional interpretation of Scripture. Furthermore, the formulation of doctrine with the words of Scripture must lead to practice and piety (*Doctrina secundum pietatum*). By implication, because of the advancing character of redemptive history, the perfect knowledge of the doctrines and practice of Scripture will occur in the eschaton. This hermeneutical approach to Scripture, with its attention to prophecy, typology, and redemptive covenant history are distinctive features of Cocceian exegesis.

Although some Voetian commentators distanced themselves from the Cocceian approach to exegesis, others of the Voetian school, such as Mastricht, D'Outrein, and Witsius, among others, combined both hermeneutical and exegetical approaches in a way that offered attention to both the historical and personal character of the work of redemption and the centrality of a Christological exegetical focus, though with less attention to typology and a rejection of the *paresis/áphesis* distinction. Thus, early modern exegesis in the Dutch Republic had a dominant presence in the post-Reformation era, in which the interpretative framework of Cocceius can be characterized as a new development in hermeneutics and exegesis. The dominant presence is particularly noticed by the influence of the Dutch Hebraists in the works of Matthew Poole (1624–1679), John Lightfoot (1602–1675), Cotton Mather (1663–1728), and others. Cocceius's redemptive-historical exegesis greatly influenced German Reformed Pietists, such as Friedrich Adolph Lampe (1683–1729), Heinrich Horche (1652–1729), Theodorus Jacobus Frelinghuysen (1691–1747), Theodor Untereyck (1635–1693), Vitringa, and Cocceian preachers of the Dutch Republic, such as Henricus Groenewegen (ca. 1640–1692), David Flud van Giffen (1653–1701), and many others. Biblical exegesis, whether philological, Voetian, or Cocceian, however, was foundational for theology and in the service of preaching.

The Dutch Bible with Annotations

The Dutch Bible with annotations, the *Statenvertaling* or *Statenbijbel* (1637), is the Dutch authorized version of Scripture—a scholarly work that was a new translation of the canonical books of the Old and New Testaments and the Apocrypha from the original Hebrew and Aramaic of the Masoretic Text and the Greek *Textus Receptus*. It was commissioned by the government of the Republic (*Staten*) upon the recommendation of the Synod of Dort (1618–19), which is more often associated with the Remonstrant and Contra-Remonstrant controversy than with Bible translation and biblical exegesis.[11] Moreover, and relevant for early modern Dutch biblical exegesis, the Synod established guidelines for the translation of biblical texts since they understood translation to be a type of interpretation. The four concise guidelines include

> (1) always a careful adherence to the original text, and that the manner of writing of the original languages be preserved, as much as the clarity and properties of Dutch speech permit. But in cases where the Hebrew or Greek manner of speech was harder than could remain in the text, that they note this in the margin, (2) add as few words as possible to complete the meaning of a sentence if it is not expressed fully, and that these words be distinguished from the text with a different font and placed between brackets, (3) formulate a short and clear summary for each book and chapter and write this in the margin at the respective locations in the Holy Scriptures, and (4) add a brief explanation providing insight to the translation of unclear passages; but the addition of doctrinal points is neither necessary nor advisable.[12]

Thus, the aim was an adherence to the words and meaning of the biblical text in the original languages, the provision of a succinct summary, and the addition of annotations in cases of unclear passages. The exclusion of doctrinal notes highlights the exegetical focus of the translation.

The translators and annotators of the Hebrew Scriptures, Johannes Bogerman (1576–1637) and Willem Baudartius (1565–1640), both studied at the Universities of Franeker and Heidelberg and complemented their studies at Geneva and Canterbury, respectively. Both worked for three years on the translation and annotation of the Old Testament.[13] The form and function of these annotations stand in a long trajectory reaching back to the medieval *glossa ordinaria*, and include commentary derived from the church fathers. Illustrative is the exegetical reflection on *Hooglied* (Song of Songs) 2:15 in a *Statenbijbel* note: "The foxes spoil the vineyard by eating the grapes. That is, the false teachers, heretics, and deceitful rulers of the true religion and Church of God."[14] Three observations can be made on this annotation. First, there is an exegetical continuity with an earlier version of the Bible in Dutch, the *Deux-aes* Bible (1581), which says, "The heretics are the true foxes, which spoil the vineyard of the Lord."[15] Second, we find interpretative continuity with Jewish, patristic, and medieval Christian exegetes who identified foxes with specific persons, nations, and schismatic groups—though these heretics may have differed among themselves in their views. The Midrash identifies the Egyptians as the foxes, while for the Targum they are the Amalekites, or, for Bernard, the Toulousans during the Albigensian Crusade (1209–29).[16] Third, the annotation by the *Statenvertalers* adds "foxes" as "deceitful rulers of the true religion," which can also be traced back to Bernard's identification of them with a fraudulent government.[17] This thought is absent in Jewish, patristic, and other medieval commentaries. These features of continuity with earlier exegetical thought, clarification of the words of the text, and an absence of theological commentary may well be representative of the annotations as a whole. The *Statenbijbel* profoundly and persistently shaped the Dutch language as well as Dutch biblical exegesis for centuries, and was not only restricted to the Dutch Republic.[18]

Homiletical Commentaries in Dutch

The biblical exegesis fostered at the Dutch universities of the early modern era resulted in a rise of publications in the second part of the seventeenth century and the early part of the eighteenth century in the Dutch Republic. Furthermore, the first years of the late orthodoxy era (ca. 1725–90) were marked by a transition in the language used for biblical exegesis from Latin to Dutch. In contrast to the theological and often technical commentaries of the Dutch Protestant scholastics in Latin, homiletical commentaries arose out of sermonic material and were more practical. As such, one should not overlook sermons as sources of biblical-exegetical commentary. The astounding number of sermons published between circa 1650 and 1750 seems to indicate an unrelenting craving for biblical exposition and application among the Lowlanders.[19] Dutch ministers published homiletical commentaries by drawing from their sermons on numerous Old[20] and New Testament[21] books of the Bible. Some of the explications of the biblical text were lengthy, as attested by the 105 sermons on the Epistle to the Hebrews by Paulus Hulsius (1653–1712) and the 145 sermons on Matthew 12:20–21 by Bernardus Smytegelt (1665–1739).[22]

Indispensable for these sermons and homiletical commentaries were the exegetical grammars, lexicons, and other aids, of which the famous and massive concordance in three volumes in folio, totaling 1,161 pages, by Abraham Trommius (1633–1719) was the apex in the Dutch language.[23]

Biblical Commentaries in Dutch

The eighteenth century, furthermore, was marked by the publication of three major commentaries on the entire Bible in Dutch. First was the *Commentary on the entire Bible, by some of the principal English divines*, edited by the Leiden professor Johann van den Honert (1693–1758).²⁴ This seventeen-volume commentary, published between 1739 and 1757, is derived from the works of the English exegetes Simon Patrick (1626–1707), Matthew Poole, and Edward Wells (1667–1727). At the same time, *A Literal and Practical Commentary on the Whole Bible* came onto the Dutch market. This ecumenical work of fifty-six volumes was edited and compiled from translations of commentaries by the English Dissenter Matthew Henry (1622–1714), the Lutheran commentator Christoph Starke (1684–1744), the Anglican exegete Thomas Stackhouse (1677–1752), and the Roman Catholic expositor Augustin Calmet, O.S.B. (1672–1757), with added annotations by the Dutch editors.²⁵

Noteworthy is Hyleke Gockinga (1723–1793), the only woman in the Dutch Republic who wrote a Bible commentary in the eighteenth century.²⁶ Her commentary on the book of Genesis consists of a verse-by-verse analysis from the translated Hebrew text, with a concluding paragraph that is practical and edifying in nature. The work was approbated by professors of theology at the University of Groningen Paulus Chevallier (1722–1795), Michael Bertling (1710–1772), and Gerardus Kuypers (1722–1798)—the former revivalist in the "Dutch Great Awakening" of 1748–52. They lauded the work as "being written with much clarity and persuasion, perceptive in biblical wisdom, balanced in interpretive judgement, very broad in knowledge, with theoretical and practical truth of our loving religion."²⁷

Last but not least, the mathematician, philosopher, pastor, and professor Jacob van Nuys Klinkenberg (1744–1812) published a twenty-three-volume *Brief Explanation with Clarifying Annotations of the Entire Bible*.²⁸

Reception and Appropriation

Early modern Dutch biblical exegesis finds its way throughout the world of the seventeenth and eighteenth centuries, directly and indirectly, as well as geographically and ecclesiastically. Biblical commentaries were translated and appropriated, and Bible translations with exegetical reflections (i.e., annotations) were favored but subsequently forgotten. Sermons, as a result of biblical exegesis, were proclaimed and printed, translated and transformed.

Sermons

The dissemination of Dutch biblical exegesis in the form of sermons took place through a (transatlantic) republic of letters among Dutch evangelicals and preachers stationed at Dutch Reformed churches around the world. Networks of Dutch publishers and German translators were instrumental in the spreading of various sermon volumes by Petrus van de Hagen (1641–1671) that were philological, theological, and devotional in essence, shaping Christian piety and practice. These were translated into German, including the 127 sermons on the Epistle to the Philippians, translated by Johann-Christoph Brößke, for the benefit of the German Pietists. The same translator was instrumental in getting *Moses and Christ* by Johannes Bierman (ca. 1675–1721) into German hands as well as into the hands of August Herman Francke (1663–1727).[29] The interecclesiastical bond between Dutch Reformed works (and, more precisely, Dutch Reformed pietistic works) and German Pietists continued into the eighteenth century, attested by the wide reception beyond the Dutch language and Reformed religion.[30] What unites these movements through these translations is the appreciation of piety or *praxis pietatis*. Furthermore, if the *Nadere Reformatie* is an appropriation of British Puritanism, the link between Puritanism, the *Nadere Reformatie*, and German Pietism is displayed through these translated works.

Concerning the preachers stationed at Dutch Reformed churches around the world, one has to consider how Dutch global trade by the East and West India Companies was connected with church planting by the Reformed Church of the Dutch Republic.[31] The Universities of Leiden and Utrecht of the seventeenth and early eighteenth centuries contributed to the exegetical formation of many pastors, including those employed by the Dutch enterprises but ordained, called, and sent by the church. These ministers served company personnel, settlers, and natives (via mission work) in Brazil, Ghana (Elmina), New Netherland, South Africa, and Formosa (Taiwan), though with differing results.[32] A selective review of the international reception of Dutch biblical exegesis through sermons illustrates this global reach.

The establishment of churches throughout Formosa (Taiwan) in the 1630s by Dutch ministers and missionaries reached more than five thousand people through their preaching in the local language rather than in Dutch. The surviving sermons in the Favorlang language by Robert Junius (1606–1655) and Jacob Vertrecht (b. 1606) were published in the Dutch Republic (1650).[33] These sermons attest early Reformed hermeneutical principles and historical-grammatical-analytical exegesis of Scripture but with practical applications concerning the opening of a new church (Isa 56:7), the work of Christ (1 Tim 2:5; John 17:3), God's care (Heb 2:6), and prayer (John 16:23).

In contrast to the biblical exegesis of early Reformed orthodoxy was the homiletical exegesis of the first Ghanese African student at Leiden University, Jacobus Elisa Johannes Capitein (ca. 1717–1747), a freed slave who became a minister and a missionary of the Dutch Reformed Church at Elmina (Ghana).

Before his departure to Ghana, two of his sermons preached in the Dutch Republic were published (2 Tim 2:8; Prov 8:8), as was his inaugural sermon on 2 Cor 4:6 that was preached at Elmina, "The great light of God's grace in his servants" (Het groote genadeligt Gods in zyne dienaaren). Characteristic of his training at Leiden University was Capitein's learned Cocceian exegetical exposition and unblemished Reformed orthodoxy.[34] The orthodoxy of these ministers, particularly in preaching, was assumed, though for some churches, like those in New Netherland (New York and New Jersey), the Voetian or Cocceian approach to biblical hermeneutics and exegesis could be a point of contention.[35]

A "transatlantic evangelical consciousness" between the Old and New World is present in Gerhardus van Schuylenborgh (1681–1770), for example, a minister near Utrecht and an advisor to the classis of Raritan.[36] The Raritan Valley in New Jersey became the new home and pastorate of the German-Dutch Pietist Theodorus Jacobus Frelinghuysen, whose Voetian inclinations promoted a strict Sabbath observance and experiential preaching—both lacking in the New World in the eyes of Frelinghuysen. Theodorus Jacobus's son, Johannes Frelinghuysen (1727–1754), stayed with Van Schuylenborgh during his study of theology at Utrecht University, married Dina van Bergh (1725–1807), and served the Reformed Church at New Brunswick, New Jersey.[37] Though little is known of Johannes's exegetical work, except that his preaching was known as Calvinistic and experiential, his wife Dina left a diary with biblical exegetical reflections throughout. Often private meditations and expositions of the preaching text of the minister following the public worship service,[38] these practical and experiential reflections exemplify the character of Reformed Pietism in eighteenth-century colonial America.

Of a different nature was the reception of a sermon of Abraham Hellenbroek (1658–1731), a pastor and preacher, a representative of the *Nadere Reformatie*, a Hebraist, and a Bible commentator in the late seventeenth and early eighteenth centuries of the Dutch Republic. In 1743, the Scots-Irish pietistic revivalist Gilbert Tennent (1703–1764) published a collection of sermons entitled *The Necessity of holding fast the Truth . . . with an Appendix Relating to* ERRORS *lately vented by some Moravians*. The title page informed prospective readers that the volume included "A Sermon of a Dutch Divine on *taking the little Foxes*."[39] The sermon was taken from Hellenbroek's extensive commentary in Dutch on the Canticle of Canticles, and it was translated into English and published in 1742.[40] Tennent's inclusion of this sermon served as an antidote to the "arrival of the Moravian Brethren in these American Regions."[41] The transatlantic reception of Hellenbroek's sermon was not restricted to the Middle Colonies but also included South Africa.[42] Furthermore, the New England divine Jonathan Edwards (1703–1758) refers to the same sermon in "Images of Divine Things" (ca. 1742). He also cross-references Hellenbroek's work in his "Blank Bible" notes on Cant 2:15 and Judg 15:4–5.[43] The reception of this little work by the "Dutch divine" in the revival context of colonial America in the 1740s, then, differs remarkably from that of the early eighteenth-century Dutch Republic in which Hellenbroek's commentary was published. Furthermore, the apologetic character of Tennent's publication contrasts with the Voetian-Cocceian exegetical nature of the biblical commentary on the Canticle of Canticles by Hellenbroek, which is considered the apex of the interpretation of the Canticles in the *Nadere Reformatie*.[44]

Early modern Dutch biblical exegesis from the mid-seventeenth century onward can be described as either Voetian or Cocceian, though adhering strictly to this demarcation would mischaracterize such exegesis. The sermons using a Voetian exegetical approach were more grammatical-analytical in nature, with a strong emphasis on the *praxis pietatis*, while those sermons arising from a Cocceian hermeneutical approach contained more "biblical theology" and were considered learned sermons. In contrast, Voetian exegetes and their preaching, as belonging to the *Nadere Reformatie*, resonated more with the Puritan, plain-style sermon. Noteworthy is the reception of the many sermons of representatives of the *Nadere Reformatie* by the German Pietists, who seem less interested in the Cocceian sermons but were receptive of Cocceius's redemption-historical approach, as noted in the works of Lampe, Untereyck, the Marburg Bible (1712), edited by Heinrich Horche, and the radical Pietist Berleburg Bible (1726–29).[45] The demarcation between Voetian and Cocceian exegesis should not be too strongly enforced, as many ministers employed around the world by the Dutch trading companies were appreciative of Cocceian exegetical hermeneutics, but not at the expense of the practice of godliness, as seen in the Middle Colonies.

Bible Translation

The importance of having a translated Bible in one's own language was articulated at the Synod of Dort (1618–19), resulting in the Dutch translation the *Statenbijbel* (1637), an annotated, interpretative work of Scripture with its exegetical insights. Not only did the synodical decision serve as an impetus for Antonius Hambroek (1606–1661), a missionary minister to Formosa, to translate the Gospels of Matthew and John with annotations in the Formosan language (ca. 1650), but the *Statenbijbel* contributed to the international recognition of early modern Dutch biblical exegesis. The fame of the annotations was not restricted to the Dutch Republic. In 1645, such Westminster Assembly divines as William Twisse (1578–1646), Cornelius Burgess (ca. 1589–1665), Stephen Marshall (ca. 1594–1655), Anthony Tuckney (1599–1670), and Samuel Rutherford (1600–1661) strongly advocated for the translation of the annotations, calling them "a treasure of knowledge and spiritual understanding."[46] Theodore Haak (1605–1690), a German Reformed scholar and a resident in England, translated not only the annotations but also the entire scriptural text of the *Statenbijbel* into English. Although Haak is perhaps most known for producing the first German translation of John Milton's *Paradise Lost*, his *Dutch Annotations upon the Whole Bible* (1657) became widely known in England, Scotland, the Middle Colonies, and New England.[47] Last but not least, the *Statenvertaling* became part of the German Pietist *Biblia Pentapla* (1711)—a polyglot Bible with five translations in German.[48]

Biblical Commentary

Many early modern Dutch Bible commentaries were written in Dutch, translated from Latin into Dutch, or translated from Dutch into German and English.[49] These works were often preserved in both private and public libraries, among them the college libraries of eighteenth-century South Africa, the American Middle Colonies, and New England.[50] One particular work in early modern post-Reformation biblical exegesis contributed to the dissemination of Dutch exegetical works, the *Synopsis Criticorum aliorumque Sacrae Scripturae Interpretum* (hereafter SSS) by Matthew Poole (1624–1679), who continued with his exegetical work in the *English Annotations on the Holy Bible* in Amsterdam at the close of his life. The works of the Dutch exegetes Henry Ainsworth (1571–1622), Cocceius, Lodewijk de Dieu (1590–1642), Johannes Drusius, Hugo Grotius (1583–1645), Franciscus Junius, Andreas Rivetus, and the Dutch Bible with annotations (*Statenbijbel*) found their way into Poole's SSS.[51]

A positive reception of the *Synopsis* can be observed in the Dutch Republic and throughout the New England valley and the Middle Colonies far into the eighteenth century.[52] Jonathan Edwards's use of the *Synopsis*, therefore, was not unusual, though Edwards read Poole's work with much discernment. Illustrative is Poole's comment on Gen 30:14 concerning mandrakes. First, one notices that he relies predominantly on Drusius's work on the book of Ruth, which contains a treatise entitled *De Mandragora Tractatus*.[53] In this treatise, addressing the question of what is understood by mandrakes, Poole follows the three suggestions offered by Drusius: the fruit of mandrakes are fruits among the leaves, or they bear the likeness of man, having the form of head and hands, or they resemble a man.[54] Although Edwards does not seem to make an immediate exegetical choice, Poole's reference should not be overlooked, noting that the word "mandrakes," besides its appearance in Gen 30, is found in Scripture only in Cant 7:13.[55] It is precisely on this biblical text that Edwards comments in *Notes on Scripture* and sermons in 1736 and 1746. In the former, he notes, "What the spouse entertains her lover with is called 'fruits' (*Canticles* 4:16, *Canticles* 7:13, and *Canticles* 8:2), as the good works of the saints abundantly are represented elsewhere as fruit, which the church brings and offers to God. The spouse is here compared to fruitful trees (*Canticles* 4:13–16, *Canticles* 7:7–8); the saints are compared to the same."[56] This understanding is also noted in a 1746 sermon on Cant 7:13: "Prop I. The precious fruits that are found in the saints are pleasant and entertaining to Jesus Christ. Prop II. 'Tis much to be desired that there should be found in those that are godly gracious fruits of all sorts. Prop III. 'Tis very desirable that there should be those exercises and fruits of grace in the souls of the saints that are new as well as old for the entertainment of Christ."[57] Additionally, in a sermon from September 1736 entitled "The Church's Marriage to Her Sons, and to Her God," he commented, "So Christ is said to feed among the lilies, *Canticles* 2:16. And *Canticles* 7:13, she speaks of 'all manner of pleasant fruits, new and old, which she had laid up for him.'"[58]

Thus, Edwards follows Drusius's exegetical understanding of the mandrakes as pleasant fruits. In sum, Poole's massive synoptic exegetical work relied on a significant amount of the work of Dutch exegetes. In other words, it mediated the work of early modern Dutch biblical exegesis, and users of Poole's commentary, such as Edwards, indirectly shared in the fruit of exegetical work originating in the Dutch Republic. Cotton Mather, furthermore, is not only an indirect but also a direct recipient of Dutch biblical exegesis. His *Manuductio ad ministerium* (1726) and "Biblia Americana" attest to his acquaintance not only with Poole, but also with Braun, Cocceius, Drusius, De Dieu, Grotius, Van Leusden, Vitringa, and Witsius, as well as the Dutch Bible with Annotations (*Statenvertaling*).[59]

In summary, early modern Dutch biblical exegesis finds its way throughout the world of seventeenth-century Dutch trade and Reformed church planting, and was heard in eighteenth-century Dutch and German Pietist communities in places like Amsterdam and New Amsterdam, Breukelen and Brooklyn, as well as Halle and Frankfurt am Main. Biblical commentaries, such as Hellenbroek's *Canticle of Canticles*, were translated and received new and different contexts—from sermonic discourse to apologetic defense. Some of the exegetical work has been largely forgotten, such as the translation of the Bible into Formosan and the sermons preached in Ghana; some work is still awaiting discovery, such as deposits from the Reformed church of Recife, Brazil, Cape Town, South Africa, and other archives. Furthermore, early modern Dutch

Reformed biblical exegesis contributed to and was mediated by major Bible commentaries, such as Poole's SSS, whose use has been noted in the seventeenth-century academic circles of the Dutch Republic, but also in eighteenth-century New England Puritanism and evangelicalism.

Conclusion

Early modern Dutch exegesis, then, was a major force within the post-Reformation era of biblical commentaries. The early attention to the technical aspects of biblical exegesis, such as attention to language (Hebraism), philology (Drusius and others), and the establishment of translation guidelines resulted in the publication of the Dutch authorized Bible with annotations (*Statenvertaling*) and the rise of commentaries in various forms, such as disputations and grammatical-analytical commentaries (in Latin, for the academy) and homiletical commentaries (in Dutch, for the church). Particularly, Dutch academic works of exegesis found their way into major, widely known commentaries, such as Poole's SSS—one that mediated early modern Dutch biblical exegesis for the Dutch Reformed, German Pietists, and British Puritans. Together, these various commentaries were understood to be in the service of Reformed theology and preaching, where doctrine and practice arose from reflection on Scripture. The Dutch academic context of biblical hermeneutics and exegesis led, however, to different interpretations of Scripture, as noted in the distinction between Voetian and Coccejan hermeneutics. Furthermore, the Dutch ecclesiastical context, particularly that of the *Nadere Reformatie*, resulted in many sermons by the Dutch Pietists being turned into commentaries and translated for the benefit of German Pietists and New England Puritans. Finally, the global reception of Dutch biblical exegesis through the efforts of the ministers in the service of the Reformed Church and trading companies around the world awaits further research.

Notes

1. On the term *Nadere Reformatie* and problems of translating it, see Herman Selderhuis, *Handbook of Dutch Church History* (Göttingen: Vandenhoeck & Ruprecht, 2014), 338–41. The author wants to express thanks to the editors of this volume for their helpful suggestions, which improved this chapter in various ways.

2. Carl R. Trueman, "Scripture and Exegesis in Early Modern Reformed Theology," in *The Oxford Handbook of Early Modern Theology, 1600–1800*, ed. Ulrich L. Lehner, Richard A. Muller, and A. G. Roeber (New York: Oxford University Press, 2016).

3. N.B.: The works referenced in this chapter have been shortened to a minimum due to word count limitations. Johannes Hoornbeeck, *Disputatio . . . Genes. 49. vers. 10* (1664); Frans Burman, *Disputatio . . . Luc. 24: 44* (1678); Burman, *Disputationum . . . Hoseæ capp. XII. XIII. XIV* (1678); Burman, *Disputationum . . . Esaiæ capp. XV. XVI. XVIII* (1678); Petrus van Mastricht, *Disputatio Exercitationum . . . in caput Jesai quinquagesimum-tertium* (1693–94, seven disputations).

4. Johannes Cocceius, *Commentarius . . . Jobi* (1644); Cocceius, *Epistolae ad hebraeos Explicatio* (1659); Cocceius, *Cogitationes de Cantico Canticorum Salamonis* (1665); Cocceius, *Sancti Apostoli Pauli Epistola Ad Ephesios* (1667); Cocceius, *Epistola ad Romanos* (1668); Cocceius, *Sancti Pauli Apostoli Epistola Ad Philippenses* (1669); Cocceius, *Prophetia et threni Jeremiae cum commentario* (1669); Cocceius, *Prophetia Ezechielis cum commentario . . .* (1669); Cocceius, *Summa doctrinae de foedere et testamento Dei explicate* (1654). Johannes à Marck, *In apocalypsin Johannis commentaries* (1699); *In Canticum Shelomonis Commentarius seu analytica exegetica . . .* (1703); Marck, *In Haggaeum, Zecharjam, & Malachiam, commentarius: seu analysis exegetica . . .* (1701); Marck, *In Micham, Nahumum, Habhakkukum, & Tsephanjam commentarius* (1694–1730).

5. The post-Reformation Reformed era is defined here as early orthodoxy (ca. 1565–1640), high orthodoxy (ca. 1640–1725), and late orthodoxy (ca. 1725–90). See Richard A. Muller, *Post-Reformation Reformed Dogmatics: The Rise and Development of Reformed Orthodoxy, ca. 1520 to ca. 1725*, 4 vols. (Grand Rapids, MI: Baker Academic, 2003), 1:31–32. The transatlantic dimension of this periodization is proposed in Adriaan C. Neele, *Before Jonathan Edwards: Sources of New England Theology* (New York: Oxford University Press, 2019), 9–18.

6. For exegetical works of these representatives, see Richard A. Muller, "Biblical Interpretation in the Sixteenth and Seventeenth Centuries," in *Dictionary of Major Biblical Interpreters*, ed. Donald K. McKim (Downers Grove, IL: IVP Academic, 2007), 22–44, http://www.prdl.org (accessed June 16, 2020).

7. Laura Cruz and Willem Frijhoff, *Myth in History, History in Myth* (Leiden: Brill, 2009), 14, 202, 219, 231, 235. The Prince of Orange was a new Moses leading the people through the Red Sea of the Revolt to the promised land of *Neerlands Israel*, "Dutch Israel."

8. See further Adriaan C. Neele, *Petrus van Mastricht (1630–1706): Reformed Orthodoxy: Method and Piety* (Leiden: Brill, 2009), 141–70 on exegesis.

9. W. J. van Asselt, "Hebraica Veritas: Zeventiende-eeuwse motieven voor de bestudering van het Hebreeuws door predikanten," *Kerk en Theologie* 46 (1995): 309–24.

10. In this paragraph I follow Johannes Cocceius, *Summa doctrinae de foedere et testamento Dei explicate* (1654); W. J. van Asselt, *Amicitia Dei, Een onderzoek naar de structurr van de theologie van Johannes Cocceius (1603–1669)* (Ede, 1988); C. Graafland, "Schrifleer en schriftverstaan in de Nadere Reformatie," in *Theologische aspecten van de Nadere Reformatie*, ed. T. Brienen and K. Exalto (Zoetermeer: Boekencentrum, 1993), 68–78.

11. *Acta ofte handelingen des Nationalen Synoden . . . tot Dordrecht 1618 ende 1619* (1621), 26.l, "De achste sessie" (November 20, 1618). This discussion at the Synod was prior to taking up the five articles of the Remonstrants.

12. *Acta ofte handelingen des Nationalen Synoden*, 26r. Unless otherwise indicated, all translations in this essay are my own.

13. M. Verduin, *Canticum Canticorum . . .* (Utrecht: Uitgeverij de Banier, 1992), 397–98.

14. *Biblia, De gantsche H. Schrifture*, "Het Hooglied van Salomo 2:15," marginal note 55.

15. *Biblia dat is, de gantsche Heylighe Schrift, grondelick ende trouvvelick verduydtschet, Met verklaringhe duysterer woorden, redenen ende spreucken* (1562), Hooghlied 2:15. The name *Deux-aes* (= the poor) is derived from the marginal notes of Neh 3:5, "Deux aes en heeft niet, six cinque en gheeft niet, quater dry die helpen vrij."

16. Cf. Verduin, *Canticum Canticorum*, 75. Bernardus, *Opera Omnia*, sermon lxv and lxvi.

17. Cf. Verduin, *Canticum Canticorum*, 442.

18. Carolus Tuinman, *De oorsprong en uitlegging van dagelijks gebruikte Nederduitsche Spreekwoorden opgeheldert* ... (1720). See below for the reception of the *Statenbijbel*.

19. Johannes Beukelman, *Uitgelezen vervolg-stoffen* ... *of Negentig leerredenen* ... (1777); Beukelman, *De lydende en verheerlykte Immanuël* ... (1775); Theodorus van der Groe, *Verzameling van een tiental godvruchtige predikatiën* ... (1818); Petrus van der Hagen, *Waere boetvaerdigheyt* ... (1687); Bernardus Smytegelt, *Acht uitmuntende practicale leer-redenen* ... (1744); Smytegelt, *Twaalf uitmuntende practicale leer-redenen over Hoogliet I. vers 2–4* ... (1750); Smytegelt, *Zes uitmuntende practicale leer-redenen* ... (1742).

20. Johannes Smith, *Het Boek Esther* (1739); Kasparus Alardin, *De geluksaligheyd van den weg der regtveerdige* ... (1738); Jan Jacob Brahé, *Ethans onderwyzinge in den negenentachtigsten Psalm* (1765); Wilhelmus à [Wilhelm von] Brakel, *Hallelujah, ofte lof des Heeren* ... *der verklaringe van den VIII. Psalm* (1737); Johannes d'Outrein, *De ziels-opheffing* ... *ofte De XXV. en CXVI. Psalm* ... (1747); Johannes Plevier, *De veerthien eerste psalmen uit het Boek der psalmen* ... (1757); Plevier, *De vyfthiende en negen volgende psalmen uit het Boek der psalmen* (1760); Plevier, *De vyf-en-twintigste en twaalf volgende psalmen uit het Boek der psalment* (1765); Plevier, *De agt-en-dertigste en elf volgende psalmen uit het Boek der psalmen*, 2 vols. (1770); Petrus Nahuys, *Leerredenen over Zacharia 5: 5–11 en Jesaias 58: 5–12* (1786); Elbertus Noordbeek, *Beknoopte uitlegginge van de prophetie Jeremie* ... (1701); Willem Teellinck, *Den hoeck-steen van het Ouden en Nieuwe Testament, ofte stichtelicke verklaringe van de propheet Maleachi* ... (1645); Campegius Vitringa Sr., *Uitlegging over het boek der profetsyen van Jezaias*, 6 vols. (1739–41); Jan Jacob Vos, *Uitlegging van het boek van den profeet Daniel*, 2 vols. (1761).

21. For the Matthean parables, see Campegius Vitringa Sr., *Verklaring van de Evangelische Parabolen* ... (1715). For the Acts of the Apostles, see Johannes Plevier, *De handelingen der H. Apostelen beschreeven door Lukas*, 2 vols. (1774). For the Pauline Epistles, see Romans: Johannes Theodorus van der Kemp, *De Theodicée van Paulus* ..., 2 vols. (1799); Galatians: Brouerius Brouwer, *Schriftmaatige verklaaring* ... (1762); Ephesians: Petrus Dinant, *De brief van den H. apostel Paulus aan die van Efeze*, 3 vols. (1721); Philippians: Petrus van der Hagen, *De Brief des H. Apostels Pauli aen de Philippensen* ... (1684); Colossians: David Knibbe, *Den Sendbrief des Apostels Pauli aan de Colossensen* ..., 2 vols. (1694); Hebrews: Paulus Hulsius, *Verklaring van de brief* ... *in hondert en vyf kerkredenen*, 2 vols. (1725); 1–2 Peter: Brouerius Brouwer, *De tweede algemeene zendbrief van den apostel Petrus* (1760); 1 John: Petrus van Staverden, *De Eerste Sendbrieff des Apostels Johannis* (1692).

22. Hulsius, *Verklaring van* ... *den Hebreen*; Bernardus Smytegelt, *Het gekrookte riet, of honderdt-vyf-en-veertig predicatiën over Mattheus XII: 20, 21* ... (1744).

23. Abraham Trommius, *Volkomene Nederlandtsche Concordantie ofte Woordt-register des Nieuwen Testaments* ..., 3 vols. (1672).

24. Jan van den Honert, *Verklaring van de geheele Heilige Schrift, door eenigen van de voornaamste Engelsche godgeleerden, Patrick, Polus, en Wells*, 17 vols. (1739–57).

25. *Letterlyke en praktikaal Verklaring over den gehele Bijbel* (1741–92). Augustin Calmet, *Commentaire littéral sur tous les livres de l'Ancien et du Nouveau Testament*, 8 vols. (1707); Thomas Stackhouse, *A new history of the Holy Bible: from the beginning of the world to the establishment of Christianity* ..., 6 vols. (1748); Christoph Starke, *Synopsis Bibliothecae exegeticae in Vetus Testamentum* ..., 10 vols. (1750)

26. Hylecke Gockinga, *Verhandeling over het eerste Bybel-boek, genoemd Genesis*, 4 vols. (1788–93).

27. Paraphrased in Gockinga, *Verhandeling over het eerste Bybel-boek*, Aprobatie, "geoeffend doorzicht in Goddelyke Bybelwysheid, van een juist wikkend oordeel, van zeer uitgebreide kunde, en in de bespiegelende, en in de gemoedelyke waarheden van onzen dierbren Godsdienst."

28. Jacob van Nuys Klinkenberg, *De Bijbel, door beknopte uitbreidingen en ophelderende aenmerkingen verklaerd*, 23 vols. (1780–88).

29. Johann Biermann, *Moses und Christus Oder / Erklärung / Der vornehmsten Fürbilder des Alten Testaments*, trans. Johann-Christoph Brößke (1706); Biermann, *Die Weissagung des Propheten Zachariae*, trans. Emanuel Mener (1710). For Francke, see https://digital.francke-halle.de/mod7/content/titleinfo/135826 (accessed June 16, 2020). For transatlantic connections, see Adriaan C. Neele, "The Reception of Jonathan Edwards in the Dutch Republic," in *Jonathan Edwards as a Transatlantic Thinker*, ed. Paul Helm (London: Palgrave Macmillan, forthcoming); Jan Stievermann, "Faithful Translations: New Discoveries on the German Pietist Reception of Jonathan Edwards," *CH* 83, no. 2 (2014): 324–66; Jan van de Kamp, "De invloed van het puritanisme in het Duitse taalgebied in de zeventiende eeuw," *Documentatieblad Nadere Reformatie* 37 (2013): 1–22; Van de Kamp, *"Op verzoek van vromen vertaald": Duitse vertalingen van gereformeerde stichtelijke lectuur 1667–1697 en de rol van netwerken* (Zoetermeer: Boekencentrum, 2012); Fred van Lieburg, "The Dutch Factor in German Pietism," in *A Companion to German Pietism, 1660–1800*, ed. Douglas H. Shantz (Leiden: Brill, 2014), 50–80.

30. Concerning this interecclesiastical bond, representative works of the *Nadere Reformatie* were translated into German as well. For example, Theodor von Brakel, *Die Staffel dess geistlichen Lebens* (1698); Theodor von Brakel, *Einige geistliche Betrachtungen* (1732); Theodor von Brakel, *Das Geistliche Leben* (1732); Wilhelm von Brakel, *Logike latreia, das ist Vernünfftiger Gottesdienst worinnen die Göttliche Wahrheiten der gantzen Theologie gründlich erkläret*, 3 vols. (1716); Jacobus Koelman, *Wecker der Lehrer* (1711); Coenraad Mel, . . . *Erklärung des Ersten Buchs Mosis* (1714); Mel, *Die Lust Der Heiligen an Jehova Oder* . . . (1768); Mel, *Posaunen der Ewigkeit* (1712); Mel, *Salems Tempel* (1724); Mel, *Wäysen-Predigt . . . Ps. 27* (1709); Lambrecht Myseras, *Unterricht vom würdigen Gebrauch des heiligen Abendmahls* (1797); Johannes d'Outrein, *Entwurff der Göttlichen Warheiten* (1698); Outrein, *Kurtzer Entwurff der Göttlichen Warheiten* (1729); Simon Simonides, *Gottselige Seelen-Ubung* . . . (1671); Jacobus Trigland, *Die Krafft der Gottseligkeit* (1651); Godefridus Udemans, *Jacobs-Leitter* . . . (1673); Trigland, *Praxis* . . . (1683); Johannes Verschuir, *Die Wahrheit im Innersten* . . . (1743); Gisbertus Voetius, *Von Eintzeler Versammlung der Christen* (1712). Concerning the wider reception of Dutch Reformed works beyond Dutch Reformed religion, see Petrus van de Hagen, *Erklärung über den Send-Brief Pauli an die Philipper in 127 Predigten* . . . (1710). Other works of Van de Hagen in German include sermons on the Heidelberg Catechism, trans. Joh. Vogelsang (Bremen, 1693), and on true repentance, trans. J. H. Winkelhäuser (Frankfurt am Main, 1701); Elbertus Noordbeek, *Erklärung Der Weissagung Maleachi* . . . (1727); David Knibbe, *Die Epistel Des Aposteles Pauli An Die Colosser In 108 Predigten* . . . , 2 vols. (1708); Knibbe, *Historie der Propheten: In vier Bücher abgetheilt* (1709); Knibbe, *Das Urtheil Gottes . . . eine Auslegung des Apostels 1 Petr. 4, 17–19* (1696). See also P. G. Hoftijzer, *Engelse boekverkopers bij de Beurs. De geschiedenis van de Amsterdamse boekhandels Bruyning en Swart, 1637–1724* (Amsterdam: APA–Holland University Press, 1987).

31. Nieuw Amsterdam (New York, 1625/28), Formosa (Taiwan, 1626), Recife (Brazil, 1631/33), Elima (Ghana, 1637), Batavia (Indonesia, 1640), Bay van Nagasaki, Deshima (Japan, 1641), Ceylon (Sri Lanka, 1642), Cape Town (South Africa, 1652), and St. Thomas (Caribbean, 1660).

32. Noorlander suggests that early seventeenth-century Dutch Calvinism was restrictive enough and the churches of the Netherlands worried enough about deviance and heterodoxy that they unintentionally undermined their own mission and reduced the Dutch footprint overseas. Cf. D. Noorlander, "The Reformed Church and the Regulation of Religious Literature in the Early Dutch Atlantic World," *Itinerario* 42 (2018): 375–402.

33. W. Campbell, ed., *The Articles of Christian Instruction in Favorlang-Formosan* (London: Kegan Paul, Trench, Trübner, 1896).

34. Jacobus Elisa Joannes Capitein, "De trouwhertoge vermaaninge . . . uit 2 Timotheus II vers 8. Te Muiderberg, den 20 Mei 1742"; Capitein, "De voornaamste goederen van de Opperste Wysheit, uit Spreuken VIII vers 18 in twee predikantien, in 's Gravenhage, de 27 Mei 1742 en t'Ouderkerk aan de Amstel, den 6 Juny 1742"; Capitein, *Het Groote Genadeligt Gods in Zyne Dienaren* . . . (Amsterdam, 1744). In the same year, Capitein translated the Lord's Prayer and

Decalogue into Mfantse, a regional language of the Gold Coast of West Africa. See also Jake Griesel, *Jacobus Elisa Johannes Capitein (ca. 1717–1747)*: The "Dissertatio Politico-Theologica de Servitute, Libertati Christianae Non Contraria" in Historical-Intellectual Context (forthcoming). *Uitgewrogte predikatien, zynde De trouwhertige vermaaninge van den Apostel der heydenen Paulus, aan zynen zoon Timotheus, uit 2 Timotheus II vers 8, te Muiderberg . . . alsmede de voornaamste goederen van de opperste wysheit, uit Spreuken VIII. vers 18 in twee predikatien* (Amsterdam: Bernardus Mourik and Jacobus Haffman, 1742).

35. Leon van den Broeke, Hand Krabbendam, and Dirk Mouw, eds., *Transatlantic Pieties: Dutch Clergy in Colonial America* (Grand Rapids, MI: Eerdmans, 2012), 20–23, 113–16; Robert A. Nahorn, "Eilardus Westerlo (1738–1790): From Colonial Dominee to America Pastor" (PhD diss., Vrije Universiteit Amsterdam, 2011), 112–14. Nahorn remarks, "The matter of labeling ministers in the New World as Voetians or Cocceians is a difficult one" (108). Dirk E. Mouw, "Moederkerk and Vaderland: Religion and Ethnic Identity in the Middle Colonies, 1690–1772" (PhD diss., University of Iowa, 2009), 524–28; James Tanis, *Dutch Calvinistic Pietism in the Middle Colonies: A Study in the Life and Theology of Theodorus Jacobus Frelinghuysen* (The Hague: Martinus Nijhoff, 1967), 97–134. *The Sermons by Theodorus Jacobus Frelinghuysen*, trans. William DeMarest (New York, 1856), a collection of twenty-one sermons by the German Pietist and Dutch Reformed "forerunner" of the Great Awakening, is not discussed here. Cf. Joel R. Beeke, ed., *Forerunner of the Great Awakening: Sermons by Theodorus Jacobus Frelinghuysen (1691–1747)* (Grand Rapids, MI: Eerdmans, 2000).

36. Susan Durden O'Brien, "A Transatlantic Community of Saints: The Great Awakening and the First Evangelical Network, 1735–1755," *American Historical Review* 91, no. 4 (1986): 813.

37. Johannes Frelinghuysen was a son of Theodorus Jacobus Frelinghuysen (ca. 1691–ca. 1747), the forerunner of the Great Awakening.

38. *The Diary of Dina van Bergh, 1746–1747*, trans. and ed. Gerard van Dyke (New Brunswick, NJ: Historical Society of the Reformed Church in America, 1993), 10, 11, 13, 27, 30, 41, 47, 55, 75.

39. Gilbert Tennent, *The necessity of holding fast the truth . . . Together with a sermon of a Dutch divine on taking the little foxes; faithfully translated* (1743).

40. *A sermon by Abraham Hellenbroek . . . from Canticles Chap. II ver. 15 . . . Being one of that Rev. Author's printed Discourses on the Song of Solomon, published at Anno 1717. Translated from the Dutch* (1742). Cf. Abraham Hellenbroek, *Het Hooglied van Salomon verklaart en vergeestelykt*, 2 vols. (1718–20).

41. Tennent, *Necessity of holding fast the truth*, [i].

42. Willem van Zyl, *Vita Verbo Dei Devota* (Cape Town: Lux Verbi, 1992), 246–47.

43. *WJE*, 11:148: "Foxes Remarkable Types of devils & other Enemies of the Church of God, see Mr. Hellenbroek's sermon on Cant. 2. 15. from p. 4. to p. 12. See also note on Cant. 2. 15." Cf. *WJE*, 24:614 and 24:338 (Judg 15:4–5): "Foxes represent heretics and heretical doctrines (See note on Cant. 2:15, and also Mr. Hellenbroek's sermon on that text, pp. 4 ff."

44. R. Bischop, "Hellenbroek, Abraham (1658–1731)," in *Encyclopedie Nadere Reformatie*, ed. W. J. op 't Hof (Kampen: De Groot Gouderiaan), 1:336, "Bovendien bereikte de mystiek Hooglied-interpretatie in de Nadere Reformatie bij hem [Hellenbroek, ACN] haar hoogtepunt."

45. See Shantz, *Companion to German Pietism*. Note also the appropriation of Vitringa's Isaiah commentary by the Halle Pietist Joachim Lange (1670–1744), *Biblisches Licht und Recht* (1732).

46. *The Dutch Annotations upon the whole Bible*, trans. Theodore Haak (1657): "1645 A copy of the certification, or attestation, about the general desire in both Kingdoms (England and Scotland) to have the Belgick or Dutch Annotations upon the Bible (come forth first anno domini 1637) translated into English, by Theodore Haak." Jan van der Kamp, "Networks and Translation Within the Republic of Letters: The Case of Theodore Haak (1605–1690)," in *Translating Early Modern Science*, ed. Sietske Fransen, Niall Hodson, and Karl A. E. Enenkel (Leiden: Brill, 2017), 41–65.

47. *Catalogus librorum Bibliothecæ Collegij Harvardini qoud est Cantabrigiæ in Nova Anglia* (1723), 2; *A Catalogue of the Library of Yale College in New Haven* (1743), 23; *Catalogue of Books in the Library of the College of New Jersey* (1760), 9. *BA*, vols. 1 and 5.

48. *Biblia Pentapla, Das ist: Die Bucher der Heiligen Schrift Des Alten und Neuen Testaments Nach funf-facher deutscher Verdolmetschung* (Hamburg: Hermann Heinrich Holle, 1711). It consists of five parts or columns. Part 1 is a translation of the Roman Catholic Caspar Ulenberg. Part 2 is a translation of the Bible by Martin Luther. Part 3 is a translation by Johann Piscator. Part 4 contains a translation of the Old Testament by Joseph Athiae and the New Testament by Johann Heinrich Reitz. The last part or column is a translation of the Dutch *Statenvertaling*.

49. Dutch: Frans Burman, *De rigteren Israels...* (1675); Johannes Cocceius, *De prophetie van Ezechiel, met de uitleggingen* (1691). English: William Ames, *An analytical exposition of both the epistles of the Apostle Peter...* (1641). German: Frans Burman, *Gesetz und Zeugnüß... oder der V. Bücher Mosis* (1693); Burman, *Alle biblischen Wercke... Der fünff Bücher Mosis, Josuae, Richter, Ruths, der zween Bücher Samuelis, der Könige, Chronicon, Esrae, Nehemiae und Esther* (1709); Burman, *Samuel, Oder Auszlegung und Betrachtung Der Bücher Samuels* (1703); Campegius Vitringa Sr., *Auslegung der Weissasung Jesaiae*, 6 vols. (1749); Salomon van Til, *Das Buch der Psalmen erkläret*, 5 vols. (1720); Heinrich von Diest, *Die Schling Davids mit fünff glatten Steinen wider den Goliath* (1648); Petrus van Hoeke, *Zergliedernde Auslegung über die 3 letzten Propheten: Haggai, Zacharia und Malachia* (1709); Noordbeek, *Erklärung Der Weissagung Maleachi*; Petrus van Staveren, *Der erste Brief des Apostels Johannis erklähret* (1697); Jean Taffin, *Kennzeichen Der Kinder Gottes* (1660); Salomon van Til, *Das Buch der Psalmen erkläret*, 4 vols. (1720); Van Til, *Das Evangelium Des heiligen Apostels Matthei Nach gehöriger Erklärung* (1705).

50. *Bibliothecæ Collegij Harvardini*, 10, 28, 41, 43, 44, 51, 57, 60, 75; *Library of Yale College*, 4, 24, 26; *Library of the College of New Jersey*, 19–22. For South Africa, see Van Zyl, *Vita Verbo Dei Devota*, 230–31, 233, 237–38, 245–47, 249, 252, 260–61, 273.

51. Matthew Poole, *Synopsis Criticorum aliorumque Sacrae Scripturae Interpretum*, 5 vols. (1669–76), "Catalogus Auctorum."

52. See, for an extensive discussion, Neele, *Before Edwards*, 106–51.

53. Johannes Drusius, *Historia Ruth* (1632).

54. Poole, *Synopsis*, 1:218.20–75.

55. Ibid., 1:218.75, "Vox exstat folùm hîc & Cant. 7.13."

56. *WJE*, 15:549.

57. *WJEO*, 51. Sermon 408 on Cant 7:13.

58. *WJE*, 25:166, 181. Sermon on Isa 62:4–5.

59. Cotton Mather, *Manuductio ad ministerium: Directions for a candidate of the ministry* (1726); *BA*, vols. 1–5, 9 (see indices).

4

READING THE BIBLE

John Owen and Early Evangelical "Biblicism"

CRAWFORD GRIBBEN

However else he might be described, the English Puritan theologian John Owen (1616–1683) was preeminently a student of Scripture, and his conclusions about the character and content of Scripture were part of his legacy to early evangelicals.[1] Biblical interpretation was at the heart of Owen's many enterprises. Although his literary and historical interests were surprisingly diverse, as a preacher, as a teacher of theology, and as the author of the longest commentary on a New Testament epistle ever published, he worked carefully, if not consistently, to draw his religious and political commitments from biblical texts.[2] He was, as the evangelical revivalist George Whitefield later put it, "the accurate Doctor Owen," formidably learned, and as precise in his philological and hermeneutical method as he was in his theological or ecclesiological conclusions.[3] Owen was well qualified as a textual critic, translator, and exegete.[4] He referred to manuscript variations, to historic and modern translations, while reading the Bible in conversation with the church fathers and medieval schoolmen and with the most capable of his Jewish, Catholic, Lutheran, and Reformed contemporaries, as well as in response to the self-taught and less than systematic theologians who sometimes did most to arouse his ire. His achievement as a Bible reader is marked in his commentary on Hebrews, which, despite having received "minimal attention," is his most significant intellectual achievement.[5] The authors he cited represented a tiny proportion of the titles that were included in the catalogue of three thousand volumes that his library may have contained, and a much smaller proportion of the contents of the Bodleian

Library, to which he had access during his student years and administrative career in Oxford.[6] In his exegetical labors, Owen was neither working *de novo* nor reading the Bible in a vacuum but was formed within the Western catholic as well as the English Protestant traditions, representing the strengths of these traditions alongside, Han Burger has claimed, some of their weaknesses.[7]

But that was not how Owen always liked to represent his reading of Scripture. While he could certainly advertise his learning, at the same time, throughout his career, he also fashioned himself as a very different kind of Bible reader, a "simple reader" like that idealized in the annotations of the Geneva Bible.[8] From his earliest polemical publications in the 1640s to the highly technical commentary on Hebrews that was published in installments at the end of his life, Owen represented himself in print as an individual bereft of scholarly resources, approaching the text as an informed but independent reader, sharing conclusions from his study of Scripture despite his "exclusion from the use of books."[9] He frequently noted his inability to access his library, during his time in Dublin in 1649–50, and especially during his dangerous peregrinations in the 1660s, in which period he moved from one safe house to another before eventually settling in Stoke Newington as the minister of a tiny congregation of washed-up republicans.[10] In his publications, Owen turned this lack of access to scholarly resources into an exegetical virtue. As he explained in the preface to the first volume of his commentary on Hebrews (1668), "I always went nakedly to the word itself, to learn humbly the mind of God in it." For, he continued, "after all searching and reading, prayer and assiduous meditation on the text have been my only reserve, and far most useful means of light and assistance. By these have my thoughts been freed from many and many an entanglement, which the writings of others on the same subject had either cast me into, or could not deliver me from."[11] Owen suggested that he combined his technical work with prayer and meditation, as if the problems raised by the former would be solved in the latter. Of course, the learning that his commentary displayed belied Owen's modesty about his intellectual formation, but it suited his purpose through much of his later life, and even in his most intellectually ambitious publications, to represent himself as depending upon the Spirit alone to read the Bible alone.

This display of depending upon the Spirit alone to read the Bible alone was widely promoted within the cultures of early evangelicalism. The "biblicism" that came to be promoted among early evangelicals drew upon the confessional and exegetical conclusions of earlier centuries, even as dependence upon these traditions slowly waned, especially with the rise of the personal and devotional Bible reading that became central to the performance of evangelical piety.[12] This biblicism reflected the sometimes individualistic tendencies that were central to what was, paradoxically, an emerging movement, even if it did not deliver the more radical transition from *sola Scriptura* to *solo Scriptura* that some scholars have observed.[13] In the early decades of the eighteenth century, evangelicals responded to the intellectual challenge of maintaining and applying in their piety a coherent doctrine of Scripture by continuing to engage with confessional and exegetical tradition while adopting what became in many cases highly subjective behaviors of biblical engagement. After the 1730s, while evangelical leaders like Jonathan Edwards continued to draw upon earlier resources and to interpret their conclusions through the lens of contemporary philosophy, others with similar theological commitments, such as the English high Calvinist John Gill, preferred to position themselves as latter-day scholastics who rejected "enlightened" claims. Other evangelicals, especially among those outside the cadre of elite leaders, grew hesitant about the limits that confessional and exegetical tradition imposed upon Bible reading. Minimizing these obligations, the response of these believers was increasingly to approach the Bible, as Owen had claimed to do, "nakedly," as if they could take Owen's rhetoric of simple piety at face value while dismissing his impressive technical work. This might explain, for example, why John Wesley included a redacted edition of some of Owen's devotional writing in his Christian Library (1750), offering his readers a model for pious Bible reading that did not contradict his decidedly anti-Calvinist convictions.[14]

Throughout the eighteenth century, evangelical leaders across the Atlantic world continued to read and promote Owen's work, alongside that of other Reformed and scholastic writers. But, in the works of Edwards and elsewhere, the print cultures of evangelicalism were shaping traditional iterations of Calvinism around new theories of conversion, with the consequence that some of the core ideas of the body of divinity that had been promoted in sixteenth-century Geneva were turned upside down by those who claimed to be its heirs.[15] Confessional denominations continued to promote traditional readings of Scripture alongside a body of divinity that was evolving to take account of new concerns, even as the intensity of some forms of evangelical piety drove many believers out of these denominations to seek fulfillment elsewhere.[16] As this approach grew in popularity in the anti-institutional structures of so much of the new movement, an individualistic and increasingly subjective practice of Bible reading became a central component of early evangelical piety—as well as a behavior that pointed to the considerable intellectual distance that had been traveled since vernacular Bible reading was first encouraged among sixteenth-century Protestants.[17]

The biblicism claimed by Owen illustrates the complex relationship that existed between the confessional commitments of English Puritan "high orthodoxy" and the piety of the early evangelicals.[18] Those involved in the debate about the relationship between these varieties of popular Protestantism have sometimes argued that these religious movements were divided by the Enlightenment, and the evangelical movement was shaped by a new confidence in the individual's ability to interpret their spiritual experience. These claims, most famously developed by David W. Bebbington in his magisterial work *Evangelicalism in Modern Britain* (1989), have been repeatedly rehearsed, but are increasingly called into question.[19] These qualifications of the Bebbington thesis require us to notice continuity as well as change in the movement from Puritanism into evangelicalism. Despite Bebbington's critics, it is still possible to argue that, whatever their theological continuity, Puritans and evangelicals fell on opposite sides of the major intellectual divide represented by the Enlightenment, and that this division exposed the differences between the precritical approaches to Scripture codified in "high orthodoxy" and the critical approaches to Scripture encouraged in the most advanced intellectual cultures of the early eighteenth century. At the same time, it is also possible to recognize that many of the most distinctive features of evangelicalism—such as its "biblicism" and its tendency toward individualism—may be found in Owen and other "high orthodox" theologians.

In this chapter, I want to notice how one very important Puritan anticipated—even if he did not exactly influence—what has come to be regarded as one of evangelicalism's most defining features. This chapter describes the cultures of Bible reading in early modern England before considering Owen's construction of the doctrine of Scripture and the ways in which that doctrine influenced his approach to the study of biblical texts. For all of his technical ability, and despite his multidisciplinary exegetical toolkit, Owen's argument for the priority of the assistance of the Spirit in Bible reading enabled the habit among evangelicals of reading the Bible apart from confessional or exegetical tradition, and without deference to uninspired aids or to the expectations of communities of interpretation. Owen always spoke highly of the authority of Scripture, but, in a period that tolerated increasing individualism and epistemological subjectivity, which was partly reflected in his increasing interest in liberty of conscience, does not always seem to have been persuaded of the sufficiency of Scripture. There are some surprising similarities between John Owen's approach to reading the Bible and that of the early evangelicals.

Bible Reading and the Cultures of Print in Early Modern England

Personal Bible reading was one of the distinctive hallmarks of Christian piety in early modernity.[20] This widespread cultural practice was enabled by the publication of massive quantities of a variety of English translations. In Owen's childhood, the most popular Bible, which circulated in the hundreds of thousands, was the translation that had been prepared by a small group of individuals who had been driven into exile by Queen Mary's persecution in the 1550s. These refugees had gathered in locations like Geneva, where they worked to prepare an edition that drew upon the best of the earlier translations to offer its readers the most accurate and detailed English Bible to date. This edition was designed for the purposes of detailed study. For the first time, chapters were broken down into verses, and the biblical text was accompanied by some three hundred thousand words of annotation that offered "simple readers" guidance in the proper interpretation of key passages as well as explanations of the key components of Reformed orthodoxy. The Geneva Bible was published in 1560 and appeared in several editions over the next eighty years. Though the last edition appeared in 1644, the Geneva Bible had a long afterlife. In the last third of the seventeenth century, writers like John Bunyan continued to make use of it as their primary translation, while its annotations continued to circulate in the margins of some editions of the translation that had been approved by King James.

Bible reading came to be particularly identified with the experience of being Protestant.[21] By the beginning of the seventeenth century, English Protestants had plenty of Bibles to choose from. In the 1640s, members of the Westminster Assembly intervened in disputes among London printers to ensure that Bibles could be published at an affordable price.[22] The policy was immediately effective. Robert Baillie noted that Bibles with marginal notes could now be purchased for two shillings and eight pence, with unbound copies being sold for slightly less.[23] Prices were driven lower by bulk purchasing by the Parliamentary army, which purchased nine thousand Bibles at prices between two shillings and four pence (1649) and one shilling and eight pence (1650).[24] Prices were higher for civilians, but still affordable: in July 1649, an Essex minister purchased a Bible for three shillings and two pence, and noted in his diary that "this booke is now very cheape."[25] There was good cause for David Dickson to note the "sweet and remarkable providence that within these not many years, such a multitude of impressions of the holy Scriptures are vented among these three united Kingdoms, and so many thousands [there] are of Scots and English who delight not only to have the holy Bible in their possession and houses, but also to carry it in their pockets, for reading of it upon all occasions."[26] These were individuals like John Hutchinson, who, his widow Lucy remembered, carried a Bible "in his pocket, [to] mark upon all occasions."[27]

Of course, the competition and innovation that drove the production of cheap and transportable Bibles encouraged some publishers to explore shortcuts in their pursuit of competitive advantage. Edward Leigh criticized "printers, who print the Bible in bad Paper, a blinde print, and corruptly," in so doing diminishing the quality of the sacred text.[28] Others, like Thomas Edwards, worried that the tendency to publish New Testaments as well as complete Bibles was encouraging readers to discount the Old Testament and was consequently promoting antinomianism.[29] Many Bible readers expressed concern about the accuracy of the most common English translation. As John Owen began his ministry, in the mid-1640s, the production of English Bibles intensified, as the quality of those Bibles came increasingly under scrutiny—not least by Owen himself.

Owen's Doctrine of Scripture

Owen was formed within this culture of Bible reading and cheap print. Throughout his life, he appears to have been an assiduous Bible reader. It is likely that, like other Puritans, he grew up reading the Geneva Bible, which would be the natural choice for someone like his father, whom Owen described as a "painful labourer in the Lord's vineyard."[30] When Owen began to preach in the 1640s, he assumed that his readers were familiar with the Geneva Bible's annotations, from which he occasionally sought to distinguish his own exegetical position.[31] In his preaching, he routinely made use of the Authorized Version. At times he offered small criticisms of its translation philosophy, and he continued to worry about its bias, especially in its choice of ecclesiological and liturgical vocabulary. But the Authorized Version was the most widely available English Bible, and Owen addressed his listeners on the basis of what he took for granted was "our translation."[32]

In his scholarly work, Owen used a great variety of Bibles, working regularly from original-language texts, with his interest in Hebrew language and literature noticeably increasing from the 1650s (Sir John Hartopp, who took notes of Owen's preaching in the 1670s and 1680s, many of which remain in manuscript in Dr Williams's Library, noted how Owen used Hebrew words even in his preaching). His work in the study and pulpit was likely supported, during his Essex pastorates in the 1640s, by the small library that had been established in Colchester to assist local clergy; in Oxford, during the 1650s, with the growing and increasingly impressive resources of the Bodleian Library, some of the content of which featured in his *Theologoumena pantodapa* (1661);[33] and, after the Restoration prevented access to such major repositories, the resources contained within what appears to have been an unusually large personal library of around three thousand volumes, which he appears to have struggled to access as he moved from one safe house to another under the protection of powerful patrons—who, presumably, had adequate library facilities of their own.[34] The content of Owen's own collection of books is known only through the catalogue that was prepared for the auction of his books after his death, which requires careful and cautious reading, as it appears to contain some material of dubious provenance. This catalogue includes surprisingly few Bibles. It suggests that Owen owned one copy of the King James translation, "interleaved, ruled and gilt" (1668); no copy of the Geneva Bible, despite the fact that he often referred to its contents; one copy each of Tyndale's New Testament and Pentateuch; and one "Welch" Bible (1677), which, despite his family's connections with the principality, he may not have been able to read.[35]

Whatever variety in the Bibles he used, Owen's doctrine of Scripture was generally consistent. He was certainly aware of the challenges involved in maintaining such a doctrine, as was attested by his familiarity with original-language texts, the manuscript tradition, the principles of text criticism, and the issues involved in providing an adequate English translation, particularly in the face of a wide variety of claims to continuing revelation. But his affirmation of Reformed orthodoxy on this point was, mostly, unambiguous. In 1645, he published two catechisms in which he described "holy Scripture" as containing "all truth concerning God, and ourselves," a statement he repeated in his revision of this catechism in *The primer* (1652).[36] He further described Scripture as "the books of the Old, and New Testament, given by inspiration from God, containing all things necessary to bee beleeved and done, that God may bee worshipped and our soules saved." He confirmed that Christians may know the Scriptures to be the word of God "by the testimony of Gods Spirit, working faith in my heart, to close with that heavenly Majesty, and cleare divine truth, that shineth in them," while a marginal note paid attention to the additional but subsidiary "unanswerable" evidences of antiquity, preservation, prophecy, the holiness and majesty of its doctrine, miracles, the testimony of the church and the blood of "innumerable Martyrs."[37]

This emphasis on the witness of the Spirit as the principal evidence for the authority of Scripture anticipated the formulation of the Westminster Confession of Faith (1647). In fact, Owen's insistence upon inspiration was so absolute, Richard Muller has noted, that he may have underestimated the role of the human author—and so pressed a very high view of inspiration "beyond its usefulness and application."[38] Owen maintained this perspective in 1652, when, as part of a committee of divines, he made his first attempt to draw up a confession of faith for the Cromwellian national church. This publication, *Some Principles of Christian Religion* (1652), stated that "the holy Scripture is that rule of knowing God, and living unto him, which who so doth not believe, but betakes himselfe to any other way of discovering truth, and the minde of God instead thereof, cannot be saved."³⁹ The statement continued, "The Holy Scriptures of the Old and New Testament are the Word of God, and the only Rule of knowing him savingly, and living unto him in all holiness and righteousness, in which we must rest; which Scriptures, who so doth not believe but rejecting them, doth instead thereof betake himself to any other way of discovering the mind of God, cannot be saved."⁴⁰ Explaining 2 Pet 1:21 in *Of communion with God* (1657), Owen argued that the "apostles forgot much of what Christ had said to them, or might do so; and what they did retain, in a natural way of remembrance, was not a sufficient foundation to them to write what they so remembered for a rule of faith to the church. For the word of prophecy is not . . . from any man's proper impulse; it comes not from any private conception, understanding, or remembrance. Wherefore, Christ promises that the Holy Ghost shall do this work; that they might infallibly give out what he had delivered to them."⁴¹ Hans Burger has argued that Owen's later position differed from this, and that *The Reason of Faith* (1677) fosters an "understanding of the authority of Scripture apart from Jesus Christ," but the implications of this claim have still to be ascertained.⁴² What is clear is that through most of his writing, Owen regarded the Scriptures as a soteriological necessity, arguing that their authority came directly from the Spirit, who witnessed to that authority in the pages of Scripture, this being evidenced only in a subsidiary way by their essential properties and qualities.

This very high view of the necessity of Scripture, and of the Spirit's attesting to its authority, explained Owen's interest in accurate translation. In 1652, he was appointed, along with several Presbyterian, Independent, and Baptist ministers, to oversee the revision of the King James Bible—a project that may have introduced him to Baptists for the first time. The committee did not produce any new translation. But Owen did think carefully about the qualities of a good translation. He did not consider that the English translation from which he preached was entirely defendable. His hesitations with the King James Version related partly to the nature of translated text, for "no translation is able in all things universally to exhibit that fullness of sense and secret virtue, to intimate the truth it expresseth to the mind of a believer, which is in many passages of Scripture in its original languages." None of the available translations "can or do express the whole excellency, elegancy, and marvellous efficacy of it, for the conveyance of its sense to the understandings and minds of men. Neither is this any reflection upon the translators, their abilities, diligence, or faithfulness, but that which the nature of the thing itself produceth." Instead, he insisted,

> translations contain the word of God, and are the word of God, perfectly or imperfectly, according as they express the words, sense, and meaning

of those originals. To advance any, all translations concurring, into an equality with the originals, so to set them by it as to set them up with it on even terms, much more to propose and use them as means of castigating, amending, altering anything in them, gathering various lections by them, is to set up an altar of our own by the altar of God, and to make equal the wisdom, care, skill, and diligence of men, with the wisdom, care, and providence of God himself.

Owen granted that "there is a frequent loss of propriety and amplitude of meaning in translations," but denied that the Scriptures would be "divested of their majesty, holiness, and spirit" if their translations were "good, true, and significant, according to the capacity and expressiveness of the languages whereinto they are translated." After all, he considered, "the majesty, holiness and spirit of the Scriptures, lie not in words and syllables, but in the truths themselves expressed in them; and whilst these are incorruptedly declared in any language, the majesty of the word is continued." Despite this qualification, and his concern about the most widely received English translation, he continued to use the King James Version, and thought highly of what he considered to be "our translation," but worried about its ecclesiastical bias, remembering the "common fault among translators, that they will accommodate the words of a text to their own apprehension of the sense and matter thereof."[43] Owen did not let his concerns about the quality of translation limit his confidence in the nature of the biblical text. The authority of Scripture was not determined by the quality of its translation.

Owen and the Sufficiency of Scripture

Owen consistently presupposed the infallibility of Scripture, even if he less consistently presupposed its sufficiency. In arguing for the infallibility of Scripture, he drew upon many centuries of Christian tradition, in contrast, he claimed, to the "universal agreement and wonderful harmony of every sort of heretic in this one point—total opposition to the infallibility of the Bible."[44] But, he realized, with growing concern, this opposition to the infallibility of the Bible was now being advanced among Puritans. From the earliest days of his ministry, he worried that this axiom of Protestant reform was being undermined by the subjective turn associated with the spirituality of such radical groups as the Quakers, whose arguments about the "inner light" seemed to many Puritans to challenge assumptions about the nature of inscripturated revelation.

Owen argued that special revelation, which began in the garden of Eden, was finally collected in Scripture. This original deposit of special revelation had, he believed, been circulated among the nations, where, in debased form, it lay behind their mythological culture. The religions of antiquity had preserved decaying memories of the original revelation, given to Adam and Eve in Eden. Although the "falsifying poets of the Greeks" had corrupted the biblical stories, Owen, in common with many of his contemporaries, believed that it was still possible to trace correlations between Scripture and mythology. This special revelation provided the key to the proper understanding of classical myth: "it can hardly be doubted that Jupiter-ammon, among the Egyptians, was no other than Ham, the son of Noah, and Bacchus Noah himself; and that Vulcan, among the other nations, was Tubal-cain," he contended, adding that "Saturn was Jephthah the Israelite," and that the "celebrated" Dutch theologian and classicist Gerardus Vossius had "clearly proved" that "Hercules was Joshua." Elsewhere, he considered that classical mythology did not only contain memories of an original revelation, but that its content had been augmented by further revelation—albeit of a diabolical kind. Owen cited the statement in Cato's *Distichs* that "it is madness to expect salvation from the death of another," adding that he had "no doubt but that this last verse is a diabolical oracle."[45]

But Quaker claims to extrabiblical revelation were also diabolical, he believed. "Our modern fanatics mutter and shout against the Bible in the streets, in temples, publicly and privately," he complained. Quakers "care not a straw for the Bible, nor do they utilize it in any way, for they neither read the Word itself, nor expound it in any way, nor make any use of testimonies drawn from it to support their teachings. . . . Of course, there would be small reason for them to do so—they are all men inspired of God themselves!" Quakers were denying that the Bible provided an unchanging rule for divine worship, and had effectively substituted Scripture with their own inspirations. Consequently, Owen believed, "all that they pronounce in religious matters they would have to be no less directly from God and His Spirit, no less infallible, no less of value to the Church than the Bible itself." If their claims were true, the Bible was no longer required. "What authority remains for a Word which may be forced in any direction by the crazy pronouncements of every fanatical vagabond and each theological featherweight?" At the end of the 1650s, Owen was clear that the canon had closed: "since the completion of the canon of Scripture . . . there can have been no new revelations concerning the common faith of the saints or the due worship of God, and so none are to be expected or admitted." It was a position he regularly restated: "What God once said to the Church through the medium of Prophets, Apostles, and other inspired writers was still spoken directly by God, and that not only in the primary sense to those to whom He delegated this task of reducing His revealed will to written form, but also, no less so in a secondary sense, He speaks to us now in His written word (Hebrews 1:1–2, Luke 1:70), as in days past He spoke through the mouths of His holy prophets (2 Peter 1:20–21)." There may have been problems in the Authorized Version, but there was no need for "novel revelations, enthusiasms, conversations with angels, and all the like manifestations of such rubbish."[46] Translations should be revised—not displaced.

But this was not a position that Owen maintained without qualification—for within a decade of denying the possibility of "conversations with angels, and all the like manifestations of such rubbish," he observed that angels might indeed communicate with the elect.[47] In 1668, in his commentary on Heb 1:14, he observed that angels had been "sent in an extraordinary manner to make revelations of the will of God," referring to several instances in the Old and New Testament as evidence for his claim.[48] This was a commonplace observation, of course, but Protestant scholastic theologians had generally insisted that extraordinary revelation had ceased, all the necessary knowledge of divine things having been provided in the Bible. Thus, for example, the Westminster Confession, which Owen and other Independents had revised as the Savoy Declaration (1658), recognized that God had once provided extraordinary revelations, but that, "for the better preserving and propagating of the Truth, and for the more sure establishment and comfort of the Church against the corruption of the flesh, and the malice of Satan and of the World," he had committed the content of this revelation "wholly unto writing: which maketh the Holy Scripture to be most necessary; those former ways of Gods revealing his Will unto his people, being now ceased" (WCF 1:1). But, by 1668, Owen was not so sure about this position. "How far God is pleased to continue the ministration of angels unto this day is hard to determine ... to say that God doth not or may not send his angels unto any of his saints, to communicate his mind unto them as to some particulars of their own duty, according to his word, or to foreshow unto them somewhat of his own approach work, seems, in my judgement, unwarrantably to limit the Holy One of Israel."[49] Owen went on to suggest that God could use angels to "suggest good motions unto the minds of his saints," though he recognized that believers would find it difficult to identify this angelical influence, which might consist in "occasional impressions in the mind, fancy, and imagination."[50] His claim was, of course, taking at face value the achievements of John Milton's *Paradise Lost* (1667), which had been published some months earlier, and which appears to have been included in Owen's library.[51] The narrator of Milton's epic presented himself as being inspired by an angel, and described detailed conversations that took place between angelic and human beings. *Paradise Lost* was encoding claims to spiritual experience that circulated widely among radical religious groups in seventeenth-century England and became a feature of some of the early communities of evangelicals.[52] Like some early evangelicals, Owen emphasized a closed biblical canon while being, at least in this instance, open to other forms of continued revelation.[53] But he did not enlarge upon his proposal that this kind of angelic communication might continue. Perhaps it was too difficult to distinguish the experience of a believer who was being influenced by angels from the experience of a Quaker whose influences were less auspicious. Owen consistently argued for the infallibility of Scripture, but, at the end of the 1660s, was prepared to think again about its sufficiency.

Owen and Biblical Criticism

Owen's high view of Scripture was reflected in positions that might be regarded as precritical and as critical.[54] At times he could sound highly conservative. In terms of authorship, for example, he was clear that Moses was the author of the Pentateuch. "Many prophets were before him, but he was the first who committed the will of God to writing after God himself, who wrote the law in tables of stone; which was the beginning and pattern of the Scriptures."[55] Owen was also quite specific about when Moses developed his literary career: in an unpublished sermon, preached in 1677, Owen explained that Moses wrote Deuteronomy about three months before his death.[56] Owen suggested that Moses might also have been the author of Job. He was not disturbed by the anonymous authorship of so many canonical texts. He believed that it did not really matter that the "writers of the historical books of the Old Testament before the captivity are unknown," for "certain it is that they were of the number of those holy men of God who of old wrote and spake as they were moved by the Holy Ghost." He explained what he understood by the experience of inspiration. Although these anonymous historians "wrote in an historical manner, as did Moses also, concerning things past and gone in their days, or it may be presently acted in their own times, yet they did not write them either from their own memory nor from tradition, nor from the rolls or records of time (although they might be furnished with and skilled in these things), but by the inspiration, guidance, and direction of the Holy Ghost." Owen's insistence upon inspiration overrode any concern that he might have had about authorial attribution.[57]

Owen's conservatism is perhaps best illustrated in his decision to build what has come to be his most enduring book—*Of Communion with God* (1657)—around 1 John 5:7, the most famous disputed text in the New Testament.[58] His conservatism was also marked in his response to the publication of the London Polyglot (1657).⁵⁹ This multivolume work presented biblical texts from multiple languages in parallel columns. Owen was both impressed and alarmed by this extraordinary achievement. On the one hand, he praised the work as reflecting unusual erudition, and used the similarities between the versions it included to make a point about the general agreement of all textual traditions.⁶⁰ On the other hand, he recognized that the London Polyglot was also presenting disagreements between the versions it included, in however minor a fashion, raising doubts about the authority of Scripture in the minds of those who had not been trained to adjudicate these competing textual claims. Most famously, of course, Owen's greatest criticism of the London Polyglot was its decision to discuss the Hebrew text without its pointing—creating ambiguities in meaning despite many centuries of convention about the proper readings of the Old Testament.⁶¹

But if some of Owen's responses could be conservative, others could be surprisingly modern. He was a careful reader of the Gospels, and paid attention to the differences as well as the similarities between individual pericopes, noting and sometimes explaining the textual differences involved. He recognized that editorial preferences were at work behind the canonical text, and that these preferences reflected the specific theological purposes of each of the Gospels. For example, he argued that the text of the Lord's Prayer was a form given to the disciples before the Pentecostal gift of the Spirit enabled them to pray extemporaneously and in accordance with the will of God, and that it was therefore not appropriate for use in public worship in the post-Pentecostal age. He also argued that Matthew inserted the Lord's Prayer into Jesus's first sermon, "by way of anticipation, and mentions it not when he comes to the time wherein it was really first delivered by him."⁶² But what mattered most to Owen was not editorial intervention in the text of the Gospel, but the direction and inspiration of the Spirit that guaranteed its work.

Of course, Owen recognized that all the superlative qualities of Scripture were ineffective without the power of the Holy Spirit. "That knowledge of God which we have by his works is but very weak and imperfect, so that which we have by the word, the letter of it, by reason of our blindness, is not saving to us if we have no other help," he explained. The Bible alone was not sufficient for salvation. "He that would utterly separate the Spirit from the word had as good burn his Bible. The bare letter of the New Testament will no more ingenerate faith and obedience in the souls of men . . . than the letter of the Old Testament doth so at this day among the Jews, 2 Cor. iii. 6, 8." He warned again and again that Christians could read the Bible as if they were Jews—without dependence upon the Spirit. For the "hammer of the word" was also the "sword of the Spirit," he argued.⁶³ The Spirit would give Scripture its power—a position that would be used to justify the tendency among those who followed Owen within the cultures of early evangelicalism to read the Bible without recourse to the confessional tradition and in reaction to the claims of "enlightened" critics. After all, as Tweeddale reminds us, "precritical exegetes were not uncritical."[64]

Conclusion

So why did Owen so often represent himself as a "simple reader" of Scripture? There may be different answers for different periods of his life. During his time in Dublin, he was physically removed from his library, and obviously perplexed by the poor resources of the library of Trinity College Dublin. His claims in that period can be taken at face value. In the 1660s, however, he may have enjoyed access to much better scholarly resources, but he was making theological arguments in favor of high Calvinism as Catholicism and the skepticism of some varieties of enlightened thinking became increasingly fashionable, and as a direct appeal to Scripture carried more weight than a reference to confessional tradition when addressing audiences that no longer found that confessional tradition to be authoritative. But, in the early eighteenth century and beyond, Owen's position on the right interpretation of Scripture was put to work in the service of agendas other than his own. In an age of "activism," and as "crucicentrism" drove early evangelical "conversionism," as Bebbington might put it, Owen's "biblicism" echoed the approaches to scriptural interpretation that facilitated the individualistic preferences of growing numbers of born-again Protestants. Owen's approach to the study of Scripture resonated within the anti-institutional contexts of large parts of the new evangelical movement. Its "democratic" impulse created new ways of ascertaining truth, and identified within the regenerate individual a new locus of hermeneutical authority. Early evangelicals made effective use of Owen.[65] In the years that followed upon his death in 1683, Owen's works continued to circulate on the secondhand market, while publishers continued to issue hitherto-unpublished Owen material, alongside second and later editions of some of his many earlier works. The decisions that publishers made to issue new material or to reissue older material shaped Owen's legacy in important ways. Early evangelicals repackaged Owen, branding the Puritan author as the theological guide of right-thinking evangelicals. The market for Owen's devotional writing appears to have remained strong, but publishers showed much less interest in reissuing editions of his polemical theology. When his theological work was reissued, it was sometimes redacted for doctrinal purposes, as when it appeared in Wesley's Christian Library (1750), as we have already noticed, or in a format that cherry-picked inspirational passages from the morass of exegetical detail, as in *Oweniana, or Select Passages from the Works of Owen* (1817), which was edited by the celebrated English economist and agricultural reformer Arthur Young after his late-in-life conversion.

But many readers continued to view Owen as exegetical guide as well as spiritual advisor. Volumes of Owen's commentary on Hebrews were reprinted in the earliest years after his death, when they were collected on both sides of the Atlantic by theologians including Increase and Cotton Mather and Jonathan Edwards, who circulated the commentary among his friends.[66] Other eighteenth-century readers preferred to engage with abridged editions of Owen's massive commentary. His influence may have reached beyond his book's circulation. Some of his conclusions came to dominate evangelical approaches to the text, including his justification for the theory that the intended readers of this epistle were in danger of relapsing into Judaism—an argument Owen rooted in a massive display of learning of first-century sources. If the details of his interpretation of Hebrews were lost in their abridgment, Owen's argument became a commonplace in later exegetical work.[67]

The theology that evangelicals inherited from Owen's work was sometimes ambiguous and subject to occasional change. Owen was confessional—most of the time. But in his engagement with early "enlightened" thought, he showed the same kinds of fluctuations as those evangelicals who would do most to perpetuate his reputation, including the English Baptist theologian Andrew Fuller, who made claims to be channeling Owen's legacy that disguised the extent to which his reading of seventeenth-century theology had in fact been shaped by Edwards and other eighteenth-century contemporaries.[68] Of course, Owen was not responsible for the variety of ways in which early evangelicals drew upon his work. Owen sustained a consistently high view of the nature and authority of Scripture, and incorporated critical perspectives within his high orthodox position, even if he was sometimes less certain of the sufficiency of Scripture. For all that Owen was a giant of Reformed orthodoxy, he bequeathed an ambiguous legacy to the early evangelicals.

Notes

1. On Owen's legacy within evangelicalism, see Crawford Gribben, *John Owen and English Puritanism: Experiences of Defeat* (Oxford: Oxford University Press, 2016), 271–72; Gribben, "Becoming John Owen: The Making of an Evangelical Reputation," *Westminster Theological Journal* 79 (2017): 311–25. On Owen's approach to the character of Scripture, see Donald K. McKim, "John Owen's Doctrine of Scripture in Historical Perspective," *Evangelical Quarterly*

45 (1973): 195–207; David J. McKinley, "John Owen's View of Illumination: An Alternative to the Fuller-Erickson Dialogue," *Bibliotheca Sacra* 154 (1997): 93–104; Carl R. Trueman, "Faith Seeking Understanding: Some Neglected Aspects of John Owen's Understanding of Scriptural Interpretation," in *Interpreting the Bible: Historical and Theological Studies in Honour of David F. Wright*, ed. A. N. S. Lane (Leicester, UK: Apollos, 1997), 147–62. For recent discussion of Owen's doctrine of Scripture, see Andrew M. Leslie, *The Light of Grace: John Owen on the Authority of Scripture and Christian Faith* (Gottingen: Vandenhoeck & Ruprecht, 2015); Hans Burger, "Why Do You Believe That Scripture Is the Word of God? Owen's Doctrine of Scripture Reconsidered," in *John Owen Between Orthodoxy and Modernity*, ed. Willem van Vlastuin and Kelly M. Kapic (Leiden: Brill, 2019), 127–47.

2. For Owen as exegete, see Barry H. Howson, "The Puritan Hermeneutics of John Owen: A Recommendation," *Westminster Theological Journal* 63 (2001): 351–76; Kelly M. Kapic, "Typology, the Messiah, and John Owen's Theological Reading of Hebrews," in *Christology, Hermeneutics, and Hebrews: Profiles from the History of Interpretation*, ed. Jon C. Laansma and Daniel J. Treier (Edinburgh: T&T Clark, 2012), 135–54; Lee Gatiss, "Adoring the Fullness of the Scriptures in John Owen's Commentary on Hebrews" (PhD diss., University of Cambridge, 2013); and John W. Tweeddale, *John Owen and Hebrews: The Foundation of Biblical Interpretation* (London: T&T Clark, 2019).

3. *The Words of that Eminent Servant of Christ Mr John Bunyan . . . with a Recommendatory Preface, by the Reverend George Whitefield, M.A.*, 3rd ed., 2 vols. (London, 1767–68), 1:iv. For discussion of Owen's learning, see Sebastian Rehnman, *Divine Discourse: The Theological Methodology of John Owen* (Grand Rapids, MI: Baker, 2002); Carl R. Trueman, *John Owen: Reformed Catholic, Renaissance Man* (2007; repr., Oxford: Routledge, 2016); Tim Cooper, *John Owen, Richard Baxter, and the Formation of Nonconformity* (Aldershot: Ashgate, 2011); and Gribben, *Owen and English Puritanism*.

4. For examples of Owen's work as a text critic, see John Owen, *The Works of John Owen*, ed. William H. Goold (1850–55; repr., Edinburgh: Banner of Truth, 1965–68), 10:164, 178.

5. Tweeddale, *Owen and Hebrews*, 5.

6. See the cautions outlined in Crawford Gribben, "John Owen, Renaissance Man? The Evidence of Edward Millington's *Bibliotheca Oweniana* (1684)," *Westminster Theological Journal* 72, no. 2 (2010): 321–32.

7. Burger, "Owen's Doctrine of Scripture Reconsidered," 134, 139–45.

8. Michael Jensen, "'Simply' Reading the Geneva Bible: The Geneva Bible and Its Readers," *Literature and Theology* 9 (1995): 30–45.

9. Owen, *Works*, 18:8.

10. Gribben, *Owen and English Puritanism*, 209–62; Crawford Gribben, "Lucy Hutchinson, John Owen's Congregation, and the Literary Culture of Nonconformity," *Review of English Studies* (forthcoming).

11. Owen, *Works*, 18:9.

12. W. R. Ward, *Early Evangelicalism: A Global Intellectual History, 1670–1789* (Cambridge: Cambridge University Press, 2006), 6–23.

13. Keith A. Mathison, *The Shape of Sola Scriptura* (Moscow, ID: Canon Press, 2001), passim; D. W. Bebbington, *Evangelicalism in Modern Britain: A History from the 1730s to the 1980s* (Boston: Unwin Hyman, 1989), 12–14.

14. Karl Ludwig Ganske, "The Religion of the Heart and Growth in Grace: John Wesley's Selection and Editing of Puritan Literature for a Christian Library" (PhD diss., University of Manchester, 2009).

15. Crawford Gribben, "Calvinism, Conversion, and the Science of the Self," in *Cultures of Calvinism in Early Modern Europe*, ed. Crawford Gribben and Graeme Murdock (New York: Oxford University Press, 2019), 37–56; Gribben, "Calvin and Calvinism in Early Modern England, Scotland, and Ireland," in *John Calvin in Context*, ed. R. Ward Holder (Cambridge: Cambridge University Press, 2020), 393–400.

16. See, for example, the turn among Calvinistic Methodists in Wales toward the ministry of an influential female prophet and communal living; Eryn M. White, *The Welsh Methodist Society: The Early Societies in South-West Wales, 1737–1750* (Cardiff: University of Wales Press, 2020).

17. For an influential discussion of this phenomenon, see Hans W. Frei, *The Eclipse of Biblical Narrative: A Study in Eighteenth and Nineteenth Century Hermeneutics* (New Haven: Yale University Press, 1974), 17–65.

18. On "high orthodoxy," see Willem van Asselt, *Introduction to Reformed Scholasticism* (Grand Rapids, MI: Reformation Heritage, 2011), passim.

19. See the modification of the Bebbington thesis proposed by the essays contained in Michael A. G. Haykin and Kenneth J. Stewart, eds., *The Emergence of Evangelicalism: Exploring Historical Continuities* (Leicester, UK: IVP, 2008).

20. See Crawford Gribben, "The Commodification of Scripture, 1640–1660: Politics, Ecclesiology and the Cultures of Print," in *The Oxford Handbook of the Bible in Early Modern England, 1530–1700*, ed. Kevin Killeen, Helen Smith, and Rachel Willie (Oxford: Oxford University Press, 2015), 224–36; Gribben, "Bible Reading, Puritan Devotion and the Transformation of Politics in the Puritan Revolution," in *The English Bible in the Early Modern World*, ed. Robert Armstrong and Tadhg Ó hAnnracháin, St Andrews Studies in Reformation History (Leiden: Brill, 2018), 141–60.

21. Alec Ryrie, *Being Protestant in Reformation Britain* (Oxford: Oxford University Press, 2015).

22. Gribben, "Commodification of Scripture," 224–36; Gribben, "Bible Reading," 141–60.

23. Robert Baillie, *Letters and Journals*, 2 vols. (Edinburgh, 1775), 2:174.

24. *The Case of William Bentley Printer at Finsbury near London, Touching his Right to the Printing of Bibles and Psalms* (1656), single sheet; W. M. Clyde, *The Struggle for Freedom of the Press: From Caxton to Cromwell* (London: Humphrey Milford for Oxford University Press, 1934), 225, 281–82.

25. *The Diary of Ralph Josselin, 1616–1683*, ed. Alan Macfarlane (Oxford: Oxford University Press, 1991), 173.

26. David Dickson, *A Brief Exposition of the Evangel of Jesus Christ According to Matthew* (1647; repr., Edinburgh: Banner of Truth, 1981), v.

27. Lucy Hutchinson, *Memoirs of the Life of Colonel Hutchinson*, ed. N. H. Keeble (1995; repr., London, 2000), 300.

28. Edward Leigh, *A Body of Divinity* (1654), 27.

29. Thomas Edwards, *Gangreana* (1646), 19.

30. Owen, *Works*, 13:224.

31. See, for example, ibid., 9:438.

32. Ibid., 18:177.

33. John Owen, *Theologoumena pantodapa* (Oxford, 1661), 321.

34. Andrew Cambers, *Godly Reading: Print, Manuscript and Puritanism in England, 1580–1720* (Cambridge: Cambridge University Press, 2011), 147.

35. See Gribben, "Owen, Renaissance Man?"

36. Owen, *Works*, 1:467; John Owen, *The primer* (1652), n.p.

37. Owen, *Works*, 1:470.

38. Muller, *PRRD*, 2:248–50, 254.

39. *Proposals for the Furtherance and Propagation of the Gospell in this Nation . . . as also, Some Principles of Christian Religion* (1652), 5.

40. *A New Confession of Faith* (London: Privately published, 1654), 1.

41. Owen, *Works*, 2:236.

42. Burger, "Owen's Doctrine of Scripture Reconsidered," 135.

43. Owen, *Works*, 10:263, 282, 308; 14:132–33; 18:50; 16:357; 14:134; 6:614; 8:257.

44. John Owen, *A Defense of Sacred Scripture Against Modern Fanaticism*, in *Biblical Theology: The History of Theology from Adam to Christ*, trans. Stephen P. Westcott (Morgan, PA: Soli Deo Gloria, 1994), 817.

45. Owen, *Works*, 10:532, 531, 540, 538.
46. Owen, *Defense of Sacred Scripture*, 792, 805, 823, 824, 826, 788, 827.
47. Ibid., 827; Owen, *Works*, 20:250 (*Hebrews*, 3:250).
48. Owen, *Works*, 20:249 (*Hebrews*, 3:249).
49. Ibid., 20:250 (*Hebrews*, 3:250).
50. Ibid., 20:251 (*Hebrews*, 3:251).
51. Crawford Gribben, "John Owen's Milton," *Milton Quarterly* 54:3 (2020): 184–90.
52. Ward, *Early Evangelicalism*, 89–161; Crawford Gribben, "Angels and Demons in Cromwellian and Restoration Ireland: Heresy and the Supernatural," *Huntington Library Quarterly* 76, no. 3 (2013): 377–92; Gribben, "'Inexpressible Horrour': The Devil and Baptist Life Writing in Cromwellian Ireland," *CH* 89 (2021): 531–48.
53. See, for example, White, *Welsh Methodist Society*, 99–102.
54. Leslie, *Light of Grace*, 181–218.
55. Owen, *Works*, 3:143.
56. Dr. Williams's Library, NCL MS 6/3, n.p. [fol. 2v].
57. Owen, *Works*, 3:143–45.
58. For this context, see Stephen D. Snobelen, "'To Us There Is but One God, the Father': Antitrinitarian Textual Criticism in Seventeenth- and Early Eighteenth-Century England," in *Scripture and Scholarship in Early Modern England*, ed. Ariel Hessayon and Nicholas Keene (Aldershot: Ashgate, 2006), 116–36.
59. Peter N. Miller, "The 'Antiquarianization' of Biblical Scholarship and the London Polyglot Bible (1653–57)," *Journal of the History of Ideas* 62, no. 3 (2001): 463–82.
60. Owen, *Works*, 14:126; see also 3:155; Muller, *PRRD*, 2:130.
61. Gribben, *Owen and English Puritanism*, 182–87.
62. Owen, *Works*, 15:15, 13.
63. Ibid., 2:108; 3:192–93; 8:171.
64. Tweeddale, *Owen and Hebrews*, 19.
65. Gribben, "Becoming John Owen."
66. Julius Herbert Tuttle, *Libraries of the Mathers* (Worcester, MA: Davis Press, 1910), 15, 75; *WJE*, 26:425. See also Cotton Mather, *Biblia Americana*, vol. 10, *Hebrews–Revelation*, ed. Jan Stievermann (Tübingen: Mohr Siebeck, forthcoming).
67. I owe this point to Philip Church.
68. Peter J. Morden, *The Life and Thought of Andrew Fuller (1754–1815)* (Milton Keynes, UK: Paternoster, 2015), 53–55, 60–67.

5

BIBLE POLITICS AND EARLY EVANGELICALISM

Scriptural Submission and Resistance in Nonconformist Commentary

ROBERT E. BROWN

In early 1685, Richard Baxter published his heavily annotated *Paraphrase on the New Testament*, a work he had been engaged with for several decades. Already free on his own recognizance (having been arrested in November of 1684 for unlicensed preaching), Baxter was rearrested in February, this time on the charge that his commentary in the *Paraphrase* constituted "seditious libel" against the Church of England. He remained in prison this time; in June the judge fined him 500 marks and remanded him to prison until the fine was paid. Baxter spent the next eighteen months there until his fine was remitted by James II in November 1686.[1] This image is arresting to the modern imagination, to be sure, in part because of the element of religious and press censorship, but also in part because Bible commentary is not something we usually associate with tense political confrontation. Yet it is difficult to exaggerate the degree of religious and political acrimony that characterized the decades after the Restoration, such that most printed works were read through the lens of the besetting conflict of the era and its implications for public life. Baxter's *Paraphrase* is a case in point. The charge was brought by Roger L'Estrange (1616–1704), Surveyor of the Press since 1663. He used that office to spy out and impound the unlicensed and heretical publications of nonconformists, as well as to subject authors, printers, and booksellers to arrest, trial, and imprisonment. He had attacked Baxter in numerous publications over many years.[2] Just three days before Baxter's arrest, L'Estrange declaimed against the *Paraphrase* in *The Observator*, his weekly broadsheet: "Mr Baxter *has broken the* Truce. *He Preaches* a New Gospel. *His* Paraphrase *on the* New-Testament. . . . *The* Faction [is] Restless *and* Cruel." It was, he concluded, "One of the Boldest; the Wickedest; The most Scandalous, and Dangerous Attempt, upon the Honour of the Government that ever I met withal since I was born."[3] The judge presiding over his trial, George Jeffreys (1645–1689), attacked Baxter as "an old schismatical knave, a sniveling parson, a hypocritical villain."[4]

Early evangelicalism was born into a bifurcated political reality that produced disparate responses among the architects of the movement. Many evangelicals found themselves a part of the state church apparatus and, not surprisingly, were prone to advocate for establishment and uniformity in religion. Others, such as Baptists, were birthed to a fully sectarian status, while still others, such as Presbyterians, found themselves in divergent politico-religious circumstances and thus possessing divergent loyalties. In the Church of England, nonconformists found themselves in an increasingly disadvantaged political standing, one that would also come to undermine the standing church in New England. This political experience of marginalization forced leaders of the emerging evangelical movement to consider anew the relation of the Christian and the Christian church to the state. They were able to draw on a long tradition of rights of conscience theory tracing back to John Calvin, a tradition elaborated upon by English Calvinists during the political upheavals of the mid-seventeenth century.[5] By the middle of the eighteenth century advocacy for the liberty of religious conscience had increasingly become part of evangelical discourse.[6] In the Revolutionary era it was used by American evangelicals to press their case for equality of religious opportunity, and to cement the identification of evangelicalism with the emerging American political identity.[7] A critical chapter in this story took place in the aftermath of the Restoration, as nonconformists were forced to articulate the basis for a right of religious conscience that was not politically revolutionary, one that considered the nature of and appropriate place for a simultaneous political submission and religious resistance within a quiescent political stance, one that paved the way for later evangelical political theory.

Nonconformists found themselves in a political and religious maelstrom in the wake of the Restoration. Their dream of a thorough reformation of the Church of England and the religious hegemony needed to effect it had foundered during the Interregnum. Their post-Restoration hope of a middle station in the form of a broad church version of national comprehension was extinguished in the wake of the failures of the Savoy Conference (1661). Having triumphed in their quest to control the reconstruction of Anglicanism, High Church clergy and their Tory allies in Parliament were in no mood to indulge nonconformity. Nonconformists were put in a seemingly untenable situation: asserting their ongoing loyalty to the state while dissenting from the religion of the state. Finding a middle ground—the ground of toleration for conscientious objection, and the concepts of religious liberty and pluralism needed to sustain it—was only accomplished painfully and slowly. It required renewed attention to those passages of Scripture that spoke to the political posture of Christians. The biblical commentary of nonconformists on both sides of the Atlantic in this era reveals an urgent political dimension. This essay will examine the contours of that interpretive world, arguing that biblical commentary played a significant role in the emerging articulation of religious pluralism and tolerance in early modernity. In particular, it will focus on the commentary of Richard Baxter and Cotton Mather, two figures whose writings were profoundly influential in early Pietism and protoevangelicalism.

The decades after the Restoration were a toxic brew of recrimination and score-settling among English coreligionists. Anglican clergy and their allies in Parliament passed a series of laws meant to punish those who had taken part in the rebellion, with the intent of exterminating nonconformist religion in any form. Opposition to the Church of England was equated with opposition to the crown.[8] In succession, the Corporation Act (1661), the Act of Uniformity (1662), the Conventicles Act (1664), and the Five Mile Act (1665) required political office holders to be communicants in the church, ordered clergy to conform to the Book of Common Prayer, banned nonconformist gatherings of more than five people, and prohibited ejected clergy from living within five miles of their former parishes. The Test Act of 1673 excluded noncommunicants from military leadership as well. In addition, the Licensing Act (1662) censored nonconformist publications.[9] The fines for violations of these laws were often deliberately punitive, and in some cases ruinous; prison terms were often the only option for those without sufficient means.

Of principal interest to Bible interpreters was Rom 13.[10] Baxter's annotations on this passage are some of the most extensive in his *Paraphrase*. In addition to his transliterative comments, Baxter appended an additional section of notes centered around fifteen questions in which he specified the relationship between resistance and subjection and the need for liberty of conscience. In contrast to traditional Anglican theory, he shifted the emphasis away from the authority of rulers over their subjects and toward the accountability that rulers have to God. Political authority is derived authority: God has bound rulers "as his Officers to see to the Execution of his Universal Laws: . . . And therefore their Office and Authority received from God, is not to be Persecutors." Rulers are "not authorised to destroy and to do mischief . . . but to take care of the Common Welfare."[11]

As those appointed by God, rulers are due the allegiance of their subjects. Baxter specifically ruled out rebellion. His commentary on verse 7 eliminated the interpretive possibility that some rulers might not be owed any due respect, and therefore could be targeted for removal: "I am not perswading you to own Usurpation . . . but that you give all their proper due."[12] Baxter took pains, however, to point out that subjection was not to be equated with unflinching servility. Christians "must not obey a sinful Command." Their subjection in such cases is to suffer the consequences of disobedience. Thus he made room for liberty of conscience; it can and must be asserted, but the consequences for doing so must not be avoided. The conscience of a citizen is sacrosanct and belongs to God; his body belongs to some extent to the state.

That said, what is perhaps most striking about Baxter's commentary is the great emphasis placed on the agency of citizens and, along with that, the right to resist. These are rooted first in the uncertainty involving political matters and thus the necessity of rendering judgment on them. Even recognizing a proper claim of the right to rule is speculative: it cannot be based on the form of government, since this is an indifferent matter; it cannot be based on succession, or the gifts of leadership. Rather, it is up to the common people "to Judge as far as they can know; else they cannot tell whom to obey or defend." In some sense, then, "the Vulgar [are] made Judges of the Princes Right." There is also an element of providence involved: if rulers have achieved power and are ruling justly, then it is reasonable to assume that they are there by God's hand. But ideally providence also has a proper political mechanism associated with it. Those present at the founding of a government must consent to the form and persons so established. "God's providence doth so manage the Affairs of the World, as shall point out the Man or Families that the People should accept of first while free, as qualified by Strength, Wisdom, and Goodness, for Authority." But all of this "shall by a Free People be chosen"—"I know therefore no remaining Title, but [the] Mutual Consent of Persons made capable by the Providence of God, at the forming of the Government." There is a strong element in Baxter's thought of the idea of the social contract, a key element in early modern political theory, a concept that depended on consent, and thus implicitly dependent on the right to withhold that consent in certain cases.

Baxter's absolute insistence that people have a natural right and duty to judge whether magistrates (including bishops) are in fact ruling justly certainly implies that there is a line that, if crossed, could necessitate action that might be termed "treasonous"—civil disobedience in matters of religion, the option of principled nonconformity. His insistence that people cannot be imposed upon religiously without their free consent made the prospect of a comprehensive national church of the sort envisioned by his critics all but impossible. Conscientious objection would always result in a certain level of social disunity or disorder—that is, religious pluralism—however modest this might be. The live questions, of course, were whether or at what point the strictures of Anglicanism would necessitate civil disobedience, who would be competent to decide this, and how such resistance would be implemented—questions Baxter leaves unanswered.[13]

A charitable reading of Baxter's commentary might conclude that he was merely creating space for the consciences of nonconformists in a time of persecution. As citizens they must be subject to the monarch, yet as conscientious Christians they must resist those elements of the state's church that run counter to their faith. Yet critics like L'Estrange were hardly in a charitable frame of mind. At Baxter's trial he identified seven offending passages from the Gospels and Acts that libeled Anglican bishops. In addition, a "certain noted clergyman" (unnamed) raised "some accusations out of Rom xiii ... as against the king, to touch his life." The passages in question (Matt 5:19, Mark 9:39, 11:31, and 12:38–40, Luke 10:2, John 11:57, and Acts 15:2) are generally those detailing the conflict between Jesus and the Pharisees; Baxter's annotations on them take issue with clergy who restrain the unfettered preaching of the gospel. His accusers read these as veiled references ("innuendo") to Anglican bishops; his lawyers objected that without having named specific bishops by name (or even bishops, a word Baxter does not use), such inferences failed to meet the legal bar of libel.[14]

But L'Estrange read Baxter's Bible commentary through the lens of the Puritan rebellion, now five decades past but still vividly resented.[15] A particular focus of his rage appears to have been Baxter's political treatise *A Holy Commonwealth*, published in 1659, at a time when the forces of revolution were reaching the point of exhaustion. In it, Baxter sought to offer a way forward that provided for the kind of government that would support his vision of a thoroughly reformed church. It contains all of the arguments that appear in his annotations on the Epistle to the Romans, perhaps most notably the right to resist for reasons of conscience.[16] The consciences of men are "out of reach" of the judgment of magistrates, thus all tolerable differences among honest men on religious matters must be endured. Baxter clearly anticipated that he and his coreligionists might be marginalized, even as he argued for a pluralized national comprehension, a hope that he held out for to his dying day.[17]

If arguing for the right to resist was not sufficiently objectionable, Baxter used the long preface to this work to rehash the history of the Civil War, a retelling that defended the actions of those implicated in the rebellion. The work was read by Royalists as an unremorseful apologetic for all of the misfortunes the nation had experienced in the war. It became so controversial that in 1670 Baxter issued a repudiation of it in print. But the so-called repudiation "retracted none of the Doctrine" in the book; Baxter rather simply "repented the writing of it as an infelicity, and as that which did no good but hurt," a concession to the "incessant bloody Malice of the Reproachers."[18]

In fact, in his charging critique L'Estrange drew a direct connection between the treason defended by Baxter in his *Holy Commonwealth* and the treason implied in his *Paraphrase*. "This Same *Paraphrase* of *Mr Baxters* upon the *New Testament*, is a . . . *Violation* of all the *Terms*, and *Measures* of *Good Manners, Society*, and *Religion*. . . . [And] His *Common-wealth Aphorisms* are no better than *Downright, Casuistical Treason*." The *Paraphrase* shares this fundamental fault. Its main aim is "to make *Broad Signs* to the *People*, that they are under a *Persecuting*, and a *Superstitious Government*." He "makes *Our Church-Governers* to be *Perverters* of the *Gospel*; and then, bids the People *Reject*, and *Forsake* them, *as Such*; wherein he makes the *People, Judges*; our *Ecclesiastical Rulers, Offenders*." What seems to have been the breaking point for L'Estrange and his collaborators was the fact that by insinuating his political theory into Scripture, Baxter was leading unsuspecting readers to conclude that his paraphrastic interpretation was to be equated with the literal meaning of the texts. "But when he comes once to turn *the Word of God* upon us; and to bring the *Four Evangelists*, and *St Paul*, to *Subscribe* to the *Divine Rights of Rebellion, and Schism*; there's no more to be said in't, but the Putting of it to the *Vote*."[19]

L'Estrange championed the claim that any expression of religious dissent was a form of sedition against the political arrangement of England, as it raised doubts about the national church headed and supported by the monarchy. The civil disobedience of nonconformists and the literature they produced justifying this was inherently treasonous. The assertion of liberty of conscience was a sham intended to buy time for plotting rebellion, in this case by the "very Patriarch" of schism, a "*Seducer* in the shape of a *Godly Minister*." Such liberty, if unleashed, would produce social chaos, since personal autonomy would trump the rule of law. The only way toward civil order was to silence and imprison Dissenters. Toleration of religious pluralism, especially extending it to those who had criminally participated in the rebellion against the state, was a non sequitur. Dissenters, he wrote, are like insects, which must be eliminated in order for the gardens of monarchy and episcopacy to flourish.[20]

Baxter articulated the doctrines of resistance and conscience in many of his works published after the Restoration as he pled the cause of nonconformity. This is pointedly the case in his *Christian Directory* (1673). In this work he raises an idea that would become important for early modern defenses of freedom of conscience: the limitations of the understanding, the inevitability of differences of opinion that result from this, and thus the need for tolerance and to refrain from coercion. "Remember that the understanding is not free ... further than as it is under the power of the will. ... A man cannot hold [an] opinion ... against what he would not have to be true." The mind is compelled by what it perceives to be evidence, not by coercion; thus conscience must be respected. Most Christians are ignorant and weak-minded. They lack the capacity to understand the finer points of theology, and so resolve their doubts—thus room must be left for their dubious opinions within the larger church. Faith is a process, and must be allowed the time to mature.[21] Furthermore, the limitations of human understanding mean that people will inevitably differ in opinion about religious matters—compelling a single set of religious beliefs would be akin to compelling a single diet, or medical treatment, or clothing for a population.[22] In the quarter century after the Restoration, Baxter repeatedly advocated for the right of liberty of conscience rooted in appeal to epistemological humility. Religious pluralism was not only good policy because the laws of nature required it; it was also necessary because the human condition prevented unanimity of agreement on religious matters.

The history of the Mather family was intimately tied to the events of the Restoration and to nonconformist leaders such as Richard Baxter. After receiving his MA at Trinity College (1658), Increase Mather served two parishes and one military chaplaincy in England. He fled for New England in 1661 when his outspoken nonconformity made it untenable to remain.[23] But "nonconformists" in New England faced a different set of political questions in the late seventeenth century as they sought to come to terms with the aftermath of the Restoration. They had achieved the kind of thorough reform of the English church that Puritans like Baxter had failed to accomplish, as well as the political hegemony necessary to enforce it. Understandably, they were not initially interested in developing strong theories of resistance and liberty of conscience. This state of affairs began to erode after Charles II's accession, however, beginning with the visitation of the king's royal commissioners (1664), continuing with the investigative visits of Edward Randolph in the 1670s, and concluding with the revocation of the charter by James II in 1684.

The revocation of the charter deeply divided the citizens of New England. The Mathers led the party of resistance, which would reach its full fruition five years later. Increase Mather publicly proclaimed that submission to this act would be a sin against God and persuaded the citizenry to reject the crown's interference.[24] But when he returned to London in 1688 to negotiate a new charter with James II, his tone had markedly changed. Instead of pleading for a return to the status quo ante, he petitioned the king for toleration of liberty of conscience in New England.[25] Cotton Mather conducted a parallel literary campaign of conciliation with the English public in the 1690s.[26] The new charter (1691) forced the introduction of Anglicanism proper as well as a broad religious pluralism in New England, bringing the experiences and interests of New World Puritans into closer alignment with their nonconformist cousins in England. From now on their religious fortunes would be dictated by the crown and by Parliament.

Thus at the outset of his professional life Cotton Mather was involved in the signal political controversies of seventeenth-century New England. In the contention over the legal status of the colony that played out between 1684 and 1691, Mather took a leading and very public role. He had a hand in the anonymous publication of his father's *Brief Discourse Concerning the Unlawfulness of Common Prayer Worship* (1687), a recitation of all of the complaints against Anglican liturgy that Richard Baxter and others had been making for nearly three decades. This polemic was directed against the Anglican services being newly held at South Church under the patronage of the recently appointed royal governor, Edmund Andros, and was the act for which Andros issued a warrant of libel against Mather two years later.[27] In the immediate aftermath of the Glorious Revolution, Mather delivered a sermon (April 1689) intimating his support for the overthrow of James II and, by implication, his royal representatives in New England.[28] Just days later Andros sought to arrest Mather for the aforementioned charge of libel; that same day the colonists began their own revolution. Mather met with the chief men of Boston in the morning; by noon their *Declaration of the Gentlemen* in favor of removing the now former king's men from power was read in public—very probably by Mather, who seems to have had a key role in writing the document as well.[29] In the ensuing months Mather preached and published in support of the colonists' actions.[30] For all these goings on Mather was later described by Andros and his associate Edmund Randolph as one of the "chief designers" of the revolt, actively giving orders to others involved. Among royalist sympathizers he became known as "the young pope," and was pilloried by them to the political classes in England for his anti-Anglican and antimonarchical sentiments.[31]

Mather owned and employed the nonconformist biblical commentaries of Baxter, Matthew Poole, and Matthew Henry in the "Biblia Americana." His professional life would also become linked to Baxter and Henry.[32] Yet his commentary on the passages related to submission and resistance is markedly different from both.

When Mather began the "Biblia" in 1693, he constructed notebooks of blank sheets to record his commentary, a practice that was typical of the time. As the pattern of the chapter headings seems to indicate, he initially allotted himself 1–2 sheets (2–4 pages) of commentary space for each chapter of a given biblical book, penciling in the chapter headings before he began introducing his notes. Since he often omitted chapter headings altogether, it appears that in the initial stage of composition he planned to skip chapters that did not hold interest for him. Mather's plan proved to be short-sighted, however, and as time passed he began to insert additional leaves for various chapters, as necessity dictated.

It is worth noting, then, that of the eleven classic passages on the subject of submission and resistance, five were later inserts and one is completely absent (1 Sam 26). It is difficult to imagine that Mather would have incidentally omitted so many passages that spoke to one of the most pressing political issues of his day, passages that were directly relevant to his own political biography, passages that would have been of intense interest to any reader.

Of the ten passages that do receive commentary (five original pages, five later inserts), eight of them do not contain any relevant comments on the key verses. In two (Mark 12, 1 Pet 2) there is no direct comment at all. For example, on 1 Pet 2 Mather comments on verses 2, 3, 5, 9, 16, 24, and 25, but passes over verse 13 entirely. In the other six passages, the commentary most often focuses on their least notable features or minimizes their political significance. For example, when David strikes down the Amalekite who reports Saul's death (2 Sam 1), rather than taking David's action to be evidence of his consciousness of the inviolability of the king's person (as was commonly done), Mather chose to focus on how the Amalekite would have known it was Saul in the first place, given that the king would have exchanged his royal robes for military clothing in battle.[33] In his commentary on Matt 22:21, he simply offered a "short and a sweet gloss" on Jesus's words "Render unto Caesar." Citing Tertullian, he wrote: "Give the man to God, and the penny to Caesar. The man bears God's image, as the penny did Caesar's. Where God and Caesar are in opposition, the whole man is God's right." His comments on Acts 5:29 border on the dismissive. Regarding the apostles' assertion that they must obey God rather than men, typically read in Protestantism as a confirmation of the right to resist religious tyranny, Mather described it as merely "a Maxim so evident unto the Natural Conscience of Man, that even a Pagan long before this, had raised it."[34]

Thus Mather seems to have studiously avoided providing commentary on nearly the entire range of these politically significant passages: first omitting them from his plan altogether, then either avoiding any comment in later insertions or making rather irrelevant or innocuous comments when he chose to weigh in. One can understand why this might be so. On the one hand, he would have had no interest in stoking dissent from the traditional New England order by schismatics such as Quakers and Baptists. Furthermore, he would have had even less interest in calling attention to his recent political notoriety under the conditions of the new charter.[35] He also had to consider that most of his anticipated readership for the "Biblia" would have been in England, not the colonies. The parties of this sharply divided audience would have respectively found strong calls to resistance or submission obnoxious.[36] Yet everything about his actions during the colonial political turmoil makes it unlikely that his commentary would have commended abject submission. Mather seems to have chosen the route of avoiding any substantive comment on the issues, as though such political concerns were hardly worth anyone's attention.[37]

It seems likely that Mather would have also taken into account the uncertain circumstances that Dissenters continued to face in the early eighteenth century. While the immediate and most onerous persecution of nonconformists came to a close with the accession of William and Mary and the Act of Toleration (1689), the underlying animus against and efforts to suppress them continued to simmer, making the security of their religious liberty uncertain.[38] With the death of William III in 1702, mobs attacked and destroyed the churches of Dissenters. It was not until the Riot Act (1715) that such activity was made illegal.[39] Queen Anne was deeply committed to High Church Anglicanism and to suppressing the Dissenters. Although she promised to maintain the Act of Toleration, she did so with qualifications. Upon her accession, the "Occasional Conformity" bill was introduced, requiring nonconformists to take Communion according to Anglican rites at regular intervals; it passed in 1711.[40] The bill also required public office holders not to attend a nonconformist church in the twelve months before their appointment. The new bill fined them for such behavior and required their continued Anglican Communion, on pain of the loss of the office. Politicians of the era spoke openly against Dissenters; Sir Humphrey Mackworth (1657–1727), among others, advocated their complete exclusion from office in his 1703 essay (*Peace at Home*) defending the conformity bill. Anglican bishops and other clergy continued to excoriate Dissenters from pulpits and in the press.[41] Mather had many reasons to restrain his political views within his biblical commentary.

As a point of comparison, one can consider the commentary of Matthew Henry (1662–1714). His father, Philip, was ejected in 1662, and thereafter arrested on several occasions for unlawful conventicles. Matthew was forced to attend an illegal Dissenting academy for his education and clerical preparation. He took a Presbyterian church in 1686 and pastored churches for the next three decades, during which he preached through the entire Bible twice. These sermons became the source of his massive Bible commentary, his six-volume *Exposition of the Old and New Testaments* (1708–10).[42] Henry provides an important marker of second-generation nonconformist biblical interpretation.

What is perhaps most striking about the substance and tone of Henry's commentary is the political passivity that he enjoined on his nonconformist readers. On the regicide passages from 1 and 2 Samuel, for example, David serves as a type of Christ in his refusal to kill Saul, recognizing that as king, Saul was "God's anointed, appointed to rule as long as he lived" and thus "under the protection of divine law." His striking down of the Amalekite who helped Saul commit suicide was similarly motivated, because "the lives of princes ought to be in a special manner, precious to us." Even Joab's decision to disobey David's command to spare the life of his son Absalom the usurper is treated sympathetically, since Joab "did a real service both to his king and country, and would have endangered the welfare of both had he not done it."[43]

In his treatment of Rom 13 and 1 Pet 2, Henry counseled submission to authority, even in the face of injustice: "Obedience to their commands in things lawful and honest, and in other things a patient subjection to the penalty without resistance—a conformity in every thing to the place and duty of subjects, bringing our minds to the relation and condition, and the inferiority and subordination of it." Paul did not want his Christian readers to be compared to the Jewish zealots, who were "factious, seditious, and turbulent," even as the "civil powers were persecuting powers, [and] the body of the law was against them." So too with nonconformists: "it is our duty in that case rather to submit to persecution for well-doing, and to take it patiently, than by an irregular and disorderly practices to attempt a redress." Hope for change is also cast in language of passive resignation: the persecuted can take hope in the thought that "divine providence [is] in a special manner conversant about those changes and revolutions of governments."[44]

Similar themes appear in Henry's treatment of other passages. Regarding tribute to Caesar (Matt 22, Mark 12), Jesus does not dispute Caesar's right to rule; his answer, rather, counsels "peaceable subjection to the powers that be." Thus he shows that Christianity is "no enemy of civil government." Furthermore, Henry took this opportunity to argue that clergy ought to remove themselves from political involvement: "he hath given an example to his ministers, who deal in sacred things, not to meddle with disputes about things secular, not to wade far into controversies relating to them, but to leave that to those whose proper business it is." The most important concern for followers of Jesus is the inner life: the "innermost and uppermost" aspects of their conscience are what God lays claim to.[45] Even the most blatant example of civil disobedience in the New Testament, Acts 5:29, is minimized: "They justified their disobedience to the command of the great Sanhedrim, great as it was ...

[by appealing to] a maxim universally owned, which every natural conscience subscribes to." That is, their insistence on following their conscience against authority was not particular to a seditious religious sect, but rather was something belonging to natural law, something having universal consent rather than a peculiar Christian color. Clearly, Henry was also speaking to the audience of his critics, trying to convince them that nonconformists were loyal citizens who supported the monarchy, social order, and peaceable religion.

Mather may have been following a similar logic in his reticence to comment or to comment provocatively upon these passages. However, there is one passage in which he allowed his political sympathies to show: Rom 13. Mather has three separate entries on the first verse, "Let every soul be subject unto the higher powers." The first of these would have been written fairly early. It is numbered "2362," which probably places it around 1698–99.[46] It contains a citation of the Portuguese Jesuit missionary Antonio Fernandes's (1570–1642) *Commentary on the Old Testament* (1617), to the effect that this verse affirms not just that humans owe their submission to rulers, but that rulers too, as those "possessing souls," are themselves subject to authority: "There are *Higher Powers*, whereto the *Magistrates* themselves are to bee *subject*. The *Highest* on Earth, must bee *subject* unto the *Most High God of, Heaven*."[47] Mather's first comment on this passage is to assert that even English kings are subject to higher authorities, and thus not absolute in their authority over subjects.

Mather's second entry is unnumbered; it is a citation of John Locke's *Paraphrase and Notes on the Epistles of St. Paul* (1705–7). It seems reasonable to suppose that this entry dates between 1708 and 1710, though a date of 1711–14 is certainly possible.[48] In his treatment of Rom 13, Locke focused on several key ideas, all of which have their origins in his *Two Treatises on Government*. First, being a part of God's kingdom does not absolve Christians from being subject to earthly rulers, even (ungodly) heathen rulers.[49] At the same time, being Christians does not prevent them from asserting their rights as citizens: "from those due rights, which by the law of nature, or the constitutions of their country, belonged to them." Furthermore, Paul takes the opportunity in this passage to offer a universal theology of government—one that explains "whence . . . all magistrates every where have their authority, and for what end they have it, and should use it"—in order to make the point that all civil power derives from God. As such, all earthly rulers are obligated to act according to divine justice, severely limiting their capriciousness: government must operate according to "the end for which God gave it, (that is) the good of the people sincerely pursued according to the best of the skill of those who share that power."[50] Only under these conditions are rulers "not to be resisted." In Locke's hands, Rom 13 becomes not a call to political passivity, but rather a bold assertion in defense of the rights of citizens to determine their own political destiny.

Mather's comments on Locke focus on those ideas with the most radical implications. First, while Christians *qua* Christians must not resist civil authorities, it seems "as if the Apostle meant here, [only] Magistrates having and exercising a *lawful* Power." Furthermore, while Christians do not have exceptional rights, neither were they deprived of any right: "They had the Common Right of others, their Fellow-citizens." Finally, and perhaps most significantly, Mather highlights Locke's most provocative point. When speaking of paying tribute, the apostle "enjoins, *Render to all their Dues*; But *who* it was, to *whom* any of these, or any other Dues of Right, belonged, he decides not. *For that he leaves them to be determined by the Lawes and Constitutions of their Countrey.*"[51] Mather follows Locke in asserting that citizens have the right to scrutinize the actions of their rulers.

Mather extended this entry at a later date, taking direct aim at the kind of abject political slavishness advocated in Anglican circles, an entry that probably dates from 1714 to 1716. In 1708, Bishop George Bull (1634–1710) directed Anglican clergy to begin using the *Book of Homilies* once again for services.[52] In 1713, after a lapse of over a quarter century, Bishop Gilbert Burnet (1643–1715) advocated the publication of a revised edition (*An Essay towards a New Book of Homilies*); in the same year a new edition composed of sixty-two sermons appeared. Coming on the heels of the Society for the Propagation of the Gospel in Foreign Parts' decade-long push to settle a bishop in the colonies (ongoing since 1704, with Queen Anne's support), one can understand Mather's consternation about what the publication of the new edition signaled. Citing an unnamed source, Mather complains, "What if the Clergy of *England* in the Book of *Homilies*, did strain [the] Text a little too far, in shewing of their extraordinary Respect unto King *Edward* VI. and Queen *Elizabeth*? Why should we keep it *still* upon the Strain, and not suffer it to come to itself, by its own elastick Motion?" Thus, Mather suggests, the best way to interpret Paul's requirement of obedience is to see it simply as a reminder about the divine authority of government, rather than a call to blind subservience, and, as Mather sharply notes, one that only entails submission to an authority constrained by its divine purpose, "the Security and Peace of all its Subjects."[53] English subjects should in no way be constrained by the hyperauthoritarian theory of submission offered in the *Book of Homilies* nearly two centuries after its original publication.

Mather's exposition of Rom 13 is thoroughly in keeping with his sentiments and activities at the time of the Glorious Revolution. The *Declaration of the Gentlemen* crafted by Mather on the day of the revolt frames the conflict as one in which the just rights of citizens are being deprived by unjust authorities.[54] Mather articulated the rationale for the political revolution in which he took part in terms of the kind of social contract theory typical of Locke and other early modern political theorists. By violating the rights of citizens, the governor had, in Lockean parlance, introduced a "state of lawlessness" in society. Under such circumstances, citizens had the right and even the duty to remove them, as an act of self-defense, in order to restore the order upon which a just society, a divinely prescribed society, is predicated.[55] His commentary on Rom 13 is in keeping with this understanding.

Why, then, did Mather wait so long to express himself politically in the "Biblia," or conversely, why did he allow his political ideas to emerge at all in his commentary on Rom 13? Perhaps the passing of time emboldened him; perhaps the uncertain ecclesiastical climate and the encroachment of Anglicanism in the colonies in the early eighteenth century alarmed him enough to speak out. Alternatively, should this last entry date from a time after the queen's death, it may reflect a lessened concern for discretion, given George I's sympathetic treatment of nonconformists. Or perhaps, since by this time his expectation of publication had all but disappeared, the "Biblia" may have become a forum where he could give voice to his true political sentiments without fear of discovery or reprisal. Whatever the case, Mather's biblical commentary offers scholars a potentially fruitful avenue for understanding the development of early American political thought. It provides further evidence that Locke's influence began well in advance of the Revolutionary period. One suspects that Mather was hardly the only figure of his era to have been absorbing such ideas; in what other sermons and commentary notebooks might such political influences be found?

Biblical commentary could and did serve as an important instrument for political expression in the late seventeenth and early eighteenth centuries, particularly for nonconformists, whose opportunities for religious expression were severely circumscribed for nearly a half century after the Restoration. Through their reflection on Scripture they were able to give voice to their discontent, make sense of their political and social marginalization, and begin to construct an alternative vision of Christian faith attuned to the principle of long-suffering in the face of persecution, while at the same time asserting their liberty of conscience. It is no coincidence, as scholars have observed, that nonconformists began to turn inward in their theology toward affective or "heart" religion as they sought to come to terms with the loss of external or societal markers of true religion such as the state church.[56] From here it was but a short step toward the revivalism of the succeeding generation of evangelicals.

Notes

1. Geoffrey F. Nuttall, *Richard Baxter* (London: Thomas Nelson, 1965), 109–11.
2. On L'Estrange, see N. H. Keeble, *The Literary Culture of Nonconformity in Later Seventeenth-Century England* (Athens: University of Georgia Press, 1987), 102–10.
3. See *The Observator* (February 25, 1685), 1–2.
4. Michael Watts, *The Dissenters: From the Reformation to the French Revolution* (Oxford: Clarendon Press, 1978), 255–56.
5. See John Witte Jr., *The Reformation of Rights: Law, Religion, and Human Rights in Early Modern Calvinism* (Cambridge: Cambridge University Press, 2007), 209, 277. See also David Little, "Constitutional Protection of the Freedom of Conscience in Colonial America," in *Christianity and Freedom*, ed. Timothy Shah and Allen Hertzke (Cambridge: Cambridge University Press, 2016), 1:237–63.
6. Thus New Light legislator and clergyman Elisha Williams, former rector of Yale: "Every man has an equal right to follow the dictates of his own conscience in the affairs of religion . . . and to follow his judgment wherever it leads him; even an equal right with any rulers be they civil or ecclesiastical." *The Essential Rights and Liberties of Protestants* (1744), in *Religion and the American Constitutional Experiment*, 3rd ed., ed. John Witte Jr. and Joel A. Nichols (Boulder, CO: Westview Press, 2011), 25.
7. Witte and Nichols, *Religion and the American Constitutional Experiment*, 26–29.
8. See Mark Goldie, "The Theory of Religious Intolerance in Restoration England," in *From Persecution to Toleration: The Glorious Revolution and Religion in England*, ed. Ole Peter Grell, Jonathan I. Israel, and Nicholas Tyacke (Oxford: Clarendon Press, 1991), 330–68; and Jonathan Scott, *Commonwealth Principles: Republican Writing of the English Revolution* (Cambridge: Cambridge University Press, 2004), 109–29.
9. See Keeble, *Literary Culture of Nonconformity*, 11ff., 96ff.
10. There are about a dozen key passages that served as foundational texts in this regard, including the regicide passages of 1 and 2 Samuel, the Gospel passages about paying tribute to Caesar, and the apostles' refusal to submit to the Sanhedrin in Acts 5, Rom 13, and 1 Pet 2.
11. Richard Baxter, *A Paraphrase on the New Testament* (Rom 13:1–7) (London, 1685). Baxter's *Paraphrase* does not have page numbers.
12. See his commentary on 1 Pet 2.13, which also alludes to the religious persecution experienced by nonconformists.
13. Matthew Poole (1624–1679) is a point of contrast to Baxter. Poole proved to be more utilitarian in his scruples about accepting political indulgences: in 1665 he took the oaths to Parliament in order to receive his preaching license, and in 1672 he submitted to Charles II's Act of Indulgence, which licensed dissenting churches and their preachers. See Thomas Harley, *Matthew Poole: His Life, His Times, His Contributions* (Bloomington: Indiana University Press, 2009). Poole's *Annotations on the Holy Bible* appeared posthumously in 1683; ministerial colleagues completed the rest of the commentary working from his notes. Thus, while it is difficult to definitively conclude about Poole's sentiments on passages such as Rom 13 and 1 Pet 2, we can be reasonably certain that those passages do not represent radical departures from his thought. On the whole, these and the other passages are much less strident than Baxter's, offering a more quiescent submission to rulers. See Poole, *A Commentary on the Holy Bible* (Peabody, MA: Hendrickson, 1985), 3:524–25.
14. Chief Justice Jeffreys was unsympathetic. He accused Baxter of being the author of books enough "to load a cart; every one [of which] is . . . full of sedition (I might say treason)." See T. B. Howell, *A Complete Collection of State Trials for High Treason: And Other Crimes and Misdemeanors* (London, 1816), 494–502.
15. His Javert-like doggedness in hounding his victims made him notorious, earning him a place in John Bunyan's novel *The Holy War* (1682) as the character "Mr. Filth," an "odious, nasty,

lascivious piece of beastliness." Keeble, *Literary Culture of Nonconformity*, 102–10. On L'Estrange's particular animus for Baxter, see Nuttall, *Richard Baxter*, 85–86.

16. Richard Baxter, *A Holy Commonwealth, or, Political Aphorisms, Opening the true Principles of Government* (London, 1659). See, for example, chap. 12, "Of Due Obedience to Rulers, and of Resistance" (346ff.).

17. Baxter, *Holy Commonwealth*, 38, 241ff., 285ff.

18. The work was nonetheless burned at Oxford in 1683, along with the works of Milton and Hobbes. The extended discussion of this matter is found in Baxter's posthumous autobiography, *Reliquiae Baxterianae, or, Mr. Richard Baxters Narrative . . . of His Life and Times*, ed. Matthew Sylvester (London, 1696), 71–72.

19. *The Observator*, February 25, 1685, 1. L'Estrange attacked Baxter regularly in *The Observator*, mentioning him some two dozen times between 1681 and 1686.

20. *The Observator*, July 18, 1685, 1–2 (issued just after Baxter's conviction).

21. Richard Baxter, *A Body of Practical Divinity, or A Christian Directory* (London: 1825), 5:168–72, 193, 195–96. There are parallels in Baxter's argument with Locke's *Letter Concerning Toleration* (1689); see John Dunn, "The Claim to Freedom of Conscience: Freedom of Speech, Freedom of Thought, Freedom of Worship?," in Grell, Israel, and Tyacke, *From Persecution to Toleration*, 171–93.

22. Baxter, *Christian Directory*, 193–96. Elements of Baxter's arguments can be found in many of his other works, such as *The English Nonconformity, Under King Charles II and King James II, Truly Stated and Argued* (1690).

23. Michael G. Hall, *The Last American Puritan: The Life of Increase Mather, 1639–1723* (Middletown: Wesleyan University Press, 1988), 44–45.

24. Kenneth Silverman, *The Life and Times of Cotton Mather* (New York: Harper and Row, 1984), 59–61.

25. It was also during this trip that he became an associate of and correspondent with Baxter. Baxter would go on to dedicate one of his last works, *The Glorious Kingdom of Christ* (1691), to Increase. Kenneth B. Murdock, *Increase Mather: The Foremost American Puritan* (Cambridge, MA: Harvard University Press, 1926), 196, 206, 266–67.

26. Silverman, *Cotton Mather*, 144–45.

27. Ibid., 68; the work describes the Book of Common Prayer as "*Popish* and *Heathenish*," which certainly bordered on libel.

28. Ibid., 69. The sermon was delivered in April, about the time news of the Revolution arrived in Boston. Mather was already under pressure from Andros; the warrant for his arrest had been issued in January of 1689.

29. Ibid., 69–71; Cotton Mather is given author credit in Evans's *Early American Imprints*.

30. An event Mather defended the following year as well, in his 1690 Election Day sermon before the General Court. See Mather, "The Serviceable Man," in *Puritan Political Ideas, 1558–1794*, ed. Edmund S. Morgan (Indianapolis: Hackett, 1965), 235–46.

31. Silverman, *Cotton Mather*, 73–74.

32. Baxter wrote a recommendation for the London edition of Mather's *Memorable Providences* (1691); he shared his interest in the invisible world and the threat of witchcraft. See Silverman, *Cotton Mather*, 87. Henry offered to help him publish the "Biblia Americana"; see Kenneth Silverman, ed., *Selected Letters of Cotton Mather* (Baton Rouge: Louisiana State University Press, 1971), 155, 181.

33. Mather proposes that his Edomite armor-bearer Doeg carried the crown with him, in case of victory in battle.

34. Mather quotes Livy's report of the Greek general Lycortas's response to the Romans: "Indeed we respect you, Romans, and if you wish it so, we even fear you; but still more do we respect and fear the immortal gods" (Livy, *History* 39.38.6). Translation from Livy, *History of*

Rome, vol. 11, Books 38–39, ed. Evan T. Sage, Loeb Classical Library 313 (Cambridge, MA: Harvard University Press, 1963), 339.

35. Mather engaged in a public relations campaign in the 1690s aimed at demonstrating the political loyalty and religious generosity of New Englanders; Silverman, *Cotton Mather*, 144.

36. It could also be that his reticence to commit his ideas to print reflected a subconscious or even a coded means of *rejecting* their traditional interpretation. That is, his refusal to employ the expected Protestant tropes about political submission might have been an indirect way of *critiquing* that tradition of interpretation. These repeated, glaring omissions on his part would hardly have gone unnoticed by his prospective readership, something he most likely would have anticipated.

37. The evidence does not seem to indicate that Mather might have removed any controversial material; his typical practice for eliminating material in the "Biblia" was simply to cross it out.

38. On the parameters of this hostility, see Hugh Trevor-Roper, "Toleration and Religion After 1688," in Grell, Israel, and Tyacke, *From Persecution to Toleration*, 389–408.

39. Watts, *Dissenters*, 264.

40. Henry W. Clark, *History of English Nonconformity from Wiclif to the Close of the Nineteenth Century*, 2 vols. (New York: Russell and Russell, 1965) 2:141ff.

41. Ibid., 148ff. Mackworth was a founding member of both the SPCK (1699) and the Propagation of the Gospel in Foreign Parts (1701), both arms of the Anglican Church's proselytism of other Protestants in the American colonies.

42. See Allan Harman, *Matthew Henry: His Life and Influence* (Fearne, UK: Christian Focus, 2012), 147–70 et passim. As with Matthew Poole's commentary, Henry's *Exposition* was unfinished at his death, and it was completed by other Dissenting clergy using his notes, including Romans and 1 Peter; see the *Protestant Dissenter's Magazine* (1797): 4:472.

43. Henry, *Matthew Henry's Commentary*, 6 vols. (Peabody, MA: Hendrickson, 1991), 2:424, 438, 462ff.

44. Henry, *Commentary*, 6:2230; so also with 1 Pet 2.

45. Ibid., 6:1728–29, 1805.

46. Entry #4849 dates from 1702, citing a work from Whiston published that year. On Reiner Smolinski's four stages of composition for the "Biblia," see *BA*, 1:51ff.

47. *BA*, 9:157.

48. Given the publication date of Locke's *Paraphrase*, the earlier date seems more likely in my judgment. It could be any time after 1707 (the 1705 edition of the *Paraphrase* included only Galatians; Romans was not included until the 1707 edition). If it were a later entry (1711–14), it seems likely he would have expressed no doubt about the authorship.

49. John Locke, *A Paraphrase and Notes on the Epistles of St. Paul*, ed. Arthur Wainwright (Oxford: Clarendon Press, 1988), 2:586.

50. Ibid., 2:587.

51. *BA*, 9:157.

52. In England, early Protestant views on political authority found a potent vehicle for dissemination in the liturgical anthology *Certain Sermons, or Homilies* (London, 1547). The title of the Tenth Homilie is "An Exhortacion concernyng Good Ordre and Obedience to Rulers and Magistrates." It amplified the idea of political submission while making civil resistance a soteriological issue. See Ronald B. Bond, *Certain Sermons or Homilies (1547) and a Homily Against Disobedience and Wilful Rebellion (1570)* (Toronto: University of Toronto Press, 1987), 163; Bond, "Cranmer and the Controversy Surrounding Publication of 'Certayne Sermons or Homilies' (1547)," *Renaissance and Reformation* 12, no. 1 (1976): 32–33. Both Elizabeth and James I would use the *Book of Homilies* to suppress Puritan ecclesial and political agitation, and for Dissenters it came to symbolize much of what was wrong with the *Via Média*.

53. *BA*, 9:157–58. This "nameless author" is not Locke.

54. See the *Declaration*, 1–4. Mather echoed these complaints in *The Serviceable Man*, an Election Day sermon given to the General Court (March 1690). See *The Serviceable Man* (Boston, 1690), 15–16.

55. See Locke, *Two Treatises on Government*, ed. Peter Laslett (Cambridge: Cambridge University Press, 1967), 431–37.

56. See Keeble, *Literary Culture of Nonconformity*, 187ff.

6

THE BIBLE IN EARLY PIETIST
AND EVANGELICAL MISSIONS

RYAN P. HOSELTON

The biblical practices of the early Pietist and evangelical movements greatly shaped, and were shaped by, their agendas for global missions. Protestant missionary initiatives had made little headway against the global spread of Catholicism in the seventeenth century.[1] The earliest Protestant ministers to travel abroad served primarily as chaplains to Europeans living and working in colonial military and trading posts, while efforts to reach non-Christian native populations remained modest. The disciples of Gisbertus Voetius (1589–1676), leader of the Dutch *Nadere Reformatie* movement, advocated mission work among Indigenous peoples in the areas colonized by the Dutch East and West India Companies, such as southeast Asia, southern and western Africa, and the New Netherlands. During the Interregnum, the Puritan-led British Parliament supported the missionary work of John Eliot (1604–1690) and Thomas Mayhew (1593–1682) among Native Americans in New England and on Martha's Vineyard, establishing the Society for the Propagation of the Gospel in New England (later called the New England Company) in 1649 to this end—but disease and conflicts such as King Philip's War (1675–1678) derailed much of their progress. The Church of England later founded the Society for Promoting Christian Knowledge (SPCK) in 1698 and the Society for the Propagation of the Gospel in Foreign Parts (SPG) in 1701, but these societies initially focused on the spiritual needs of Anglican colonists and had little success converting non-Europeans. Recent studies have shown that Native American and Black missionaries made far greater strides than Europeans in the late seventeenth- and early eighteenth-century Atlantic world.² The chief accomplishment of the early European Protestant missionaries (with the help of Indigenous partners) was Bible translation. Eliot produced his Algonquin New Testament in 1661 and finished the Old Testament in 1663, and Dutch chaplains produced a Malay translation in 1688.³ Committed to the Reformation principles of *sola Scriptura* and vernacularization, Protestants made Bible translation and biblical literacy central priorities in their missionary labors.

The Pietist and evangelical movements changed the picture in the eighteenth century, when their quest to renew the Protestant world inspired greater measures to missionize the rest of the world. Despite national, denominational, and geographical boundaries, their shared zeal to spread the Bible's message of salvation bound them together in transatlantic networks and collaborations and gave them a sense of collective mission and unity in the Spirit's redemptive operations. The turn began in 1705, when King Frederick IV of Denmark sent the Halle-trained German Pietist missionaries Bartholomäus Ziegenbalg (1682–1719) and Heinrich Plütschau (1676–1747) to the Danish colony at Tranquebar, India. They and their German, Scandinavian, and British successors (who expanded the mission throughout South India) enjoyed the support of the London-based SPCK—mediated by the Halle-trained chaplain at Saint James Palace, Anton Wilhelm Böhme (1673–1722)—and like-minded advocates in New England such as Cotton Mather (1663–1728). The connection between Germany, England, and British North America continued through Böhme's successor in London, the Halle-trained Friedrich Michael Ziegenhagen (1694–1776), who worked with both the SPCK and the Francke Foundations in Halle to send the Salzburg Protestants to Georgia in the 1730s and cosponsor Heinrich Melchior Mühlenberg (1711–1787) as a missionary to Pennsylvania in 1742. Over the long eighteenth century, Pietist missionary initiatives expanded around the globe and across Europe as they also amplified efforts to missionize Jews, Muslims, and Catholics closer to home.⁴ Although the Moravians' doctrinal and cultural idiosyncrasies limited collaboration with churchly Pietists and Anglophone evangelicals, their extensive missionary networks spread to Greenland, Labrador, the Danish and English Caribbean, British North America (esp. Georgia, Pennsylvania, and New York), Latin America (esp. Suriname and Guyana), South Africa, the Gold Coast, Ceylon (Sri Lanka), Persia, Egypt, Algeria, Russia, and more.⁵

The Anglophone transatlantic awakenings of the 1730s and 1740s energized the alliances between colonial evangelicals and British missionary organizations such as the New England Company (NEC) and the Presbyterian Society in Scotland for Propagating Christian Knowledge (SSPCK, 1709), and Pietists followed their work closely. The NEC sponsored the Stockbridge Mission, led by John Sergeant (1710–1749) from 1735 to 1749 and then by Jonathan Edwards (1703–1758) from 1751 to 1758, and the SSPCK enlisted David Brainerd (1718–1747) as a missionary to Native Americans in the middle colonies. Edwards's publication of Brainerd's *Diary* was translated into multiple languages and inspired scores of evangelical and Pietist missionaries across the Atlantic.[6] These organizations also trained and employed Native American evangelical missionaries such as Samson Occom (1723–1792) and Samuel Kirkland (1741–1808). Thanks in part to his friendship with the English revivalist George Whitefield (1714–1770), Occom enjoyed great success with his preaching tour through England and Scotland to raise money for Eleazar Wheelock's (1711–1779) missionary-training school for Native Americans in Lebanon, Connecticut (which relocated and became Dartmouth College, to Occom's dismay).[7]

As these Pietists and evangelicals emphasized the new birth and an experiential biblical piety over confessional tradition as the main basis of true global Christianity, they contributed to the construction of a new mental framework that recent scholarship has termed the "Protestant International."[8] They imagined themselves as part of a spiritual, pan-Protestant, global community of like-minded colaborers who were participating in and advancing Scripture's redemptive drama. By the power of the Spirit and the Word, together they would reverse the spread of Catholicism, revive Protestant Christendom, and channel Christ's salvation to the world.

While their traditions, cultures, contexts, and interests produced great variety among them, parallel transformations in Pietist and evangelical biblical practices shaped their aspirations for global missionary expansion in broadly similar ways. First, their interpretation of Scripture and their times led them to believe that their work of revival and mission inaugurated a unique stage of sacred history in which the Holy Spirit would soon be poured out on the heathen in extraordinary measure before Christ's return to establish his kingdom. Second, their heightened emphasis on the Spirit's use of means—in particular, the Holy Scriptures—to accomplish God's redemptive purposes motivated an activistic urgency to propagate the Word among non-Christians through preaching, translation, printing and distributing Bibles, and education. Third, Pietist and evangelical pieties and their quest for true biblical Christianity formed their missionary objectives and practices in critical ways.

Biblical Sacred History

In contrast to the widespread view among the early Protestant reformers that Christ's great commission in Matt 28:19–20 to "teach all nations" applied only to the apostles, eighteenth-century awakened Protestants increasingly emphasized its continuation and future fulfillment. As Edwards's grandfather Solomon Stoddard (1643–1729) declared in 1723, "The Command was not given to the Apostles alone, but to their Successors also throughout all generations."[9] However, early Pietist and evangelical interpretations of Scripture's missionary imperative did not hinge on a few verses. Building on a long tradition of redemptive-historical exegesis, they read the entire Bible as a grand sacred drama of God's plan of salvation—one in which they were both observers of God's sovereign workings and actors as God's instruments—that spanned from before the creation to the end of time. The entire Old Testament shadowed forth the coming of the Messiah who would save all nations and peoples. The New Testament then related Christ's life, death, resurrection, and ascension to fulfill this salvation, after which Christ sent the Holy Spirit to assist the church to proclaim the good news to all the world until his Second Coming. Contrary to some skeptical philosophical circles and historicizing exegetical trends of their early Enlightenment context, Pietists and evangelicals saw abundant evidence of the Spirit's supernatural progression of this salvation history in their day as promised in divinely inspired Scripture.[10]

According to their framework of sacred history, the early church had faithfully continued the mission after the apostolic age. But then the Roman Catholic Church emerged—which they regarded as the "whore of Babylon" of Rev 17—and spread poisonous idolatries for most of the Middle Ages. While a small remnant of the true spiritual church had persisted through these years, it was not until the Protestant Reformation when the authority of the Word was restored in greater fullness. In their day, however, they feared that the Protestant project was faltering as churches succumbed to spiritual lethargy and as Catholicism continued to spread around the globe. Yet they held out hope that the Spirit was at work in a remarkable renewal of Protestant Christendom, and this momentum was awakening the church to fulfill its mission to the world in anticipation of Christ's return and the establishment of the kingdom.[11]

While Pietist and evangelical views on chiliasm varied, many shared a general optimism that Christ's return was not far off. However, certain scriptural prophecies had to be fulfilled first. Many followed Philipp Jakob Spener (1635–1705) in reading Rom 11 and Old Testament prophecies such as Hos 3:4–5 to promise a future conversion of the Jews to Christianity, rejecting the predominantly preterist stance of seventeenth-century Protestant Orthodoxy, which asserted that this promise had been fulfilled in the first century. Moreover, Rev 18–19 promised the downfall of papal Rome ("Babylon") before Christ's return. Yet these things could never come to pass with the Protestant churches in such a dire state—they needed spiritual renewal.[12] As W. R. Ward explains, in order to allow time for these fulfillments to take place, Pietists and evangelicals suspended the end times to "the middle distance"—it was neither immediate nor far off, but just soon enough to spur urgent reform and activism in preparation for it.[13] They were not the first Protestants to speculate about the imminent return of Christ with one eye on Scripture and the other on world events. But their eschatological hopes laid increasing emphasis on the spiritual revival and global expansion of the church as key conditions for Christ's return, and they saw promising signs that they lived in the dawn of that day.

For Böhme, the tasks of renewing Protestant Christendom and expanding the mission abroad were interconnected and mutually integral for moving the church toward its latter-day glorification. In his preface to part 3 of *The Propagation of the Gospel in the East*, an English edition of the Tranquebar mission reports, *Merckwuerdige Nachricht aus Ost-Indien*, he declared that the "Conversion of the Gentiles" throughout the *"parched Wilderness of the Pagan World"* should be of central interest to any who *"wish to see the Church in a better and more flourishing State, than that wherein it doth appear at present."* Following a long tradition of Christian exegesis in reading Canticles—a love poem about King Solomon and his betrothed—as an allegory of Christ and the church, he interpreted Cant 6:10 to represent the church's progress toward glory. As the morning dawn was a *"Fore-runner"* of the brighter day, so was the current *"gloomy State of the Church a Fore-runner of a more Glorious Display of the Gospel, which, by a gradual Increase of Light shall succeed."* The advancement of world missions was critical to this progress. Referencing Rom 11:25, Böhme declared that the *"glorious State of the Church will then doubtless appear, when the Fulness of the Gentiles is come in and all Israel is saved at last."* He saw positive signs of dawning light in his day that shadowed forth the fulfillment of this promise. He observed God stirring up reform-minded laborers throughout the Protestant world *"who do not only grieve"* for the *"Decay of True Piety, but do also contrive Means to repair it."* Moreover, the recent attempts to propagate Christianity *"in the East and West-Indies"* boosted the "Reformation and Enlargement of the Church." Although the work was *"but an Embryo, and a Seed as it were,"* the Spirit would raise up more laborers to grow the kingdom.[14]

In his correspondence with Ziegenbalg and Johann Ernst Gründler (1677–1720), the Bostonian minister Cotton Mather suggested that the Spirit might soon renew the miraculous Apostolic gifts to assist the missionaries' work in fulfillment of "the Prophecy in *Joel* [2:28], *I will pour out my* SPIRIT *upon all Flesh."*[15] While Mather's speculations would have struck most churchly oriented Pietists and evangelicals as uncomfortably bordering enthusiasm, most nonetheless believed that the Spirit was doing something remarkable in their time. The correspondents of the SSPCK rejoiced in the "uncommon Effusion of the divine Spirit" in blessing David Brainerd's "plain and faithful Preaching of the Gospel" among the Native Americans. In the preface to Brainerd's missionary journal, *Mirabilia Dei inter Indicos*, the Correspondents interspersed several scriptural phrases that cast the mission as part of a critical turning point in redemptive history: "When we see such Numbers of the most ignorant and barbarous of Mankind, in the Space of a few Months, *turn'd from Darkness to Light, and from the Power of Sin and Satan unto God* [Acts 26:18], it gives us Encouragement to wait and pray for that blessed Time" when Christ shall "march on from *conquering to conquer* [Rev 6:2], *till the Kingdoms of this World, are become the Kingdoms of our Lord* [Rev 11:15]." They looked to Brainerd's reports of Native American conversions with "hope that it may be the Dawn of that bright and illustrious Day" when, "to use the Language of the inspired Prophets, *the Gentiles shall come to his Light, and Kings to the brightness of his Rising* [Isa 60:3], in Consequence of which, *the Wilderness and solitary Places shall be glad; and the Desert rejoice and blossom as the Rose* [Isa 35:1]."[16]

Long before he became a missionary himself, Jonathan Edwards tied together the religious awakenings, the spread of missions, and millennial hopes within a sweeping biblical sacred history. In his 1739 sermon series *A History of the Work of Redemption*, he charted the Spirit's advancement of God's redemptive plan as one continuous history from creation through biblical times to modern day. The Reformation was a critical turning point in this story, but the outpourings of the Spirit in his day signaled something even more extraordinary still to come. He pointed to the progress of Christian missions in Muscovy, among Native Americans, and the Halle Pietist mission in the "East Indies." Moreover, the revival of religion in Saxony under Francke and the Halle Pietists, combined with the awakenings in New England, gave him hope that the Spirit was inaugurating the final stages of the history of redemption.[17] In his 1742 treatise defending the revivals as a work of the Spirit, he interpreted these developments as the "dawning, or at least a prelude, of that glorious work of God, so often foretold in Scripture, which in the progress and issue of it, shall renew the world of mankind." He not only believed this age "must be near" but also interpreted the prophecy of Isa 60:9 to mean "that this work will begin in America."[18] Later, in his 1747 tract *An Humble Attempt*, he interpreted the apocalyptic prophecies of Revelation alongside the workings of the Spirit in world events and the transatlantic awakenings to conclude that the dawn of Babylon's downfall and the church's golden age was likely upon them. He thus urged Christians in all places to pray for revival by the Spirit, promote the Protestant interest against Catholic powers, and advance the kingdom abroad.[19]

While Moravian missionaries laid less emphasis on the imminence of the coming Kingdom and the uniqueness of their era than other Pietists and evangelicals, they too framed their missionary work within an expansive biblical sacred history. In August Gottlieb Spangenberg's (1704–1792) history of Moravian missions (1780), he cast the Bible's entire story line as revolving chiefly around the salvation of the world. Throughout the Old Testament, God had "always thought of the salvation of the Gentiles," and the New Testament then narrated the Messiah's fulfillment of the promise and the commission to spread the good news to all nations. After charting the apostle Paul's missionary work among the Gentiles and briefly acknowledging the church's expansion over the centuries, Spangenberg resumed his narrative with the "labour of the evangelical brethren [*Unitas Fratrum*] among the heathen" in his lifetime, incorporating their missionary efforts in the very same biblical salvation history.[20]

Evangelicals creatively absorbed non-European converts in their biblical sacred histories—not merely as evidential confirmations of the progress of God's salvation plan but also as key actors moving the story line forward. Reflecting on the prophetic promises of Isa 32:3–4, Edwards anticipated a glorious age when "many of the Negroes and Indians will be divines, and that excellent books will be published in Africa, in Ethiopia, in Turkey" to further the "light and knowledge" of God in the non-Christian world.[21] As Edward Andrews explains, European Protestants incorporated African and Native American converts as "vital *participants*" in a grander "sacred genealogy" that charted the temporal and spatial spread of missions from the apostolic period to the millennial kingdom. Ironically, the "very attributes that many English commentators perceived as cultural liabilities" that justified "transatlantic slavery and Indian dispossession"—namely their "native languages, arduous lifeways, geographic mobility, and strong bodies"—came to be viewed as assets by mission-minded Protestants who wished to commission non-European converts to evangelize their own peoples. Language was especially key. According to Acts 2, the apostles received the spiritual gift of glossolalia at Pentecost to proclaim the good news in other languages—signaling both the reversal of the curse of Babel (Gen 11) and the extension of God's salvation promises to the world. However, most Protestant ministers believed that glossolalia had ceased after the Apostolic age. Consequently, they relied on non-European converts to carry out the Apostolic commission to spread the Word in the languages of the nonevangelized world.[22]

At the same time, many non-European converts reconceived and narrated their lives according to Scripture's sacred history in ways that served their own interests. For instance, in the early 1740s, the Moravian missionary Christian Heinrich Rauch (1718–1763) brought a group of Mohican converts from New York to Oley, Pennsylvania, to visit the founder of the Hernnhuter Brüdergemeine, Nicolaus Ludwig von Zinzendorf (1700–1760). At their baptismal ceremony, as Rachel Wheeler explains, the converts renamed themselves after Israel's patriarchs Abraham, Isaac, and Jacob, marking their new roles as "patriarchs of a new nation of believers." Their wives later changed their names to Sarah, Rebecca, and Rachel. Another prominent convert in the group was renamed Johannes, a "Mohican John the Baptist paving the way for the emergence of a new Christian community."[23] Non-European Christian converts narrated their lives and destinies into the Bible's sacred history in ways that elevated their spiritual authority and status as key participants in God's story line of salvation. In the 1780s, Samson Occom preached from Exodus as he led a group of Algonquian Christians to their new settlement in Brothertown, New York, drawing parallels with the Israelites' exodus from Egypt for inspiration to press on in their sacred journey.[24]

According to some scholarship, the rise of critical biblical scholarship in the eighteenth century entailed an "eclipse" or decline of spiritual hermeneutics as exegetes increasingly subjected the Bible to external historical frameworks rather than attempting to fit history (and their individual story) into the Bible's narrative.[25] Yet this was not the trajectory for all Bible readers. Pietists and evangelicals—many of whom embraced historical-contextual biblical scholarship—still very much conceived of their lives and times as part of a grander sacred and redemptive history arising from Scripture that expanded from creation to the new creation, even as this conception transformed since the times of the Reformation to embrace a more central role for the progress of world missions.

Spreading the Word

Pietist and evangelical schemes of sacred history and their longing for Christ's return propelled a missionary activism to propagate the Word to all the world. They emphasized that the task should concern not only trained ministers and missionaries but every believer. Inspired by Brainerd's example, the Correspondents of the SSPCK stressed that it "is doubtless the Duty of all, in their different Stations, and according to their respective Capacities, to use their utmost endeavours to bring forward this promised—this desired Day," until the *"whole Earth is Filled with the* Glory of the Lord [Num 14:21]."[26] Böhme called for "an effectual Reformation *at Home"* that would inspire *"European* Christians" to financially support the work at Tranquebar and thereby advance "the Propagation of our holy Faith in the pagan World." He explained that the apostles benefited from *"miraculous* Powers" to advance the mission, but today all Christians must rely on the ordinary *"Means"* at their disposal to help "prepare the way towards an Accomplishment of those glorious *Predictions* that are recorded by the Prophets, and which do set forth that *vast Extent* of the Kingdom . . . in the latter Days."[27] Like their Protestant Orthodox predecessors, they believed that God was the primary cause behind the establishment of the kingdom, but God achieved his redemptive plan through secondary or instrumental causes—that is, through means. Evangelicals revamped this conviction into a fervent missionary activism intent on maximizing the proper means to advance the kingdom.

They held that the primary means used by the Spirit was the Bible. In the Pietist manifesto *Pia Desideria* (1675), Spener affirmed that "the diligent use of God's Word" was "the chief means" for true reform.[28] In a sermon on Hos 5:15, Edwards declared that the "Spirit of God in all his work upon the souls of men works by his Word"—a theme he emphasized throughout his ministry.[29] While the increased priority on the experience of the Spirit led some to transgress the scriptural conservatism of the Reformers, most leaders of the transatlantic Protestant awakenings insisted on the inseparability of the Spirit and the Word as they sought to inculcate vital piety while countering enthusiast fixations on revelatory visions and impressions. The Spirit always worked by means of the Word. This principle underlay not only their agendas of reform and renewal but also their missionary ambitions to spread true piety throughout the world. Wishing to facilitate the outpouring of the Spirit on non-Christian peoples, Pietists and evangelicals amplified their efforts to spread the Word through translation, print, distribution, and education.

Seeking to carry out Spener's dictum to "bring the Word of God more richly among us,"[30] Halle Pietists pursued an ambitious program of printing and education. Under Francke's leadership, the Halle Foundations established various innovative institutions (some building upon Dutch models), including orphanages, schools for all economic classes, vocational training centers, a university, and laboratories, with the intention of shaping individuals to live out the teachings of Scripture in all levels of society. Moreover, in 1710, Baron Carl Hildebrand von Canstein (1667–1719) worked with Francke to establish a Bible institute and printing house (later referred to as the Cansteinsche Bibelanstalt) at Halle with the aim of making the Bible more accessible and affordable. Halle printed and distributed about two million complete Bibles and one million New Testaments in the eighteenth century, far surpassing the production of previous German Bible publishers.[31] The influence of Halle's institutions spread around the world, due in large part to its mission endeavors.[32] In 1728, Johann Heinrich Callenberg (1694–1760) established the Institutum Judaicum et Muhammedicum in Halle for the purpose of furthering research, translating and distributing Christian texts in "oriental" languages, and training missionaries to Christianize adherents of monotheistic religions. By century's end, Halle had sent out over twenty missionaries to Jewish populations—especially in eastern Europe and the Middle East—and their model inspired similar institutes elsewhere, such as in Darmstadt under Johann Philipp Fresenius (1705–1761). They placed particular priority on producing evangelistic resources that advanced a Christocentric exegesis of the Hebrew Scriptures. For instance, Callenberg urged lay Christians to fund and distribute a tract that sought to convince Jews from Old Testament passages such as Isa 53 and Jer 23:6 that Jesus was their promised Messiah.[33]

Pietist missionaries brought these impulses to spread the Word through printing and education to India. With the aid of local Tamil teachers, Ziegenbalg soon mastered the Tamil language and completed his translation of the New Testament in 1711 (he died before he completed the Old Testament). Thanks to Böhme's advocacy and organization, the London-based SPCK sent a printing press to Tranquebar in 1712. Using Tamil fonts produced in Halle, they printed the Tamil New Testament along with other translated works, such as Luther's *Small Catechism*, in 1714/15.[34] In a letter to the SPCK, Ziegenbalg and Gründler expressed their thanks for the press and voiced their prayer "that the Truths of Christianity to be printed by this Means on Paper, may be all deeply impress'd by his holy Spirit on the Minds of such Pagans and Infidels as shall happen to read them!"[35] The *Wortspiel* delivered the point: the Spirit worked by the Word to transform the minds of non-Christians anywhere in the world.

To facilitate knowledge of the Bible, they undertook a holistic program of education. Beginning in 1707, Ziegenbalg established a network of schools on the model of Francke's charity schools in Halle, teaching children of all economic classes literacy, practical skills, sciences, and other arts. The Bible stood at the center of their education. In a letter from October 1709, the missionaries explained their daily routine—a program that relied heavily on native teachers. The day began at six o'clock with prayers and catechizing. At seven o'clock, "One of the *Malabarick* Masters reads to the Children a Chapter out of the *Malabarick* New-Testament," and the "Children learn the Places of Scripture by Heart." The morning and early afternoon continued with catechizing, reading, spelling, writing, knitting, arithmetic, and Bible memorization. In the mid–late afternoon, they taught the children "to understand *Poetry*" by using poems that "contain the *History of the Bible*." The school day concluded with catechizing, recreation, "useful Histories" or "discourses upon the Heavens, and other celestial Bodies," and review. In the evening, the four German missionaries attended to their own spiritual nourishment with a conventicle-like Bible study: "There is a Chapter of Scripture read and practically applyed, and everything concluded with a hearty *Prayer*, wherein the Conversion of the Heathens is particularly offer'd up to divine Providence." During supper, one of the schoolmasters read out of the New Testament to the children, after which they prayed and went to bed.[36]

In his letter to Mather, Gründler expounded their methods for training the more advanced "Catechists" to become teachers themselves. To impart the "Word of Truth," the missionaries guided the students through a "*Biblical Exercise*, an *Exegetical*, and a *Theological*." For the "*Biblical Exercise*," they had the students work through books, chapters, and subsections of the New Testament: "First, they Expound the Matters, and the Context. Then . . . they apply to the proper Edification of the Soul, those things that appear to be most Subservient unto it." The design of the method was twofold: for students to acquire a "more Solid, and Stable Knowledge of the Truth, out of the Sacred Scriptures," and second, to attain "a greater Ability for Preaching" in order to "propound the Truth of GOD among the Nations." The "*Exegetical Exercise*" then focused on interpreting particular "Sentences of the Bible . . . according to the Rules of Interpretation." The students derived "Meditations" from this study to use in a "Sermon for the Publick." Finally, the "*Theological Exercise*" taught the main "Articles of our Faith" with "Proofs" from "Scripture."[37] By fusing biblical study with spiritual application, Pietist missionary education transmitted the thrust of Halle Pietism's exegetical program.

The bibliocentric educational model of Halle Pietism was also replicated in colonial American schools, such as George Whitefield's orphan schools in Georgia and Wheelock's Moor's Indian Charity School in Connecticut.[38] Regrettably, these education programs were deeply entangled with colonial-era biases against Native Americans and Blacks and with White Protestant agendas to "civilize" them according to European ideals. Yet it is important to not overlook how Africans and Native Americans pursued their own interests in these cultural exchanges. Native Americans sent their children to mission schools with hopes that they would acquire skills to promote their tribe's welfare in its dealings with colonists. Moreover, many had genuine religious motivations and found tremendous value in literacy because it gave them access to divine revelation. The ability to read and teach Scripture afforded many Native

Americans and enslaved Blacks considerable spiritual enrichment and power in the context of eighteenth-century colonialism.[39]

The Pietist and evangelical stress on employing means to advance world missions and the stimulus to translate and propagate the Word long preceded the work of the famous evangelical Baptist missionary William Carey (1761–1834), who has often been erroneously dubbed the father of modern missions. Seeking to overcome the high Calvinistic English Baptist resistance to missions, Carey leaned heavily on the theology of Jonathan Edwards to argue for the compatibility of God's sovereignty in salvation and the necessity of human responsibility to employ means in advancing the gospel abroad. This design infused his highly influential tract *An Enquiry into the Obligations of Christians to Use Means for the Conversion of the Heathens* (1792). In 1792, Carey coestablished the Baptist Missionary Society, which inspired the founding of similar voluntary mission agencies in Britain and America—such as the London Missionary Society (1795) and the American Board of Commissioners for Foreign Missions (1810)—and he labored many years as a missionary in Calcutta, where he helped facilitate translations of the Bible into forty-four languages. The Word-centric missionary activism of early Pietists and evangelicals laid a foundation for generations to come: by the end of the twentieth century, evangelical missions had given rise to Bible translations in over two thousand languages as well as hundreds of schools around the world.[40]

Biblical Piety and Mission

As Pietists and evangelicals spread the Word, they sought to engender a lively piety of the Word. Throughout their work of reform and revival, they stressed that a mere theoretical or doctrinal knowledge of Scripture was insufficient—true faith entailed vital, experiential, and spiritual knowledge of the Word by the Spirit.[41] They were not the first to voice this point, but the ways they harnessed it to advance true religion in the context of the early eighteenth century contributed to key transformations in piety. They downplayed the authority of inherited hierarchies, scholarly sophistication, and doctrinal and ecclesiological subtleties while elevating the authority of personal experience, the Spirit's illumination and indwelling guidance, revivalism, crucicentrism, lay devotion and participation, spiritual affections, evangelistic zeal, immediate conversion, biblical (quasi-restorationist) simplicity, emotive rhetoric, Christocentric hermeneutics, and voluntary activism.[42] Their pursuit of true Christianity via these modes of piety greatly shaped their methods and aims in propagating the Word on the mission field. In a letter from 1713, Ziegenbalg and Gründler explained that the chief design of their schools was for the children to "not attain to a bare *historical* Knowledge, or even an outward Practice of many Christian Truths," but ultimately "that their Minds, by means of what they learn, may be sanctified, regenerated, and renew'd, feeling within themselves the good and lively Word of God." To this end, they infused their teaching with "continual Precepts, Admonitions, and Prayers."[43] This drive for inculcating experiential piety and spiritual knowledge of the Word pervaded Pietist and evangelical missions.

David Brainerd's *Diary* brims with illustrations of evangelical piety at work in the mission field. Like many evangelicals, Brainerd looked to his experiences as evidential confirmations that the Spirit was doing something remarkable by means of the living Word to awaken the world: "God seems still to vouchsafe his divine presence and the influence of his blessed Spirit to accompany his Word, at least in some measure, in all our meetings for divine worship." He filled his entries with highly emotive episodes of him opening Scripture, preaching the new birth, and observing the power of the Spirit at work among the Native Americans. For instance, on one occasion, Brainerd preached with the help of his interpreter on 1 John 4:10, "Herein is love." At first, the response was not "remarkable," but toward the end of the sermon "the divine truths were attended with a surprizing influence, and produced a great concern among them." As he "discoursed of the love and compassion of God in sending his Son to suffer for the sins of men," the crowd, "as one, seemed in an agony of soul to obtain an interest in Christ." He recorded that two Native Americans "obtained relief and comfort" as they entreated Christ to "wipe their hearts quite 'clean' [1 John 1:7]." Their reaction he judged "solid, rational, and scriptural," reinforcing a common and calculated evangelical attempt to authenticate such emotional outbursts as rational and biblical and thereby distinguish them from enthusiast delusions. Finally, he employed biblical phrases to interpret and substantiate the episode as "the 'doings of the Lord' [Ps 77:12]," convinced that "the 'arm of the Lord' was powerfully and marvelously 'revealed' [Isa 53:1; John 12:38]" that day.[44]

Evangelical and Pietist missionaries labored to apply Scripture to bring about real conversion, which was above all Christocentric and experimental. Spangenberg described how the earliest Moravian missionaries in Greenland developed their strategy accordingly. Initially, their tactic was to first prove God's existence and then present the Bible's teachings starting with creation, humankind's fall into sin, the law, and finally their need for a savior. However, this approach yielded little success, so the Herrnhuter Brüdergemeine recommended they shift their tactic to foreground Christ's atonement. "The brethren began to translate some parts of the gospel," Spangenberg explained, "especially what relates to the sufferings and death of Jesus, and read that to the heathen." This method produced results: "God opened their hearts, that they attended to the word." From this point on, the Moravians followed Paul's words in 2 Cor 2:2 as their "firmly established rule" to preach "Jesus Christ and him crucified." They began to exposit all of Scripture to teach "the blood and death of Jesus," finding the biblical "prophets" and "apostles" alike to present it in such "plain terms." In a lengthy footnote, Spangenberg cited numerous missionary accounts to illustrate the effectiveness of the method, namely David Cranz's (1723–1777) history of the Moravian mission in Greenland, C. G. A. Oldendorp's (1721–1787) account of the mission in the Caribbean, Johann Lucas Niekamp's (1707/8–1742) history of the Pietist mission in East India, and David Brainerd's *Mirabilia Dei inter Indicos*, as translated and excerpted in Fresenius's journal *Pastoral-Sammlungen* in 1749. In each instance—in Greenland, the Caribbean, India, and American colonies—the missionaries initially had little success. But when they began to preach the Word in plain, experimental, and vernacular terms and focused on the sufferings and crucifixion of Christ for sinners, spiritual awakening ensued.[45]

At times, the evangelical pursuit of true religion led missionaries to apply Scripture in order to identify and overcome colonial abuses done in the name of Christianity. In a 1751 sermon to a Mohawk audience, Jonathan Edwards (albeit a slaveholder who, like others, challenged the biblical warrant for the racialized slave trade but not slavery itself) sought to differentiate between "two sorts" of people "that have the Bible." The first sort of "white people [who] came over the seas and settled in these parts" had disregarded the Bible's light and consequently had failed in their duty to share and apply the Word rightly among the Native Americans. The French, Dutch, and English alike had withheld the Word and the power of literacy and had chosen instead "to keep you in the dark for the sake of making a gain of you," he warned. But another sort cherished the Word and acknowledged that they "are no better than you," for sin had ruined all mankind equally. This latter sort of true Christians wished to share the light and blessing of the Word with the Native Americans as others had done for them in the past. "When the light of God's Word shines into the heart," Edwards declared, "it gives new life to the soul" that "is sweeter than honey." Edwards wished to share that honey freely.[46] Early evangelical uses of Scripture thus wielded tremendous potential for liberation and egalitarianism.

For many, however, a simplified prioritization of conversion conditioned their reading and application of Scripture in ways that reinforced colonial-era inequalities and oppression. While they applied Scripture to promote spiritual freedom for non-Whites, they seldom advocated for their social freedom and equality. When Moravian missionaries in the Danish Caribbean received resistance from slaveholders who were concerned that baptism and literacy would motivate enslaved converts to demand emancipation, they considered the matter "according to the scriptures." They found "no where that the apostles commanded the masters to emancipate their slaves." Even the apostle Paul sent Onesimus back to his master after he escaped and became a Christian. They thus resolved not only to refrain from encouraging emancipation but also to instruct enslaved converts to be all the more obedient and submissive. It was their duty to "set before the negroe the doctrines which the apostles preached to servants," namely that God has ordained "that one man is a master and another a slave, and that therefore they ought to acquiesce with the ways of God."[47] Their minimalistic, conversionist-oriented exegesis failed to apply Scripture to confront the sins of colonialism. Intent on furthering evangelism among the enslaved, they assured slaveholders that conversion would not entail emancipation but rather make the enslaved more obedient and hard-working. Early awakened Protestants thus bequeathed a mixed legacy to later generations. On the one hand, their emphasis on biblical themes of spiritual liberation and equality provided fuel for the Protestant antislavery movement that arose in the 1770s.[48] On the other hand, early to mid-eighteenth-century missionary applications of Scripture to sanction yet "Christianize" slavery also helped lay the foundations for antebellum paternalistic ideologies that viewed racialized slavery as intrinsic to a thriving, biblically based Christian society.[49]

As mentioned, non-European converts were not passive observers in these exchanges. They capitalized on the resources of evangelical piety to serve their own spiritual and practical concerns in ways that helped them navigate and confront the challenges of dispossession, slavery, disease, alcoholism, cultural diminution, and economic exploitation wrought by colonialism. Like those of European Pietists and evangelicals, their biblical practices empowered and guided their quest to distinguish pure Christianity from the corrupt religion of European cultures. But they pursued this agenda on their own terms, as illustrated in the ministry of Samson Occom. Converted under the preaching of New Light revivalist James Davenport (1716–1757), Occom attended Wheelock's Moor's Charity School, toured Britain, and labored as a missionary to Native Americans. His thought and practice were heavily shaped by New Light revivalist Christianity, and he channeled evangelical biblical practices for the benefit of his own people as a minister of the new birth. To cater to audiences of "poor Negroes" and "my poor kindred the Indians," he downplayed his learning and honed a "common, plain, every-day talk" in his preaching and writing. Yet he also employed evocative metaphors to appeal to Native

American imaginations, often utilizing the English Baptist Benjamin Keach's work *Tropologia: A Key to Open Scriptural Metaphors* (1682) to mine biblical symbols to this end. Toward the end of his life, he increasingly interpreted Scripture to distinguish true religion from the deceptions of White Europeans. In 1772, Occom was asked to preach at the execution of a Native American convict. Selecting Rom 6:23 for his text, "The wages of sin is death," Occom addressed all "Indians, English, and Negroes," using sin, as Joanna Brooks observes, "as a leveler of racial and class distinctions." As he called upon Native Americans to turn from drunkenness, he took the opportunity to denounce the "develish men" who brought alcohol in the first place: "we find in sacred writ, a wo denounced against men, who put their bottles to their neighbors mouth to make them drunk, that they may see their nakedness" (Hab 2:15).[50]

In a sermon in the late 1780s on Luke 10:26–27, "Thou Shalt Love They Neighbor as Thyself," Occom amplified this logic as he preached fire and brimstone against all "oppressors, over reachers, Defrauders, Extortioners, with holders of Corn," with express aim at Europeans who failed to love their African and Native American neighbors. Whereas the "Savage Indians, as they are so calld, are very kind to one another, and they are kind to Strangers," he found "those who are Calld Christians, Void of Natural affection." This applied above all to slaveholders and those who approved of slavery. They "are not Neighbours to anyone," he proclaimed, "and Consequently they are not Lovers of God, They are no Christians, they are unbelievers, yea they are ungenteel, and inhumane." For Occom, obedience to Scripture determined one's status as a true believer. "I think I have made out by the Bible, that the poor Negroes are your Neighbours," he challenged Christian slaveholders, and unless they could "prove it from the Bible that Negroes are not the Race of Adam," they should repent and release them from enslavement. Occom's Bible guided his pursuit of true Christianity. "If I understand the gospel a wright," he concluded, "I think it is a Dispention of Freedom and Liberty, both Temporal and Spiritual." The Bible taught him not only that White slaveholders and manipulative extortionists were not real Christians, but also that they were more barbaric than the Native Americans they sought to convert. No wonder he warned in another sermon on Isa 58:1 that the English were endangering their status as "the Covenant People of god."[51]

Early Pietists and evangelicals read, propagated, and practiced the Bible in ways that not only shaped their missionary ambitions and methods but also constructed their pan-Protestant identity as the true people of God. They viewed themselves as pivotal partakers in the history of redemption, carrying the same torch of the New Testament church closer to its latter-day glory as they spread the light of the Word around the globe. Their efforts never led to the demise of Catholicism, nor did they precipitate the return of Christ as soon as hoped. Their biblical and missionary practices also bequeathed mixed legacies mired in colonial inequalities. Despite these realities, their labors helped lay the foundation for generations of an increasingly globalized missionary force that has zealously carried on the errand to spread the light of God's Word.

Notes

1. For studies demonstrating that the sixteenth-century Protestant reformers were more missions-minded than many have assumed, see Ingemar Öberg, *Luther and World Mission: A Historical and Systematic Study with Special Reference to Luther's Bible Exposition*, trans. Dean Apel (St. Louis: Concordia, 2007); Andrew Buckler, *Jean Calvin et la mission de l'église* (Lyon: Editions Olivétan, 2009); and Robert L. Gallagher and Edward L. Smither, eds., *Sixteenth-Century Mission: Explorations in Protestant and Roman Catholic Theology and Practice* (Bellingham, WA: Lexham Press, 2021).

2. See esp. Edward E. Andrews, *Native Apostles: Black and Indian Missionaries in the British Atlantic World* (Cambridge, MA: Harvard University Press, 2013).

3. Dana Roberts, *Christian Mission: How Christianity Became a World Religion* (Chichester, UK: Wiley-Blackwell, 2009), 41–42.

4. For more on early Pietist missions, see esp. Hermann Wellenreuther, "Pietismus und Mission: Vom 17. bis zum Beginn des 20. Jahrhunderts," in *GdP*, 4:168–76; Douglas H. Shantz, *An Introduction to German Pietism: Protestant Renewal at the Dawn of Modern Europe* (Baltimore: Johns Hopkins University Press, 2013), 237–69. For more on Pietist missions and transatlantic networks, see, among others, Ernst Benz, "Pietist and Puritan Sources of Early Protestant World Missions (Cotton Mather and A. H. Francke)," *CH* 20, no. 2 (1951): 28–55; Daniel L. Brunner, *Halle Pietists in England: Anthony William Boehm and the Society for Promoting Christian Knowledge* (Göttingen: Vandenhoeck & Ruprecht, 1993); the essays in Andreas Goss, Y. Vincent Kumeradoss, and Heike Liebau, eds., *Halle and the Beginning of Protestant Christianity in India*, 3 vols. (Halle: Frankesche Stiftungen, 2006); Robert Eric Frykenberg, *Christianity in India: From Beginnings to the Present* (New York: Oxford University Press, 2008), 142–68; and Ulrike Gleixner, "Remapping the World: The Vision of a Protestant Empire in the Eighteenth Century," in *Migration and Religion: Christian Transatlantic Missions, Islamic Migration to Germany*, ed. Barbara Becker-Cantarino, Chloe: Beihefte zum Daphnis 46 (Amsterdam: Rodopi, 2012), 77–90.

5. For Moravian missions, see esp. Peter Vogt, "Die Mission der Herrnhuter Brüdergemeine und ihre Bedeutung für den Neubeginn der protestantischen Missionen am Ende des 18. Jahrhunderts," *PuN* 35 (2009): 204–36; Shantz, *Introduction to German Pietism*, 253–68; and Katherine Gerbner, *Christian Slavery: Conversion and Race in the Protestant Atlantic World* (Philadelphia: University of Pennsylvania Press, 2018), 138–88. For a comparison between evangelical and Moravian missions in British North America, see Rachel Wheeler, *To Live upon Hope: Mohicans and Missionaries in the Eighteenth-Century Northeast* (Ithaca: Cornell University Press, 2008).

6. John A. Grigg, *The Lives of David Brainerd: The Making of an American Evangelical Icon* (New York: Oxford University Press, 2009); Jan Stievermann, "The German Lives of David Brainerd: The Beginnings of Pietist Interest in an American Evangelical Icon," in *Zwischen Aufklärung und Moderne: Erweckungsbewegungen als historiographische Hreausforderung*, ed. Thomas K. Kuhn and Veronika Albrecht-Birkner (Münster: Lit, 2017), 119–39; Stievermann, "Faithful Translations: New Discoveries on the German Pietist Reception of Jonathan Edwards," *CH* 83, no. 2 (2014): 324–66; Stievermann, "Halle Pietism and Its Perception of the American

Great Awakening: The Example of Johann Adam Steinmetz," in *The Transatlantic World of Heinrich Melchior Mühlenberg in the Eighteenth Century*, ed. Hermann Wellenreuther, Thomas Müller-Bahlke, and A. Gregg Roeber (Halle: Verlag der Franckeschen Stiftungen, 2013), 213–46.

7. For more on Black, Native American, and Indigenous missionaries, see Andrews, *Native Apostles*; John F. Sensbach, *Rebecca's Revival: Creating Black Christianity in the Atlantic World* (Cambridge, MA: Harvard University Press, 2006); Linford Fisher, *The Indian Great Awakening: Religion and the Shaping of Native Cultures in Early America* (New York: Oxford University Press, 2012); and Heike Liebau, *Die indischen Mitarbeiter der Tranquebarmission (1706–1845): Katecheten, Schulmeister, Übersetzer* (Tübingen: Max Niemeyer Verlag, 2008).

8. For more on the "Protestant international," see the endnotes in the introduction to this volume.

9. Stoddard, *Question whether God is not angry with the country for doing so little towards the conversion of the Indians?* (Boston, 1723), 7. See Ronald E. Davies, "The Great Commission from Calvin to Carey," *Evangel* 14, no. 2 (1996): 44–49.

10. For more on early evangelical spiritual exegesis in the context of the early Enlightenment, see Ryan P. Hoselton, "Spiritually Discerned: Cotton Mather, Jonathan Edwards, and Experiential Exegesis in Early Evangelicalism" (PhD diss., Ruprecht-Karls-Universität Heidelberg, 2019).

11. James A. De Jong, *As the Waters Cover the Sea: Millennial Expectations in the Rise of Anglo-American Missions, 1640–1810* (Laurel, MS: Audubon, 2006).

12. Philipp Jakob Spener, *Pia Desideria* (Frankfurt am Main, 1676), 72–91; excerpted in Veronica Albrecht-Birkner, Wolfgang Breul, and Joachim Jacob, eds., *Pietismus: Eine Anthologie von Quellen des 17. und 18. Jahrhunderts* (Leipzig: Evangelische Verlagsanstalt, 2017), 165–69.

13. W. R. Ward, *Early Evangelicalism: A Global Intellectual History, 1670–1789* (New York: Cambridge University Press, 2006), 32.

14. Bartholomaeus Ziegenbalg, *The Propagation of the Gospel in the East . . .* , ed. A. W. Boehme [Böhme] (London: J. Downing, 1718), 3:iii–vii, xi, xiii.

15. Cotton Mather, *India Christiana* (Boston: B. Greene, 1721), 72. For more on Mather's affinity with Pietism and evangelicalism, see Richard F. Lovelace, *The American Pietism of Cotton Mather: Origins of American Evangelicalism* (Grand Rapids, MI: Christian University Press, 1979).

16. David Brainerd, *Mirabilia Dei inter Indicos* (Philadelphia: William Bradford, 1746), vi–viii.

17. *WJE*, 9:433–36.

18. Ibid., 4:353–54. Some have misconstrued Edwards's meaning here as a statement about American exceptionalism. However, he never identified America with the millennial kingdom but merely held that the Spirit's work of revival in the final phases before Christ's return would *begin* there and then spread throughout the world. In any case, Edwards repudiated and never repeated the claim.

19. *WJE*, 5:363–64.

20. August Gottlieb Spangenberg, *An Account of the Manner in which the Protestant Church of the Unitas Fratrum, or United Brethren, Preach the Gospel, and Carry on their Missions Among the Heathen* (London: H. Trapp, 1788), 7–9, 31.

21. *WJE*, 9:480.

22. Andrews, *Native Apostles*, 11–12.

23. Wheeler, *To Live upon Hope*, 76, 91.

24. See Andrews, *Native Apostles*, 224; Samson Occom, *The Collected Writings of Samson Occom, Mohegan: Leadership and Literature in Eighteenth-Century Native America*, ed. Joanna Brooks (New York: Oxford University Press, 2006), 300, 305.

25. See Hans W. Frei, *The Eclipse of Biblical Narrative: A Study in Eighteenth and Nineteenth Century Hermeneutics* (New Haven: Yale University Press, 1974); Peter Harrison, *The Bible, Protestantism, and the Rise of Natural Science* (Cambridge: Cambridge University Press, 1998); and Michael C. Legaspi, *The Death of Scripture and the Rise of Biblical Studies* (New York: Oxford University Press, 2010).

26. Brainerd, *Mirabilia*, viii.
27. Anton Wilhelm Boehme [Böhme], "Preliminary Discourses on the Character of a Missionary" (1718), in Ziegenbalg, *Propagation*, 1:xv, xxxiv–xxv.
28. Spener, *Pia Desideria*, 101.
29. *WJE*, 17:155.
30. Spener, *Pia Desideria*, 94.
31. Frykenberg, *Christianity in India*, 143–45; Martin Brecht, "Die Bedeutung der Bibel im deutschen Pietismus," in *GdP*, 4:106; Karl Hildebrand von Canstein, *Ohnemaßgeblicher Vorschlag / Wie gottes Wort denen Armen zur Erbauung um einen geringen Preiß in die Hände zu bringen* (Berlin: Schlechtiger, 1710).
32. Johannes Wallmann, *Der Pietismus* (Göttingen: Vandenhoeck & Ruprecht, 2005), 128–35.
33. Johann Heinrich Callenberg, *Bericht an einige Christliche Freunde von einem Versuch Das arme Jüdische Volck zur Erkäntniß und Annehmung der Christlichen Wahrheit anzuleiten* (Halle: Krottendorff, 1730), viii–ix, excerpted in Albrecht-Birkner, Breul, and Jacob, *Pietismus*, 494–97. See Cristoph Rymatzki, *Hallischer Pietismus und Judenmission: Johann Heinrich Callenbergs Institutum Judaicum und dessen Freundeskreis (1728–1736)* (Tübingen: Harrassowitz, 2004).
34. Shantz, *Introduction to German Pietism*, 240–53.
35. Ziegenbalg, *Propagation*, 3:24. Edwards applauded their educational initiatives and their "printing press to print Bibles." *WJE*, 9:435. For more on Edwards's connection to Halle Pietists, see Ryan P. Hoselton, "Jonathan Edwards, Halle Pietism, and Benevolent Activism in Early Awakened Protestantism," in *Edwards, Germany, and Transatlantic Contexts*, ed. Rhys Bezzant (Göttingen: Vandenhoeck & Ruprecht, 2021), 51-68.
36. Ziegenbalg, *Propagation*, 2:54–58.
37. Gründler, in Mather, *India Christiana*, 82–83.
38. Andrews, *Native Apostles*, 155; Eleazor Wheelock, *A Plain and Faithful Narrative of . . . the Indian Charity-School at Lebanon, in Connecticut* (Boston: Richard and Samuel Draper, 1763).
39. Gerbner, *Christian Slavery*, 182–87; Andrews, *Native Apostles*, 117–23, 162–67; Frank Lambert, "'I Saw the Book Talk': Slave Readings of the First Great Awakening," *Journal of Negro History* 77, no. 4 (1992): 185–98. Fisher notes that most Indian Christian schools after the Great Awakening were run by Native Americans themselves and wielded far greater influence. Fisher, *Indian Great Awakening*, 137.
40. Roberts, *Christian Mission*, 48.
41. See Jan Stievermann and Ryan P. Hoselton, "Spiritual Meaning and Experimental Piety in the Exegesis of Cotton Mather and Jonathan Edwards," in *Jonathan Edwards and Scripture*, ed. David P. Barshinger and Douglas A. Sweeney (New York: Oxford University Press, 2018), 86–105.
42. See esp. Ward, *Early Evangelicalism*; Douglas L. Winiarski, *Darkness Falls on the Land of Light: Experiencing Religious Awakenings in Eighteenth-Century New England* (Chapel Hill: University of North Carolina Press, 2017); D. Bruce Hindmarsh, *The Spirit of Early Evangelicalism: True Religion in a Modern World* (New York: Oxford University Press, 2018).
43. Ziegenbalg, *Propagation*, 3:102.
44. *WJE*, 7:341, 306–7.
45. Spangenberg, *Account*, 60–61, 64, 67, 68–71. *The History of Greenland: Containing A Description of the Country, and Its Inhabitants: and Particularly, a Relation of the Mission, carried on for above these Thirty Years by the Unitas Fratrum, at New Herrnhuth and Lichtenfels, in that Country* (London: Brethren's Society for the Furtherance of the Gospel Among the Heathen, 1767); C. G. A. Oldendorp, *Geschichte der Mission der evangelischen Brüder auf den caraibischen Inseln S. Thomas, S. Croix und S. Jan* (Barby: Christian Friedrich Laur, 1770); Johann Lucas Niekamp, *Kurtzgefaßte Missions-Geschichte, Oder Historischer Auszug der Evangelischen Mißions-Berichte aus Ost-Indien . . .* (Halle: Waisenhaus, 1740). See also Wheeler, *To Live upon Hope*, 86; Stievermann, "German Lives of Brainerd," 121–22.

46. Jonathan Edwards, "To the Mohawks at the Treaty, August 16, 1751," in *The Sermons of Jonathan Edwards: A Reader*, ed. Wilson H. Kimnach, Kenneth P. Minkema, and Douglas A. Sweeney (New Haven: Yale University Press, 1999), 105–10. See Rachel Wheeler, "'Friends to Your Souls': Jonathan Edwards' Indian Pastorate and the Doctrine of Original Sin," *CH* 72, no. 4 (2003): 736–65.

47. Spangenberg, *Account*, 42–43.

48. John Coffey, *Exodus and Liberation: Deliverance Politics from John Calvin to Martin Luther King Jr.* (New York: Oxford University Press, 2013), 79–106.

49. Gerbner, *Christian Slavery*.

50. Occom, *Collected Writings*, 177, 160–64, 193.

51. Ibid., 202, 206, 215.

PART 3

INTERPRETIVE APPROACHES,
ISSUES, AND DEBATES

7

THE EVANGELICAL SUPERNATURAL IN EARLY MODERN BRITISH PROTESTANTISM

Cotton Mather and Jonathan Edwards on the Miracles of Jesus

DOUGLAS A. SWEENEY

Early modern Europe was a theater of prodigies, portents, signs, and wonders. The age of "the Enlightenment," ironically, was nonetheless an age of miracles. To the chagrin of conventional Protestants and liberal skeptics alike, it teemed with testimony and rumor about levitating saints (such as Joseph of Cupertino), bilocating mystics (such as María, abbess of Ágreda), missionary healers (such as Julian Maunoir), and assorted exorcists (such as Johann Joseph Gassner). Even in early modern England and its North American colonies, the period from the Civil War to the eighteenth-century awakening saw a surge in signs and wonders. Congregationalists and Baptists claimed to heal the sick by faith. A few Quakers raised the dead. A "Derbyshire damsel," Martha Taylor, starved herself for over a year. A group of "French prophets" in London trod through fires unscathed, healed the sick, raised the dead, and claimed all manner of spiritual ecstasies. Cotton Mather filled his famous history of New England with *"thaumatographia pneumatica,"* accounts of spiritual wonders known to Puritans in the region. Even King Charles II gave the royal touch for scrofula to tens of thousands of people, thousands more than any other king or queen in British history. In the words of Jane Shaw, "Miracle claims were revived and indeed increased at just the moment that the new philosophy and the experimental method were developing; though it may seem counter-intuitive to the usual historical story, the evidence suggests that miracles and science 'grew' together" in this era.[1]

Sixteenth-century Protestants had been cautious around miracles, nervous as they were about the ways in which Catholics had often used them to justify their extrabiblical teachings. In a comment on a saying of Jesus in John 14 ("the one who believes in me will also do the works that I do and, in fact, will do greater works than these," etc., verses 12–13), Luther told his congregation "the day of miracles is past." He allowed that the Lord still employs Word and sacrament to do marvelous things. But the exorcisms and healings worked in apostolic times—mainly to validate the ministries of Jesus and the apostles—came to an end after the closing of the New Testament canon. Similar deeds done today were most likely tricks of the devil. John Calvin said the same. As he penned in a "Prefatory Address to King Francis" at the opening of the *Institutes of the Christian Religion*, Roman Catholics "act dishonestly" in rows with Protestant rivals over present-day miracles. We are "forging" no "new gospel," the French reformer claimed, "but are retaining that very gospel whose truth all the miracles that Jesus Christ and his disciples ever wrought serve to confirm." Like Luther, then, he granted that the Lord works wonders through the everyday ministries of Word and sacrament. But because few of the magisterial reformers advanced new teachings, they wanted no signs and wonders to confirm them.[2]

By the mid-seventeenth century, things had clearly changed. Supernaturalistic Protestants in state-church Europe had grown more worried about the dangers of a tepid Christian faith and conventional Protestant practice than about their right to organize and worship on their own. And their warmhearted, effervescent Christian faith and witness soon softened their resistance to the notion of modern miracles. Puritans and Pietists, not to mention freer Protestants, now showed a greater openness to what their cautious members dubbed special providences, but others called omens, signs, wonders, even miracles.[3] This led to what became a great debate about miracles, which started shortly after the execution of Charles I, picked up steam with the deists in the late seventeenth century, and culminated during the Great Awakening.

To rehearse only the best-known lines of this debate, Thomas Hobbes, in *Leviathan* (1651), a defense of social contracts, sturdy central governments, and reasonable religion, warned readers of credulity regarding miracle claims, and enthusiasts who make them. Baruch Spinoza, in *Tractatus theologico-politicus* (1670), ruled most such claims out of play in public life. He defined alleged miracles as events whose natural causes are not known to believers. He said that miracles in Scripture were exceptional events meant to inspire faith and piety among the common people, but averred that physical laws govern all that ever happens (in the natural order of things) and that so-called acts of God would prove explicable eventually by means of second causes. John

Locke, in *A Discourse of Miracles* (1706), proved to be less skeptical than this. He, too, defined miracles as sensible operations that *appear* to believers to transcend laws of nature. But he affirmed that they had happened, especially in the Bible. He contended that the miracles of Jesus were inscrutable to first-century observers, and succeeded thus in generating trust in his teaching, validating his ministry and spreading Christian faith through the ancient Roman world—just as God had intended. But even Locke granted the difficulty of demonstrating rationally that miracles could not occur through secondary causes. And David Hume, in *Enquiry concerning Human Understanding* (1748), defined miracles (or so-called miracles, at any rate) as *violations* of nature, writing them out of the realm of empirical validity. He said that no one can attain sufficient evidence to warrant trust that miracles occurred (because belief in the miraculous rests on human testimony, which is never as reliable as scientific proof, such as that for laws of nature), and concluded that Christianity rests on faith, not reason.[4]

Cotton Mather (1663–1728) and Jonathan Edwards (1703–1758) spent a great deal of time on this early modern debate. They engaged its principal arguments, and many others like them (although Hume published twenty years after Mather died). As New England's leading apologists for evangelical faith, they cared deeply about the scientific evidence for miracles, especially those in Scripture. They did not pursue such data, though, as ends in themselves, mere proofs of the historicity of Christian claims or the reasonableness of trust in evangelical institutions—and the scholarship suggesting that they did needs revision. Peter Harrison and others argue that early modern Protestants underwent "a clear shift" in their understanding of miracles. In the period under review, their faith grew far more "propositional" and evidentiary, seeking approval far more frequently in natural philosophy. Miracles, for them, "gradually cease[d] to be understood within the context of faith and increasingly play[ed] a primary role in the rational justification of religious beliefs."[5] There is truth in this assertion. Many Christians did respond to Enlightenment-era critics with a greater degree of evidential reason than before. But the now common notion that modern Protestantism—or, rather more ironically, evangelicalism—was secularized by fixating on evidence for faith, assessing miracles primarily with tools borrowed from scientists, does not account well for the likes of Mather and Edwards.[6]

The most pious, supernaturalistic Protestant divines proved much less concerned about adjudicating rival views of miracles with science, or using modern-day miracles to justify their churches' most contested propositions, than with using signs and wonders to advance an ancient faith in the reality of God's vital presence in the world and quickening work in human souls. They were not even worried about the question whether miracles are better understood as interruptions of nature or results of natural systems not yet fully understood. Church fathers like Augustine had contended long ago that whereas God governs the natural realm, even signs and wonders that cannot be explained transpire in and through natural forces he controls.[7] So for Mather, Edwards, and many of their early modern kin, most miracle accounts deserved scientific scrutiny, but mainly for the sake of perpetuating rationally, defensibly, compellingly—in the face of modern critics—an older vision of the world and transcendent way of life that their naturalizing peers now struggled to appreciate. Miracles were not seen as ultimate solutions to the challenges of faith, the primary means by which to justify belief, or as only flashes in the pan of institutional religion, important to the hoi polloi but negligible to others. They were types of resurrection, redemption, and rebirth, stirring signs of God's presence and activity in the world, worth defending first and foremost for their spiritual potential in a world losing touch with the divine.

I want to unpack this argument in three main stages, looking closely at the miracles of Jesus in the Bible (the most central signs and wonders to the piety and vision Mather and Edwards maintained). First, I want to scan my subjects' use of rational evidence in favor of these miracles, which showed, they said, that Jesus is the savior of the world. Second, I will demonstrate their use of such evidence to champion a traditional and spiritual view of the world. And finally, I will highlight the end to which this led: an ultimate fixation in the work of Mather and Edwards on the ways in which these signs point to spiritual rebirth and a divine form of life to which they thought Jesus beckoned those who followed him.

"Every Rational Man Must Conclude as Nicodemus Did"

If miracles were to point persuasively to spiritual power—at least to large numbers of people—public evidence was required of their existence and legitimacy, and not just from believers. After all, as Mather wrote in a vade mecum on rationality, "he that would approve himself a Reasonable man, must hearken to Reason." Indeed, "the voice of *Reason*," he stressed in a homiletical flourish aimed at like-minded Protestants, "is the *Voice* of God."[8] Evangelicals like Mather and Edwards endeavored to be reasonable—not rationalists, but publicly accountable intellectuals. They deployed several batches of their home-brewed ink assessing evidence of the quality and force of Jesus's signs.

Mather scouted such evidence with ceaseless curiosity, seeking strategies to exploit it in support of the divinity of Jesus and his ministry. In the words of Rick Kennedy, Mather's "biblical enlightenment was open-minded to a wide range of experiences that moderate Protestants increasingly insisted were impossible. For [Mather] there was no reasonable foundation in the Bible for assuming that miracles would stop, angels would cease to be active, the dead were completely out of reach, or that God would slumber into semi-retirement." And as Mather said himself of the miracles of Jesus in his book *The Quickened Soul* (1720), which treats the healing by Jesus of a man's withered hand (as found in Matt 12:13), "the Miracles were such as to demonstrate, That God was with Him; yea, that He was very God."[9]

The best place to find Mather's analysis of the evidence of Jesus's own miracles is his hitherto unpublished commentary on the Bible, "Biblia Americana," in which he wrote hundreds of pages on Jesus's life and work. In its lengthy introduction to the study of the Gospels, Mather gathered an array of ancient data from "the most professed Enemies of Christianitie," and a few of its adherents, underwriting the historicity of "many wonderful things" claimed of Jesus by the evangelists. Celsus, Julian the Apostate, and Porphyry "deny not the Miracles" performed by the Lord, he wrote. "Mahomet ... that imposter bears Witness" to them too. "The Jewes in their Talmuds" and the Sibylline oracles allowed and even vouched for the savior's best-known signs. Pontius Pilate wrote the Emperor Tiberius about them. Church fathers Hegesippus, Justin Martyr, and Tertullian employed Pilate's letters to attest similar works. And then, later in the "Biblia," while expositing historically a verse in Matt 4 ("And Jesus went about all Galilee ... healing," verse 23), Mather added that the Roman scholar Tacitus and Jewish sage Josephus testified to the wonders of the Lord.[10]

In addition to ancient authors, Mather engaged modern scholars on the miracles of Jesus: John Locke most famously, but also the Reformed divine Benedict Pictet, the nonjuror Robert Jenkin, the physician Guilhèm Adèr, and the Anglican Newtonian philosopher Samuel Clarke. He engaged Locke's *Discourse of Miracles* at length, extracting, rearticulating, and celebrating Locke's affirmation of Jesus's signs. "Oh! how triumphant the *Miracles* of our Saviour!," he ejaculated during a sustained reading of Locke. The disputed "business of *Miracles*," he quoted from the *Discourse*, "has no Manner of difficulty." Every "rational Man," in fact, Mather paraphrased now, "must conclude as *Nicodemus* did" in John 3:2: "*no Man can do those Signs which thou dost, except God be with him.*" From Pictet and especially Jenkin, he took encouragement regarding the uniqueness of these signs, preceded as they were by several centuries without any miracles in Scripture. From Adèr he determined that, by early modern standards, the people healed by Jesus stood "past all humane help" and were "gone beyond the Cure . . . of any Physician in the World."[11] And from Clarke, he wrung sophisticated philosophical aid on the nature, possibility, and reality of the miracles of Jesus in the Bible.[12]

With assistance from these writers, Mather claimed throughout his section on the Gospels in the "Biblia" that Jesus's best-known miracles hailed him as the heaven-sent savior of the world, the divinely appointed king prophesied in Hebrew Scripture. He accomplished all "those Works, which the Messias was to do according to the Prædictions of the divine and ancient Oracles," said Mather. He fulfilled the law and the prophets, becoming everything the faithful had expected their long-awaited liberator to be.[13]

Edwards's evidence of the quality and force of Jesus's miracles is strewn throughout his corpus, primarily in manuscript sermons and private notebooks, and based in the main upon the spadework of others and his trust in the cogency of Scripture (the evidence for which he addressed in other places). Like Mather, he recalled that even unfriendly sources from the premodern world—the Quran, for example—lent support to Christian claims regarding Jesus's signs and wonders. And like Mather, he engaged modern authors on the subject, though his list of interlocutors was, as usual, distinctive: Dean of Norwich John Sharp (later archbishop of York), Anglican bishop Richard Kidder, Irish priest Philip Skelton (of the Anglican Church of Ireland), and the Swiss Reformed theologian Johann Friedrich Stapfer. By Sharp he was assured that Jesus's miracles attested his unique, divine status. From Kidder he acquired episcopal confirmation that "such a sort of miracles as Christ wrought, and which he most abounded in, viz. his healing the bodies of men when diseased, were a proper and good evidence of a divine mission." With Skelton he agreed that Jesus's resurrection, especially, authenticated his ministry. And from Stapfer he gained confidence that Scripture features so many miracle accounts that "if . . . in one deed or another some doubt could arise about whether it had been produced from physical causes or whether some fraud was present, there are uncounted others where it is plainly impossible to explain them thus."[14]

To a greater degree than Mather, though, Edwards built his case for the miracles of Jesus on the witness of the subjects, writers, and compilers of the Old and New Testaments. He reiterated in "Miscellanies" no. 382, "there is no kind of miracle can be thought of that would be more evidential, than those that Christianity has been confirmed by," a common theme of apologists for sixteen hundred years.[15] But the bulk of the evidence to which he paid attention lay within the friendly confines of the canon. Edwards trusted that the Bible brimmed full of signs and wonders that typified, led to, and culminated in Christ and his mission of redemption. He considered its account of salvation, to be sure, an extended, "constant miracle," symbolized dramatically by several "standing miracles." God's preservation of Israel (and the line of the Messiah) as it languished in Egypt, wandered in the wilderness, conquered the Canaanites, fended off threats to its national security, atrophied in Babylon, and rebuilt Zion proved a centuries-long, suspense-filled "constant miracle." And his presence over the mercy seat atop the ark of the covenant, guidance of his people with the Urim and the Thummim, and gift and spirit of prophecy were "standing miracles."[16]

All of these prepared the way for Jesus's own miracles, which Edwards thought completed the magnalia that preceded them and marked him as the long-awaited messianic king. In a sermon on the healing of the Gadarene demoniac, Edwards told his people that this supernatural exorcism proved "a notable evidence that . . . Jesus was the person by whom mankind were to be delivered from Satan," for example. In another Sunday sermon, he assured his congregation that the miracles of Jesus were indeed "divine works" and that the "end" for which he "wrought" them "was to confirm his doctrine" and "induce man to [entertain] and practice" what he preached. In an early private notebook, he reflected on the role of the resurrection of Jesus in attesting his authority. "I can think of no other miracle whatever," he recorded, "that would be so full an evidence and manifestation of the finger of God; it must therefore be a certain evidence of the truth of that that it is done in confirmation of. And especially the resurrection of the person himself in proof of his own authority, foretold by the person that he would rise and thereby give a demonstration of it."[17] In a few different contexts, he suggested that the Lord used the power of his miracles—especially the resurrection and sending of the Spirit—to inculcate gradually his most troubling doctrines. In his "Miscellanies" notebooks, while recalling John 16:12–15, he wrote that "Christ had many things to say which he said not, because the disciples could not bear them yet; Christ revealed his gospel to them by little and little." And in a sermon to his people preached six years later, he said that Jesus taught people counterintuitive things carefully. "He took such opportunities to tell 'em of his death and sufferings when they were full of admiration for some signal miracle, and were confirmed in it that he was the messiah," Edwards preached. "He told 'em much more plainly after his resurrection than before; but he did not tell them all yet, but left more to be revealed by the Holy Ghost at Pentecost." For both Mather and Edwards, Jesus's miracles had evidentiary and authorizing power.[18]

"I See My Saviour Doing . . . Miracles upon the Children of Men"

But for neither Mather nor Edwards were the miracles of Jesus dazzling ends in themselves, meant to secure the authority of faith by natural means. Rather, they indicated the *supernatural* wellspring of reality, the essentially spiritual nature of the universe itself, which depended every moment on a Maker who is real, transcendent, and ever near. Brooks Holifield's depiction of Mather's worldview is apt, and applies to Edwards as well. They shared an "intense supernaturalism" that "counterbalanced" their early modern "commendations of reason." They invested quite heavily in physico-theology, natural typology, and providential history. Mather, especially, was fascinated with catalogues of prodigies, accounts of curiosa, and scientific treatments of the soul's role in bodily health and physiological therapy. Both thinkers demonstrated what D. Bruce Hindmarsh dubs "the spirit of early evangelicalism." That is, they showed an "aspiration" to know and even feel the "presence of God" in a modernizing, naturalizing European culture "that was sharply separating nature (including human nature) and spirit."[19]

Mather thrilled at the thought of God's presence and activity in the mundane world. As he scribbled on a page once possessed by his son and first biographer Samuel Mather, "I see my Saviour doing illustrious Miracles upon the Children of Men in their Distresses: I feel the *Power* of it in my own Experience of the *Divine Works* upon my Soul, answerable to what was in those ancient Operations of the Lord." While declaiming to his people on the miracles of Jesus in a sermon series preached early in 1692—on the eve, we should note, of the Salem witch trials—Mather wondered to himself in the leaves of his diary, "who can tell what *miraculous* Things, I may see, before this Year bee out!" He retained this expectation through the latter years of his life, when he contemplated another sermon series on the signs. "Who can tell," he asked, "what Wonders" Jesus "may be going to shew" in the cosmos today? His reliance on magnalia rarely wavered.[20]

In one of his best-known jeremiads, an election day sermon published in 1696, Mather generated hope in his region's wayward Protestants by fleshing out his trust in the wonders of the Lord. Hinting that the Roman Catholic Antichrist was tottering, he predicted that the Second Coming of Christ would happen soon and that a spate of new miracles would herald his return. "Lift up your Heads then," he cried, "O you that Love the Appearing of the Lord Jesus Christ: For there seems as if there were an Age of Miracles now Dawning upon us. Proper Miracles were continued in the Church of God," he said, "for Two or Three Hundred years" after Jesus's first coming, "even until the Antichristian Apostasy was come to some Extremity. And when that Apostasy is over, tis possible," he suggested, "there may be a Return of proper Miracles." Mather spied this return on the European horizon, where a growing number of people testified to special healings. "These Persons," he reported, "as they have been Reading the Ancient Miracles of our Lord Jesus Christ, the Spirit of Christ hath wonderfully given them, the Faith of His doing the like for them; and Behold, they have, to the Astonishment of mankind, been by the like Miracles, perfectly and presently recovered out of all their Maladies." In a postscript added to the sermon's publication, Mather offered a description of a few of these cures. And in his diary two years later, he rejoiced over the healing of a Massachusetts widow that was triggered by her reading of this narrative itself. Mrs. Joan Ellis of Medfield had lost most of her hearing. She strained to hear preaching and suspected the judgment of God. But after reading Mather's sermon, she believed that God could heal her. Petitioning the Lord for a supernatural blessing, "shee had her *Hearing* suddenly restored unto her: and to this Day can *hear* very well, and doth with great Comfort attend upon the public Ordinances of Christ."[21]

Mather's notes on Samuel Clarke's interpretation of Jesus's miracles testify further to his trust in God's power. "We know," Mather cogitated, "that such is the *Power of God*, and such is the *nature* of things in themselves a lying before that all-powerful One; that all things are *alike easy* to Him. A *Miracle* therefore is not to be distinguished, by the *difficulty* in the *nature* of the thing itself to be done; as if, what we call *natural*, were in its own proper *nature* easier to be effected, than what we call *miraculous*." Indeed, "strictly speaking," Mather copied in the "Biblia," if "we regard only the *Power* of God, there is *nothing miraculous*" (read bizarre or fantastic). Everything that happens transpires "either immediately," produced "by GOD Himself," or through the mediation of other, already created things. And all that is ascribed "to the *Lawes* and *Powers* of *Matter*" is "but the Effect of GOD acting upon *Matter*, continually." What we call the "*course of nature*," then, is "but the *Will of God*, producing certain Effects in a Manner" that is "uniform" and constant. In Clarke's Boyle lectures, this logic bore nonenthusiastic implications. It was a providential way of moving past the God of the gaps. But for Mather and many other evangelical supernaturalists, it implied that signs and wonders, whether biblical or modern, should appear perfectly natural or only to be expected from a provident, personal, and supernatural deity.[22]

Edwards, too, trusted in a God who worked miracles that pointed to the spiritual constitution of reality. Like Mather, he believed, as he wrote to one of his friends, "that we live in an age, wherein divine wonders are to be expected."[23] He did not speak much about miracles of healing. He was more cautious than Mather about charismatic excess, living as he did amid the tumult of revival.

He believed that the special gifts of the Holy Spirit had ceased.[24] And he doubted that the Lord would use miracles again for "the healing of the nations of their idolatry."[25] But he ruminated frequently on military miracles that God used to undermine the Roman Catholic "Antichrist" and make a way for the golden age of the Spirit yet to come—the millennial age, that is, a massive miracle itself. In the letter just quoted, he reported, for example, on the recent British victory at Cape Breton Island, interpreting the win over the French Catholic forces as "a dispensation of providence, the most remarkable in its kind, that has been in many ages, and a great evidence of God's being one that hears prayer; and that it is not a vain thing to trust in him; and an evidence of the being and providence of God, enough to convince any infidel." And in his *Humble Attempt* to underwrite a concert of prayer for revival "and the advancement of Christ's kingdom on earth" (1747), he interpreted several other recent English victories as "a manifest interposition" of God in human affairs. "It appears to me," he wrote, "that God has gone much out of his usual way . . . in these instances." He has "wrought great things for us, . . . dispensations of providence . . . so wonderful . . . that they come perhaps the nearest to a parallel with God's wonderful works of old, in Moses', Joshua's, and Hezekiah's time, of any that have been in these latter ages of the world."[26]

Like Mather, Edwards taught that signs and wonders drew a curtain on the coming kingdom of God, which would outlast the earth and its vaunted general laws. As he put this in a sermon on Heb 9:27, "all those wondrous miracles . . . wrought from the beginning of the world, have been wrought for the confirmation of the truth of a world to come." And in his "Controversies" notebook, in response to an argument advanced by Bishop Butler and the liberal George Turnbull "that all that God does, and even miracles themselves, is according to 'general laws,' such as are called the laws of nature," Edwards posted a demurral. "According to this," he retorted, "all signification of the divine Mind, even to the prophets and apostles, must be according to general laws without any special interposition at all of the divine agency." A world without wonders was not the world that Edwards knew, where a personal God spoke and governed supernaturally.[27]

For Edwards, even the laws of nature themselves were supernatural, a paradox that rankles modern readers to this day. Everything that happened transpired under God, who created and sustained natural systems incessantly, directly, arbitrarily. As he penned in "Miscellanies" no. 1263, "of the two kinds of divine operation, viz. that which is arbitrary and that which is limited by fixed laws, the former, viz. arbitrary, is the first and foundation of the other, and that which all divine operation must finally be resolved into, and which all events and divine effects whatsoever primarily depend upon. Even the fixing of the method and rules" of natural laws and systems was, to Edwards, "an instance of" the sovereignty of God. Of course, ever since the beginning God has acted in the world *in relation to* the rules, laws, and systems he created. Creation *ex nihilo* is "the only divine operation that [is] absolutely arbitrary, without any kind of use made of any such antecedently fixed method of proceeding as is called a law of nature." For Edwards, there were grades of God's action in the world. And "the higher we ascend in the scale or series of created existences, and the nearer in thus ascending we come to the Creator, the more the manner of divine operation with respect to the creature approaches to arbitrary in these respects." Nevertheless, the whole scale—the entire chain of being—comes from God and depends upon his care every moment. Or as he put this in the pulpit late in 1738, "the gifts of common providence, such as the rain, the light of the sun, and the fruits of the earth, are gifts of God as much as if they were immediately sent from heaven. They are as entirely owing to God's bounty as though they were given by some miracle."[28]

"A Figure of His Opening the Eyes of Men's Souls"

Saving knowledge of this gracious God, gained by means of repentance and spiritual rebirth, was the end game for both men in the contest over miracles. The portents in the Bible drew attention to the sovereignty of God over physics, but the Savior ruled a kingdom that transcended the physical world. Jesus warned Nicodemus, "except a man be born again, he cannot see the kingdom of God" (John 3:3), a dictum that was central to the thought of Mather and Edwards. God's reign was eternal. And the bulk of signs and wonders he had given us on earth aimed at regeneration—spiritual awakening—the portal through which pilgrims had to pass in order to find it.

Mather was obsessed with the quest for spiritual life and the tumult of conversion that inspired it. In the words of Richard Lovelace, he "returned to [this] theme ... with hypnotic regularity." Nothing had distressed him more than apathy from Christians with respect to the spiritual anemia of others. As he vented to his diary in 1711, "we have religious People, whose nearest Relatives are poor, vain, carnal Creatures, utterly destitute of the Symptoms of Regeneration. And yet they seem very easy and thoughtless about them." He pledged himself not only to evangelize his kin, but "awaken all religious People" everywhere to vigilance for their loved ones.[29]

Mather preached scores of homilies and published several essays on the blessings of conversion and spiritual vitality: *Unum Necessarium: Awakenings for the Unregenerate*, a book full of sermons on the subject of rebirth (1693); *The Spirit of Life Entring into the Spiritually Dead: An Essay, to Bring a Dead Soul into the Way, wherein the Quickening Spirit of God & of Grace, Is to Be*

Hoped and Waited for (1707); *The Quickened Soul* (1720); *Vital Christianity: A Brief Essay on the Life of God, in the Soul of Man* (1725); and many, many others.[30] He portrayed the new birth as the one thing needful, the *sine qua non* of eternal life with God. He defined it as "a Real and Thorough Change, wrought by the Holy Spirit, in a Fallen Man, through the Infusion of a Gracious Principle into him, which Restores in him, the Lost Image of God, and therewithal Inclines him to comply with . . . the Gospel." And he specified further that "there is in the Regenerate . . . that which is called in 2 Pet 1.4, the divine nature; that is, a principle which is Divine for the Original of it."[31]

The miracles of Jesus, in Mather's estimation, were meant to open people up to such gracious spiritual life. They were not grand displays meant to silence opposition, advance propositions, or generate applause. Jesus knew that they would oftentimes fail to win belief. In fact, he hid them from the crowds, especially around Jerusalem, in order to be sure that they would send him to the cross.[32] He refused to work wonders for the sake of "ostentation."[33] To the contrary, as Mather maintained in the "Biblia," his "Corporal Miracles were Pledges" of the "*Spiritual*." The "Greatest Work of our Saviour is on the *Souls* of Men." Mather made this point next to Matt 11:5, where the Lord had responded to the query of John the Baptist whether he was the Messiah: "The blind receive their sight," the Savior had reported, ordering the corporal in relation to the spiritual, "the lame walk, the lepers are cleansed, . . . the deaf hear, the dead are raised up, and the poor have the gospel preached to them." Or as Mather put the matter in his book *The Quickened Soul*, in healing people's bodies Jesus also healed their souls, which provided them with health for all eternity.[34]

Edwards, too, was keen to facilitate awakening. He was a tax-supported servant of his colony's state church, an institution he knew was full of culture Protestantism. So he spoke about the difference between mundane religion and authentic faith in Christ—and taught that spiritual rebirth was the key to the kingdom of God. "There is such a thing as conversion," he pleaded. "'Tis the most important thing in the world; and they are happy that have been the subjects of it and they most miserable that have not." The subjects of conversion had the Spirit guiding their lives, rehabilitating their souls and giving them spiritual understanding. They had acquired a taste for God, a new and profound sense of joy and confidence in divine things. Or, as he put this in his sermon "A Divine and Supernatural Light," they had "a true sense of the divine excellency of the things revealed in the Word of God, and a conviction of the truth and reality of them."[35]

Like Mather, Edwards trusted that the miracles of Jesus gestured toward the new birth and eternal life with God. As he preached in a sermon on 1 Pet

2:9, Jesus's healing of the blind was a symbol of conversion. "Christ several times wrought this miracle upon men's bodies while he was here upon earth," Edwards stressed to his people. "He opened the eyes of the blind, and sometimes the eyes of those that were born blind, which miracles were only a figure of his opening the eyes of men's souls." Other miracles, as well, served as signs of conversion. "As I have often observed to you," Edwards stated in a discourse on Rom 11:10, "the diseases & Calamities that [Christ] by his miracles healed persons of were all of them figures & Representations of those sp[iritual] diseases that he came into the [world] to heal men's souls of." The raising of the woman "bowed down eighteen years & enabling her to lift up herself & ... walk Erect [Luke 13:11] was an Image of the w[ork] of Conv[ersion]," for instance, "as almost all [Christ's] miracles were," Edwards told his flock. For, as he added in another sermon, preached as he strived toward the first signs of revival he would shepherd in Northampton, "restoring a dead soul to Life" is "a Greater work than External miracles."[36]

More frequently than Mather, Edwards warned fellow Protestants of counterfeit miracles, especially those he thought had been conjured by Catholics to delude devotees. He addressed this problem in his treatise on the affections. "When the images of Christ, in popish churches, are ... made by priestcraft to appear to the people as if they wept, and shed fresh blood, and moved, and uttered such and such words," many claim to see miracles and trust in the church. But the "tendency" of such tricks has worked great harm, promoting "atheism" among less credulous observers. He repeated this notion in his "Notes on the Apocalypse." When priests draw attention to their fictitious wonders, they distract people's attention from the one thing needful—trading life with God for a mess of bread and pottage.[37]

Still, despite such warnings about counterfeit miracles—redolent of Reformation battles of religion—neither Mather nor Edwards wanted to throw the spiritual baby out with what they deemed the bathwater of Catholic superstition. They inhabited a different time and place than Luther and Calvin, and faced new demons. Discontented with the disenchanted world of modern naturalism, worried about the attenuation of Christian faith and piety its skepticism wrought, they affirmed modern miracles, or some of them, at any rate, and yearned for revival of the vibrant spiritual life to which they thought true signs and wonders pointed. They defended the miraculous—partly in support of the veracity of Scripture and the teachings it conveyed, but mostly in the service of a spiritual sensibility receptive to their message of transcendence and conversion. Our scholarship has yet to elucidate the presence and resilience of their modern supernaturalism.

Notes

1. Jane Shaw, *Miracles in Enlightenment England* (New Haven: Yale University Press, 2006), 12. For Mather's account of spiritual wonders, see Cotton Mather, *Magnalia Christi Americana: Or, the Ecclesiastical History of New-England, from Its First Planting in the Year 1620, unto the Year of Our Lord, 1698* (London: Thomas Parkhurst, 1702), unpaginated front matter and all of book 6 (pp. 1–88).

2. Martin Luther, *Sermons on the Gospel of St. John: Chapters 14–16*, in *Luther's Works*, vol. 24, ed. Jaroslav Pelikan (St. Louis, MO: Concordia, 1961), 78 (see also Luther's comments on John 16:13, pp. 367–70); and John Calvin, *Institutes of the Christian Religion*, 2 vols., ed. John T. McNeill, Library of Christian Classics (Louisville, KY: Westminster John Knox Press, 1960), 1:16–17. See also Calvin, *Institutes* 4.17.24–25, 4.19.6, and 4.19.18–19 (2:1390–92, 1453–55, 1465–67). For Luther's original German, see *D. Martin Luthers Werke: Kritische Gesamtausgabe*, 136 vols. (Weimar: Hermann Böhlaus Nachfolger, 1883–2009), 45:532 ("the day of miracles is past") and 46:60–65 (for the relevant material on John 16:13).

3. It will become clear below that these Protestants never agreed on a definition of miracles (or even whether miracles are always supernatural and immediate acts of God). For them, the word "miracle" referred rather generally (sometimes even vaguely) to an amazing act of God meant to draw people's attention to his redemptive activity in the world.

4. Thomas Hobbes, *Leviathan, or The Matter, Forme, & Power of a Common-Wealth, Ecclesiasticall and Civill* (London: Andrew Crooke, 1651; rev. Latin ed., 1668), chap. 37 ("Of Miracles and Their Use"); Benedict Spinoza, *Tractatus theologico-politicus* (Amsterdam: Henricum Künraht, 1670), chap. 6 ("Of Miracles"); John Locke, *A Discourse of Miracles* (1706), in *Posthumous works of Mr. John Locke . . .* (London: W. B. [William Bowyer] for A. and J. Churchill, 1706), 217–31; and David Hume, *Enquiry concerning Human Understanding*, published originally as *Philosophical Essays concerning Human Understanding* (London: A. Millar, 1748), §10 ("Of Miracles").

5. Peter Harrison, "Miracles, Early Modern Science, and Rational Religion," *CH* 75, no. 3 (2006): 494–95.

6. This essay is not an effort to refute metahistorical work on Western secularization. But it does seek to revise the brilliant work of Peter Harrison (now widely influential), who says that early modern Protestants contributed to the spread of modern science and secularization by disenchanting the world of medieval Roman Catholicism, valorizing the literal sense in scriptural exegesis, and investing more than their forebears in scientific evidence for miracles—putting religion on the defensive in the process, ironically, by suggesting that it needed scientific justification. I do not deny any and all truth to Harrison's narrative; on the contrary, I think it has explanatory force. But it fails to illuminate the still-enchanted worldviews (and biblical exegesis) of spiritually fulsome Protestants like Mather and Edwards as brightly as it sheds light on Protestants who gave more ground to the critics of supernatural Christianity. It also fails to account for the enormous investment in beliefs and propositions that had always characterized Christianity. For more on Harrison's narrative of Western secularization, the rise of modern "science," and its gradual exclusion of "religion" from its sphere, see Peter Harrison, *The Bible, Protestantism, and the Rise of Natural Science* (Cambridge: Cambridge University Press, 1998); Jitse M. van der Meer and Richard J. Oosterhoff, "God, Scripture, and the Rise of Modern Science (1200–1700): Notes in the Margin of Harrison's Hypothesis," in *Nature and Scripture in the Abrahamic Religions: Up to 1700*, ed. Jitse M. van der Meer and Scott Mandelbrote, Brill's Series in Church History (Leiden: Brill, 2008), 2:363–96; Harrison, *The Territories of Science and Religion* (Chicago: University of Chicago Press, 2015); and Harrison, ed., "Narratives of Secularization," special issue, *Intellectual History Review* 27, no. 1 (2017), released in book form by Routledge in 2018. By implication, of course, my research also suggests that we should qualify the most dramatic arguments attributing secularization, disenchantment, and/or desacralization to a Protestant "revolution" in European metaphysics and epistemology—for example, Carlos

Eire, "Incombustible Weber: How the Protestant Reformation Really Disenchanted the World," in *Faithful Narratives: Historians, Religion, and the Challenge of Objectivity*, ed. Andrea Sterk and Nina Caputo (Ithaca: Cornell University Press, 2014), 132–48. It finds greater continuity with the historiographical trends surveyed by Alexandra Walsham, "The Reformation and 'the Disenchantment of the World' Reassessed," *Historical Journal* 51, no. 2 (2008): 497–528, who views desacralization as "a complex cycle in which opposing impulses interacted dynamically and played off each other in a reciprocal and dialectical fashion" (p. 517).

7. See especially Augustine, *City of God* 21.8.

8. Cotton Mather, *A Man of Reason: A Brief Essay to Demonstrate, That All Men Should Hearken to Reason* . . . (Boston: John Edwards, 1718), 2, 7.

9. Rick Kennedy, *The First American Evangelical: A Short Life of Cotton Mather*, Library of Religious Biography (Grand Rapids, MI: Eerdmans, 2015), 119; and Cotton Mather, *The Quickened Soul: A Short and Plain Essay on, the Withered Hand Revived & Restored* . . . (Boston: B. Green, 1720), 1. On Mather and Jesus's miracles, see also Grace Sara Harwood, "'Perhaps No One General Answer Will Do': Cotton Mather's Commentary on the Synoptic Gospels in 'Biblia Americana'" (PhD diss., Georgia State University, 2018), 83–106, who argues that Mather tries to have it both ways with respect to the miracles of Jesus—upholding a Calvinist worldview while defending them historically—and proves inconsistent and unconvincing.

10. Mather, "Biblia" (unpaginated but organized in keeping with the canon of the Old and New Testaments as ordered by Protestants, a running gloss on Scripture), found in the section of prolegomena to the study of the Gospels and in a comment on Matt 4:23.

11. Mather, "Biblia," all at Matt 4:25 except the (tacit) engagement with Jenkin, which is at John 3:2. For the sources of this material, see Locke, *Discourse of Miracles*, 221; Benedict Pictet, *Theologia Christiana* (Geneva: Cramer et Perachon, 1696), 8.7–8; Robert Jenkin, *The Reasonableness and Certainty of the Christian Religion*, 5th ed., 2 vols. (London: W. B. for Richard Sare, 1721), 1:243–46; and Guillelmi Ader, *Medici Enarrationes De Ægrotis & Morbis in Evangelio* . . . (Toulouse: Raymundi Colomerii, 1620), passim.

12. Mather, "Biblia," at the end of Matt 12. See Samuel Clarke's Boyle lectures, given two years in a row (1704–5) in the form of sixteen sermons in the cathedral church of St. Paul: *A Discourse concerning the Being and Attributes of God* (1704) and *Evidences of Natural and Revealed Religion* (1705), published together as Samuel Clarke, *A Discourse concerning the Being and Attributes of God, the Obligations of Natural Religion, and the Truth and Certainty of the Christian Revelation* . . . , 7th ed. (London: W. Botham for James and John Knapton, 1728), especially the second set of lectures, Proposition XIV. Edwards also knew of both sets of Clarke's lectures, and owned, used, and lent the second set. See *WJE*, 26:214, 325, 419–20, 436–37.

13. See, for example, Mather, "Biblia," at Matt 11:5 (where the quotation was taken from) and Luke 9:3.

14. See *WJE*, 18:63–64 (Sharp); *WJE*, 23:108 (Kidder); *WJE*, 23:159–60, 165–66 (Skelton); and *WJE*, 23:273–74 (Stapfer). Cf. *WJE*, 20:520–24. For the sources of this material, see John Sharp, "Sermon VI, Preached at White-Hall on the Twentieth of March, 1684–5," in John Sharp, *Fifteen Sermons Preached on Several Occasions*, 6th ed. (London: Mary Kettilby for W. Parker, 1729), 1:178; Richard Kidder, *Demonstration of the Messias*, 2nd ed. (London: John Osborn et al., 1726), part 2, p. 5; Philip Skelton, *Deism Revealed* . . . , 2nd ed., 2 vols. (London: A. Millar, 1751), 1:24, 2:16–17; and Johann Friedrich Stapfer, *Institutiones Theologiæ Polemicæ Universæ*, 5 vols. (Zurich: Heideggerum et Socios, 1743–47), 2:1103–4.

15. *WJE*, 13:451.

16. For Edwards on "constant" and "standing" miracles, see *WJE*, 9:186–280; and *WJE*, 28 (unpaginated "Defense of the Pentateuch as a Work of Moses"). And for a sampling of his other work on the miracles of Scripture that pointed to, led to, and culminated in Jesus, see his sermon on Matt 12:41 (May 1747) on the prophetic work of Jonah among the Ninevites (*WJE*, 65, unpaginated); his "Notes on Scripture" nos. 207–9 and 387 on the sun standing still for Joshua's

victory at Gibeah (*WJE*, 15:129–35, 371); and various notes jotted in his "Blank Bible" (*WJE*, 24:227, 230, 799–800). Edwards also deemed "the preserving" of the Jews as a nation after the New Testament age—"when in such a dispersed condition for above sixteen hundred years" (from the fall of Jerusalem to Edwards's own era)—a "continual miracle." World history "affords nothing else like it," he claimed. "There is a remarkable hand of providence in it" (*WJE*, 9:469–70). For more on Edwards's defense of the miracles of redemptive history charted in the Old and New Testaments, see the fine essay by Corné Blaauw, "Redemptive History as a Paradigm for Jonathan Edwards' Exposition of Miracles," *Jonathan Edwards Studies* 4, no. 1 (2014): 4–20.

17. Edwards, sermon on Mark 5:16–17 (April 1737), L. 4v, in *WJEO*, 52 (unpaginated); Edwards, sermon on John 10:37 (March 12, 1740, and December 4, 1756), L. 2r and L. 12v, in *WJEO*, 55 (unpaginated); and Edwards, "Miscellanies" no. 313, in *WJEO*, 13:394–95. For more from Edwards on the power of the miracles of Jesus to confirm his identity and authorize his mission, see his sermon on Luke 8:28 (n.d.), L. 1r, in *WJEO*, 43 (unpaginated); Edwards, sermon on Heb 12:2–3 (1731–32), L. 2v, in *WJEO*, 47 (unpaginated); Edwards, sermon on Luke 4:38–39 (January 1739), in *WJEO*, 54 (unpaginated); Edwards, sermon on Matt 16:15 (January 1749 and October 1756), in *WJEO*, 67 (unpaginated); Edwards, "Miscellanies" nos. 1286 and 1288, in *WJE*, 23:230–31, 232–33; Edwards, "Blank Bible" (at numerous texts), in *WJE*, 24:896, 915–16; and Edwards, "Subjects of Inquiry," in *WJEO*, 28 (unpaginated), one of which pertains to the ways that Jesus's miracles, especially raising of the dead, provided "evidence" of "the truth of his mission."

18. Edwards, "Miscellanies" no. 160, in *WJE*, 13:317; and Edwards, "The Perpetuity and Change of the Sabbath" (on 1 Cor 16:1–2), in *WJE*, 17:241. On Jesus's use of miracles to teach difficult things, see also "Miscellanies" no. 475, in *WJE*, 13:517–18.

19. E. Brooks Holifield, "The Abridging of Cotton Mather," in *Cotton Mather and "Biblia Americana"—America's First Bible Commentary: Essays in Reappraisal*, ed. Reiner Smolinski and Jan Stievermann (Tübingen: Mohr Siebeck, 2010), 86; and D. Bruce Hindmarsh, *The Spirit of Early Evangelicalism: True Religion in a Modern World* (New York: Oxford University Press, 2018), 268.

20. Samuel Mather, *The Life of the Very Reverend and Learned Cotton Mather* . . . (Boston: Samuel Gerrish, 1729), 100; and *Diary of Cotton Mather*, 2 vols., American Classics (New York: Frederick Ungar, [1957]), 1:144, 2:620.

21. Cotton Mather, *Things for a Distress'd People to Think upon, Offered in the Sermon to the General Assembly of the Province, of the Massachusetts Bay, at the Anniversary Election, May 27, 1696* . . . (Boston: B. Green and J. Allen for Duncan Campbell, 1696), 36 (for the narrative of healings, mostly in England and France, see "A Postscript, Giving an Account of some late Miracles, wrought by the Power of our Lord Jesus Christ," 77–86); and Mather, *Diary*, 1:274–75.

22. Mather, "Biblia," at Matt 12:50.

23. Edwards to a correspondent in Scotland (probably the Reverend John McLaurin), November 1745, in *WJE*, 16:197.

24. Edwards, "Divine Love Alone Lasts Eternally" (on 1 Cor 13:8), in *WJE*, 8:355–58.

25. Edwards, "Miscellanies" no. 1223, in *WJE*, 23:156.

26. Edwards to a correspondent in Scotland, November 1745, in *WJE*, 16:197; and Edwards, *An Humble Attempt to promote Explicit Agreement and Visible Union of God's People in Extraordinary Prayer*, in *WJE*, 5:361–62. Like the Puritans before him, Edwards often distinguished between general and special providence. The latter was miraculous. The former was exercised via secondary causes. But as explained at length below, even secondary causes, for Edwards, obtained by means of God's supernatural superintendence of the world.

27. Edwards, "The Importance of a Future State" (on Heb 9:27, ca. 1721–22), in *WJE*, 10:362; and Edwards, "Controversies," in *WJE*, 21:297–98. Edwards was responding in the latter note to Bishop Joseph Butler, *The Analogy of Religion* (London: James, John and Paul Knapton, 1736), esp. 144–48; and George Turnbull, *Christian Philosophy* . . . (London: J. Noon, 1740), 173–92,

where the following proposition is defended: "The divine, infinitely wise, just, faithful, good providence governs the whole universe by general laws; nor is what is said in Scripture of special, miraculous interpositions of providence inconsistent with such government."

28. WJE, 23:202–4; and Edwards, sermon on 1 John 4:12 (December 1738), L. 5r, in WJEO, 53 (unpaginated). On this theme, cf. "Miscellanies" no. 136, in WJE, 13:295.

29. Richard F. Lovelace, *The American Pietism of Cotton Mather: Origins of American Evangelicalism* (Grand Rapids, MI: Christian University Press, 1979), 74; and Mather, *Diary*, 2:120.

30. Cotton Mather, *Unum Necessarium: Awakenings for the Unregenerate* . . . (Boston: Duncan Campbell, 1693); Mather, *The Spirit of Life Entring into the Spiritually Dead* . . . (Boston: Timothy Green, 1707); Mather, *Quickened Soul*; and Mather, *Vital Christianity: A Brief Essay on the Life of God, in the Soul of Man* . . . (Charles-Town, MA: Samuel Keimer for Eleazer Phillips, 1725).

31. Mather, *Unum Necessarium*, 7, 16, 43; Mather, *Quickened Soul*, 7–9.

32. Mather, "Biblia," at Matt 12:50, Matt 13:58, Mark 1:44, the end of Mark 5, Mark 6:6, Luke 3:23, Luke 4:41, and Luke 11:33.

33. As Mather insisted in the "Biblia" at Mark 6:6, Jesus "wrought not his *Miracles* upon the designs of *Ostentation*." And as Edwards said a number of times with help from Thomas Sherlock, the learned bishop of London, "Christ would not work miracles for ostentation. . . . He favored not the multitude, who were so greatly affected with his miracles and appeared so ready to assist him to set up a temporal kingdom at Jerusalem. . . . He chose rather to go and be crucified"—and we should follow his example by refusing to tout miracles in pursuit of vainglory. Edwards, "Christ's Example," WJE, 21:514, 518–19 (quotation from p. 518); and Edwards, "Miscellanies" no. 1342, in WJE, 23:378–80, an extract from Sherlock's *Several Discourses Preached at the Temple Church* (London: J. Whiston and B. White, 1756), 1:210–17.

34. Mather, "Biblia," at Matt 11:5; Mather, *Quickened Soul*, passim. On this theme, see also Mather's now more famous publication, finished in 1724 but published in 1972, *The Angel of Bethesda*, ed. Gordon W. Jones (Barre, MA: American Antiquarian Society and Barre, 1972).

35. Edwards, "The Reality of Conversion" (on John 3:10–11), in *The Sermons of Jonathan Edwards: A Reader*, ed. Wilson H. Kimnach, Kenneth P. Minkema, and Douglas A. Sweeney (New Haven: Yale University Press, 1999), 83, 92; and Edwards, "A Divine and Supernatural Light" (on Matt 16:17), in WJE, 17:413. For more from Edwards on the Spirit as a supernatural light and source of spiritual vitality in twice-born souls, see his *Treatise on Grace*, in WJE, 21:149–97.

36. Edwards, "Christians a Chosen Generation" (on 1 Pet 2:9), in WJE, 17:321–22; Edwards, sermon on Rom 11:10 (June 1740), L. 2v, L. 4v, in WJEO, 55 (unpaginated); and Edwards, sermon on John 1:41–42 (December 1733), L. 13r, in WJEO, 48 (unpaginated).

37. Edwards, *Religious Affections*, in WJE, 2:309–10; and Edwards, "Notes on the Apocalypse," in WJE, 5:112–13.

8

LAY APPROPRIATIONS AND FEMALE INTERPRETATIONS OF THE BIBLE IN GERMAN PIETISM

RUTH ALBRECHT

The Bible for All

"It would be hoped that all Christians strove more diligently to study the Hebrew and Greek language in which Scripture is written (as is custom with other foreign languages which are acquired for worldly usage) and thereby hear, as much as possible, the Holy Spirit in his own tongue."[1] This admonition is part of Philipp Jakob Spener's writings on the tasks of the spiritual priesthood—that is, the priesthood of all believers—"As much as it was the task of priests to deal with the law of God, it is the duty of the spiritual priesthood to ensure that the Word of God lives abundantly among them."[2] In his 1677 tract on *Spiritual Priesthood*, Spener leaves no doubt that women are implied in his remarks as much as men.[3] This tract revisits some of the fundamental prerequisites that the Frankfurt pastor delineated in his 1675 *Pia Desideria* regarding the doctrinal and practical reformation of the church. In his explanations on *Spiritual Priesthood*, he repeats almost verbatim what he only briefly and programmatically formulated two years prior. Of Spener's six proposals in *Pia Desideria* on how the church may implement the core truths of the Reformation, the first enjoins "that we may be more intent on spreading the Word of God more abundantly among us." Harking back to Luther, Spener then points out the necessity of exercising spiritual priesthood.[4] Both of these foundational Pietist texts—*Spiritual Priesthood* and *Pia Desideria*—thus link together the need for everyone who has been baptized to assume personal spiritual responsibility and read the Bible. In Spener's view, one cannot lead to fruition without the other.

On the one hand, these works from the mid-1670s may be read as expressions of Spener's theological views as they had been developing since he came to Frankfurt in 1666. During those years he took the first tentative steps toward putting his reform ideas into practice.[5] On the other hand, they may be seen as a reflection of what was going on in the pious circle that had begun to take shape in that city. Together with Spener, the leading Frankfurt theologian, its members were striving toward a form of Christian life that would rise above the perceived deadness of the established church. The Pietist call for returning to Holy Scripture as the sole normative orientation in ecclesiastic life and doctrine does, of course, stand in continuity with the Reformation. At the same time, Pietists interpreted the Bible anew in response to challenges of the seventeenth century, in which the confessional churches intently focused on setting themselves apart from each other.

The fact that this essay starts out with a reference to Spener, however, should not be seen as a return to a historiographic model that centers Pietist history around his life and thought. Rather, it illustrates how the basic outlines of the Pietist program had already become discernible at this early point in the movement in Frankfurt.[6] Spener's statements make it unambiguously clear that all Christians alike—that is, clergy and laymen of both genders—must devote themselves to the Bible. This explicit inclusion of all baptized persons marks the early modern horizon of these ideas. Over the course of the seventeenth century, various laymen spoke out concerning church reforms. Examples for this include Ahasver Fritsch[7] and Johann Jakob Schütz. The debates associated with the moniker "Querelle des femmes" illustrate how female lay theologians had also firmly established themselves within early modern learned discourse. From the very beginning, laypeople took on a central role in the development and spread of the Pietist reform movement. While academics had initially outlined and disseminated Pietist ideas, formally uneducated men and women increasingly gained in significance. According to the fundamental principle of the spiritual priesthood, their experiences were assuming the same weight as that of theologians and ordained pastors. The spaces that opened up for women within the movement may thus be considered especially characteristic of the modernizing impulses that came out of Pietism. Whether as authors, correspondents, networkers, or patrons, they contributed decisively to the composition and propagation of the Pietist movement.[8]

It is within this context that Spener's aforementioned statements calling for the acquisition of Hebrew and Greek must be situated. In his work on the

Spiritual Priesthood, he elucidates this demand and outlines his vision for reform through questions and concise answers: "Are then all Christians entitled to read Scripture diligently? Yes, since it is the letter of the Heavenly Father to all His children. Thus, no child may be excluded; instead, all are entitled and obligated to read it." He thereby also reduces deference to the ordained ministry and its male representatives, which had also come to characterize the churches of the Reformation: "Would it not be better if they simply believed their preacher and what he taught them? No, instead they, too, should study Scripture in order that they may examine their preacher's teachings and so their faith does not rest on the view and beliefs of a person but on divine truth."[9] However, the standing order of early modern society set firm limits to this idea. Only a few persons without formal education had the opportunity to study these languages and thus discern the Holy Spirit on their own.

A different but equally powerful limitation of Pietist reform was created by critics of the movement from within their own churches. Already in 1677, Spener was forced to confront such charges. Among other things, he defended himself against the accusation that "everything is in grave confusion and a great many people—men and women—dare to hold strange *conventicula* or *collegia* and interpret Scripture and its difficult places, which theologians would find hard to explain. During these strange gatherings women and maids preach for many hours and in numerous ways interfere with the *ministerio*."[10] In their opponents' eyes, the Pietist idea that all persons should read and interpret the Bible in the same manner was an assault on the ordained ministry—especially when women interpreted and taught it.

These basic conditions shaped how Pietists approached the Bible,[11] as this chapter will illustrate with three examples: Schütz, a formally educated lawyer; Anna Catharina Scharschmidt, a female writer of mystical texts; and Johanna Eleonora Petersen, the most significant female theologian and author of early Pietism. Significantly, all three examples evince the close connection between the self-empowerment of laypeople in radical Pietism, with its spiritualist tendencies and millennialist eschatologies.[12]

Biblical Purism—Johann Jakob Schütz

"Hopeful to encourage the growth of a few souls in Christ, I have compiled some present short sayings from Scripture conducive to life and godliness, written by his holy evangelists and apostles under particular chapters and headings." These sentences are part of the "Manual" with which the Frankfurt lawyer Johann Jakob Schütz (1640–1690) prefaces his *Rules of Christian Life*, published in 1677.¹³ He primarily addresses those willing truly to follow biblical teachings. While bearing in mind the conversion of "the enemies of the cross of Christ," he chiefly cares about like-minded believers. "It is you in particular, my dear brothers and sisters, whose hearts have been inscribed by the Lord with the obedience of Christ so that you may recognize that the laws of the Lord are sweeter than honey and honeycomb. Let us therefore be diligent to grow constantly and completely in these words of life, never ceasing to encourage and admonish each other in every way and stir each other in love and good works; never caring what the impenitent worldly crowd may think or how they may try to impede the truth of Jesus and his innocent discipleship."¹⁴

Schütz's work reflects not merely a biblical purism but a New Testament purism. His selection exclusively consists of verses from the New Testament since they alone (as he saw it) provide the true instructions on how to follow Christ. Apart from the preamble—which includes the "Preface," a "Warning," the index, and an "Afterword"—the book spans seven hundred print pages in duodecimo format. The pages are filled with Bible passages and divided into thematic sections.¹⁵ The verses are all cited verbatim, and the index serves as a directory to understand the book. *Rules of Christian Life* propagates Schütz's ideals for Christian living and likewise functions as a compendium of Pietist ethics.¹⁶

Spener's reputation as the architect of the Pietist reform movement and the *Collegia pietatis* in Frankfurt long overshadowed Schütz. However, in his groundbreaking study building on the work of Johannes Wallmann, Andreas Deppermann positions Schütz as the most important impetus for change in the Frankfurt area. Schütz descended from a prestigious Frankfurt family and after his legal studies established himself there as a lawyer. By reading mystical texts, especially by Johannes Tauler, he developed a new understanding of Christianity that transformed his approach to the Bible. Deppermann even speaks of a "rediscovery of the Bible." Schütz's fascination with mystical traditions, alchemy, and Kabbalah deeply shaped his subsequent career. His global network of correspondence included, among others, William Penn, Anna Maria van Schurmann, Pierre Poiret, and Christian Knorr von Rosenroth. Along with Juliana Maria Baur von Eyseneck and Johanna Eleonora von Merlau, he belonged to the core group of Saalhof Pietists who became increasingly radical and separatist. In a concerted effort, they purchased land in Pennsylvania in order to emigrate there and live according to Christian principles without any authoritarian intrusion. Starting in 1676, Schütz no longer partook in Holy Communion in his hometown, which would later lead to his break with Spener. The *Rules of Christian Life* from 1677 mark his development in the mid-1670s as he sought to apply his personal understanding of

Christianity. With this book, Schütz put forth "a catalogue of Christian virtues that programmatically displayed the biblicism so characteristic of him and Frankfurt Pietism: New Testament instructions and rules are here compiled verbatim; their literal content without any 'artificial' additions outlines the certain path to God."[17]

The thematic compilation of biblical texts is divided into sixty-one chapters that are in turn allocated to four larger thematic units. Section 1 establishes the basics of how God addresses humankind and how believers should respond. Section 2 focuses on the "Christian's duty" in regard to the "inclination or motion of our will." The third main section describes the "gifts of the Spirit, which consist mainly in the illumination of the soul and mind." Under the theme of "characteristics of Christendom," the fourth section delves into aspects such as vigilance, mindfulness, interiority, earnestness, industriousness, and steadfastness. First, Schütz lays out his Christological and soteriological concept, upon which the concrete implications of the following sections are based. The introductory abstract for chapter 1 reads, "On the state and promises of the New Covenant; which the disciples of the Lord Jesus Christ should obtain for themselves and take comfort in today, and thereafter in the next world, and in eternal life." The page header throughout the chapter is "On Christian Vocation." Schütz begins his compilation of citations with the Gospel of Matthew and ends with Revelation. The Beatitudes of Matt 5 commence the Bible compendium. They are followed by Matt 8:11 and selected verses from Matt 10–11, 19–20, and 23–26. Thematically, the passages revolve around the standards that Christ exemplified for his disciples. Schütz resumes this topic by examining Mark 8:31–33. After citing additional passages from the Gospel of Mark, he continues the Beatitudes with Luke 6:20–26. He follows the order of the New Testament and cites from almost every single book, completing the first chapter with Rev 22:4–5, "And they shall see his face; and his name *shall be* on their foreheads. 5. And there shall be no night there, and they need no candle, neither light of the sun; for the Lord God giveth them light: and they shall reign for ever and ever."

The second main part includes further subdivisions: "On Duty toward Ourselves and toward Others" (chaps. 35–39) and "On the Duty Toward Particular Estates" (chaps. 40–53). A close examination of the latter chapters illuminates how Schütz's process of selecting Bible verses underlay his ideal for Pietist discipleship and fellowship. In these chapters, women explicitly appear as wives, mothers, and widows. Chapter 43 is titled "On male and female servants for the needy." This wording harks back to Phil 2:25, in which Epaphroditus in the Luther Bible is referred to as "meiner Nothdufft Diener" (the servant of my needs). By incorporating women in this passage, Schütz highlights the equal duty of all Christians to serve one another—a fundamental Pietist reform idea that also underlies the argument for the priesthood of all believers. The detailed list of Bible passages on Christian servanthood begins in Acts 6, which describes the appointment of the seven deacons. This is followed by Rom 12:7–9, Rom 15:25–28, 1 Cor 16:3;15, 2 Cor 8:18–22, the aforementioned passage Phil 2:25, 29, 30, as well as 1 Tim 3:8–10, 1 Pet 4:11, and Heb 6:10, "For God is not unrighteous to forget your work and labor of love, which ye have shewed toward his name, in that ye have ministered to the saints, and do minister." Both Acts 6 and 1 Tim 3 are nowadays considered descriptions of early Christian diaconal ministry.

Since Schütz found terminology of servanthood in all of these texts, he could easily adapt them to his concept of Pietist ethics. In his elaborations on female servants, he incorporated several famous New Testament women: Phebe, Tryphena, Tryphosa, and Persis (Rom 16:1–2; 12), as well as Euodias (Phil 4:2). The third Bible passage given is 1 Tim 5:9–10, which lists the tasks of a widow in the congregation. In his chapters on bishops, elders, and teachers, Schütz held to the classic view that these offices were reserved for men since he found no references to females in these roles throughout the New Testament. Yet his selection on the theme of teachers (chap. 44) illustrates how broadly he understood this task. Beginning with Matt 5:9 ("Blessed be the peacemakers: for they shall be called the children of God"), he references fifty-three Bible passages in total, all the way to Jas 3:1–2, "My brethren be not many masters knowing that we shall receive the greater condemnation. For in many things we offend all." Both teaching and learning are fundamental aspects of Christian life. Accordingly, Schütz refers to 1 Cor 15:3 on the topic of "Teaching," "For I delivered unto you first of all that which I also received, how that Christ died for our sins according to the scriptures." Similar to how all Christians are called upon to teach and learn, they are also called upon to fashion their life through listening to the Word of God. He thus elaborates on listening to God's Word and to each other in chapter 45 ("On Listening") and substantiates it with fifty-five biblical references. Matt 9:37 demonstrates that such listening may be seen as a fundamental feature of obedience in faith: "The harvest truly is plenteous, but the laborers are few."[18] Furthermore, Schütz lists the parallel passage in Luke 10:2 and thus underscores the centrality of its message. It is evident throughout all of his writings that the author of *Rules of Christian Life* placed the Christian faith center stage; it must permeate every aspect of the disposition and behavior both of the individual and the Christian community.

Between Mysticism and the Bible—Anna Catharina Scharschmidt

A fascinating example of female appropriations of the Bible in the Pietist movement is Anna Catharina Scharschmidt of Quedlinburg.[19] Toward the end of the 1690s, a Pietist subculture with specific characteristics began to take shape in that small town on the eastern edge of the Harz Mountains.[20] In the post-Reformation period, the abbess of the Protestant imperial abbey of Quedlinburg also had governing rights in the city.[21] At the time, Anna Dorothea von Sachsen-Weimar (1657–1704), a fierce opponent of Pietism, headed the abbey.[22] However, several canonesses, especially the provost[23] as well as servants, maintained close relations with Pietist groups. Quedlinburg's geographical location allowed for good connections to Halberstadt, Halle, and Magdeburg. The Pietist circles emerging in these bigger cities stood in close contact with their sympathizers in Quedlinburg.[24] Anna Catharina Heidfeldt descended from a prestigious Quedlinburg family that owned significant property in the city. Her date of birth unknown, she died on February 2, 1730.[25] In 1679, she married the lawyer Johann Christian Scharschmidt (1658–1721), who also descended from a clerical and ruling family of Quedlinburg.[26] The pair were key figures in the development of Pietism in Quedlinburg.[27]

Scharschmidt's underresearched work from 1704 offers a significant contribution to the history of biblical interpretation. As far as we can tell, Scharschmidt published three books between 1702 and 1704. While Scharschmidt published her first book anonymously, the cover of her second book bore the letters A.C.S.G.H.: Anna Catharina Scharschmid, née Heidfeldt. Only her third and final publication carried her full name. All three emerged from the Quedlinburg Pietist discourse. Her first work, *The All-Important Work of Rebirth*, outlines the steps to salvation.[28] Published in 1703, *A Plain Testimony of the Spirit's True Duties in the New Covenant* connects typical Pietist criticism of the church to an androgynous concept of creation and salvation.[29] The third book, *Useful Excerpt from Joh. Angeli Silesii's "The Cherubinic Wanderer,"*[30] revisits and comments on the famous mystical collection of sayings by Angelus Silesius (birth name Johannes Scheffler, 1624–1677).[31] A general fascination with the mystical tradition also led to the reception of *The Cherubinic Wanderer* in Quedlinburg. This is demonstrated by the fact that in her 1703 work, Scharschmidt seizes upon three verses from this opus as she urges every Christian to personally believe in the incarnation and redeeming death of Christ: "This is what Johann Angelus in Cherubinic Wanderer talked about so agreeably in these verses: 'If Christ had been born a thousand times in Bethlehem but not inside of you, you would still be eternally lost.'"[32] The two subsequent Silesius citations further underline the necessity of individually acquiring salvation so that it may take place "in us."[33] By characterizing Silesius as a witness of truth, Scharschmidt takes up a central motif of Pietist historiography used especially by Friedrick Breckling and Gottfried Arnold.[34] It can be assumed that the members of the Quedlinburg network closely collaborated and that perhaps several people engaged with the same mystical text prior to their respective publications. In 1701, Gottfried Arnold published an edition of *The Cherubinic Wanderer* with an interpretive preface.[35] It remains unclear whether additional Quedlinburg Pietists dealt with Silesius, but it is probable.[36]

Scharschmidt's first two works frequently refer to biblical texts and cite verses verbatim. However, there is no discernible central theme. Several passages display the author's knowledge of Greek and Hebrew, which is not surprising given the Quedlinburg milieu.[37] When referring to the Bible, she seems to have relied on the Luther translation, yet she slightly alters it in numerous places. Compared to her prior commentary, the *Useful Excerpt* bears several distinguishing features in how she presents herself as an author. In a published letter from 1703, she responds to a Quedlinburg clergyman who accuses her of making "an audacious female challenge" when expressing her theological opinions. While she may be "a woman in regard to her gender," she admits, "the masculine power" of the spirit of Jesus speaks through her.[38] This self-characterization corresponds to the androgynous anthropology and soteriology prevalent in the Quedlinburg network.[39] In *The All-Important Work of Rebirth*, she further portrays herself as a self-confident author certain of her mission: "I want to report with obedient love what the Spirit of truth has shown and revealed to my spirit for my awakening and that of the other members."[40] *A Plain Testimony* includes a preliminary report, written perhaps by Gottfried Arnold. It does not address the authorship of the tract, merely stating that it is "a simple and honest child of God."[41] Yet, within the text, the author draws attention to herself and speaks with a distinctive voice, particularly in the passages in which she defends her Pietist orientation and harshly strikes out at the church and clergy. She feels called upon to show her opponents "how I have been taught and guided by God and have remained in the sanctification with other believers."[42]

The 1704 work does not include any preface or commentary on the author. Nonetheless, in her edition of *Cherubinic Wanderer*, she occasionally inserts references to women that do not appear in the original. For instance, whereas Arnold reproduces epigram no. 192 ("One Must Be Righteous") of the Scheffler text verbatim, Scharschmidt adds the key word "sister:" "O brother/sister please be transformed: Why do you remain wrapped up in haze and false appearances? We have to become something substantially new."[43] Brother and sister are highlighted by the use of a parenthesis and positioned directly alongside each other.[44] Furthermore, in the epigram on the subject of listening to God's Word (book 1, no. 85), Angelus Silesius speaks of a gender-neutral "you." However, Scharschmidt's comments on it incorporate females by referring to John 8:47 and Ps 45:10: "Hearken, O daughter, consider, and incline thine ear"—a phrase from a bridal song at the wedding of the king. The analysis that follows thus approaches Scharschmidt's edition as a form of Pietist Bible reading.

Following the structure of the original, all six chapters use excerpts from *Cherubinic Wanderer* and supplement them with one or two Bible verses.[45] Scharschmidt's selection also closely follows the original and sticks to the numbering of the epigrams. However, while *Cherubinic Wanderer* consists of 1,675 verses overall, the Pietist author reduces them to 814.[46] Each epigram is followed by a Bible text, which is printed in a much larger font and thus appears more prominent. Scharschmidt does not seem to favor any of the six books of *Cherubinic Wanderer*, yet she prioritizes certain content. If we look only at book 1, the criteria for the author's selections become apparent at several points. She excludes all epigrams that relate to the veneration of Saint Mary and the saints.[47] On subjects such as death, the sun, or adoption as God's children, she selects only a few. Scharschmidt omits elaborations on certain items relating to theological issues or literature—in contrast to Arnold, who keeps with the original.[48] Instead, she adds explanations that target an uneducated readership and promote practical piety. Relatedly, Scharschmidt also omits or replaces some difficult terms and phrases from Arnold's edition with simpler ones. For instance, in her edition, no. 182 is titled "Whoever serves for a wage is not a son," instead of Arnold's version, "The hireling [*Löhner*] is not a son." She simplifies the syntax of the title of an epigram on paradise to "First it must be in you" (no. 295). When Arnold mentions an "entmilchtes Kind" (unmilked child), Scharschmidt talks about a weaned child (no. 67). Finally, she changes the title of epigram no. 41 from "God knows no end to himself" to "God is without end," further illustrating her aim for simplicity and clarity.

In book 1 of *Cherubinic Wanderer*, Scharschmidt consults twelve books from the Hebrew Bible and twenty from the New Testament. Most citations are from the Gospel of John (19), followed by Matthew (15), Ephesians (13), and Romans (12).[49] In her comments on the first epigram, "Pure as the finest gold, firm as a rock, and clear as a crystal shall be your disposition," she connects the word "pure" with the beatitude in Matt 5:8 for the pure in heart and cites Eph 4:23 to call upon readers to renew their spirit and mind.[50] Later, in her comments on epigram no. 158 on the fountain of life, she refers to the promise in Matt 5:6 to those who hunger and thirst after righteousness. From the outset, the tenor of Scharschmidt's selections underscores the call to convert in the Pietist sense of the term. To this end, the Quedlinburg author favors Jesus's "I am" declarations from John and any statement that highlights the close connection between Christ and believers (nos. 26, 30, 79, 81, 85, 117, 146, 167, 173, 209, 237, 244). Her tendency to summon readers to pursue a conspicuous Christian lifestyle centered on Christ is particularly poignant in two places in book 1. Epigram no. 87, titled "At the Cornerstone Lies the Treasure," states, "Why do you torment the ore? It is the cornerstone at which health, gold, and all arts lie." Undoubtedly, Silesius also refers to Eph 2:20. Scharschmidt thus does not add any Bible passages but instead writes in brackets under the text, "The cornerstone is Christ." Later on, she supplements epigram no. 252, "Heaven Belongs to the Children,"[51] with Mark 10:15, "Whosoever shall not receive the kingdom of God as a little child, he shall not enter therein." Commenting in turn on the citation, she includes an explanation in brackets, "This does not mean the form of a child but rather childlike innocence and simplicity in Christ." She cites Eph 5:30 in two places to illustrate the close connection between Christ and believers by calling them "members of his body, of his flesh, of his bones."[52] She also employs two different renderings of Eph 3:19 to stress the superiority of the love of Christ over knowledge (while also displaying her familiarity with various versions of the Luther Bible).[53]

The educated theologian Gottfried Arnold edited an entire version of *Cherubinic Wanderer*. In the preface, he addresses confessional concerns and urges a wide reception among the heirs of the Reformation even though Johann Scheffler was Roman Catholic. Working on her edition around the same time, Scharschmidt approached her selections and commentary from the perspective of *praxis pietatis*. She combines the pretext of the mystical original with a biblical exegesis that functions as a continuous, spiritual reading—similar to the later Daily Watchwords[54] of the Moravian Church—as befits an exemplary life of discipleship to Christ. Through this publication strategy, the Quedlinburg Pietist network underlined the various facets that characterized not only their milieu but also Pietism more generally. Their incorporation of mystical traditions went hand in hand with the reception of Jakob Böhme's works and the impact of Johann Georg Gichtel and Jane Leade.[55] For Scharschmidt and her circle, Scripture remained central, but it was no longer the sole authority. Rather, it became one revelatory source among others. This includes an openness to new, divine communication.

Between Biblical Exegesis and Continuing Revelation— Johanna Eleonora Petersen

"I am the Alpha and Omega, the beginning and the end, saith the Lord, who is, and who was, and who is to come, the Almighty (who has the same honor, name, and glory as the Father, and through whom all things came into being and will be completed, and through whom everything was created and will be revived and restored)." This is how Johanna Eleonora Petersen (1646–1724) rendered Rev 1:8 in her 1706 treatise *Die verklährte Offenbahrung JEsu Christi nach dem Zusammenhang des Geistes deutlich gezeigt* (The Revelation of Jesus Christ Explained and Made Clear According to the Spirit). By the time she wrote the treatise, Petersen (née "von und zu Merlau") had already made a name for herself in German and international Pietist networks by tirelessly advocating her convictions.[56] Early on in her career, she and her husband, Johann Wilhelm Petersen (1649–1727),[57] had defended the possibility of new divine revelations, but then shifted their focus to the imminent millennial kingdom and, eventually, the apocatastasis, or final restoration of all things. While Petersen's great opus and commentary on Revelation (1696) attracted great attention and furnished biblical proofs for her chiliasm, her 1706 publication did not spark much public interest.[58] Yet she saw a close correlation between the two publications: "I was asked by various people to shorten the blessed book (which I published on a few years ago with the *Einleitung zur gründlichen Verständniß der heiligen Offenbahrung* [Introduction/Guide to a Thorough Understanding of the Holy Revelation]), but I had to begin my work anew since I was unable to shorten anything from the book *Introduction to Revelation*, despite the fact that I wrote it myself." She ends the foreword on a humble note, reminding readers of God's special work for the poor and feeble, such as herself: "May the Lord our God, who sealed and guarded his truth in his wretched handmaid, also lead you to salvation so that the beloved reader may thus flee all evil and come to stand before the Son of Man in his world to come!"[59]

Johanna Eleonora was part of the Pietist circles of the 1670s and married the notable Pietist theologian Johann Wilhelm in 1680.[60] Following a relatively quiet phase in Eutin, the family lived a few years in Lüneburg until he was divested of his office as Lutheran pastor and superintendent in 1692. Under the protection of the Brandenburg court, the couple lived off their own estate near Magdeburg and freely pursued their various theological projects. Among many other issues, they were concerned with the connection of chiliasm and apocatastasis.[61] Johanna Eleonora dedicated the majority of her written work to biblical interpretation, always seeking to ground her specific claims in Holy Scripture.[62] In her autobiography, for example, she associates her discovery of apocatastasis as a biblically anchored doctrine to a correspondence that she and her husband had led with Jane Leade and her circle.[63] According to her account, Leade and Petersen arrived at an identical insight—revealed to Leade through visions, but to Petersen through prayer and reading Scripture. She thus admonished Leade and the other English followers of Jakob Böhme "that you must prefer Holy Scripture over visions and carefully examine everything according to this divine rule. Similarly, I do not take the visions I see in my dreams as the basis of divine truth, although I do see them as truthful guidance by which the Lord leads me in examining Holy Scripture."[64] According to Petersen, God revealed himself to her both through the Bible as well as dreams. This twofold path to the truth follows a long line of Pietist interest in charting continued revelations from God and underlies their openness to enthusiastic phenomena.

In *The Revelation of Jesus Christ Explained*, the author interprets the New Testament book of Revelation in different ways. As we saw with her rendering of Rev 1:8, Johanna Eleonora puts additional words in the mouth of the apostle John. She continues in verse 9 as follows: "I John, who also am your brother and companion in tribulation, and in the kingdom (that will succeed the tribulation) and in the patience of Jesus Christ (through whose power we endure with him that we may reign with him, I) was in the isle that is called Patmos (where I was in exile)." After Rev 1:11, the seer John again hears a voice that says, "I am the Alpha and the Omega." Petersen then takes on the role of a commentator explaining the passage to the readers: "(here something very profound is uttered, which is why it is repeated so that John may learn to recognize that Christ is the true God and the eternal life, for He is called the beginning and the end, the first and the last, in whom all things exist, have their beginning, and find their consummation)."[65] In the following verses on John's mission to write the churches, Petersen intersperses long elaborations about the specific locations. On the name "Philadelphia," she fills an entire print page with her interpretation of the eschaton's beginning events:

> unto Philadelphia (which prefigures the time when the nature of the Antichrist becomes more recognized, and the faith which is at work through love arises once again, which had ceased in Sardis and which instead was filled with the carnal teachings, as is reflected by the name. [During this Philadelphian dispensation], brotherly love is again extended out of faith and the few who were suppressed in Sardis are encouraged and prevail by faith. The Reformation advances and many are turning to the gospel, even though it will also once again be fiercely denied by others. But at the end of this time, as prefigured by the congregation [of Philadelphia], faith and love will flourish most gloriously, since those who grow in the divine life and give evidence of it, will thus be able to receive the seal of God, as ch. 7 will show you . . .).[66]

As these publications illustrate, Petersen believed that she was already living in the times described in Revelation as the Philadelphian dispensation. Her commentary following Rev 22:6 conveys her eager expectation of the latter-day final restitution and redemption of all things, "in which things are being progressively renewed until everything has become new." During the millennial age, those who had been reborn in faith "will first reign for a thousand years and then in the eternity of eternities with their prince who rules over all kings; and as priests in and with Christ they exercise their office in the final restoration and carry out their office as priests of God and Christ until everything is restored, and God is all in all." The uncovering of this truth about the restitution of all things, according to Petersen, had been preserved until the latter days.

Similar to how Petersen amends what the apostle John says, she also puts words in Jesus's mouth when she comments on Rev 22:13 as follows: "I am the Alpha and Omega, the beginning and the end (and thus together with the Father the one true God, am the beginning, through whom all things were created, and the end, as the restorer of all things), the first (in the goings forth, Mic 5:1) and the last." By making Christ proclaim her views on the apocatastasis, she seeks the ultimate legitimacy for her claim. She also utilizes her variant reading of Revelation to prove the millennial kingdom and expectation of the final restoration as necessary for salvation. In *The Revelation of Jesus Christ Explained*, she comments on Rev 22:19, writing that in the last days "many will deny that this great book is a divine book and demean it, as if it was not essential to the faith, although it is in this book that one obtains the blessedness of one's soul." In another interpretive variant in her 1706 edition, Petersen writes herself into the book of Revelation as a speaking persona by rendering the last verse as follows: "Even so, come, Lord Jesus (says his loyal witness John and she, who writes this, cries with him from the depths of the heart: Even so, come, Lord Jesus. This is followed by the apostolic blessing:) The grace of our Lord Jesus Christ be with you all. Amen. AMEN."[67]

While *The Revelation of Jesus Christ Explained* may be based on the New Testament book of Revelation, the original text is at times barely discernible through her extensive annotations. Petersen presents a de facto new Revelation documenting her readings and interpretations of the Bible. Her biblical exegesis thereby combines the Pietist maxim to examine all Christian teaching and life according to the Bible with the Pietist drive for personal, direct access to God and Christ. As an early modern Pietist, she connects these elements with her understanding of the continuing nature of God's revelation. In this way, she presents her biblical interpretations as legitimate and necessary for salvation, although only few contemporary Pietists actually shared her specific beliefs.

"Spreading the Word of God More Abundantly Among Us"— Concluding Remarks

Spener's quest from 1675 to spread "the Word of God more abundantly among us" can be found in almost all Pietist undertakings, although in very different forms. Their attempt to base all Christian teachings and practices on Holy Scripture is only one characteristic that explains Pietism. The three examples examined in this chapter illustrate how other factors besides the biblical text itself affect its interpretation. Their aspiration to follow the Word of God directly displays the breadth of biblical hermeneutics common in Lutheran churches in the late seventeenth and early eighteenth centuries. The contributions of international networks played a central role, as the examples of Johann Georg Gichtel, Jane Leade, Anna Maria von Schurmann, and William Penn show. Laypersons—in this case, a highly educated lawyer and two exceptionally well-educated women—were more limited due to their status. However, they also had more freedom since they were not held to the same standards as ordained, male theologians. They could deviate from doctrinal standards, such as the *Confessio Augustana*, without endangering their professional and material livelihood. The two female authors did not pursue specific interpretive strategies to highlight their positions as women, even if they occasionally mentioned their gender in their works. Rather, their primary aim was to present themselves as members and representatives of their networks in order to espouse and defend the aims of these Pietist communities. Scharschmidt, Schütz, and Petersen formulated Pietist maxims in the conviction that they were genuinely doing justice to the correct interpretation of Holy Scripture. What all of their works published between 1677 and 1706 have in common is that they refer back to the Luther Bible translation even though they knew it contained flaws. While other Pietists during this time period published their own translations, these three continued to use the edition approbated by the Lutheran Church, thereby signaling a certain ongoing adherence to this tradition—in spite of all other deviations. Yet their insistence on a *praxis pietatis* that strictly followed the Bible increasingly distanced them from the practices of piety common in the church communities they had grown up in.

Although at the time Schütz, Scharschmidt, and Petersen were well connected with Pietist groups in their respective regions and beyond, they hardly exerted any influence on later generations. While Spener's and Francke's writings continued to be read in the "awakening movements" (*Erweckungsbewegungen*) of the nineteenth century, those of the authors discussed in this chapter were not. Except for Johanna Eleonora Petersen, they were all but forgotten. And even Petersen became a marginal figure in the history of radical

Pietism, remembered mostly in association with her husband. It was only with the recent rise of women's history and gender studies that a new culture of memory began to develop that also includes these female Pietists.

Notes

1. Philipp Jakob Spener, *Das Geistliche Priesterthum Auß Göttlichem Wort Kürtzlich beschrieben* . . . (Frankfurt am Main: Johann David Zunner, 1677), 37–38.
2. Ibid., 27.
3. Ibid., 63–64. Spener refers to Gal 3:28.
4. Philipp Jakob Spener, *Pia Desideria oder Hertzliches Velangen Nach Gottgefälliger Besserung* . . . , ed. Kurt Aland, 3rd ed. (Berlin: De Gruyter, 1964), 53, 58.
5. Martin Brecht, "Philipp Jakob Spener, sein Programm und dessen Auswirkungen," in *GdP*, 1:278–389.
6. Klaus vom Orde, "Frankfurt am Main," in *Pietismus Handbuch*, ed. Wolfgang Breul and Thomas Hahn-Bruckart (Tübingen: Mohr Siebeck, 2021), 212–15.
7. Susanne Schuster, *Aemilie Juliane von Schwarzburg-Rudolstadt und Ahasver Fritsch: Eine Untersuchung zur Jesusfrömmigkeit im späten 17. Jahrhundert* (Leipzig: Evangelische Verlagsanstalt, 2006).
8. Ulrike Gleixner, "Pietism and Gender: Self-Modelling and Agency," in *A Companion to German Pietism, 1660–1800*, ed. Douglas H. Shantz (Leiden: Brill, 2015), 421–71; Pia Schmid, ed., *Gender im Pietismus: Netzwerke und Geschlechterkonstruktionen* (Halle: Verlag der Franckeschen Stiftungen, 2015); Ruth Albrecht, Ulrike Gleixner, and Corinna Kirschstein, eds., *Pietismus und Adel: Genderhistorische Studien* (Halle: Verlag der Franckeschen Stiftungen, 2018).
9. Spener, *Geistliches Priesterthum*, 29.
10. Philipp Jakob Spener, *Sendschreiben An Einen Christeyffrigen außländischen Theologum* . . . (Frankfurt am Main: Johann David Zunner, 1677), 77–78.
11. Thomas Hahn-Bruckart, "Bibel," in Breul and Hahn-Bruckart, *Pietismus Handbuch*, 420–27.
12. On these characteristics, see, among others, W. R. Ward, *Early Evangelicalism: A Global Intellectual History, 1670–1789* (Cambridge: Cambridge University Press, 2006).
13. Johann Jacob Schütz, *Christliche Lebens=Reguln / Oder vielmehr Außerlesene Sprüche auß dem N. Testament* . . . (Frankfurt am Main: Johann David Zunner, 1677), b2v; Andreas Deppermann, *Johann Jakob Schütz und die Anfänge des Pietismus* (Tübingen: Mohr Siebeck, 2002), 171–80.
14. Schütz, *Christliche Lebens=Reguln*, b4r-v.
15. See Deppermann, *Johann Jakob Schütz*, 172–74.
16. Ibid., 171.
17. Ibid., 62; 58–60; 62–65, 327–35, 180–95, 175.
18. Schütz, *Christliche Lebens=Reguln*, 620, 635, 628, 635–36.
19. Other forms of her name include Scharschmied and Schaarschmid.
20. Martin Schulz, *Johann Heinrich Sprögel und die pietistische Bewegung Quedlinburgs* (DTheol diss., Martin-Luther-Universität Halle-Wittenberg, 1974); Katja Lißmann, *Schreiben im Netzwerk: Briefe von Frauen als Praktiken frommer Selbst-Bildung im frühen Quedlinburger Pietismus* (Halle: Verlag der Franckeschen Stiftungen, 2019).
21. Lißmann, *Schreiben im Netzwerk*, 81–180.
22. Although she is remembered this way, other sources show that she was, at first, quite open to Pietism. See Klaus vom Orde, "Die ersten Kontakte Johann Heinrich Sprögels und

Anna Dorothea von Sachsen, Stiftäbtissing zu Quedlinburg, mit Philipp Jakob Spener," *PuN* 42 (2017): 65–86.

23. Magdalena Sophie von Schleswig-Holstein-Sonderburg-Wiesenburg (1664–1720); see Lißmann, *Schreiben im Netzwerk*, 94–96.

24. Cf. ibid., 128–38. Quedlinburg Pietism was characterized by women who garnered attention through their ecstasies and prophesies. See Ulrike Witt, *Bekehrung, Bildung und Biographie: Frauen im Umkreis des Halleschen Pietismus* (Tübingen: Niemeyer, 1996); Ryoko Mori, *Begeisterung und Ernüchterung in christlicher Vollkommenheit: Pietistische Selbst- und Weltwahrnehmung im ausgehenden 17. Jahrhundert* (Halle: Verlag der Franckeschen Stiftungen, 2004); Claudia Wustmann, *Die "begeisterten Mägde": Mitteldeutsche Prophetinnen im Radikalpietismus am Ende des 17. Jahrhunderts* (Berlin: Kirchhof & Franke, 2008); Ruth Albrecht, ed., *Begeisterte Mägde: Träume, Visionen und Offenbarungen von Frauen im frühen Pietismus* (Leipzig: Evangelische Verlagsanstalt, 2018); Markus Matthias, "Der Geist auf den Mägden: Zum Zusammenhang von Enthusiasmus und Geschichtsauffassung im mitteldeutschen Pietismus," *PuN* 43 (2019): 71–99.

25. Information provided through a letter by Christoph Schröter from January 13, 2020, who consulted the church books at St. Nikolai Church. I thank Katja Lißmann for this information.

26. The birth and death of this child the following year are also verifiable by the church records. Ibid. On F. C. Scharschmidt, see Lißmann, *Schreiben im Netzwerk*, 108–13.

27. Lißmann, *Schreiben im Netzwerk*, 136. While we know that Schütz's reading of Tauler was decisive in his conversion, we know virtually nothing about Scharschmidt's religious biography up until the 1690s. On the diverse interpretations of the conversion process in German Pietism, see Jonathan Strom, *German Pietism and the Problem of Conversion* (University Park: Penn State University Press, 2018).

28. Anna Catharina Scharschmidt, *Das Hochwichtige Werck der Wiedergeburt: Aus Christlichem Hertzen geflossen* (n.p., 1702). See Ruth Albrecht and Katja Lißmann, "Mit Freude, Angst und Qual auf dem Weg zur Wiederherstellung der Androgynität: Anna Catharina Scharschmidts Hochwichtiges Werk der Wiedergeburt (1702)," in *Gefühl und Norm. Religion und Gefühlskulturen im 18. Jahrhundert. Beiträge zum V. Internationalen Kongress für Pietismusforschung 2018*, ed. Daniel Cyranka et al. (Halle: Verlag der Franckesche Stiftungen 2021), 623–36.

29. Anna Catharina Scharschmidt, *Einfältiges Zeugniß Von dem wahren Dienste des Geistes im Neuen Bunde* . . . (n.p., 1703). Albrecht and Lißmann are currently preparing a critical edition of this tract for the series Edition Pietismus Texte, published by Evangelische Verlagsanstalt in Leipzig.

30. Anna Catharina Scharschmidt, *Nützlicher Auszug Aus Joh. Angeli Silesii, Cherubinischen Wandersmann* (n.p, 1704). The first edition of Silesius's work, in five books, was published in 1657, and the extended edition was published in 1675. See Angelus Silesius (Johannes Scheffler), *Cherubinischer Wandersmann: Kritische Ausgabe*, ed. Louise Gnädinger (Stuttgart: Philipp Reclam, 2000), 355–64. For the English edition, see Silesius, *The Cherubinic Wanderer*, ed. Maria Shrady (Mahwah, NJ: Paulist Press, 1986).

31. Dieter Breuer, "Angelus Silesius," in *Religion in Geschichte und Gegenwart* (Tübingen: Mohr Siebeck, 1998), 1:483.

32. Scharschmidt, *Einfältiges Zeugniß*, 99; Johannis Angeli Silesii [Angelus Silesius], *Cherubinischer Wandersmann*, ed. Gottfried Arnold (Frankfurt am Main: Johann David Zunner, 1701), book 1, no. 61. All following details on this work refer to Arnold's edition, if not specifically labeled as Scharschmidt's or Gnädinger's.

33. Scharschmidt, *Einfältiges Zeugniß*, 99; and *Cherubinischer Wandersmann*, book 1, nos. 62 and 63.

34. Scharschmidt, *Einfältiges Zeugniß*, 100.

35. Gnädinger, in her edition of *Cherubinischer Wandersmann*, 355, mentions Gottfried Arnold's edition but not Scharschmidt's.

36. An example of this may be the opus thought to have been written by Susanna Margaretha Sprögel, Johann Heinrich Sprögel's wife. Arnold edited the work without mentioning the author. It consists of short treatises that are not closely related. Jakob Böhme's influence is clearly identifiable: *Consilia und Responsa Theologica: Oder Gottsgelehrte Rathschläge und Antworten . . . , gemein gemacht von Gottfried Arnold* (Frankfurt am Main: Thomas Fritsch, 1705).

37. Scharschmidt, *Einfältiges Zeugniß*, 65; and Lißmann, *Schreiben im Netzwerk*, 315.

38. *Frauen Annen Catharinen Scharschmiedin gebohrnen HeydFeldin*, 91–92. Printed in Johann Heinrich Sprögel, *Gründliche Beantwortung derer so genanten Unverwerfflichen Zeugnüße . . .* (n.p., 1703)

39. Ruth Albrecht and Katja Lißmann, "Undoing gender als Bibelinterpretation im Quedlinburger pietistischen Netzwerk," in *La Querelle des Femmes: Die Bibel und die Frauen; Eine exegetisch-kulturgeschichtliche Enzyklopädie*, vol. 6.3, ed. Angela Munoz Fernandez and Xenia von Tippelskirch (Stuttgart: Kohlhammer, forthcoming).

40. Scharschmidt, *Das Hochwichtige Werck*, 53.

41. Scharschmidt, *Einfältiges Zeugniß*, Vorwort, 5r.

42. Ibid., 106; cf. 105–12.

43. Ibid., 54.

44. Scharschmidt refers to Eph 4:15.

45. The appendix contains excerpts from *Geistliche Hirtenlieder* by the same author. However, the publisher is not given. On these shepherd songs, see *Cherubinischer Wandersmann* (ed. Gnädinger), 381.

46. As reference, the numbers of the six books by Arnold and Scharschmidt are given: (1) 302/132; (2) 258/128; (3) 249/139; (4) 229/129; (5) 374/175; (6) 263/106.

47. *Cherubinischer Wandersmann*, book 1, no. 23, 169, 210, 286.

48. Ibid., book 1, no. 74.

49. The findings in the other books are somewhat similar: In book 2, fifteen citations derive from John and fifteen from Romans; in book 3, twenty verses derive from Matthew and thirteen from John. Book 4 puts a special emphasis on the Psalms, book 5 on 1 Corinthians, and book 6 on Matthew.

50. Scharschmidt, *Nützlicher Auszug*, 1.

51. Scharschmidt's edition here mistakenly lists no. 252, which thereby occurs twice.

52. *Nützlicher Auszug*, nos. 17 and 216.

53. Ibid., nos. 24 and 284.

54. Shirley Brückner, "Die Providenz im Zettelkasten: Divinatorische Lospraktiken in der pietistischen Frömmigkeit," in *Geschichtsbewusstsein und Zukunftserwartung in Pietismus und Erweckungsbewegung*, ed. Wolfgang Breul and Jan Carsten Schnurr (Göttingen: Vandenhoeck & Ruprecht, 2013), 351–66; Hahn-Bruckart, "Bibel," 425–27.

55. Aira Võsa, *Johann Georg Gichtel—teosoofilise idee kandja varauusaegses Euroopas*, Dissertationes theologiae Universitatis Tartuensis 10 (Tartu: Tartu Ülikooli Kirjastus, 2006), 298–305 (these pages contain a summary of the work in German). On Gichtel's correspondence with partners from Quedlinburg, see Gertraud Zaepernick, "Johann Georg Gichtels und seiner Nachfolger Briefwechsel mit den Hallischen Pietisten, besonders mit A.M. Francke," *PuN* 8 (1982): 74–118, esp. 114–18. See also Julie Hirst, *Jane Leade: Biography of a Seventeenth-Century Mystic* (London: Routledge, 2005). The work *Consilia und Responsa* is especially characterized by Sophia-mystical aspects that could be explained by Scharschmidt knowing Leade's work and perhaps even Leade herself.

56. Johanna Eleonora Petersen, *Die verklährte Offenbahrung JEsu Christi nach dem Zusammenhang des Geistes deutlich gezeigt* (n.p., 1706).

57. Markus Matthias, *Johann Wilhelm und Johanna Eleonora Petersen: Eine Biographie bis zur Amtsenthebung Petersens im Jahre 1692* (Göttingen: Vandenhoeck & Ruprecht, 1993).

58. Albrecht, *Johanna Eleonora Petersen: Theologische Schriftstellerin des frühen Pietismus* (Göttingen: Vandenhoeck & Ruprecht, 2005), 245–64, 295–98.

59. Petersen, *Verklährte Offenbahrung*, Vorrede, a2r.

60. Albrecht, *Petersen*; Albrecht, "Johanna Eleonora Petersen," in Breul and Hahn-Bruckart, *Pietismus Handbuch*, 114–21. Petersen's turn to Pietism was influenced by the devotional life at the court of the family of Schleswig-Holstein-Sonderburg-Wiesenburg. However, we have little information on Petersen's religious development before she arrived in Frankfurt. See Albrecht, *Petersen*, 42–57.

61. Markus Matthias, "Das Ehepaar Petersen und die theologische Aufklärung," in *"Erinnern, was vergessen ist": Beiträge zur Kirchen-, Frömmigkeits- und Gendergeschichte; Festschrift für Ruth Albrecht*, ed. Rainer Hering and Manfred Jakubowski-Tiessen (Husum: Matthiesen Verlag, 2020), 83–98.

62. Ruth Albrecht, "Pietismus und Mystik: Verknüpfung von Bibellektüre und visionären Erleben bei Johanna Eleonora Petersen," in *"Dir hat vor den Frauen nicht gegraut": Mystikerinnen und Theologinnen in der Christentumsgeschichte*, ed. Mariano Delgado and Volker Leppin (Fribourg: Kohlhammer, 2015), 192–216.

63. On Gichtel's role as a mediator in this correspondence, see Ruth Albrecht, "Zum Briefwechsel Johann Georg Gichtels mit Johanna Eleonora Petersen," in *Der radikale Pietismus: Perspektiven der Forschung*, ed. Wolfgang Breul, Marcus Meier, and Lothar Vogel (Göttingen: Vandenhoeck & Ruprecht, 2010), 327–58.

64. Johanna Eleonora Petersen, *Leben, von ihr selbst mit eigener Hand aufgesetzt*, ed. Prisca Guglielmetti (Leipzig: Evangelische Verlagsanstalt, 2003), 41; Barbara Becker-Cantarino, ed., *The Life of Lady Johanna Eleonora Petersen, Written by Herself: Pietism and Women's Autobiography in Seventeenth-Century Germany* (Chicago: University of Chicago Press, 2005).

65. Petersen, *Verklährte Offenbahrung*, 5–6.

66. Ibid., 7.

67. Ibid., 172, 175, 178–79, 280.

9

"MY BELOVED IS WHITE AND RUDDY"

Particular Baptist Readings of the Song of Songs
in the Long Eighteenth Century

MICHAEL A. G. HAYKIN

"The Canonicalness of Solomon's Song"

The long eighteenth century saw the publication of some thirty-five English translations or paraphrases of the Song of Songs.[1] Toward its close yet one more was added by the Calvinist preacher Thomas Williams (1755–1839), a theological author whose rebuttal of Thomas Paine's *The Age of Reason* had enjoyed a mild degree of popularity in the mid-1790s.[2] In the long term, Williams's translation of the Solomonic text did not prove to be especially noteworthy, but an anonymous review of this translation in the short-lived journal *The Biblical Magazine* piqued the interest of the Particular Baptist divine Andrew Fuller (1754–1815).[3] The reviewer had raised the question as to Solomon's intent in writing the poem: did he have any "spiritual intentions in reference to the Messiah," or had this interpretation of the text as an allegory been introduced by "some pious teachers in the Jewish church to illustrate the sublime connection between the Son of God and his church," in a manner similar to Paul's allegorical treatment of Sarah and Hagar in Gal 4?[4]

This question particularly intrigued Fuller, for a few years earlier he had penned a defense of the allegorical reading of the Song of Songs in a series of six letters to a close friend that came to be entitled *Strictures on Some of the Leading Sentiments of Mr. R. Robinson*.[5] Fuller's antagonist in this latter work, Robert Robinson (1735–1790),[6] was a well-known preacher and author in the English Particular Baptist and Nonconformist communities, though during the 1780s serious questions had arisen over his commitment to the classic formulation of Nicene Trinitarianism.[7] Fuller's first pastorate in the 1770s had been in the village of Soham, Cambridgeshire, twenty or so miles from Robinson's church in the university town of Cambridge, but neither of the two men nor their congregations were especially close.[8] By the mid- to late 1780s, in fact, Fuller had come to be critical of Robinson's thinking in a number of areas, including the latter's conviction that common sense is entirely sufficient to understand the Bible and that, therefore, to resort to allegory is "all froth and nonsense."[9] For proof of Robinson's categorical rejection of allegorical exegesis, Fuller turned to Robinson's "A Brief Dissertation on the Ministration of the Divine Word by Publick Preaching," which formed something of a preface to his translation of Jean Claude's (1619–1687) manual on sermon composition, *An Essay on the Composition of a Sermon* (*Traité de la composition d'un sermon*).[10] Discussing preaching and exegesis in the patristic era, Robinson observed, "The fathers were fond of allegory, for Origen, that everlasting allegorizer, had set them the example. I hope they had better proofs of the canonicalness of Solomon's Song, than I have had the pleasure of seeing."[11] On the basis of Robinson's conviction that the Scriptures must be plainly interpreted, Fuller deduced from this remark that Robinson was calling into question the canonicity of the Song of Songs, for both men regarded it as an impossibility that "a mere love-song [had been added] to the sacred canon."[12] Robinson's singling out of Origen (ca. 185–254) as the exemplar of a defective exegete was commonplace in the Protestant tradition of exegesis. John Calvin (1509–1564), for example, accused him of "distorting Scripture ... away from its natural meaning." François Turretini (1623–1687) also believed the Alexandrian author to be guilty of unwarranted allegorization, for "he failed to observe proper limits" in his exegetical discussions.[13]

Fuller was prepared to admit that the soil from which the Song of Songs sprang was the genre of the Ancient Near Eastern epithalamium. But he was also convinced that there were expressions in the canonical book that "are totally inapplicable to anything but what is Divine." For instance, Fuller argued that when the bride is compared to "a company of horses in Pharaoh's chariots" (Song 1:9), this, if referring to the church, is "a fine representation of her union, order, and activity, in her social capacity." But taken literally, "how a female ... can be likened to 'a company of horses,' I am at a loss to conceive." Fuller was similarly nonplussed at the idea of the bridegroom declaring his beloved to be "terrible as an army with banners" (Song 6:10): "How this could be a recommendation of one of Solomon's wives I cannot conceive. But apply it to the church of Christ, and it beautifully sets forth the terror with which their testimony, attended with unity, order, zeal, and inflexible piety, strikes the enemies of God. Mary, queen of Scots, declared that she feared the prayers of John Knox more than an army of ten thousand men!"[14]

Further examples that Fuller cited were not discussed in any detail: "I am the rose of Sharon, and the lily of the valley [Song 2:1]—white and ruddy—the chief among ten thousand [Song 5:10], and the altogether lovely [Song 5:16]." Such expressions, Fuller averred, are "impossible to drop from the pen of any mere creature," for if applied to oneself, they would bespeak "a stark fool." In fine, Fuller was conscious that his position was one that had been held by "holy men ... in all ages" who have found in this portion of the Old Testament "a holy tendency ... to raise in their minds a flame of genuine and ardent affection towards Him who is the subject of the Song—'The chief among ten thousand, the altogether lovely' [cf. Song 5:10b, 16]."[15]

This essay focuses on one of the passages cited by Fuller that he did not choose to exposit, namely Song 5:10a, "My beloved is white and ruddy."[16] The biblicism of the eighteenth-century English Particular Baptist community has long been known and to a certain degree demonstrated,[17] but the exact shape of its biblical exegesis remains almost wholly terra incognita. This essay is a small step toward the exploration of this realm of Particular Baptist exegesis, which, it will be seen, is far more complex than might be assumed. Of course, Particular Baptist reflection on the Song of Songs was not unique to them: they, along with other Protestant and evangelical commentators in the eighteenth-century transatlantic world, were regularly reading and reflecting on this biblical text, both as an aid to devotion and as a source of Christological and ecclesiological principles.[18] What is notable about eighteenth-century exegesis of the Song is the absence of the historico-prophetic readings that were so popular with Anglophone Puritans, continental Pietists, and Dutch Reformed exegetes in the seventeenth century. A more personal and devotional reading of this book appears to have triumphed over an older reading that was sometimes apocalyptic. After a brief overview of various readings of Song 5:10a in two eras in the history of interpretation—the patristic and Puritan—this essay focuses on three Baptist commentators from the eighteenth century: Joseph Stennett I (1663–1713), a widely respected denominational leader from a Seventh-day Baptist background; John Gill (1697–1771), the gifted autodidact who was considered by many as the iconic doyen of the denomination for much of the eighteenth century; and Anne Dutton (1692–1765), who had significant links to the evangelical revival and was the most-published female theological author of that era.

"Holy Men in All Ages"

Fuller's statement that his reading of the Song of Songs, and in particular Song 5:10a, was one held by "holy men ... in all ages" places him in a long line of Christian interpretation stretching back to the patristic era. The Alexandrian exegete Origen, for example, established a basic line of interpreting this text when he understood the two colors to be speaking about distinct elements of the person of Christ and his work.[19] The twofold description of the beloved as *leukos kai pyrrhos* is a reference first to Christ's divinity—"white, because he is the true God"—and then to his salvific work on the cross—"red on account of the blood which was poured out on behalf of the church."[20] Fortunatianus of Aquileia (ca. 300–ca. 360) similarly saw the reference to redness in this verse to be an allusion to the outpouring of "blood with water from his [i.e., Christ's] side when he had been struck by the soldier's spear."[21] This line of exegesis is crystallized for many in the Middle Ages by the Anglo-Saxon commentator Bede (673–735), for whom Christ is "white because when he appeared in the flesh 'he committed no sin, and no deceit was found in his mouth' [1 Pet 2:22], and ruddy because 'he washed us from our sins by his blood' [Rev 1:5]. And appropriately is he first white, then ruddy, because he first comes into the world innocent of blood and afterward goes out of the world bloody from his passion."[22]

With the Cappadocian theologian Gregory of Nyssa (ca. 335–ca. 395), however, the interpretation of this text took a different trajectory. He noted that "the mingling of these two colors" of Song 5:10a produces a hue characteristic of "flesh,"[23] which bespeaks the humanity assumed by the divine Word, ever a central concern of the Cappadocian author. In Nyssen's words, Christ is called "white and ruddy" since he "made our life his own through flesh and blood ... in being born of virginal purity."[24] It needs to be noted that the use of a term like "mingling" to describe the relationship between the humanity and divinity does not entail a monophysite Christology. Nyssen's firm rebuttal of Apollinarianism as well as his employment of definite diphysite terms reveals a "rich and balanced Christology" that is in harmony with the Symbol of Chalcedon.[25]

Here, then, we have two interpretative pathways: an Origenist one that keeps the white and the red of Song 5:10a separate and sees them speaking of contrasts in the person and work of Christ, and a Gregorian one that highlights the color that results from the blending of white and red together, what we call "pink," and sees this as a reference to the incarnation, which united divinity and humanity in one person.

He "Became Ruddy for Our Sakes"

As noted above in connection with Origen's allegorization, Protestant hermeneutical practices in principle were overtly hostile to allegorical interpretation. This hostility was due in large measure to the conviction, well expressed by the English Reformed theologian William Perkins (1558–1602), that "there is one full and entire sense of every place of Scripture, and that is also the literal sense, sometimes expressed in proper, and sometimes in borrowed or figurative speeches," for "to make many senses of Scripture, is to overturn all senses, and to make nothing certain."[26] But, as Keith Stanglin has noted, it would be an interpretative error to identify what Perkins here called "the literal sense" with the modern notion of human authorial intent.[27] Perkins, and the Protestant tradition in the early modern era, allowed for "figurative" readings, for as Perkins noted a few lines after the above statement, "Scripture is not only penned in the proper terms, but also in sundry divine figures and allegories. The song of Solomon is an allegory borrowed from the fellowship of man and wife, to signify the communion of between Christ and his Church: & so is the 45th Psalm."[28] In trying to determine whether or not a text admits of a figurative interpretation, Perkins gave three hermeneutical boundaries: "If the proper signification of the words be against common reason, or against the analogy of faith, or against good manners [morals], they are not then to be taken properly, but by figure."[29] In the world of early modern exegesis—as typified by Fuller's comments noted earlier—it seemed obvious that a literal interpretation of the Song of Solomon was against "good manners."

Thus, in a posthumous work on the communion between Christ and his people, the Puritan author Richard Sibbes (1577–1635) described Song 5:10a as a "misticall portion of Scripture,"[30] and followed, knowingly or unknowingly, Nyssen's interpretative line. Sibbes noted that white and red together make the "carnation colour,"[31] a chromatic designation that dated from the mid-fifteenth century and would later be termed "pink."[32] This most beautiful of colors, in Sibbes's judgment—he called it "the purest and the best" of the color range—was the most appropriate way to set forth "that excellent and sweet mixture" of divine and human that "makes such a gracefulness in Christ."[33]

In 1642, Sibbes's student John Cotton (1584–1652) also published a series of sermons on Solomon's Song. Like Sibbes, he was convinced of a Christological reading of Song 5:10a, but, following the interpretative path laid down by Origen, he differed from his mentor in seeing a contrast between the two colors. The whiteness of Christ spoke of his "innocency of true holinesse," while the red foreshadowed "the ruddy scarlet dye of his death."[34]

Nearly ten years later, Cotton's fellow Congregationalist John Owen (1616–1683) agreed with Sibbes that "white and ruddy" are "a due mixture of... colours" that constitute "the most beautifull complexion." In the same context, Owen maintained that the particular beauty of Christ owed much to the union of natures in his one person. One would expect Owen then to link the "carnation colour" to the incarnate Christ, and follow the Gregorian interpretation of Song 5:10a. Instead, in the Origenist vein of interpretation, Owen focused on the two colors and saw them as representative of three distinct contrasts. First, Christ is "white in the glory of his deity," but red "in the preciousness of his humanity." Then, the Messiah is "white in the beauty of his innocency, and holinesse," but ruddy "by being drenched all over in his own blood" and having our sins, "whose colour is red and crimson"—a reference to Isa 1:18—imputed to him. He "who was white, became ruddy for our sakes," Owen declared with Puritan pithiness. Yet a third contrast was that the Lord Jesus is "white in love and mercy" to his people, but "red with justice and revenge towards his enemies."[35]

"In My Love's Cheeks"

One of the first translations/paraphrases of the Song of Songs in the long eighteenth century was that by the Particular Baptist Joseph Stennett I, who was one of the most prominent Dissenters of his day.[36] It says much for the general respect in which he was held that an Anglican prelate once remarked that if Stennett were willing to relinquish his Baptist convictions and join the Established Church, no post within that church would be beyond his merit.[37] He had received a superb education at Wallingford Grammar School, Berkshire, which enabled him to become fluent in French and Italian and extremely proficient in the Hebrew and Greek Scriptures. Stennett was converted at a young age and had an early desire to be a theologian like his father, Edward Stennett (1627/28–1705), a leading Sabbatarian apologist. His theological reading included an extensive study of the church fathers, which would have exposed him to their interpretation of the Song of Songs. He joined Pinner's Hall Seventh-day Baptist Church in London in the autumn of 1686 and four years later was ordained as a pastor of this congregation, where he served for the next twenty-three years till his death in 1713.

Stennett was also active as a scholar, translating works from French and publishing his own paraphrase of the Hebrew Song of Songs in 1700, which he wrote in such a way that it could be sung in worship. Stennett was well aware that there had been a slender thread of opinion among exegetes in the history of the church—Stennett specifically named Theodore of Mopsuestia (ca. 350–428) and the Dutch jurist and exegete Hugo Grotius (1583–1645)—who regarded Solomon's design in writing this book as little more than "celebrating his Amours with Pharaoh's Daughter, or some other person." The vast majority of commentators, though, understood the book in a "Mystical Sense," setting forth "the mutual Love of Christ and his Church." Supporting this majority opinion, Stennett argued, were Ps 45, which "celebrates the same mystical Espousals and very much in the same strain," and the use of marital imagery with reference to God's relationship to his people throughout the Scriptures. Moreover, if Solomon were actually one of the principals in the Song, "is it to be imagined that he would speak so largely in his own praise, and magnify his own Beauty in so high a degree?"[38]

Illustrative of this latter point was Song 5:10a, which Stennett renders thus: "In my Love's Cheeks pure White and Red / In just degrees their mixture spread."[39] Here Stennett localized the colors of Song 5:10a to the Bridegroom's cheeks, added the adjective "pure"—an influence of the Origenist tradition's contrast of the colors?—and spoke of "their mixture," a phrase used by both the Origenist and Gregorian hermeneutical perspectives.[40] Now, Stennett's reflection might seem a paltry one compared to those of John Gill and Anne Dutton discussed below, but it serves to reinforce the continuity between the Particular Baptist tradition and earlier exegetes all the way back to Origen.

"The Compleatest Beauty"

The most famous Baptist author for much of the eighteenth century was undoubtedly the London pastor John Gill, whose insatiable desire for learning was foundational to his voluminous literary output.[41] Gill was born in Kettering, Northamptonshire, at the end of the Puritan era in 1697, and his early schooling was at a local grammar school. This formal education came to an abrupt end in 1708, though, when the school's headmaster demanded that all of his pupils attend Anglican morning prayer. Gill's parents were decided Dissenters and consequently withdrew their son from the school. His parents had limited financial resources—Gill's father, Edward, was a wool merchant—and could not afford to send their son to a Dissenting academy, so Gill's formal studies were over. But this did not check their son's hunger for learning. Gill had acquired a good working knowledge of Latin and Greek before leaving school, and by nineteen he was not only adept in both of these languages, but also well on the way to becoming proficient in Hebrew. Knowledge of these three languages gave him ready access to a wealth of scriptural and theological knowledge, which he used to great advantage in the years that followed as he pastored Goat Yard Chapel, Southwark (later Carter Lane Baptist Church), in London from 1719 to 1771 and became what the American preacher Samuel Davies once described as "the celebrated Baptist Minister."[42] Gill, a High Calvinist, has been seen as implacably hostile to the evangelical revival. Yet he counted among his close friends the evangelical hymn writer Augustus M. Toplady (1740–1778), and numerous evangelicals avidly read his works. For instance, when William Williams Pantycelyn (1717–1791), one of the central figures of eighteenth-century Welsh Calvinistic Methodism and the author of "Guide Me, O Thou Great Jehovah," was dying in 1791, he thanked God for the "true religion" that he had found particularly in the writings of "Dr. Goodwin, Dr. Owen, Dr. Gill, Marshall, Harvey, [and] Usher."[43]

Gill's first major work was an exposition of the Song of Songs in 1728, which, according to John Rippon (1751–1836), who succeeded him as pastor, "served very much to make Mr. Gill known."[44] Gill's robust defense of Calvinism in the late 1730s, *The Cause of God and Truth* (1735–38), issued at a time when British Calvinism was very much a house in disarray, and then his commentary on the entire New Testament—his deeply learned *Exposition of the New Testament*, published in three folio volumes between 1746 and 1748—helped secure his fame as a theological author. Later, of course, there was Gill's companion to his New Testament commentary, his four-volume *Exposition of the Old Testament* (1763–66), and his magnum opus, *The Body of Doctrinal and Practical Divinity* (1769–70).

Gill's comments on Song 5:10a consisted mostly of his delineation of four main ways in which commentators in the history of Christian interpretation have understood the distinction between the two colors in this text. In other words, his discussion is fully in line with the Origenist tradition of interpretation. According to Gill, some readers of this passage have seen in them Christ's two natures, the white representing his divinity and the redness, his humanity. The union of such natures in one person reveals Christ to be "no mean, common and ordinary person," but "a glorious and extraordinary one."[45] For others, the white depicts first his "innocence, purity and holiness" and the red, his bloody sufferings for sinners. One of those who held to this interpretation, Gill noted, was the Northumbrian scholar Alcuin (ca. 735–804). Gill himself clearly favored this reading of the verse, for, as he went on to say in distinctly personal terms, "there cannot appear a more beautiful and delightful sight" to sinners than

> to see the just Jesus suffering for unjust ones, him that knew no sin, made sin for them, and the holy, harmless, innocent and unspotted lamb of God, shedding his blood for the vilest of sinners.... Would you know

what my beloved is, and wherein he excels others? I'll tell you, he's not black with original and actual sin, as you and I are; for though you see him red with sufferings, yet he was not cut off for himself, but was "wounded for our transgressions, and bruised for our iniquities" [Isa 53:3]; for in his nature and actions he is white, pure and spotless; and such a mixture of white and red, of innocence and sufferings, render him extremely amiable and lovely to me.[46]

A third reading saw in the white and the red Christ's "different administrations of mercy and justice." Though sinners' "sins be as scarlet," Christ can make them "white as snow," a reference to Isa 1:18, and clothe them in "white robes" and so enable them to "walk with [him] in white," as stated in Rev 3:4 and 7:9. Red, on the other hand, speaks of the execution of divine justice, as Gill deduced from Isa 63:1–2 and Rev 19:13. The final interpretation was that the colors spoke of "Christ's battles and victories," a view derived from the white and red horses of Rev 6:2 and 4.[47]

In the final analysis, though, Gill reckoned that while none of these interpretations violated biblical orthodoxy—"the analogy of faith"—they might be considered by some to be "too nice [that is, not readily apprehended] and curious."[48] Gill therefore opted for a simpler explanation of the pairing of the two colors. Taken together, "white and ruddy" depicted "the most healthful constitution, and the compleatest beauty," and as such must have reference to "the beauty, glory and excellency of Christ, as mediator." Gill found support for this reading in 1 Sam 16:12, where David is described as "ruddy, and withal of a beautiful countenance, and goodly to look to" (KJV). The link between Song 5:10a and 1 Sam 16:12 in Gill's mind had to be the use of the term "ruddy" in both verses, the beauty of David's countenance, and the fact that "David was an eminent type of Christ . . . in Scripture."[49]

"The Most Beautiful Person"

Possibly the most detailed eighteenth-century reflection on the Song 5:10a is that by the Baptist author Anne Dutton in her treatise *Hints of the Glory of Christ* (1748), one of a number of literary works that made her fairly well known throughout the world of transatlantic evangelicalism in the long eighteenth century.[50] Among Dutton's friends were a number of key figures in that era's evangelical revival: the remarkable preacher George Whitefield (1714–1770), the Welsh preacher Howel Harris (1714–1773), and the redoubtable Selina Hastings, the Countess of Huntingdon (1707–1791).[51] While Harris was convinced that the Lord had entrusted Dutton "with a talent of writing for him,"[52] Whitefield, who helped promote and publish Dutton's writings, once said after meeting with her, "her conversation is as weighty as her letters."[53] By 1740 she had written seven books. Another fourteen followed between 1741 and 1743, and fourteen more by 1750.[54] And there were yet more, for she continued to write up until her death in 1765. She was clearly the most prolific female Baptist author of the eighteenth century. Her writings are typical of eighteenth-century Particular Baptist piety: robustly Christ- and cross-centered.

In *Hints of the Glory of Christ*, which is a detailed study of Song 5:10–16, Dutton devoted forty-four pages to specifically noting five contrasts between Christ's whiteness and his redness, some of which had been noted by Gill in his exposition of Solomon's Song.[55] First, white bespeaks deity, while redness is a reminder of his humanity. Whiteness also stands for "the purity of his human nature, in his spotless conception, and birth, and in the whole of his life," while his being ruddy points to "the greatness of his sufferings." White also refers to Christ's victory over his enemies, while his redness, in contrast, is "his just vengeance against them, in his resurrection, ascension, and session at God's right hand." Then, whiteness is a reference to Christ's "heavenly glory as the head of the Church, both in its personal and relative branches; and [his being] ruddy, as the exalted savior." Finally, whiteness alludes to the Second Coming of Christ "as the Church's bridegroom, to save her completely from all her enemies, and marry her openly unto himself in glory," and his ruddiness depicts him "as the tremendous judge of wicked men and devils." Put all of this together, Dutton commented, and "it appears that Christ's beauty is incomparably great!"

Now, from the first of these contrasts, it is patent that Dutton had read and reflected upon John Owen's comments on this text from the Song of Songs. For as she put it, Christ is

> White: with regard to the glory of his deity. Ruddy: with respect to the truth of his humanity. His divine, and human nature, hypostatically united, are hereby intended.... Oh, this glorious mystery of the incarnation of the Son of God, in which he appears both white and ruddy! This is such a mixture that renders him the most beautiful person, in both worlds, to the eye of faith. I say, mixture: not that the divine and human natures in the person of Christ, were in the least mixed by way of confusion. The divine nature, by assuming the human, sustain'd no change. Nor was the human, by that assumption, absorpt, swallow'd up, or lost any of its essential properties. But both these natures, so vastly different,

are closely join'd in Christ. So that tho' they remain two entire, distinct natures, yet in him, they make but one person for ever.[56]

Sibbes had discussed the incarnation through the imagery of mixing together the white and the red of Song 5:10a—hence his "carnation colour." Did Dutton know of this discussion? She never used the term "carnation," but she was aware that the incarnation is a truth that can be easily misunderstood and taken to imply that an essential change occurred in one or both of the two natures in Christ. After all, when white and red are blended together to produce pink, the latter is neither white nor red, but a different color entirely. She thus stressed that in the "mixture" of the incarnation, there is neither change nor confusion of natures, an understanding wholly in sync with Chalcedonian Christology.

Coda

Richard Sibbes's opinion that "carnation," or as we would call it, pink, is the most lovely of all colors implied, in light of his exposition of Song 5:10a, that he viewed Christ as the loveliest of persons. The English Particular Baptist tradition, especially exemplified in John Gill and Anne Dutton, was in wholehearted agreement with Sibbes's estimation of the Lord Jesus. As a tradition, though, it did not follow Sibbes in his Gregorian and "pink" reading of Song 5:10a, but preferred the Origenist tradition of contrasting the two colors mentioned in this verse. In taking this tack, this Baptist tradition was in harmony with other evangelical commentators in the eighteenth-century transatlantic world, notably Jonathan Edwards (1703–1758).[57] And so it was that the Alexandrian hermeneut Origen, whom Robert Robinson snidely termed an "everlasting allegorizer" and whose exegesis was regularly cited by Protestants as a deeply flawed method of biblical interpretation, came to be the ultimate fount of Particular Baptist readings of the "white and ruddy" of Song 5:10a.[58]

Notes

For help with locating some of the resources used in this essay, I am indebted to Dr. Adam Winters and Mr. Chris Fenner, the Archivist and Digital Archivist respectively of Archives & Special Collections, Southern Baptist Theological Seminary, Louisville, Kentucky.

1. William J. Chamberlin, *Catalogue of English Bible Translations: A Classified Bibliography of Versions and Editions Including Books, Parts, and Old and New Testament Apocrypha and*

Apocryphal Books (New York: Greenwood Press, 1991), 406–11. See also Elizabeth Clarke, *Politics, Religion and the Song of Songs in Seventeenth-Century England* (London: Palgrave Macmillan, 2011).

2. Thomas Williams, *The Song of Songs, which is by Solomon: A New Translation; with A Commentary and Notes* (London: C. Whittingham for Thomas Williams, 1801).

3. *The Biblical Magazine* ran from 1801 to 1805 and was published by one of Fuller's Baptist friends, John Webster Morris (1763–1836). For studies of Fuller's life and thought, see especially E. F. Clipsham, "Andrew Fuller and Fullerism: A Study in Evangelical Calvinism," *Baptist Quarterly* 20 (1963–64): 99–114, 146–54, 214–25, 268–76; Michael A. G. Haykin, *One Heart and One Soul: John Sutcliff of Olney, His Friends, and His Times* (Darlington, UK: Evangelical Press, 1994), passim; Paul Brewster, *Andrew Fuller: Model Pastor-Theologian*, Studies in Baptist Life and Thought (Nashville, TN: B&H, 2010); Peter J. Morden, *The Life and Thought of Andrew Fuller (1754–1815)*, Studies in Evangelical History and Thought (Milton Keynes, UK: Paternoster, 2015).

4. "Review: *The Song of Songs, which is by Solomon: A new translation; with a commentary and notes*. By T. Williams," *Biblical Magazine* 3 (1803): 392. See also two other discussions of this translation in this journal, the first signed with a pen name: Ekaw, "Query on Solomon's Song," *Biblical Magazine* 3 (1803): 327–28; and "Answer to the Query on Solomon's Song," *Biblical Magazine* 3 (1803): 368.

There was also a response to the review of William's translation, which was signed with a pen name: Alpha, "Queries on Solomon's Song," *Biblical Magazine* 3 (1803): 416–17. Joseph Belcher, the editor of Fuller's works, intimates that Fuller wrote this reply. See *The Complete Works of the Rev. Andrew Fuller*, ed. Joseph Belcher (Harrisonburg, VA: Sprinkle, 1988), 3:605n*. But Fuller normally used the pen name "Gaius" when submitting pieces to journals.

5. Five of the six letters of Fuller's *Strictures on Some of the Leading Sentiments of Mr. R. Robinson* first appeared in *The Baptist Magazine* 20 (1828): 97–102, 145–50, 199–203, 241–46, and 341–47. What became the first letter, "On the Importance of Truth and a Right Belief of It," was not included. They were submitted to the magazine by Fuller's son J. G. Fuller, who noted that they were written to "a highly-esteemed Christian friend now deceased" ("Letters of the Late Rev. Andrew Fuller," *Baptist Magazine* 20 [1828]: 97). By the 1830s, the first letter was included with the other five in various editions of Fuller's works. I am indebted to Dr. Timothy Whelan for the location of the original appearance of the letters.

Fuller's *Leading Sentiments of Mr. R. Robinson* will be cited as they appear in *Complete Works of the Rev. Andrew Fuller*, 3:588–615. Fuller's thoughts on the Song of Songs can be found in "Letter V. On the Canonicalness of Solomon's Song," in *Complete Works of the Rev. Andrew Fuller*, 3:605–10.

6. On the career and thought of Robert Robinson, see especially Graham W. Hughes, *With Freedom Fired: The Story of Robert Robinson, Cambridge Nonconformist* (London: Carey Kingsgate Press, 1955); L. G. Champion, "Robert Robinson: A Pastor In Cambridge," *Baptist Quarterly* 31 (1985–86): 241–46; Len Addicott, "Introduction," in *Church Book: St Andrew's Street Baptist Church, Cambridge 1720–1832*, ed. Len Addicott, L. G. Champion, and K. A. C. Parsons (London: Baptist Historical Society, 1991), viii–xviii; Karen Smith, "The Liberty Not to Be a Christian: Robert Robinson (1735–1790) of Cambridge and Freedom of Conscience," in *Distinctively Baptist: Essays on Baptist History; A Festschrift in Honor of Walter B. Shurden*, ed. Marc A. Jolley and John D. Pierce (Macon: Mercer University Press, 2005), 151–70.

7. In a letter to Mary Hays (1759–1843) written less than a year before his death, Robinson told Hays:

> I am neither a Socinian nor an Arian. I do not know among what class of heretics to place myself. Sometimes I think I am a Paulianist or Samosaatenian, for I think Jesus a man in whom the fullness of the Godhead dwells, and give him more dignity than they do who ascribe to him only a third part of the Deity. Years ago, reverence for great names misled

me. I said after [Samuel] Clarke there was a *Scripture Trinity*, and I would say so still if I could tell what I meant; and as I cannot, I cast that phrase also to the bats and moles. There is, there can be, only one First Cause, Jesus is his Son, his representative, and, if you please your God,—the vice-regent of the Supreme, whom you honour by honouring him. I do not think God ever proposed the question of the nature of Jesus to us to determine; it is a child of the schools, born in litigation and subsisting by it to this day, to the utter ruin of genuine piety and Christian benevolence."

Letter to Mary Hays, September 16, 1789, in *Christian Reformer* 11 [1844]: 943–44. I am indebted to Dr. Timothy D. Whelan for sending me his transcription of this letter. See also the discussion of this area of Robinson's thinking in the sources cited in not 6 above.

8. Morden, *Life and Thought of Andrew Fuller*, 28, 36. Fuller did seek Robinson's advice in 1781 regarding a call he had received to take up the Baptist pastorate in Kettering. See Morden, *Life and Thought of Andrew Fuller*, 46. Fuller also wrote up Robinson's remarkable conversion story under the preaching of George Whitefield (1714–1770) in "Anecdote," *Evangelical Magazine* 2 (1794): 72–73. The story was written under the name of "Gaius," a pen name that Fuller regularly used.

9. Cited in Fuller, *Leading Sentiments of Mr. R. Robinson*, 3:605.

10. Jean Claude, *An Essay on the Composition of a Sermon*, trans. Robert Robinson, 2 vols. (Cambridge: Francis Hodson, 1778–79). Robinson's translation went through at least three editions before his death and was later republished by Charles Simeon (1759–1836) in the nineteenth century. The French original is in *Les oeuvres posthumes de Mr. Claude* (Amsterdam: Pierre Savouret, 1688), 1:163–492. For an online discussion of this translation by Robinson, see Fred Sanders, "A Protestant Preaching Tradition (Claude, Robinson, Simeon)," *Scriptorium Daily* (http://scriptoriumdaily.com/a-protestant-preaching-tradition-claude; accessed September 9, 2018).

11. Robert Robinson, "A Brief Dissertation on the Ministration of the Divine Word by Publick Preaching," in his translation of John [sic] Claude, *An Essay on the Composition of a Sermon* (Cambridge: Francis Hodson, 1779), 2:xlviii.

12. Fuller, *Leading Sentiments of Mr. R. Robinson*, 3:605–6.

13. John Calvin, *Commentarius in Epistolam ad Galatas* 4:22, in *Ioannis Calvini Opera*, ed. William Baum, Edward Cunitz, and Edward Reuss, Corpus Reformatorum 78 (Braunschweig: C. A. Schwetschke & Son, 1893), 50:236; François Turretini, *Institutio Theologiae Elencticae* 2.19.15 (Leiden: Frederick Haring; Utrecht: Ernest Voskuyl, 1696), 1:168. My attention was drawn to these comments on Origen by Keith D. Stanglin, *The Letter and Spirit in Biblical Interpretation: From the Early Church to Modern Practice* (Grand Rapids, MI: Baker Academic, 2018), 136 and 145.

14. Fuller, *Leading Sentiments of Mr. R. Robinson*, 3:607–9.

15. Ibid., 3:608, 610.

16. Influencing Fuller in his reading of Song 5:10a would certainly have been the interpretation of John Gill, discussed below. But Fuller also possessed a copy of the third edition of Matthew Henry's (1662–1714) commentary on the entire Bible. See "Appendix A: Books in Fuller's Library, 1798," in *The Diary of Andrew Fuller, 1780–1801*, ed. Michael D. McMullen and Timothy D. Whelan, Complete Works of Andrew Fuller 1 (Berlin: De Gruyter, 2016), 224. In his comments on Song 5:10a (*An Exposition Of the Five Poetical Books of the Old Testament*, 3rd ed. (London, 1721], 3:631), Henry took the colors "white and ruddy" to depict the "complete beauty" of Christ, but was at pains to emphasize, following Isa 53:2, that this beauty was not discernible in his incarnate body. Rather, it was the Spirit who enabled a person to see in Christ as Mediator and God the whiteness of impeccability, deity, and tender love to his people and the redness of a vicarious death, humanity, and judgment of his enemies. Henry's interpretation of this text is clearly dependent on that of John Owen. See below. Also in Fuller's library was a copy of Joseph

Hussey, *The Glory of Christ Vindicated* (London: J. Fuller; Coventry: T. Luckman, 1761), on pages 48–51 of which was a Christological reading of Song 2:1, "I am the rose of Sharon."

17. See, for example, the magisterial study of L. Ross Bush and Tom J. Nettles, *Baptists and the Bible: The Baptist Doctrines of Biblical Inspiration and Religious Authority in Historical Perspective* (Chicago: Moody Press, 1980). For the biblicism of some specific Baptists, see also John H. Watson, "Baptists and the Bible as Seen in Three Eminent Baptists," *Foundations* 16 (1973): 239–54; Peter Morden, *Offering Christ to the World: Andrew Fuller (1754–1815) and the Revival of Eighteenth-Century Particular Baptist Life*, Studies in Baptist History and Thought (Carlisle, Cumbria: Paternoster Press, 2003), 36–38; Michael A. G. Haykin, "'A Great Thirst for Reading': Andrew Fuller the Theological Reader," *Eusebeia* 9 (Spring 2008): 7–10.

18. See, for example, the discussion of Cotton Mather's exegesis of the Song by Jan Stievermann, *Prophecy, Piety, and the Problem of Historicity: Interpreting the Hebrew Scriptures in Cotton Mather's "Biblia Americana,"* Beiträge zur historischen Theologie 179 (Tübingen: Mohr Siebeck, 2016), 241–57 and 361–80, and that of Jonathan Edwards's interpretation of this biblical text by Douglas A. Sweeney, *Edwards the Exegete: Biblical Interpretation and Anglo-Protestant Culture on the Edge of the Enlightenment* (New York: Oxford University Press, 2016), 113–33.

19. Cf. Elizabeth A. Clark, "Origen, the Jews, and the Song of Songs: Allegory and Polemic in Christian Antiquity," in *Perspectives on the Song of Songs / Perspektiven der Hoheliedauslegung*, ed. Anselm C. Hagedorn (Berlin: De Gruyter, 2005), 274–93.

20. Origen, *Procopius' Excerpts from Origen on the Song of Songs* 5.10, in *Patrologiae cursus completus . . . Series Graeca*, ed. J.-P. Migne (Paris, 1857), 13:205C. It was common in patristic exegesis to associate the death of Christ with biblical references to red. See V. Pavan, "Colour, Symbolism and Liturgy," in *Encyclopedia of Ancient Christianity*, ed. Angelo Di Berardino et al. (Downers Grove, IL: InterVarsity Press, 2014), 573.

21. Fortunatianus of Aquileia, *Commentary on the Gospels* 82, trans. H. A. G. Houghton and Lukas J. Dorfbauer, Corpus Scriptorum Ecclesiasticorum Latinorum (Berlin: De Gruyter, 2017), 68. On Fortunatianus, see Lukas J. Dorfbauer and Victoria Zimmerl-Panagl, *Fortunatianus redivius: Bischof Fortunatian von Aquileia und sein Evangelienkommentar* (Berlin: De Gruyter, 2017).

22. Bede, *On the Song of Songs* 3.23, trans. Arthur Holder, in *The Venerable Bede: On the Song of Songs and Selected Writings* (Mahwah, NJ: Paulist Press, 2011), 155.

23. Neither ancient Greek nor Latin had a distinct term for what has come to be called "pink." See Michel Pastoureau, *Red: The History of a Color*, trans. Jody Gladding (Princeton: Princeton University Press, 2017), 144–46.

24. Gregory of Nyssa, *Commentary on the Song of Songs*, Homily 13, trans. Richard A. Morris (Atlanta: Society of Biblical Literature, 2012), 406–7, 409.

25. Lucas Francisco Mateo-Seco, "Christology," trans. Seth Cherney, in *The Brill Dictionary of Gregory of Nyssa*, ed. Lucas Francisco Mateo-Seco and Giulio Maspero (Leiden: Brill, 2010), 142–44.

26. William Perkins, *A Commentarie, or, Exposition upon the five first chapters of the Epistle to the Galatians* (London: John Legatt, 1617), 304. The spelling has been modernized.

27. Stanglin, *Letter and Spirit*, 142–43.

28. Perkins, *Galatians*, 305. For the interpretation of the Song of Songs during the sixteenth century, see the definitive work by Max Engammare, *Qu'il me baise des baisiers de sa bouche: Le Cantique des Cantiques à la Renaissance; Étude et bibliographie* (Geneva: Librairie Droz S.A., 1993).

29. Perkins, *Galatians*, 305. See also the helpful discussion of Stanglin, *Letter and Spirit*, 141–44.

30. Richard Sibbes, *Bowels Opened, or, A Discovery of the Neere and deere Love, Union, and Communion betwixt Christ and the Church, and consequently betwixt Him and every beleeving soule* (London: George Edwards, 1639), 344.

31. Ibid., 345.

32. Pastoureau, *Red*, 144–47. See also *The Oxford English Dictionary*, 2nd ed., s.v. "carnation."

33. Sibbes, *Bowels Opened*, 345–46.

34. John Cotton, *A Brief Exposition Of the whole Book of Canticles, or, Song of Solomon* (London: Philip Nevil, 1642), 154.

35. John Owen, *Of Communion with God The Father, Sonne and Holy Ghost, Each Person Distinctly; in Love, Grace, and Consolation* (Oxford: Thomas Robinson, 1657), 52–53.

36. For the life and ministry of Stennett, see "Some Account of the Life Of the Reverend and Learned Mr. Joseph Stennett," in *The Works of the late Reverend and Learned Mr. Joseph Stennett* (London, 1732), 1:3–36; R. L. Greaves, "Stennett, Joseph (1663–1713)," in *Biographical Dictionary of British Radicals in the Seventeenth Century*, ed. R. L. Greaves and Robert Zaller (Brighton, UK: Harvester Press, 1984), 3:205–6; B. A. Ramsbottom, "The Stennetts," in *British Particular Baptists, 1638–1910* (Springfield, MO: Particular Baptist Press, 1998), 1:136–38; Allen Harrington and Martha Stennett Harrington, "Joseph Stennett—Life," https://www.blue-hare.com/stennett/joseph/josephl.html (accessed September 9, 2018); Elizabeth Clarke, "Hymns, Psalms, and Controversy in the Seventeenth Century," in *Dissenting Praise: Religious Dissent and the Hymn in England and Wales*, ed. Isabel Rivers and David L. Wykes (Oxford: Oxford University Press, 2011), 28–32.

37. Bryan W. Ball, *The Seventh-Day Men: Sabbatarians and Sabbatarianism in England and Wales, 1600–1800* (Oxford: Clarendon Press, 1994), 120–21.

38. Joseph Stennett, *A Version of Solomon's Song of Songs: Together with The XLV. Psalm* (London: Daniel Brown and Andrew Bell, 1700), xvii, iii, vi–vii.

39. Ibid., 21.

40. It is noteworthy that the ideal cosmetic look for many late seventeenth- and eighteenth-century women, and even some men, involved the face being whitened with a lead-based white makeup and the cheeks reddened with a rouge made from vermilion, ceruse, or various vegetable sources. See "Women's Makeup in the 17th Century," http://madameisistoilette.blogspot.com/2014/12/womens-makeup-in-17th-century.html (accessed September 17, 2018); and "Women's Hairstyles and Cosmetics of the 18th Century: France and England, 1750–1790," http://demodecouture.com/hairstyles-cosmetics-18th-century (accessed September 17, 2018). In comments on Song 5:13, John Gill noted that the comparison of the cheeks of the bridegroom to "beds of spices" is like "spices . . . set in rows by the confectioner in vessels, placed in his shop in rows to be sold; which being of various colours, especially white and red, the cheeks, for colour and eminence, are compared unto them." Commentary on the Song of Songs 5:13 in his *An Exposition of the Old Testament* (London: Mathews and Leigh, 1810), 4:671.

41. The standard biographical sketch of Gill is John Rippon, *A Brief Memoir of the Life and Writings of the late Rev. John Gill, D.D.* (1838; repr., Harrisonburg, VA: Gano Books, 1992). For more recent studies of Gill and his theology, see Graham Harrison, *Dr. John Gill and His Teaching*, Annual Lecture of The Evangelical Library (London: Evangelical Library, 1971); Tom Nettles, *By His Grace and for His Glory: A Historical, Theological, and Practical Study of the Doctrines of Grace in Baptist Life* (Grand Rapids, MI: Baker, 1986), 73–107; George M. Ella, *John Gill and the Cause of God and Truth* (Eggleston, UK: Go, 1995); Michael A. G. Haykin, ed., *The Life and Thought of John Gill (1697–1771): A Tercentennial Appreciation* (Leiden: Brill, 1997); and Timothy George, "John Gill," in *Theologians of the Baptist Tradition*, ed. Timothy George and David S. Dockery, rev. ed. (Nashville, TN: Broadman and Holman, 2001), 11–33.

42. George William Pilcher, ed., *The Reverend Samuel Davies Abroad: The Diary of a Journey to England and Scotland, 1753–55* (Urbana: University of Illinois Press, 1967), 65.

43. Cited in Eifion Evans, "William Williams of Pant Y Celyn," *Evangelical Library Bulletin* 42 (Spring 1969): 6.

44. Rippon, *Brief Memoir*, 24.

45. John Gill, *An Exposition of the Book of Solomon's Song, Commonly called Canticles*, 2nd ed. (London: John Ward, 1751), 345. See also Gill, *Exposition of the Old Testament*, 4:669.

46. Gill, *Solomon's Song*, 346. See also Gill, *Exposition of the Old Testament*, 4:669. The theological employment of the color black for human sinfulness has a long history that would be a topic worthy of examination. It is noteworthy that the Scriptures never talk of sin in terms of black or blackness. Rather, sins are likened to the color red. See, in this regard, Isa 1:18. Gill, of course, is very aware of this use of the color red, as noted below.

47. Ibid., 346–47.

48. *Oxford English Dictionary*, 1st ed., s.v. "nice," 9, which cites a 1789 example from the political theorist William Belsham: "a very nice and curious question."

49. Gill, *Solomon's Song*, 347–48.

50. For Dutton's life and thought, see especially J. C. Whitebrook, "The Life and Works of Mrs. Ann Dutton," *Transactions of the Baptist Historical Society* 7, nos. 3–4 (1921): 129–46; Stephen J. Stein, "A Note on Anne Dutton, Eighteenth-Century Evangelical," *CH* 44 (1975): 485–91; Michael D. Sciretti Jr., "'Feed My Lambs': The Spiritual Direction Ministry of Calvinistic British Baptist Anne Dutton During the Early Years of the Evangelical Revival" (PhD diss., Baylor University, 2009). Most of Dutton's works have survived in only a few copies. Thankfully many of her works are currently available in a series of volumes compiled by JoAnn Ford Watson, *Selected Spiritual Writings of Anne Dutton: Eighteenth-Century, British-Baptist, Woman Theologian*, 7 vols. (Macon: Mercer University Press, 2003–15).

51. See the discussion of these links by Stein, "Note on Anne Dutton," 485–90, Sciretti, "Feed My Lambs," 198–280, and Andrew Michael Pisano, "'To Speak for Myself': Eighteenth-Century Writers of Color and the First Great Awakening" (PhD diss., University of North Carolina at Greensboro, 2014), 36–46.

52. Cited in Stein, "Note on Anne Dutton," 487–88.

53. George Whitefield, letter to Mr. [Jonathan] B[ryan], July 24, 1741, in *Letters of George Whitefield for the Period, 1734–1742* (1771; repr., Edinburgh: Banner of Truth Trust, 1976), 280.

54. Sciretti, "Feed My Lambs," 100–101.

55. Anne Dutton, *Hints of the Glory of Christ* (London: J. Hart, 1748), 64.

56. Ibid., 18, 23–24.

57. See *WJE*, 24:621: "His whiteness represents his infinite holiness and perfect righteousness. His being red represents the great sufferings and extreme trials under which his righteous and most excellent virtue was manifested. It may also signify his incarnation. The word is אָדֹם, a word of the same derivation as Adam, man."

58. This small slice of exegetical history well reveals that evangelical biblicism was not reducible to *nuda Scriptura* and subjectivism.

10

COTTON MATHER, JONATHAN EDWARDS, AND THE RELATIONSHIP BETWEEN HISTORICAL AND SPIRITUAL EXEGESIS IN EARLY EVANGELICALISM

KENNETH P. MINKEMA

Scholars such as W. R. Ward, and more recently Bruce Hindmarsh,[1] have identified distinguishing features of an "early" phase of evangelicalism, running roughly from the late seventeenth to the late eighteenth century, that set it off from "modern" evangelicalism. Extending this effort to define an early evangelicalism, other scholars have begun examining biblical interpretation among European and American figures in that long century. Are there features of exegesis that are a subset of the characteristics of early evangelicalism generally, or are there features that fall outside the circumference? If the latter, would that lead us to shift the defining characteristics of early evangelicalism? This chapter will consider some examples of biblical exposition by two preeminent colonial New England theologians, Cotton Mather and Jonathan Edwards, to see how they formed, and were formed by, early evangelicalism.

For the early modern period, roughly comprehending the sixteenth through the eighteenth centuries and including the Puritan and Pietist movements, interest in the role of the Bible, and the way it was interpreted and preached, has been nourished to no small extent either by a reappraisal of existing primary sources or by the availability of new sources. These efforts have opened up new possibilities for the study of early transatlantic evangelical exegesis, including that of Mather and Edwards: for Mather, focusing on the massive and multilayered "Biblia Americana," and for Edwards, on the phalanx of expository notebooks including "Notes on the Apocalypse," "Notes on Scripture," and especially the "Interleaved [or Blank] Bible."[2] By way of comparison and contrast, this essay brings these two figures into conversation within the context of early modern biblical commentary, centering on their respective glosses on certain passages in the historical books of the Bible.[3] In this way, it lifts up these two figures, both shaped by late Reformed Orthodoxy, Pietism, and the emerging revivalistic culture, as a way of helping to isolate some features of early evangelical exegesis.

The following examines several tableaus in which Mather and Edwards provided their observations on the same biblical passage, event, or figure. The scene opens on the battle in the valley of Ajalon, where Joshua bid the sun and moon to stand still; the next act considers Jephthah's "rash vow"; it then moves to the refugee drama of Ruth, and finally to the deadly gambit of Esther and Mordecai to save their people from annihilation.

"Sun, Stand Thou Still" (Joshua 10)

Mather was a vital inlet of Pietism into the New World, and his "Biblia Americana" was meant, in part, to show that the provinces could contribute to the discussions of "religion of the heart" taking place in Europe.[4] But it was also intended, in the spirit of the Enlightenment, to be a digest of the learning of all time, including the most recent discoveries and ideas as they bore on the sacred texts, to examine Scripture in light of science so as to affirm the verity of the biblical narratives. In the "Biblia Americana," in which Mather sought to give a fair hearing to the latest materialist and skeptical thought, he revealed some ambivalence about the compatibility of religion and science. This conflict must have been particularly keen when it came to defending miraculous events in the context of the new historical-critical approach, which, perhaps not coincidentally, arose during evangelicalism's early phase.

One such biblical episode to explore, told in Josh 10, was the Israelite commander's ordering the sun and moon to stay in place, so that the day would be extended for the purpose of giving the people of Israel the opportunity to complete the slaughter of the armies of five opposing cities. Mather wrote no less than eight entries, from all four phases of his composition of the "Biblia Americana," on this passage.[5]

One subject that fascinated Mather was how biblical characters and events were taken up by "pagans"—Greeks and Romans—and turned into mythology. Thus Joshua, it was thought, was morphed into none other than the mighty

Hercules. The point for Mather and other biblical scholars of the time was that the Hebrew Scriptures comprised the "ancientest history," the one from which all other histories, real or fictionalized, derived. That is one trajectory that lay behind his treatment of the prolonged day, which in "Pagan Antiquitie" was described as "the Nights being Doubled or Trebled, by *Jupiter*, for the Sake of *Alcmaena*."[6] According to the Roman playwright Plautus, after Alcmene's husband had lain with her, Jupiter (Zeus) also came to her, lengthening the night to make his conjugal visit with her possible.

Mather also loved philology. One theme that he visited several times in this cluster was that the language and terms in which the Scriptures were couched were adapted by God to the understanding of the people of the time. To make all the machinations of the universe understandable to "the Vulgar Conceptions of Men," Mather explained, would have required "a large System of Philosophy, & have rendred the Scriptures a Book unfit for Common Capacities." Paraphrasing from Robert Jenkin's *Reasonableness and Certainty of the Christian Religion* (1708), Mather observes, "The Scriptures were not written with a Design to teach us Natural Philosophy, but to shew us the way how to Live and Dy well."[7]

Even allowing for this accommodation, Mather maintained that Joshua's command to the moon argued the movement of the earth, since "a Stop given to the *Diurnal Motion* of the Earth, unavoidably produces the *Phaenomena*, of the *Moon standing still*." He also noted that the word in the text concerning the sun was "Metaphorical," because that body only "seems" to move. Despite the caveats about the Bible being a book of faith and not of science, Mather affirmed that there was nothing in it inconsistent with "present Notions of philosophy."[8]

Mather further considered the position of the twelfth-century Spanish rabbinic scholar Maimonides, who submitted that Joshua's words were a "poetic turn of phrase" from the book of Jasher, and so not to be taken literally. To discredit such a notion, Mather brought to bear a battery of recent English, German, and French authorities, including Stephen Nye, Ezekiel Spanheim, Pierre-Daniel Huet, Thomas Jackson, and John Owen, who all criticized the "Talmudic doctors" for their efforts to provide natural or metaphorical explanations.[9]

Mather was incredibly well read; his erudition is breathtaking, his networking dense. Although Edwards, who too was a product of the early Enlightenment, had his stable of authors on whom he relied, his field was notably narrower than Mather's. One important difference was that while Mather produced his "Biblia Americana" with an eye to publication, Edwards's "Blank Bible" was, as Stephen Stein describes it, "a personal professional tool."[10] So

Edwards was not interested so much in presenting and harmonizing a broad spectrum of past and present views as in developing the meanings of a text that informed his particular outlook or priority—his sensibility, we might say, perhaps even his personal spiritual concerns.

While the mechanics of the sun and moon arresting their motions did not occupy Edwards's attention to the extent it did Mather's, he did present an explanation.[11] Interestingly, when he preached, Edwards retained the language of an earth-centered system, but in his private writings he assumed a heliocentric one in keeping with the most recent learning. Thus, in entries in the "Blank Bible" and "Notes on Scripture" made during the period from 1728 to 1733, Edwards spoke of the sun and moon "appearing" to stand still. He did not doubt the reality of the event. Indeed, in a separate entry, Edwards claimed the account influenced the mythological story of Phaethon, who, rather like an overeager teenager in his first time behind the wheel of a car, persuaded his father to let him guide the chariot of the sun for one day, only to set the world on fire. Edwards also cited a story (found in Arthur Bedford's *Scripture Chronology*) from ancient Chinese history that asserted that during the reign of a distant emperor the sun did not set for "ten days together," which, allowing for accumulated layers of exaggeration in ancient accounts, was thought to coincide chronologically with Joshua's lifetime.[12] (Both Mather and Edwards subscribed to the then-conventional assumption that the Earth was less than six thousand years old.) Quite contrary to doubting the miraculous nature of the event, Edwards found further evidence of its veracity in its description: "such a circumstance," he wrote, "must be wholly unknown in those days to the Jews, which argues the truth of the fact: for nothing but the real fact, the means of which was wholly unknown, could have put this into the head of the historian."[13] Like Mather, Edwards, whether he knew it or not, argued that the apparent "halting" of those celestial bodies was actually the effect of the "staying of the earth's diurnal revolution"; that is, "the earth was stopped, and so all the heavenly bodies ... kept their position with respect to the horizon."[14]

Yet Edwards's real interest in the event, and in other miraculous events, was elucidated in a series of intricately cross-referenced entries in his commentaries. First, it seems Edwards could not resist typologizing, but this was integral to his larger vision of finding connections across texts, across time, and within the very fabric of being that informed his Christocentric faith. In an entry in "Notes on Scripture," he asserted that the standing still of the sun and moon was typical; that the sun "was made" to be a type of Christ, the Sun of Righteousness, the Light of the World; and that Joshua himself was a type of Christ, whose name was the same with Jesus, leading God's people as a captain. So, too, the moon was a type of the church, which fought alongside

Christ against the "spiritual [Amorites]." Describing the battle, Edwards sums up: "There was Joshua and Israel fighting God's enemies on earth, and there were the sun and moon fighting against them in heaven; and both represented Jesus and his church fighting against their spiritual enemies."[15]

Edwards's overarching rubric, like that of the seventeenth-century Dutch covenantal theologian Johannes Cocceius and his followers,[16] was God's ordering of the work of redemption through the works of creation for the benefit of the saints. In the arresting of the sun and moon at the word of Joshua, "God thereby showed that all things were for his church; all was theirs," all was "made for them." This particular instance in Joshua merely highlighted the larger principle that "God's providence . . . is an operation and work of his superior to the work of creation." Interventions in universal natural law by the Father-Creator demonstrated "that the whole frame of the universe was by him put in subjection to Christ's redeemed church."[17] Even more, "the creation of the visible world was in order to the work of redemption"; it was made by and for Jesus Christ in anticipation of this great work that Christ agreed to undertake. The numberless material and immaterial parts of the creation were really only so many "appendages," as Edwards called them, to the plan of redemption. In a lengthy "Miscellanies" entry, he wrote, "That the works of creation and the laws of nature, and that course of nature that God established in creation, is subordinate to the work of redemption, is confirmed by this, that the laws of the course of nature have often been interrupted to subserve to the designs of the great work of redemption, and never for any other purpose."[18] All would eventuate in the glory and happiness of Christ and of the saints.

Jephthah's Vow

Mather referred to the issue of the vow of Jephthah as "That Noble and Vexed Quæstion." Judges 11 tells the story of Jephthah, one of the judges of Israel, who had to sacrifice his own daughter because he promised God that, if he was victorious over Israel's enemies, he would offer up the first thing that came out of his house when he returned. But did he actually have her killed? The thorny matter of human sacrifice has long been debated in both the Jewish and Christian traditions, with Mather and Edwards, though so close to each other in heritage, location, and time, nonetheless choosing different solutions. For his part, Mather has three entries on the issue, the longest taking up five folio pages. The first contains a common theme in the "Biblia Americana": the sacred account, as we saw with Joshua, provided the original basis for a mythological adaptation. In this case, the parallel was the sacrifice of Iphigenia by Agamemnon during the siege of Troy, which Mather asserted was "contemporaneous with the Government of *Jephthah*." Indulging his love of etymology, Mather asked, "what is the very Name of *Iphigenia*, but *Iphthigenia*, or, *Iephthigenia*; that is, the Daughter of *Jephthah*?"[19]

However trying the "Quæstion," Mather consented that Jephthah did indeed make "a Real & Bloody *Sacrifice* of his Daughter." He sought to ameliorate the act by historical contextualization, citing the "Notions & Practices" of the ancient world as well as recent theology to show that human sacrifice as a means of appeasing divine justice had long been and still was common across cultures and throughout the world, even among the Hebrews, as Abraham's near slaying of Isaac illustrated. Within the Israelites' sacrificial rites, there were two sorts of "Devoted Things": those that could be "redeemed" at a price paid to the priests, and *cherem*, those that had to be put to death. So Mather, though with evident unease, concluded that "a *Rational Creature*" could be "made a *Cherem*," and that Jephthah's daughter was proof. One mitigation he allowed was that she was most likely not subject to the cutting and burning that the rites of offering prescribed, but simply "slain." Why would God have allowed this? From the New Testament commentary of French Huguenot and Saumur professor Louis Cappell, Mather drew three reasons: to teach the power of life and death that parents have over children, to give parents and masters pause in jumping to violent declarations, and to lead believers to consider how God devoted his Son to be a sacrifice on the cross.[20]

Edwards had only to go to Matthew Poole's detailed entry in *Synopsis Criticorum*, his main resource for annotating his biblical commentary, to know about the mythological parallels and the etymological permutations that Mather mentioned, and to be informed about the reasons to deduce that the daughter was indeed killed.[21] But in a lengthy entry in "Notes on Scripture," Edwards began by asserting "that Jephthah did *not* put his daughter to death and burn her in sacrifice."[22] He constructed an essay that, rather than outsourcing, relied on frequent and close scriptural analysis, first on the nature of oaths, and then on Nazaritism.

The "tenor of his vow," Edwards began, did not oblige Jephthah to sacrifice his offspring. If it had been an unclean beast that had come out of the house, then, as outlined in Lev 27, he would have had to redeem it, because the law of God forbade offering something unclean as a sacrifice. Likewise, "when it was his daughter that met him," he would have acted in accordance with his vow without making a burnt sacrifice of her, because "the law of God directed" that "a dedicated person" was not in a "capacity" to be offered as a burnt sacrifice. Edwards observed several things concerning Old Testament laws relating to consecrated persons: first, the eldest offspring "of men and of unclean beasts were to be redeemed"; second, those devoted by their parents to God "by a singular vow . . . were to be brought before the priest" to be "estimated" and redeemed; third, such dedicated persons, though redeemed, "were yet to remain persons separate," which included Nazarites, who were to give their lives to religious exercises, were not to cut their hair, and were to "abstain from all legal pollutions."[23] Female Nazarites were not to have sex or to marry.

This, Edwards contended, was what happened to Jephthah's daughter: she became a Nazarite, possibly a servant of the sanctuary, which is why the Scripture states that she went up and down "bewailing her virginity"—and not, Edwards pointed out, "her untimely end"—and that when she returned from her journey, "she knew no man." Jephthah's grief can be explained not only by his reproaching himself for his vow, but by his realization that in so dedicating his daughter, his only child, he would have no one "to keep his name in remembrance, which in those days was looked upon an exceeding great calamity."[24]

It would not be right to conclude, from this instance, that Edwards was somehow more "humane" or "sentimental" than Mather, or that Mather felt that God was any less "reasonable" than Edwards did. After all, Edwards was fully capable of stern statements on God's behalf, such as consigning unconverted children to hell. No, the answer as to why they diverged on this "Vexed Quæstion" lies elsewhere. Perhaps Edwards sought a different solution because of mounting criticisms of high Calvinism's fatalism by advocates of "new-fashioned" schemes in divinity, including Arminians and crypto-deists. This, with changing formulations of the doctrine of God and of Old Testament law and the nature of sacrifices, or hermeneutical shifts, or the effects of education and exposure to specific sources, combined to bring Mather and Edwards down on alternative sides of the interpretational divide. Here, they reflected the potential for diversity within early evangelical exegesis.

Ruth as Exemplar and Type

Ruth was a Moabite who, after her Jewish husband's death, chose to accompany her mother-in-law Naomi to Israel and adopt Judaism as her religion. In his commentary on Ruth 1, Mather agreed with fifth-century Christian writer Prosper of Aquitaine's "elegant" observation that Ruth was "a Type of the *Gentile*-Church." The "Church of *Israel*," Mather continued, "did not the Duty that was owing to her," and so became "*The House of him that hath his Shooe loosed*." This referred to Deut 25, which laid out the duty of a younger brother to marry his deceased brother's wife and bear children in order to perpetuate his name (the importance of which we saw with Jephthah); a brother who refused was publicly and ceremoniously to have his shoe taken off by his sister-in-law. However, Mather added, the apostles and their disciples later did accept the gentiles, "having their *Feet shod with the Praeparation of the Gospel of Peace*," quoting Eph 6:15, which for Mather provided the fulfillment of the Deuteronomic matrimonial stricture, making it relevant to the expansion of the Christian church.

In further entries, Mather showed a concern, as he does throughout his commentary on the historical books, with idols and with cultural aspects of the ancients, such as clothing and foodways. But his longest entry on Ruth is a nearly four-thousand-word unpacking of Ruth 4:17 on "The Business of the Marriage between *Boaz* and *Ruth*." After Ruth and Naomi had come to Israel, they were impoverished, so Ruth went out and gleaned in the fields of her mother-in-law's kinsman Boaz, who, attracted to her, not only allowed her to glean but gave her additional tokens of friendship. In return, she came to him in the night and offered herself to him sexually (euphemistically, she "uncovered his feet"), which amounted to offering herself to him in marriage. Boaz could have refused her outright, but he did not. However, under Leviratic law, there was a nearer kinsman who could have claimed Ruth as his wife; probably knowing how things stood, he declined, setting in motion the public ceremony and clearing the way for Ruth and Boaz's nuptials. Throughout the "Biblia Americana," Mather showed sustained interest in various aspects of Hebrew culture, including legal matters. Here he exemplified the trend in what Jonathan Sheehan calls "antiquarian biblical scholarship" of the seventeenth century, which emphasized thick understanding of ancient social and political contexts in order to explicate the Scriptures.

It is instructive to see how our two subjects exported their exegesis into sermons for public consumption. Ruth appeared at many points in Mather's sermons, especially in patriarchal, eulogistic pieces on deceased females whose real or idealized examples of piety and duty he wished to recommend, and in sermons that described "family government." An elegiac poem of Mather's composition from 1704 gives us a good idea of his assumptions. Entitled *Eureka: The Vertuous Woman found*, it was delivered in memory of Mary Brown, wife of Benjamin, most likely of Salem Town, who died in childbirth along with her infant—a tragically common occurrence in those days. The memorial takes Ruth 3:11 for its motto, the words of Boaz to Ruth when he wakes up and finds her sleeping next to him: "All the City of my People does know, that thou art a Vertuous Woman." As the poet, Mather invoked Truth in describing what he considered the epitome of Puritan womanhood: modest, demure, prudent, humble, obedient, and yet, Ruth-like, willing to challenge her right because of her virtue. Thus, Mather proclaimed, "*Grammar* makes TRUTH, a SHEE": "we shall with care / Nothing but very *Truth* of *Her* declare." A reader not of romances but of the Bible, spare of speech but expansive of piety, who did not "patch" or paint her face but rather ornamented her heart, this latter-day Mary our pastor-poet compared to the Virgin—a logical end of Mather's invocation of Ruth on the title page, since Ruth, though not a Jew, was considered one of the "mothers" of Christ and of the church.

In his commentary on the first chapter of Ruth, Edwards, like Mather, affirmed that she "typifies the calling of the Gentile church." Unlike Mather, however, he saw Naomi as a type of the Jewish church, not the part that was rejected, but "the true church of God in Israel." He also observed that Ruth typified "the universal church, and the conversion of believers everywhere. We are all born in sin, as Ruth was born in Moab," Edwards observed; "A state of sin is as it were our father's house, and sinners are our own people. When we are converted, we forsake our own people and father's house."[25] Here we can make two observations: first, though saying that Naomi was a type of the Jewish church would not have raised many eyebrows among Edwards's contemporaries, this multiplying of types shows how Edwards was not afraid to extend typological meanings further than someone like Mather, and in ways that sometimes violated accepted Reformed and Puritan norms.

Second, as a progenitor and product of the age of revivals, Edwards, rather than exploring the anthropological details of Hebrew culture, brings his own presentist, conversionist emphasis to the interpretation. While Mather occasionally digressed to present some "evangelical illustrations" in his comments on the Historical Books, Edwards regularly included them. So, in his gloss on 1 Chr 11:39, regarding Zelek the Ammonite, Edwards noted that the law of Moses forbade an Ammonite or a Moabite, such as Ruth, from entering into the congregation of the Lord (Deut 23:3). The cases of Zelek and Ruth show, however, that "evident piety prevailed for persons' admission, notwithstanding this law. When the case was so, they were no longer Ammonites or Moabites in the eye of the law. By these things and many others it appears that evangelical qualifications always prevailed over legal ones."[26] Mather and Edwards were both products of New England's conflicted ecclesiastical experiment, including the much-debated implementation of the Half-Way Covenant; Mather even feuded publicly with Edwards's grandfather, Solomon Stoddard, over the nature of entry into the sacraments.[27] Yet both Mather and Edwards came to realize in common, albeit in different circumstances, that the prerequisites for church membership had to take into account "evangelical qualifications," that is, individual experience and expression in light of the teachings of Scripture.

It is worth considering Edwards's noted sermon *Ruth's Resolution*. Originally preached in April 1735 toward the end of the Connecticut Valley Revival, which Edwards made famous in his *Faithful Narrative*, this sermon was one he chose to include in *Discourses on Various Important Subjects*, a 1738 collection memorializing the awakening. Here, Edwards stated publicly what he committed to his private commentaries: Ruth was a mother of Christ and a type of the gentile church. But she was also a type of "every sincere convert" and, again, of the conversion process itself. As Ruth did, "every true Christian forsakes all for Christ," departing from "the tents of wickedness, to dwell in the land of uprightness," leaving behind family and friends, and all by a firm resolution to pledge oneself to Christ. In the context of the waning revival, Edwards used Ruth's resolution to exhort those left unconverted to join with their loved ones, companions and neighbors who were going to the land of uprightness, never to be parted.

Esther

Esther was a woman in very different circumstances from Ruth. The new queen of Persian king Ahasuerus, she, with the help of the king's trusted Jewish counselor Mordecai, turned the tables on evil Haman, who sought the destruction of the Jews. In his commentary on Esther, Mather dwelt at some length on matters such as the nature of Persian court practices, their luxurious building materials, incredible wealth, decadent eating habits, postal network, royal edicts and archives, and other details. As Harry Clark Maddux points out, Mather wished to explore "how custom and law dictate behavior," and yet that "all should be responsive to the will of God."[28] Mather also presented two reasons for Mordecai's refusal to prostrate himself before Haman: first, because Haman was an Amalekite, a people "*Accursed* of God," and second, because he wanted to "arrogate" the sort of respect of which only God was worthy.[29] In contrast to how the Jews had lost their original purity (with the exception of Mordecai) and were copying the lavish habits of the nations where they lived, Mather held up the interrelationship of history and providence, and how God can bring things to pass through an ordinary course of events rather than through miracles.

Yet again, information that Mather deemed to be significant found its way into both the "Biblia Americana" and into sermons. For example, his comment on Esth 7:8, about the "Original" of the "*Covering of Hamans Face*," is found nearly word for word in his sermon *A good man making a good end*, delivered to eulogize a fellow minister who died in 1698. Mather related the story that a malefactor about to be executed in ancient Persia asked to look on the king's face one last time and, through pleading, was able to obtain pardon. Afterward, the Persians altered executions such that the condemned's face was covered. In the sermon, Mather continued, "I will not now Enquire, how far this passage, will Illustrate the Story of *Haman*; but I will observe, That the *Face of God*, is the Name of the *Messiah*; and in this observation, I have given you a Golden Key, to come at New Treasures in stores of Scriptures."[30] Likewise, in *An history of seasonable interpositions* (1719), as in his "Biblia Americana" entry on Esth 9:10, Mather hinted at Haman as a type of Antichrist, asserting that the deliverance from Haman's "Bloody Decree" was but one of many of God's "interpositions" on behalf of his people. "And what became of *Haman*, and his *Ten Sons?*" Mather rhetorically inquired. "*Antichrist* and his *Ten Sons*, have cause to think of That!"[31] Thus, Mather could be a pretty mean typologist in his own right.

We have an even more dramatic sermonic employment of Esther by Mather. In the late winter and early spring of 1690, French soldiers and their Indian allies, for the most part Abenakis, attacked Schenectady, New York, and Salmon Falls, New Hampshire, setting off a panic throughout New England. This was but the latest round in an ongoing conflict that had its immediate origins in the winter of 1688–89, coinciding with the Glorious Revolution and the overthrow of Edmund Andros. News of the attack reached Boston the day before Mather was set to preach a lecture on March 20. His quickly devised sermon, *A publick spirit recommended unto the inhabitants of New-England*, took as its text Mordecai's words to Esther in 4:14, "If thou altogether hold thy peace at this time, thou and thy Father's house shall be destroyed." The "fresh News of our *Distress* and *Danger* which within this four and twenty Hours arrived unto us" compelled Mather to choose this text. Esther was called on to "venture *All*, for the service of her People." Perhaps, Mather speculated, God had allowed the Jews to come close to extermination because they had grown "a little too secure and careless" and were neglecting God's ordinances "for the sake of their own Secular Accommodations," implying that New England, the new Israel, was being chastised for similar reasons. Upon learning that all the Jews were to be killed, Mordecai told Esther that she had to go before the king and supplicate for her people. This was risky; to go before the king unbidden was to court death. Fortunately, when Esther approached him, he held out the golden scepter, signifying acceptance. From this, Mather declared, the people of God can learn that they have a duty, a necessity, and an encouragement to approach God's throne of grace for relief. This ancient predicament led Mather to the general lesson "that every Christian should

Readily and Chearfully Venture his All to serve the people of God, when a Time of Distress and Danger calleth for it."[32]

Edwards too saw the reason for Mordecai's refusal to bow to Haman as arising from his being an Amalekite, but focused much more on Haman as a type of Antichrist. For Edwards, biblical figures and events were sometimes important not so much for what they were but for what they represented. So we should not be surprised to hear that he was also much more fulsome than Mather in teasing out typological, even anagogical (or mystical) meanings, claiming that "this book of Esther is an history that is a shadow of gospel things and times."[33] Thus, Ahasuerus's great feast was "the gospel feast," representing "Christ's life, incarnation, and death," offered to "great and small, agreeing [with] the universality of the gospel offer," and held in a king's palace—that is, the house of God. Vashti, the former queen, curiously, was both "the church, or God's people," the Jews, but also "the wife of God, the great King"; she, like the Jews, refused to come to the gospel feast, upon which Ahasuerus "repudiated" her and gave the "royal estate" to another, who delighted the king even as Christ is delighted with the church—the rejection of the Jews and the calling of the gentiles was confirmed and foreseen in this relationship. Further, Mordecai, in presenting Esther to the king, embodied the "gospel ministry," which presented the church to Christ.

Haman, on the other hand, typified Antichrist. Mather had said as much too, but here again Edwards was more expansive. Haman was haughty, sought dominion, loved to have everyone pay homage to him, persecuted any who did not. The king gave power to Haman, just as God did and will give Antichrist power over his people, at least for a time. But eventually Haman, as Antichrist was and will be, was thrown down and humbled, made to serve Mordecai the minister, who was elevated above him, and made to serve God's people who are exalted after their suffering. The gallows that Haman prepared for Mordecai was used to execute Haman. "So," Edwards asserted, "it will be for Antichrist." But he went further: Haman, like the pope, "dispenses God's curses, but at length falls into it." And just as Haman's house was given to Queen Esther, so Europe, the bastion of Catholicism, "the house of Antichrist," will be given to the Protestants.[34] To be sure, Mather would not have disagreed with such a pro-Protestant reading of the end times, though he and Edwards definitely had distinctive elements in their eschatologies.[35]

But Haman, for Edwards, also represented Satan. Both were once high in position and power, Haman in the court of Ahasuerus and Satan in heaven, where he was next only to God in authority. They both manifested enmity to God's people. Both "fell suddenly from this height to the lowest disgrace,"

Haman to the gallows and Satan to hell. In their place, Mordecai, Christ, was appointed and given the greatest honor, dressed in royal robes and crowned. As it had been for Haman, the means by which Satan sought to destroy the church became the means of his own destruction.[36] Thus, we see in Edwards an imaginative (some might say overly imaginative) penchant to find parallels as part of his effort to confirm the promises and prophecies of the Scripture.

In addition, just as Mather enjoined the duty of prayer after the French and Indian attack of 1690, so for Edwards the efficacy of prayer emerged as an important lesson from the book of Esther. Esther's earnest prayer obtained deliverance for the Jews, even as prayer constituted a means by which God's saints will be saved from Antichrist. Edwards amplified this theme in *An Humble Attempt*, his 1747 treatise that, in cooperation with Scottish revivalists, called for organized, transatlantic quarterly days of prayer to perpetuate the recent outpourings of the Spirit. Arguing that "great and particular encouragement" was given to God's people in the Word of God "to express union and agreement in prayer," he cited, among many instances, Esther's request, "for the saving of the church of God, and the whole nation of the Jews," that all the Jews in Shushan pray and fast with her and her handmaidens. Later, in considering that the church would undergo a time of persecution before the "glorious times," Edwards gathered evidence from Scripture and from history to show that the worst period—the slaying of the witnesses—was past, and that with the Reformation, Antichrist "hath fallen, at least, halfway to the ground, from that height of power and grandeur, that he was in before." Thus, many, though by no means all, historical threats to God's people, including Babylon, Antiochus Epiphanes—and Haman—have passed.[37]

Conclusion

Bearing these vignettes in mind, what conclusions can we draw about the nature of early evangelical exegesis as seen in Mather and Edwards? In their commentarial concerns, the pair certainly had more areas in which they overlapped than in which they differed, and seem to have had them in common with other early evangelical exegetes. They both believed that biblical exposition was a cumulative and collaborative affair; that an exegete had to rely on deep and broad study; and that one's own work stood on the shoulders of generations upon generations—even if Mather's style was baroque while Edwards's harked back to the "bookless," plain style of Owen.

They both incorporated the latest learning in the sciences and other disciplines. Bob Brown's and Reiner Smolinski's work has demonstrated that, in the importation of natural philosophy into their commentaries, both figures, as part of the Christian Enlightenment, were also very eclectic, in terms of both whom they read and the issues they pursued in response to the ascendant critical method, among other factors.[38] Think of Mather's wide reading in science, physics, botany, and geography, which he brought to bear on verses of the Bible, and Edwards's collection of religious "data" in the Baconian mode, as Sarah Rivett has shown.[39] In terms of the more esoteric sorts of pursuits that Ward portrays as integral to early evangelicalism, such as alchemy, Paracelsianism, hermeticism, and Kabbalah, those occult, secret funds of ancient knowledge, Mather was more of a student than Edwards, though Edwards did pursue the *prisca theologia*, as Gerry McDermott first informed us, and revealed at least a passing knowledge of Kabbalah.[40]

The extent to which both Mather and Edwards looked to other Christian traditions, as well as other religions, for illuminating Scripture is impressive. As we saw with Joshua and Jephthah, for them—though perhaps more for Mather than Edwards—"Pagan Antiquitie" and mythology were rich fields for comparative study with the Bible. Still, Mather as an expositor was more committed to pansophism and had a staggering range of interests on which he could speak authoritatively—as historian, scientist, naturalist, numerologist, archaeologist—reflecting his method, which was nothing less than to unite all branches of knowledge in service of the gospel.[41] In Mather's study of the historical books, he was concerned with such things as the minute exploration of false deities, or the many meanings of the elements of the Temple, or the diaspora of the Jews, subjects in which Edwards showed much less interest.

They also saw their endeavors as part of a larger effort to defend the Bible against its enemies and also against those who defended it in incompetent ways. Both compiled massive amounts of information for their apologetic stances on the verity of the biblical narratives—its "historicity," its groundedness in real events and places. Etymology was a concern of both, admittedly of Mather more than Edwards, though for both a thorough grounding in the original languages was essential, as was ongoing reexamination of the texts. They treated in detail aspects of Hebraic law, whether ceremonial or moral. For this, and other concerns, they turned extensively to rabbinic learning. Both defended the supernatural and the miraculous, even if, as Ava Chamberlain has observed, Mather was more apt to seek a natural explanation, while Edwards more dogmatically affirmed God's hand in events.[42] And both had distinctive views on the millennial and on the apocalyptic that reached far beyond their strictly exegetical repositories, and indeed permeated much of what they did. Here, as Americans, they may have been different from other, more amillennial early evangelicals.

Moving to "interior" religion, and devotionalism, we see certain authors that were held in high regard by both Mather and Edwards: à Kempis, Scougal, Bayly, Allestree, and Gearing among them. Outright appeals to interiority, self-examination, or "evangelical illustrations" are not seen so much in Mather's entries on the Historical Books, but in other commentary these topics are more prevalent; Edwards, meanwhile, writing from the nexus of British empiricism and developing revival culture, via British Pietism, cultivated the "spiritual sense." Jan Stievermann and Ryan Hoselton point to Mather's "regenerate hermeneutic of piety," on which Edwards expanded, making it his own, privileging the heightened ability of the regenerate to read Scripture and the types.[43] And their biblical contemplations fed their faith lives in constant and sometimes remarkable ways: think of Mather in an ecstasy rolling on the floor of his study, or of Edwards seated on a tree stump chanting his meditations while a thunderstorm approached. For Edwards, this experientialism merged into the aesthetic, the "sweet," the beautiful. There are elements of mysticism here, as Rhys Bezzant has pointed out,[44] though not of the radical stripe; for that, we need to look to Sarah Pierpont Edwards, with her reading of Guyon, Fénelon, and Elizabeth Singer Rowe. All the same, it is interesting to see scholars today asserting that Edwards affirmed the legitimacy of kinesthetic manifestations as positive rather than merely neutral signs of grace.[45]

Speaking of behavior, there was also a pastoral dimension to their exegesis. This is the "practical" aspect of doing theology that Adriaan Neele so helpfully emphasizes. As we saw with the stories of Ruth and of Esther, both Mather and Edwards imported passages from their commentaries into their sermons, or vice versa. This speaks to how the local church experience strongly informed the direction and possibly the content of biblical interpretation. Both skillfully related their interpretation of Scripture to their congregants' lives in very pragmatic, sometimes challenging, sometimes affirming ways.

But most characteristic, perhaps, is the blended providential-prophetic-typological hermeneutic that both of these exegetes employed in their reflections on all of the biblical vignettes we have considered. Doug Sweeney and David Barshinger's work has confirmed how Edwards arranged his thought within the rubric of redemptive history, which bears close relation to this approach.[46] Prophetic interpretation permeated Mather's *Triparadisus* and Edwards's "Prophecies of the Messiah" and "Fulfillment of the Prophecies of the Messiah," a shared concern stemming from their biblicism that has yet to be explored.[47] Mather and Edwards likewise had an abiding interest in providence and typology, though Edwards was more experimental. Indeed, while the typological persuasion reemerged in later writers such as Emily Dickinson and Marianne Moore, as seen in Jennifer Leader's recent study,[48] it may be that Edwards, with his expansive method, was the last of the great typologists, whether in early evangelicalism or otherwise.

As rich as this matrix of interpretation was, it did not endure, or at least did not endure in its entirety. Among later evangelicals, engagement with the latest scientific advancements, with the aesthetic, mystical, and varied dimensions of interiority, with several exegetical "senses," with providentialist assumptions about causality, and with typological conceptions of reality's discursive nature receded. Meanwhile, they placed increasing emphasis on other approaches, including a narrowing of acceptable exegetical senses, premillennialism, and the necessity of a locatable, even embodied religious experience. Certainly there were continuities in the evangelical tradition, but it is questionable whether Mather and Edwards would have been able to comprehend, or even to abide, their later counterparts.

Notes

1. W. R. Ward, *Early Evangelicalism: A Global Intellectual History, 1670–1789* (Cambridge: Cambridge University Press, 2006); D. Bruce Hindmarsh, *The Spirit of Early Evangelicalism: True Religion in a Modern World* (New York: Oxford University Press, 2018).

2. For Mather's main commentaries, see Reiner Smolinski, ed., *The Threefold Paradise of Cotton Mather: An Edition of "Triparadisus"* (Athens: University of Georgia Press, 1995); and the critical editions in the "Biblia Americana" series. For Edwards's, see "Notes on the Apocalypse," in *WJE*, 5:305–96; "Notes on Scripture," in *WJE*, 15; and *The "Blank Bible,"* in *WJE*, 24.

3. See Stephen J. Stein, "Cotton Mather and Jonathan Edwards on the Number of the Beast: Eighteenth-Century Speculation About the Antichrist," *Proceedings of the American Antiquarian Society* 84 (October 1974): 293–315; and Stein, "Cotton Mather and Jonathan Edwards on the Epistle of James: A Comparative Study," in *Cotton Mather and "Biblia Americana": America's First Bible Commentary*, ed. Reiner Smolinski and Jan Stievermann (Tübingen: Mohr Siebeck, 2010), 363–82.

4. See Richard F. Lovelace, *The American Pietism of Cotton Mather: Origins of American Evangelicalism* (Grand Rapids, MI: Christian University Press, 1979); Douglas H. Shantz, *An Introduction to German Pietism: Protestant Renewal at the Dawn of Modern Europe* (Baltimore: Johns Hopkins University Press, 2013); Jan Stievermann and Oliver Scheiding, eds., *A Peculiar Mixture: German-Language Cultures and Identities in Eighteenth-Century North America* (University Park: Penn State University Press, 2013).

5. Reiner Smolinksi identifies four periods during which Mather composed and added layers to the "Biblia": 1693–1706, 1706–the latter part of 1711, the end of 1711–February 1714, and 1716–28. See Smolinski, "Introduction," *BA*, 1:51–61.

6. *BA*, 3:113, entry on Josh 10:13.

7. Ibid., 3:109, entry on Josh 10:12.

8. Ibid., 3:113, 110. See also Winton U. Solberg, ed., *The Christian Philosopher* (Chicago: University of Illinois Press, 1994), 84.

9. *BA*, 3:111–12, entry on Josh 10:12.

10. Stein, "Mather and Edwards on James," 367.

11. See Ava Chamberlain: "A Fish Tale: Jonathan Edwards and Cotton Mather on Jonah's Whale," in *Jonathan Edwards and Scripture: Biblical Exegesis in British North America*, ed. David P. Barshinger and Douglas A. Sweeney (New York: Oxford University Press, 2018), 144–62.

12. Edwards, "Scripture," no. 209, on Josh 10:12–14, in *WJE*, 15:134–35.

13. Edwards, "Blank Bible," entry on Josh 10:12–13, in *WJE*, 24:326.

14. Ibid., and Edwards, "Scripture," no. 117, on Josh 10:13, in *WJE*, 15:83.

15. Edwards, "Scripture," no. 207, on Josh 10:12–14, in *WJE*, 15:129–31, quote from p. 131.

16. See chapter 3 in this volume.

17. Edwards, "Scripture," no. 167, on Josh 10:13, in *WJE*, 15:98; and "Miscellanies," no. 702, in *WJE*, 18:283–309.

18. Edwards, "Miscellanies," no. 702, in *WJE*, 18:284, 289, 290.

19. *BA*, 3:192, entry on Judg 11:40.

20. Ibid., 3:192, 193–99, 197, 200.

21. See "Blank Bible," entry on Judg 11:39, which refers to "SSS," Edwards's abbreviation for Poole's *Synopsis*, on "fables of the heathen from hence," *WJE*, 24:334; also, Edwards later added references to Poole in "Scripture," no. 223, his essay on Judg 11:30–40, in *WJE*, 15:162, 169.

22. "Scripture," no. 223, in *WJE*, 15:160 (my emphasis).

23. Ibid., 161, 162–64.

24. Ibid., 168, 169.

25. Edwards, "Notes on Scripture," no. 125, in *WJE*, 15:85.

26. Edwards, "Blank Bible," note on 1 Chr 11:39, in *WJE*, 24:405–6.

27. On the controversy, see, for example, Paul J. Lucas, *Valley of Discord: Church and Society Along the Connecticut River, 1636–1725* (Hanover: University Press of New England, 1976).

28. Harry C. Maddux, "Introduction," in *BA*, 4:20.

29. *BA*, 4:148; see also entry on chap. 9:6 (p. 159).

30. Cotton Mather, *A good man making a good end: The life and death, of the Reverend Mr. John Baily, comprised and expressed in a sermon, on the day of his funeral. Thursday. 16.d. 10. m. 1697* (Boston, 1698), 21; see also *BA*, 4:155, on chap. 7:8.

31. Mather, *An history of seasonable interpositions; especially relating to the twice-memorable fifth of November* (Boston, 1719), 9–10.

32. Mather, *The present state of New-England. Considered in a discourse on the necessities and advantages of a public spirit in every man; especially, at such a time as this* (Boston, 1690), 2, 5, 9.

33. Edwards, "Scripture," no. 46, "The Book of Esther," in *WJE*, 15:60.

34. Ibid., 60–63.

35. On the conflagration, see *Threefold Paradise of Cotton Mather*; and Kenneth P. Minkema, "The End of the World: Edwards on the Apocalypse and the Environment," in *Jonathan Edwards on the Environment: The Relevance of the Thought of Jonathan Edwards to Our Current Environmental and Ecological Concerns*, ed. Richard A. S. Hall (Lewiston, NY: Edwin Mellen Press, 2016), 87–104.

36. Edwards, "Miscellanies," no. 702, in *WJE*, 18:305–6.

37. Edwards, *An Humble Attempt to promote Explicit Agreement and Visible Union of God's People in Extraordinary Prayer*, in *WJE*, 5:361, 363, 383.

38. Robert E. Brown, *Jonathan Edwards and the Bible* (Bloomington: Indiana University Press, 2002); Smolinski, "Introduction," *BA*, 1.

39. Rivett, *The Science of the Soul in Colonial New England* (Chapel Hill: University of North Carolina Press, 2011).

40. Gerald R. McDermott, *Jonathan Edwards Confronts the Gods: Christian Theology, Enlightenment Religion, and Non-Christian Faiths* (New York: Oxford University Press, 2000). For Edwards on Kabbalah, see "Catalogue of Reading," entry no. [237], in *WJE*, 26:165–66; and "Types Notebook," in *WJE*, 11:24–27, 151.

41. Jan Stievermann, "Introduction," *BA*, 5:9.

42. Chamberlain, "Fish Tale," 157–58.

43. Jan Stievermann and Ryan P. Hoselton, "Spiritual Meaning and Experimental Piety in the Exegesis of Cotton Mather and Jonathan Edwards," in *Edwards and Scripture*, 86–105.

44. Rhys Bezzant, "'Wrapt and Swallowed Up in God': Edwards as Mystic?," paper read at American Society of Church History conference, Washington, DC, January 2014.

45. See, for example, Kathryn Reklis, *Theology and Kinesthetic Imagination: Jonathan Edwards and the Making of Modernity* (New York: Oxford University Press, 2014).

46. Douglas A. Sweeney, *Edwards the Exegete: Biblical Interpretation and Anglo-Protestant Culture on the Edge of the Enlightenment* (New York: Oxford University Press, 2016); David P. Barshinger, *Jonathan Edwards and the Psalms: A Redemptive-Historical Vision of Scripture* (New York: Oxford University Press, 2014).

47. See *Threefold Paradise of Cotton Mather*; "Miscellanies," nos. 1067 and 1068, in *WJEO*, 30. See also Jan Stievermann, *Prophecy, Piety, and the Problem of Historicity: Interpreting the Hebrew Scriptures in Cotton Mather's "Biblia Americana,"* Beiträge zur historischen Theologie 179 (Tübingen: Mohr Siebeck, 2016).

48. Jennifer L. Leader, *Knowing, Seeing, Being: Jonathan Edwards, Emily Dickinson, Marianne Moore, and the American Typological Tradition* (Amherst: University of Massachusetts Press, 2016).

11

READING REVELATION AND REVELATORY READINGS IN EARLY AWAKENED PROTESTANTISM

A Transatlantic Comparison

JAN STIEVERMANN

This essay examines a basic tension arising from the spiritualistic tendency in how German Pietism and British evangelicalism engaged with the Bible. It will consider a wide range of examples from the early, formative phases of Pietism and colonial evangelicalism, focusing especially on August Hermann Francke, Johann Wilhelm and Johanna Eleonora Petersen, Heinrich Horche, Cotton Mather, and Jonathan Edwards, who were all in conversation with each other, directly or indirectly. Their discussions reveal a fine and highly contested line between reading with the Spirit and having quasi-revelatory experiences that were usually rooted in Scripture but transcended it. This dividing line became blurry especially when reading the Book of Revelation and other biblical prophecies thought to foretell latter-day events preceding the millennium. Of particular importance was Joel 2:28, which many understood to promise an eschatological outpouring of the Spirit that would potentially bring a restitution of the charismata, including the gift of prophecy. Given these hopes, the elucidation of Scripture potentially became a form of prophetic discourse, yielding new mystical insights and predictions about the future.

The Spiritualistic Tendency in Early Pietist and Evangelical Exegesis

Early German Pietists and British evangelicals inherited a high view of the Bible as the inspired, authoritative, and final Word of God. They felt loyal to the Reformers' scriptural principle, which understood the Bible as the necessary means of salvation and the grace of God as mediated through the interplay of Word and Spirit. Like their "Orthodox" colleagues, Pietist and evangelical theologian-scholars devoted enormous energy to scriptural apologetics and learned exegesis. They did not shy away from new historical-critical methods that were emerging in the early Enlightenment. At the same time, Pietism and evangelicalism were part of a pneumatological revival fostering a piety of the Spirit and an openness to what Cotton Mather called *thaumatographia pneumatica*.[1] This pneumatological emphasis distinguished them from both the magisterial Reformers and their more conservative contemporaries. Johannes Wallmann's description of "all forms of early Pietism" fully applies to early evangelicalism as well: it was informed by a deep dissatisfaction with the perceived "dearth of the Spirit" in their churches, and characterized by a "striving and longing for a new and richer experience (both individually and collectively) of the work of the Holy Spirit."[2]

Pietists and evangelicals also invigorated a spiritualistic tendency in biblical interpretation.[3] Their most important forerunners already showed this tendency—for example, the classics of medieval mysticism, the *devotio moderna*, the Reformation-era spiritualists, Jacob Böhme, the Christian theosophic tradition, Johann Arndt, and mystically inclined Puritan practical divinity writers.[4] David R. Como notes how seventeenth-century British Puritan devotional culture was characterized not only by a strong biblicism but also a "spiritist enthusiasm," which some radical circles took to an extreme by maintaining that "believers needed to submit to the unmediated power of the Holy Spirit."[5] The hermeneutics of Pietists and evangelicals drew on these sources and traditions. Consequently, many came to emphasize the Spirit's indwelling as necessary for unlocking and experientially grasping the Word's mysteries. Reading the Word in this way went beyond received notions of the *testimonium internum* and opened the possibility for enthusiastic, even revelatory readings of Scripture.

The early conversation between German Pietism and British evangelicalism on this subject was especially fostered by Anton Wilhelm Böhme, the London-based ambassador of Halle Pietism and English translator of several major Pietist works. Bruce Hindmarsh notes that these works were crucial for

Whitefield, the Wesley brothers, Edwards, and other evangelicals who were developing their distinct practices of piety, conversionist theology of mission, and, importantly, their "mode of devotional Bible reading."[6] Böhme published a London edition of Francke's important hermeneutical handbook for theology students, *Manuductio Ad Lectionem Scripturae Sacrae* (1693),[7] as well as his own *Plain Directions for Reading the Holy Bible* in 1708, which went through numerous editions.

Twenty years before Whitefield and the Wesleys, Cotton Mather—who also exchanged letters and publications with Böhme, Francke, and other Halle Pietists between about 1710 and his death in 1728—fully engaged with the *Manuductio*.[8] He found it so congenial to his own exegetical theory that he incorporated key arguments and long citations into the "Essay for further Commentary, on the Sacred Scriptures" appended to his "Biblia Americana."[9] The essay subsequently furnished the main source for the chapter "Of Reading the Sacred Scriptures" in Mather's oft-reprinted handbook for ministerial candidates, *Manuductio ad ministerium* (1726).[10] Like Francke and Böhme, Mather distinguished between the "rind" and the "kernel" of the Word. The former was constituted by Scripture's literal sense, and was accessible to historical-contextual, grammatical, philological and logical analysis. Far from disparaging these approaches, Mather, Franke, and Böhme's works all devote much space to them. Mather, Francke, and Böhme also heartily promoted learned biblical studies among divinity students. Still, the Halle Pietists and Mather firmly believed that the *sensus literalis* was mere preparation for truly understanding Scripture's spiritual core.

This hermeneutic ideal of reading the Bible with the Spirit had consequences. Consider the prayer for scriptural devotion from Böhme's *Plain Directions*: "*Give me Thine Holy Spirit, which is the Spirit of Wisdom and Revelation; that he may write with his own Finger thy Words, which are Spirit and Life, in my Heart; and I may so inwardly and deeply relish the Spiritual Power of thy Word.*"[11] Word and Spirit are still inextricably tied together. But in contrast to the magisterial Reformers, the prayer shifts more emphasis to "*the Spirit of Wisdom and Revelation.*" Genuine Christians must have vital communion with the Spirit, who directly and inwardly imparts the spiritual power of the Word.

This emphasis was primarily introduced to distinguish between true Christians personally appropriating the gospel's saving truth and nominal Christians, who could only attain head knowledge. However, unlike Spener, who was wary of straying too far from the plain sense of Scripture, Francke, Böhme, and Mather also assumed that the pious experiences of regenerate Christians would "*obtain a lively Knowledge of the wonderful and hidden Mysteries*" underneath the *sensus literalis* of all biblical texts.[12] Personal piety thus became an instrument to illuminate dark, difficult places of Scripture. In their exegetical practice, the Halle Pietists, and even more so Cotton Mather, developed a strong penchant for typological, prophetic, and allegorical-mystical readings, often drawn from patristic and medieval, but also Kabbalistic and theosophical sources. These readings they often verified by their own experiences and those of other pious Christians. While over- and misinterpretation was a real concern, the bigger concern was robbing the Word of God of its spiritual riches.

The principal features of this spiritualistic hermeneutic were widely shared by Pietists and evangelicals of all stripes. For the most part, differences between more moderate churchmen and so-called radicals were in degree rather than kind.[13] In the New England tradition, for instance, Jonathan Edwards would be more wary than Mather about searching for Scripture's hidden mysteries. But Edwards took for granted the distinction between unconverted and converted readers. Only true Christians, endowed by the power of the indwelling Spirit and given a new spiritual sense, could obtain spiritual knowledge from Scripture.[14]

On the German side, the key figures of Pietism—whether Lutheran or Reformed, moderate or radical—all shared this basic assumption. For example, in the preface to his early *Spruch-Catechismo* (1689), Johann Wilhelm Petersen argued that effective teachers of the Word needed to be holy men, "as they had themselves heard and learned it from God in the school of the Holy Spirit."[15] The two monuments of radical Pietist exegesis, the *Marburg Bible* (1712) and the *Berleburg Bible* (8 vols., 1726–42),[16] pushed this Pietist hermeneutics to an extreme, suggesting that an inward revelation by the same Spirit who had given forth the Scriptures was required to truly take hold of their secret mystical and prophetic meanings.[17]

Like the "Biblia Americana," the two Pietist commentary Bibles extensively explored tropological-moral, allegorical-mystical, typological, and prophetic meanings. Such meanings elucidated the history of redemption believed to be encoded in Scripture. While unusual in the length to which their respective commentators went, these were not per se unusual pursuits. Significant divergences arose, however, with regard to sources Pietist and evangelical exegetes used for these mystical and prophetic readings and the conclusions they drew from their application. For instance, the Philadelphianism and theosophical speculations that informed many of the glosses in the Marburg and Berleburg bibles would have been unacceptable both to the more "churchly" Halle Pietists and to Mather or Edwards. Interpreting end-time prophecies also produced pronounced differences. How much did one feel emboldened by the indwelling Spirit to pinpoint historical events leading up to the parousia, or to predict its date and the precise nature of the millennial kingdom? Interpreters' boldness on these topics was closely related to their hopes for the imminent millennium, and their expectations (or skepticism) about a new apostolic age of the Spirit.

Millennialism and the Debates over the Restoration of Spiritual Gifts

The resurgence of futurist millennialism originated in Reformed Protestant circles of the mid-seventeenth century and especially flourished among Puritans in old and New England.[18] Turning away from the still dominant Augustinian amillennialism, these exegetes put the thousand-year binding of the dragon (Rev 20) back into the future as an actual reign of Christ on earth before the general resurrection and the Last Judgment. The book of Revelation as a whole was read as a prophetic church history of the postapostolic period. The mysterious cycles of visions prefigured a chronological sequence describing the rise, dominance, decline, and ultimate fall of the Antichrist, the great antagonist of the true church. The end of his reign, which Rev 11 foretold to last for 1,260 days or years, was widely believed to have been initiated by the Reformation. Its completion and the church's triumph over its enemy were thought to be predicted by the final chapters of the book. This understanding of Revelation anchored the redemptive-historical interpretations of a wide range of other biblical prophecies, particularly from Daniel.

Reformed millennialist exegetes differed widely on the details of their chronologies, and methods of interpreting various latter-day historical events. While modern historians often sort millenarians of the period according to a simple pre- or post distinction, the question of whether Christ would return before or after the thousand years was only one among many debated points. Others included the nature of the apocalyptic tribulations, the slaying of the witnesses, and the resurrection of the saints before the millennium. Would there be an eschatological gathering and conversion of the Jews? In what ways exactly would Christ rule on earth, and how was one to imagine the millennial earth? And, most pertinent to our topic, would the looked-for revival of Christ's pure church in the last day be accompanied, as Joel 2:28 and Acts 2:17 suggested, by an outpouring of the Spirit "on all flesh," bringing back the charismata of the apostles? On each of these issues, exegetes discussed whether a preterist or a futurist understanding, and whether a more literalist-factualist or more allegorical interpretation, applied.

The wide range of responses and positions reflects the ubiquity of these questions in transatlantic Anglophone Protestant circles. The years before and after the Glorious Revolution (1688) marked a high tide of apocalyptic excitement, especially but not exclusively among Dissenters. It produced a slew of works predicting the supernatural destruction of Antichrist's reign and personal return of Christ—sometimes as soon as the 1690s or early 1700s.[19] After the turn of the century, these imminent expectations receded somewhat. A more gradualist "postmillennialism," which emphasized continuity with rather than disjuncture from the present age, emerged as the dominant evangelical paradigm during the Great Awakening. In the British colonies, Cotton Mather and Jonathan Edwards embody this development and illustrate the close connection between eschatology, pneumatology, and hermeneutics.

Mather's many works on millennialism document considerable change in some of his views, notably on the national conversion of the Jews. Yet, overall, he stayed true to the kind of hyperliteralist premillennialism first developed in *Things to be Look'd for* (1691). Mather initially expected Christ's earthly reign to begin in 1697, following the remaining apocalyptic tribulations. In "Problema Theologicum" (1703), he adjusted his timetable for 1716 as the *annus climacticus*. Disappointed a second time, Mather stopped making public pronouncements on dates, but privately continued to speculate that 1736 might be the year of the Antichrist's destruction, to be completed by the Petrine conflagration.[20]

Mather expected the impending revolution to involve a new outpouring of the Spirit. In another essay appended to the "Biblia," titled "VATES. Or, some Remarks upon the SPIRIT of PROPHECY," Mather argued that the early church's charismata and proper miracles continued well into the fourth century, until the Spirit finally withdrew in response to the Antichristian apostasy.[21] While "the plentiful Rain with which the Lord once comforted His Heritage, has been Stopt by the Ingratitude of Mankind; and so, for three Years and an half (the M.CC. LX dayes of Antichrist) it has not rained," as Mather succinctly put it in a diary entry from May 1717, this period was quickly drawing to an end now, and so "there will be a Sound of Abundance of Rain."[22] Mather did respect and also gave extensive consideration in his "Biblia" to the traditional Protestant vindication of cessationism. He summarized that position in a long entry on 1 Chr 29 dealing with prophecy, writing that the closing of the canon meant the "Church of God" was "now being furnished with so Compleat a *Rule* of *Beleef* and *Practice*, as the Holy Scriptures, we must not wonder, if those Gifts are not now granted, as they were in former Ages."[23] Mather was never convinced, however, that Joel's eschatological prophecy had been fully accomplished in the days of the apostles (Acts 2:16–18).

To be sure, Mather did not believe that actual new scriptures or teachings were to be added in this last age. He nowhere hinted at such a possibility in the "Biblia," and affirmed the completeness and sufficiency of the canon in many publications, most strongly perhaps in his polemical writings against the Quakers. For instance, in *The Principles of the Protestant Religion maintained* (1690), Mather specifically targeted the Friends' dangerous "Fancy of *New Divine Revelations and Inspirations*." While Mather emphasized the central and active role of the Spirit, he simultaneously asserted "that the Word of God in Scripture is that which to us in Gospel Times, since the Canon was perfected, Answers all other wayes of Revelation."[24] In response to George Keith's capacious understanding of the light of Christ within, Mather drew a sharp distinction between an immediate revelation by inspiration and a mediate revelation by the Spirit, "called *Illumination*." The latter applied the promises and duties of Scripture to the heart and mind of all believers, while enabling teachers to uncover and expound the sometimes hidden meanings of God's Word. "That in this sense, there are new Revelations made from time to time to God's Children, i.e. *subjectively*, 2 Pet. 3.18," Mather readily granted. By contrast, the kind of extraordinary inspirations given to the prophets and apostles, yielding new objects of faith or duty, had "ceased, before *John* the Apostle, *deceased*, though his other extraordinary gifts did continue" for at least two more centuries.[25]

In theory, Mather never wavered from this position. However, especially during phases of heightened spiritual fervor, the distinction between subjective illumination and revelatory inspiration could, at times, become blurry in Mather's practice of biblical interpretation and devotion. He came to give great importance and an elastic meaning to the gifts of the Spirit that he believed were being restored to the church in the latter days. And he was convinced that without the Spirit's supernatural aid the completion of the church's reformation by restoring "primitive" Christianity and spreading it to the far ends of the earth seemed well-nigh impossible in the short time that remained.[26]

By the 1710s, Mather had grown confident, as he wrote in a letter to Bartholomäus Ziegenbalg—the Halle-trained pastor in Tranquebar, India—that the rapid extension of revivals and missions amongst Jews and heathens "will be accomplished, by Granting over again, those *Extraordinary Gifts of the Prophetic Spirit*, by which the Holy Spirit watered the Primitive Church, and at first spread and confirmed the *Christian Religion* in the World."[27] Mather knew that the Halle Pietists, like others among his associates, treaded carefully around this subject. At the end of the "Biblia Americana" essay on the "SPIRIT of PROPHECY" he cited Böhme's pronouncement of the official Halle position: the question "whether these *Gifts* will revive in the latter Ages," one ought to "leave to the supreme Disposer of all things" and focus on doing good in the world inspired by the "*Spirit* of LOVE."²⁸ But Mather could not let things rest there. He considered it likely "that the *Effusions* of the Holy SPIRIT in the *primitive Times*, in Proportion to what are to be in the *latter Dayes*, were to be no more than a *Few Drops* that go before the falling of a *mighty Showre*."²⁹

By contrast, a strict cessationism characterized the postmillennialism that Jonathan Edwards helped establish among the more moderate "New Light" evangelical pastors of the next generation. Edwards pushed back the onset of the millennium to somewhere around 2000. In his *Notes on the Apocalypse* and elsewhere, he argued for a figurative and gradualist understanding of the coming kingdom and most of the remaining latter day events leading up to it. He denied that the dawning of the last age would be accompanied by either apocalyptic tribulations or supernatural wonders, and read Joel's prophecy in a preterist fashion. Commenting on the Holy Spirit's special visitation on Pentecost, Edwards pointed out that the apostles' endowment with spiritual gifts fulfilled Joel 2:28, "Which prophecy the apostle Peter takes notice is accomplished in this dispensation, Acts 2:17."³⁰ Edwards also believed that the charismata had ceased at the end of the apostolic age. With the canon complete, the church now possessed a "perfect and complete standing rule, sufficient to guide her in all things."³¹ In his sermon on 1 Cor 13:8, "Divine Love Alone Lasts Eternally," which he preached as a caution against enthusiasm in the context of the Great Awakening, he argued that cessation was not a punishment for the church's corruption, but came about because the Spirit's extraordinary gifts were no longer needed.

In the last third of the seventeenth century, futurist millennialism and the exegetical debates surrounding it also appeared in the emerging German Pietist movement—including its Lutheran branch, despite the Augsburg Confession's condemnation of chiliasm. However, the "hope for a better state of the church here on earth," first formulated in Spener's *Pia Desideria* (1675) and then expanded in the *Behauptung Der Hoffnung künfftiger Besserer Zeiten* (1693), was very intent on avoiding the faults of a *chiliasmus crassus*. Francke, as well as Spener, avoided speculations about the kingdom's precise nature or date of arrival. Whether the church's progressive triumph would cause or be preceded by the Roman Antichrist's fall and the national conversion of the Jews was a matter of doubt. But, like Edwards, the Halle Pietists were convinced that no dramatic disjuncture would mark the transition from the present to the millennial age, and that Christ would only return at its conclusion.³²

As the Pietist movement developed and diversified, this programmatically moderate, vague form of postmillennialism soon found itself in competition with much more concrete visions. In German-speaking lands, too, the 1690s became a decade of imminent apocalyptic expectations. The radical branches of Pietism were particularly committed, with many looking to the turn of the century as the eschatological turning point. For example, Heinrich Horche's mystical and prophetic readings of Scripture—which drew on many of the same sources as Mather—also predicted 1697 as the likely dawning of the millennial age.[33] Similar expectations also emerged in the circle of Johann Wilhelm and Johanna Eleonora Petersen (née von und zu Merlau), which had separated from Spener's *collegium pietatis* in Frankfurt. In 1685, the Petersens came to embrace a version of premillennialism that owed much to the Puritan-Dissenting tradition. Through the 1690s, the Petersens published a series of hefty and learned exegetical works, including Johann Wilhelm's *Schriftmäßige Erklärung und Beweis der Tausend Jahre* (Frankfurt, 1692) and Johanna Eleonora's *Anleitung zu gründlicher Verständniß der Heiligen Offenbahrung Jesu Christi* (Frankfurt, 1696). Like Mather, they predicted an impending revolution, ushered in by a literal first resurrection of the saints and a personal appearance of Christ. Their vision of the millennial reign was less corporeal than Mather's and more akin to Edwards's, though. Toward the end of the decade, the Petersens added two major components to their millennialism that Mather, Edwards, and the majority of churchmen would have rejected: a Philadelphian, dispensationalist ecclesiology and the doctrine of universal salvation.

Significantly, the Petersens believed that with the parousia drawing near, the spiritual gifts were now being restored and that Joel's prophecy would have its full accomplishment with the coming millennium.[34] Heinrich Horche's 1698 *Send=Schreiben* on divine dreams and revelations similarly argued that the spiritual gifts were still needed as long as so many heathens and Jews remained unconverted.[35] Similarly, the Berleburg Bible glossed on the eschatological fulfillment of Joel 2:28 "that Acts 2 was only a token of it and the first fruits, whereas the full harvest was still to come."[36] While Spener and especially Francke sympathized with the Petersens' positions, such topics required considerable delicacy in the protracted debates with "Orthodox" critics. Speculating too freely about the end times could endanger the respectability of the entire Pietist movement.

The Gift of Prophecy, Revelatory Readings, and New Revelations

The belief in an eschatological restitution of spiritual gifts was accompanied by a heightened experiential supernaturalism. This was embraced by some laypeople, especially women,[37] as well as learned theologian-pastors like Mather, Petersen, and Horche. Other churchmen showed more skepticism and restraint, as they worried about the effects of enthusiasm on ecclesial politics. Reports about supernatural and spiritual experiences reached periodic heights on both sides of the Atlantic during the revivals of the 1690s and 1740s. Especially common were accounts of special providences, signs, and wonders directly attributed to God's interventions; dreams, ecstatic visions, and auditory experiences that were understood as premonitions, or outright prophetic revelations. Somewhat rarer were reported miracles performed by humans and associated with other spiritual gifts, such as glossolalia, healings, and even exorcisms. In many cases, these extraordinary experiences were attributed to the help or mediation of angels, who played a central role in the supernaturally charged piety of many awakened Protestants.[38]

The accounts of prophetic dreams and visions ranged from threats of God's punishment and admonitions for repentance to joyous promises of temporal deliverance and eternal salvation—either for individuals or communities. These basic variants and their many combinations usually appeared in the context of apocalyptic-millenarian expectations. Almost without exception, these revelatory experiences were rooted in certain eschatological Scripture passages, which assumed new, acute, and intensely personal meaning. For instance, many dreams and visions reported during the 1690s and 1740s described being transported to heaven, meeting Christ the bridegroom, or seeing names written in the "Book of Life" and "Book of Death" of Revelation. Such visions, like the frequent auditory phenomenon of hearing heavenly music while meditating on Scripture, were almost indistinguishable from what was called "biblical impulses"—individuals having a particular, personally relevant Bible verse impressed on their mind and heart. Awakened Protestants consistently explicated these experiences through scripturalizing language; that is, through a bricolage of biblical citations and allusions. Expressing and explicating such experiences became another form of mystical and prophetic interpretation. Besides their intensely personal meanings, many experiences were understood as general "signs of the times": predictions of the imminent fulfillment of certain biblical prophecies. Thus, these revelatory experiences arose from the general culture of experiential-illuminated exegesis. They constituted a particular mode of reading the Bible with the Spirit, which, however, occasionally began to cross the line between scriptural illuminations and new revelations and thus stretched the boundaries of the canon.

For example, the "Begeisterte Mägde" appeared in several central and northern German cities during the early 1690s, claiming to be blessed with visions and signs.[39] These "Inspired Women" were part of a larger wave of enthusiasm then circulating through Pietist groups in cities such as Gotha, Erfurt, Halberstadt, and Quedlinburg. The best known of them was Rosamunde

Juliane von der Asseburg. Since her youth, she had experienced heavenly journeys and visions of Christ as her approaching spouse, which she communicated to the world in language heavily derived from Revelation, Isaiah, and Canticles. The Petersens saw a kindred spirit and strongly supported her, even taking her into their Lüneburg parsonage.[40] Johanna Eleonora herself was no stranger to supernatural experiences that inspired and undergirded many of her distinct interpretations of the Scriptures. For example, in 1664 she had a dream about the eschatological conversion of the Jews, and in 1662 she received a prophetic vision: an angel-like figure pointed to a gilded number 1685 and promised that, in that year, great things would start to happen and something important would be revealed to her.[41] She understood this vision to be fulfilled, for in that very year, she and her husband embraced the true system of millenarianism. In 1691, Johann Wilhelm published an anonymous "Letter to some theologians regarding the question whether God, after the ascension of Christ, was no longer revealing himself to his children today through divine visions," in which Petersen argued for an ongoing revelation of God through elect believers even after the closing of the canon. The tract also contained some of von der Asseburg's visions, which Petersen took as experiential confirmations of his own interpretations of the end-time prophecies. If women were having dreams and prophesying as a fulfillment of Joel 2:28, he thought, this demonstrated the trustworthiness of his own predictions that the parousia must be near.[42]

The tract triggered a heated discussion about the possibility of extrabiblical, immediate revelations and their relation to the canonical Scriptures.[43] Von der Asseburg's visions were branded as heretical by defenders of Lutheran "Orthodoxy," and in 1692 Petersen was stripped of his offices as minister and superintendent. Yet the Petersens continued to follow their callings as eschatological prophets, spreading what they now understood as the "eternal gospel" of Rev 14:6. This long-hidden spiritual kernel of Scripture containing the secrets of the Philadelphian millennial dispensations and the *apokatastsis panton* had been finally revealed as the last days were drawing near.[44]

In the pamphlet war of the early 1690s, Spener and Francke attempted to steer a middle course. They defended belief in God's special providences, extraordinary spiritual experiences, and even the ministry of angels. However, while affirming the possibility of prophetic dreams and visions, they insisted that God would not reveal new doctrines or duties. And they never claimed such experiences for themselves. Spener in particular expressed significant skepticism about accounts of visions and dreams: they could be caused by the devil, evil spirits, or mental illness. Hence, Spener and Francke publicly urged utmost caution. Spener never affirmed the authenticity of any specific new revelation, and denounced some self-declared prophets as frauds. However, he refrained from judging von der Asseburg. While Francke agreed with his mentor on most cases, he thought von der Asseburg genuine, along with some of the other "Mägde." After the mid-1690s, however, Francke began differentiating his brand of "churchly" Pietism from the unrulier, separatist kinds, which were associated with revelations and ecstatic phenomena.[45] Francke became guarded and never again defended a living prophet.

Freshly removed from his offices as minister and professor of theology in Marburg, Heinrich Horche offered a spirited defense of new revelations in his 1698 *Send=Schreiben*. He, like Spener and Francke, emphasized the need to measure dreams and visions against the canonical Bible when discerning whether a new revelation was from God or a mere figment of the imagination. Like other radical Pietists, however, Horche believed that inspired revelations could help uncover Scripture's deepest mysteries, especially the prophecies that still remained to be fulfilled. The Marburg Bible is testimony to that conviction. With the millennial dawn drawing near, such prophetic discoveries would grow. As the preface of the Berleburg Bible proclaimed, glossing Zach 14:7 ("at evening time it shall be light") and Dan 12:4 ("and knowledge shall increase"), on the eve of history "God will illuminate the hearts of the faithful. From which will follow, according to Daniel's prophecy, that many will go over the prophetic books and the entire Holy Bible and knowledge shall increase."[46]

The debate surrounding spiritual gifts and new revelations was further galvanized by the Camisards or French Prophets and by the spread of "Inspirationist" conventicles among British Dissenters and German Pietists. There is no room to treat this here. Suffice it to say that the "Inspirationists" pushed the Halle Pietists in a more conservative direction, although they found many sympathizers and followers in more radical circles. Mather's response was a mixture of openness, curiosity, genuine excitement, and skeptical reservation.[47] This was very much consistent with how he generally dealt with potential spiritual experiences and supernatural phenomena—including his own.

On the one hand, Mather actively searched for signs and wonders to confirm his interpretations of Scripture. On the other hand, he always urged thorough discernment of the spirits, and he was careful about sharing or assigning evidential weight to his personal experiences. His diaries regularly describe his "presagious impressions" (i.e., premonitions) or "particular faiths": moments of assurance that a prayer would be answered or a certain event come to pass. At one time, he called these assurances "a little degree of the spirit of prophecy." During his days of prayer and fasting, Mather also recorded experiences he variably described as "ecstasies," "irradiations," or "effusions of the spirit."[48] Such spiritual illuminations could concern general matters of faith (e.g., trust in God's providence) but also the particular meaning of Scripture texts. In this respect, Mather's *praxis pietatis* stood in the tradition of the more radical strands of seventeenth-century Puritanism. Here, apocalyptic and spiritualist enthusiasm already "opened up a space for progressive divine revelation, channeled through the Holy Ghost," by which God would disclose "hitherto hidden truths" as the new age of wonders dawned.[49] Even some of the more moderate Puritan churchmen of the seventeenth century believed that their readings of Revelation were quite literally revelatory readings. Thomas Brightman, for instance, programmatically titled his commentary *Apocalypsis Apocalypseos* (1609). He and others thought that it had been composed under divine inspiration. Similarly, James Ussher was widely regarded as a latter-day prophet on account of his eschatological predictions about the future.[50]

Mather grew up in an environment where his own father nurtured hopes that new revelations regarding the apocalyptic prophecies might be given to pious souls living "in an exiled condition" in the American "wilderness." Increase Mather also implanted in his son a belief in the imminent fulfillment of Joel's prophecy in a restitution of the extraordinary gifts and a latter-day outpouring of the Spirit that would enable the mass conversion of Jews and heathens,[51] as well as in the decisive role of the ministry of angels during the end times. Accordingly, Cotton Mather often attributed his spiritual illuminations to the mediation of angels, and, on several occasions, reported actual angelic visitations in his diary. The most spectacular and famous one occurred in February 1685. It is best understood as a potential experience of prophetic calling in conjunction with an inspired reading of Scripture. The angel's revelation reads like a "targumic" version of Ezek 31:3–5, 7, 9, with omissions, alterations, and a very personal application (the young man's election, the many books he would publish, and the "great works" he "should do for the church of Christ in the revolutions that are now ahead"). Even as he marveled at this extraordinary blessing, however, Mather worried that this vision might really be the product of his vainglorious imagination, or, worse, be of demonic origin.[52] For the rest of his career, he struggled to know if this sense of calling was genuine.

The question became especially acute in the 1690s and then again in the mid-1710s, when Mather's apocalyptic expectations and spiritual intensity rose to a fever pitch. He was constantly on the lookout for signs of Antichrist's raging or the latter-day revolutions in the church that would confirm his predictions for the *annus climacticus*. This concern drove his interest in the Huguenots and the Camisard prophets, but also his engagement with possessed young women during the Salem witchcraft affair. In their spiritual struggles, Mather found ample proof for the reality of demons and angels alike. He was convinced that the evil spirit could not have been cast out, and the women converted, without the Spirit's extraordinary gifts mediated by angels. In such successes as well as his "irradiations" and "particular faiths," Mather saw harbingers of the great eschatological outpouring of the Spirit. At the same time, Mather expected God to humble and correct his servants. Despite many misfortunes and setbacks (most dramatically the repeated disappointment concerning the predicted dates for Christ's parousia), Mather continued hoping that God had indeed appointed him as a latter-day prophet. He did not long to speak in ecstasy like the Camisards, but to be granted inspired readings of the Bible, especially the end-time prophecies.

In keeping with his spiritualistic hermeneutics, Mather expected that the prophetic Spirit's return would enable a deepened understanding of the Word of God, especially Revelation. As his father had put it, "the Un-sealing of these Mysteries is a sign that the Time of the End is at hand, Dan. 12.9."[53] Such was the hope for his own "Biblia Americana," as Mather made clear in an advertising pamphlet for subscriptions. With unmistakable millennialist fervor, it presents the "Biblia" as both a sign and a fruit of an eschatological increase in knowledge as promised in Dan 12:4: "An Age of *Light* comes on; *Explications* and *Discoveries* are continually growing; which all that will but *shew themselves* Men cannot but imbibe with Satisfaction. The *Path of the Just One*, in his gracious Approaches toward us, causes the *Light* which opens His Oracles unto us, *to shine more and more toward the perfect Day.* . . . And, Lo, there is Light, and the Illustrations of the Sacred Scriptures are carried on to Wonderment!* The Instruments by whom this Light is brought down upon us, have of late been greatly Multiplied." Mather included various branches of biblical studies among the "Instruments," but highlighted two approaches in particular: illustrating "the Scriptures from EXPERIMENTAL PIETY, or the Observation of Christian Experience"; and explicating the *"Book of the Kingdom"* as the "true Doctrine of the CHILIAD which more opens & breaks in upon the more considerate Enquirers, *as the Day approaches.*"[54]

Around the turn of the century, Mather, like the Petersens, developed the idea that pious, inspired biblical interpreters could work with the Spirit and the support of angels to effectively propagate the "eternal Gospel" of Rev 14:6. Mather was no Philadelphian and not, as far as we know, in conversation with the writings of Jane Leade and her English or German followers. Instead, he came up with his own related but independent notion of an *evangelium aeternum*. Mather's gospel consisted of a few, fundamental biblical principles or, as he called them, "Maxims of Piety." All regenerate Protestants could converge around these principles without having to abandon their confessional homes before the return of Christ. This project preoccupied the last two decades of

Mather's life, as he refined and reduced his "Maxims of Piety" in numerous publications. One, which he also appended to his "Biblia Americana" as a kind of *summa summarum*, clearly reflects how he considered this "eternal gospel": *The Stone Cut out of the Mountain* (Boston, 1716), which would help to crush the kingdom of Antichrist as prophesied in Dan 2:45.

Mather also advocated the "Maxims of Piety" to his many correspondents, notably the Halle Pietists and a large network of British Dissenters. In a 1715 letter to his Scotch-Presbyterian correspondent Robert Wodrow, he wrote that among the signs of the advancing "Kingdom of God" he expected God to "raise up some Instruments, who from the Mines of the Sacred Scriptures, will dig and run the maxims of the everlasting Gospel . . . wherein all the children of God really are united," and on the basis of which they will "associate for the Kingdome of God." To quickly spread this "everlasting gospel" near and far, "*Joels* prophecy is also to receive its full Accomplishment."[55]

During the last two decades of his life, Mather's prophetic self-understanding increasingly focused on this notion of propagating the *evangelium aeternum* with the help of the Spirit and, as he put it in his diary in May 1717, the "Angels whom our ascended Lord having received the Command of them, sends with their various Gifts to possess the Children of Men." For years, Mather would set aside special days to pray for the return of the prophetic spirit, without which "the Kingdome of God, which we are to look for, and long for, will not come." He had concluded "that all other Wayes to introduce Piety into the World, or establish Unity among the People of God, are by sad Experience found ineffectual." For fear of spiritual pride, Mather was careful on such occasions not to ask God, "that I may myself enjoy any Share in the gifts of the prophetic Spirit." "I desire nothing extraordinary for myself," he emphasized, "but extraordinary Holiness."[56] As we have seen, however, Mather definitely believed he had received drops of the Spirit, even if he never claimed to be fully endowed with the prophetic spirit himself.

Clearly, Mather was aware of the dangers of investing all one's hope in the prophetic spirit. "The Affectation of *Extraordinaries*," Mather wrote at the very end of his essay on "The PROPHETIC SPIRIT," may lead "to very dangerous *Temptations* and *Illusions*," including the introduction of heretical novelties. He then approvingly quoted a tract by "the memorable *Franckius*," titled *Programma, De Donis Dei Extraordinariis* and published in response to the activities of the Inspired in Halle. The tract cautioned against "a very great danger for those who will not have grown firm and deep roots in humility. But who can claim that for himself?"[57] While Mather agreed, he believed that cultivating a God-fearing, humble piety through his "Maxims" could offer the necessary protection and purely scriptural principles of the Everlasting Gospel.

Maxims could serve as the "Infallible *Touchstone*, by which we are to *Try the Spirits*." Whatever "marvellous Communications from the Heavenly World" one received, it should be asked, "*How far do the* MAXIMS *of Piety, the Establishment, and Propagation of which is intended by the Holy* SPIRIT *in all His extraordinary Gifts, receive Encouragement from these Communications?*"[58]

Twenty years later, Edwards was much more cautious than Mather or the radical Pietists in giving credence to any "marvellous Communications from the Heavenly World." Indeed, he took a position even more absolute than that of the "churchly" Lutheran Pietists, denying even the possibility of the Spirit's extraordinary gifts and new revelations. Historians have explained this as Edwards's growing concern over the Great Awakening's ecclesial and social upheaval, driven by enthusiastic phenomena among laypeople. In many ways, the wave of enthusiasm unleashed by George Whitefield was a large-scale replay of the religious fervor that arose in millenarian circles during the 1690s. The Great Awakening was an unruly popularization of the kind of biblical piety that aimed for Spirit-filled readings. Biblical impulses and ejaculatory biblical outbursts, as Douglas Winiarski has shown, were a regular feature of the revivals. For many of these inspired lay readers, the Word did not just come alive with new personal relevance. Instead, readers received direct revelation about the Bible's mystical and prophetic meanings through dreams, trance visions, or angelic mediation. Once again, celestial journeys and experiential explications of the end-time prophecies were widespread. "Aided by special illumination of the indwelling Holy Spirit, visionists fervently believed that they were living in the last days," as Winiarski writes, "and in their trances found themselves facing Father and Son on their throne, as foretold in Rev. 20"; or saw "the appearance of the Son of Man descending from the clouds and throwing open the Book of Life for all to see." In the early 1740s, these visions "emerged as a crucial battleground in an increasingly fractious print war between revival opposers and apologists."[59]

While more radical New Light preachers, like James Davenport, embraced these biblical impressions and revelations, Edwards became a leading spokesperson for a more conservative faction that denounced them as false and dangerous. Even more than emotional eruptions and bodily agitations, the pretensions to gifts of the Spirit and new prophecies were helping critics to dismiss the revivals as a whole. Worse, such pretensions threatened to undermine the authority of the canonical Scripture and lure Christians away from what was "a perfect rule already by which to walk."[60]

Edwards had no doubt, as Darren Pollock argues, that the Spirit was "indeed working in the hearts of Christians in the present age." But his ministry was not to reveal new meanings behind or hidden within Scripture, but rather to inspire a "'new sense and understanding of the same truths'" apparent to every reasonable reader.[61] Like Mather and the Pietists, Edwards believed that knowledge would increase as the final age approached. As his *Notes on the Apocalypse* and other writings display, Edwards no doubt entertained highly speculative and figural interpretations of Revelation and the events leading up to the end times—interpretations that are not, to the modern observer, categorically different from those of a Mather or Horche. Yet Edwards did not attribute these insights to revelatory communications of the Spirit. Rather, in line with his gradualist postmillennialism, he understood the fruits of his exegetical labors as growing from deepening spiritual knowledge of Scripture, which did not require extraordinary gifts. Through careful study, the church would progress to "a very glorious state here in this world and to a very great degree of perfection in knowledge and resemblance of an heavenly state of perfect light and knowledge."[62] More than any of the other awakened Protestants treated in this essay, Edwards thus kept a jealous watch over the line between Spirit-enabled, illuminated Bible readings and purported revelations leading to yet-undisclosed meanings of Scripture, whether mystical or prophetic. The line was fine, but to him it made, as Douglas Sweeney notes, "a world of difference."[63]

Conclusion

Like the Halle Pietists after the turn of the century, Edwards and the other moderate New Light ministers struggled to contain a dynamic that originated from their own biblical piety and its inherent spiritualistic tendency. The Word was to come alive with the Spirit, but not take on a life of its own in the kind of "targumizing impulse" that animated many of the hotter awakened Protestants.[64] The search for personal appropriations, inspired readings, and hidden meanings could inadvertently blur the boundaries of the canon, not just by attention to apocryphal books (which received ample treatments in the commentaries of radical Pietists!), but, more significantly, by ongoing revelations and prophetic predictions. The sense of living in the end times brought a new sensitivity to seeing spiritual gifts. To be sure, a man like Mather always maintained *"that all new Revelation is ceased,"* in the sense that no new objects of faith were to be expected.[65] However, for him, as for the Petersens, elaborate interpretations of the Scriptures and revelatory, visionary experiences mutually confirmed each other. This belief generates a peculiar tension. One the one hand, the absolute authority of the Bible was the foundation and framework of all they believed, and their eschatology more specifically. They spent an incredible amount of labor explicating even the minutest details of the prophecies. On the other hand, the pronounced spiritualism and experientialism in their approach could hardly be contained in that framework and overflowed it with enthusiastic energy. The stronger the accentuation of the Spirit's inward work and immediate revelations to the soul, one might conclude, the more many, if not all, Pietists and evangelicals loosened its connection with the Word as defined by the scriptural principle of the Reformers.

Notes

1. Cotton Mather, *Magnalia Christi Americana: Or, the Ecclesiastical History of New-England, from Its First Planting in the Year 1620, unto the Year of Our Lord, 1698* (London: Thomas Parkhurst, 1702), book 6:1–88.
2. Johannes Wallmann, "Geisterfahrung und Kirche im frühen Pietismus," in *Charisma und Institution*, ed. Trutz Rendtdorff (Gütersloh: Gütersloher Verlagshaus, 1985), 132.
3. Martin Brecht, "Die Bedeutung der Bibel im deutschen Pietismus," in *GdP*, 4:102.
4. For a very helpful survey of the German side, see Volkhard Wels, "Unmittelbare göttliche Offenbarung als Gegenstand der Auseinandersetzung in der protestantischen Theologie der Frühen Neuzeit," in *Diskurse der Gelehrtenkultur in der Frühen Neuzeit: Ein Handbuch*, ed. Herbert Jaumann (Berlin: De Gruyter, 2010), 747–808.
5. David R. Como, "Radical Puritanism, c. 1558–1660," in *The Cambridge Companion to Puritanism*, ed. John Coffey and Paul C. H. Lim (Cambridge: Cambridge University Press, 2008), 248–49.
6. D. Bruce Hindmarsh, *The Spirit of Early Evangelicalism: True Religion in a Modern World* (New York: Oxford University Press, 2018), 24–27.
7. For reviews of the scholarship on the hermeneutics of Pietism and Francke in particular, see Susanne Luther, "Schriftverständnis im Pietismus," in *Pietismus-Handbuch*, ed. Wolfgang Breul and Thomas Hahn-Bruckart (Tübingen: Mohr Siebeck, 2020), 349–59; and Thomas Hahn-Bruckart, "Bibel," in Breul and Hahn-Bruckart, *Pietismus-Handbuch*, 420–27.
8. Mather used the 1706 London edition, containing a preface by Anton Wilhelm Böhme and a commendation by the Huguenot theologian Pierre Allix: *Manuductio Ad Lectionem Scripturae Sacrae, Augustu Hermanni Franckii . . . Commendata, A Petro Allix, S.T.P., Cum Nova Praefatione, De Impedimentis Studii Theologici* (London: R. Burrough, 1706).
9. See "Appendix. Containing Some general stores, of Illustration; and a Furniture which will richly Qualify a Person to be a reader of the bible," *The Mather Family Papers*, Cotton Mather Papers, "Biblia Americana," reel 13, following Revelation. This essay, like the other ones mentioned below, will be published in Cotton Mather, *Biblia Americana*, vol. 10, *Hebrews–Revelation*, ed. Jan Stievermann (Tübingen: Mohr Siebeck, forthcoming).
10. Cotton Mather, *Manuductio ad ministerium: Directions for a candidate of the ministry* (Boston: Hancock, 1726). For a fuller discussion, see Jan Stievermann and Ryan P. Hoselton, "Spiritual Meaning and Experimental Piety in the Exegesis of Cotton Mather and Jonathan Edwards," in *Jonathan Edwards and Scripture*, ed. David P. Barshinger and Douglas A. Sweeney (New York: Oxford University Press, 2018), 86–105.
11. Anton Wilhelm Böhme, *Plain Directions for Reading the Holy Bible, To Promoting of Mens Salvation, Part I* (London: Joseph Downing, 1708), 23.

12. Ibid., 23.

13. Hans Schneider has observed that churchly and radical Pietist hermeneutics alike tended toward experiential, subjectivist, and enthusiastic approaches. See Schneider, "Der radikale Pietismus im 17. Jahrhundert," in *GdP*, 1:391–437, at 402.

14. *WJE*, 17:413–14; see also *WJE*, 17:408–26; 14:70–96.

15. Johann Wilhelm Petersen, *Spruch-Catechismus: Aus dem Catechismo des seel. Lutheri in Fragen vorgestellet / Die mit den unmittelbahren Sprüchen der Heiligen Schrifft beantwortet werden* (Frankfurt: Lipper, 1689), 32, 65.

16. *Mystische und Profetische Bibel, . . . Sampt Erklärung Der fürnemsten Sinnbilder und Weissagungen, Sonderlich Des H. Lieds Salomons Und der Offenbarung J.C.* (Marburg: Joh. Kürßner, 1712), Vorwort, i–ii. For literature on the two Bible commentaries, see Shantz's essay in this collection.

17. See *Der Heiligen Schrifft Neuen Testaments Achter Theil . . .* (Berleburg, 1742), Vorrede, ii.

18. See Jeffrey K. Jue, "Puritan Millennarianism in Old and New England," in Coffey and Lim, *Cambridge Companion to Puritanism*, 259–76.

19. Warren Johnston, *Revelation Restored: The Apocalypse in Later Seventeenth-Century England* (Woodbridge: Boydell and Brewer, 2011).

20. On the development of Mather's eschatology, see Reiner Smolinski, "Introduction," in *The Threefold Paradise of Cotton Mather: An Edition of "Triparadisus"* (Athens: University of Georgia Press, 1995), 3–78.

21. Significantly, this essay was based on the work of a controversial follower of the French Prophets in London, John Lacy, *The General Delusion of Christians, touching the Ways of God's revealing Himself, to, and by the Prophets* (1713).

22. *The Diary of Cotton Mather*, ed. W. C. Ford (Boston, 1911–12), 2:453.

23. *BA*, 3:735.

24. Cotton Mather, *The Principles of the Protestant Religion maintained, and churches of New-England, in the profession and exercise thereof defended, against all the calumnies of one George Keith, a Quaker, in a book lately published at Pensilvania, to undermine them both* (Boston: Richard Pierce, 1690), 21, 15.

25. Ibid., 23–27.

26. It is not entirely clear which gifts Mather expected to be restored, but in his diverse writings on the topic he tends to focus on the prophetic. For Mather's understanding of the gift of prophecy, see the entries on the various *charismata* in his annotations on 1 Cor 12 (*BA* 9: 287–91). Here Mather connects prophecy not only with foreknowledge but also with the "Word of Knowledge" as the "gift of understanding certain special Mysteries" of faith and especially "the Mystical Sense of the Scriptures of the Old Testament."

27. Cotton Mather, *India Christiana . . .* (Boston: Green, 1721), 69.

28. Mather cites Anthon [Anton] Wilhelm Böhme, *The Character of Love: Set Forth in a Sermon Preach'd on the Third Sunday After Easter* (London, 1713), 30.

29. To the same effect, Mather's gloss on Rev 2:16.

30. *WJE*, 9:365. My understanding of Edwards's spiritualistic hermeneutics and its continuities as well as discontinuities with that of Mather is much indebted to Ryan P. Hoselton, "Spiritually Discerned: Cotton Mather, Jonathan Edwards, and Experiential Exegesis in Early Evangelicalism" (PhD diss., Ruprecht-Karls-Universität Heidelberg, 2019), here esp. 143–78.

31. *WJE*, 21:232.

32. On the varieties of millennialism in German Pietism, see Ulrich Gäbler, "Geschichte, Gegenwart, Zukunft," in *GdP*, 4:19–48; Wolfgang Breul, "'Hoffnung besserer Zeiten': Der Wandel der 'Endzeit' im lutherischen Pietismus um 1700," in *Frühe Neue Zeiten: Zeitwissen zwischen Reformation und Revolution*, ed. Achim Landwehr (Bielefeld: Transcript, 2012), 261–82; Hans Schneider, "Die unterfüllte Zukunft: Apokalyptische Erwartungen im radikalen Pietismus

um 1700," *Jahrhundertwenden: Endzeit- und Zukunftsvorstellungen vom 15. bis zum 20. Jahrhundert*, ed. Manfred Jakubowski-Tiessen et al. (Göttingen: Vandenhoeck & Ruprecht, 1999), 187–212.

33. See Heinrich Horche, *Das A und das O oder Zeitrechnung der gantzen Hl. Schrift*. . . . (Leipzig: Thomas Fritsch, 1697).

34. See Johanna Eleonora Petersen, *Anleitung zu gründlicher Verständniß* (Frankfurt, 1696), 293.

35. Heinrich Horche, *Send=Schreiben Von Wahrhaffter Beschaffenheit und Deutung Göttlicher Träume und Gesichter* (Offenbach am Main, 1698), 19–20.

36. *Der Heiligen Schrifft Alten Testaments Vierter Theil* . . . (Berleburg, 1732), 722.

37. On the English side, see Phyllis Mack, *Visionary Women: Ecstatic Prophecy in Seventeenth-Century England* (Berkeley: University of California Press, 1992). For German Pietism, see Ruth Albrecht, ed., *Begeisterte Mägde: Träume, Visionen und Offenbarungen von Frauen des frühen Pietismus* (Leipzig: Evangelische Verlagsanstalt, 2018).

38. See Peter Marshall and Alexandra Walsham, eds., *Angels in the Early Modern World* (Cambridge: Cambridge University Press, 2006).

39. For further discussion and relevant literature on the "Begeisterte Mägde," see Ruth Albrecht's essay in this collection.

40. Markus Matthias, *Johann Wilhelm und Johanna Eleonora Petersen: Eine Biographie bis zur Amtsenthebung Petersens im Jahre 1692* (Göttingen: Vandenhoeck & Ruprecht, 1993), 254–300.

41. Albrecht, *Begeisterte Mägde*, 48–49, 59–62; and Albrecht, *Johanna Eleonora Petersen: Theologische Schriftstellerin des frühen Pietismus* (Göttingen: Vandenhoeck & Ruprecht, 2005), 201, 233–70.

42. Johann Wilhelm Petersen, *Send=schreiben An einige Theologos und Gottes=gelehrten / Betreffend die frage / Ob GOtt nach der Auffahrt Christi nicht mehr heutiges Tages durch göttliche Erscheinung den Menschenkindern sich offenbahren wolle und sich dessen gantz begeben habe?* . . . (n.p., 1691).

43. The debate surrounding the Petersens became part of a larger discussion over spiritual gifts and new revelations in German Pietism that extended well into the eighteenth century. See Oskar Füller, *Pietismus und Enthusiasmus: Streit unter Verwandten; Geschichtliche Aspekte der Einordnung und Beurteilung enthusiastisch-charismatischer Frömmigkeit* (Wuppertal: Brockhaus, 1998); Jonathan Strom, "Jacob Fabricius, Friedrich Breckling und die Debatte um Visionen und neue Offenbarungen," in *Der Radikale Pietismus: Perspektiven der Forschung*, ed. Wolfgang Breul, Marcus Meier, and Lothar Vogel, 2nd ed. (Göttingen: Vandenhoeck & Ruprecht, 2011), 249–70.

44. See, for instance, *Das Ewige Evangelium der Allgemeinen Wiederbringung Aller Creaturen*, which was published anonymously in 1698 and 1699, but was clearly authored by Johanna Eleonora Petersen. The work was reprinted in 1700 in her *Mysterion Apokatasteseos*.

45. Wallmann, "Geisterfahrung und Kirche," 140–43.

46. *Der Heiligen Schrifft Neuen Testaments Erster Theil* . . . (Berlenburg, 1726), Vorrede, 2r–3r.

47. On Mather's views of and collaborations with the Huguenot refugees, see chap. 6 of Catherine Randall, *From a Far Country: Camisards and Huguenots* (Athens: University of Georgia Press, 2001).

48. See Kenneth Silverman, *The Life and Times of Cotton Mather* (New York: Harper and Row, 1984); and Richard F. Lovelace, *The American Pietism of Cotton Mather: Origins of American Evangelicalism* (Grand Rapids, MI: Christian University Press, 1979), 180–92.

49. Como, "Radical Puritanism," 248.

50. Ute Lotz-Heumann, "'The Spirit of Prophecy Has Not Wholly Left the World': The Stylisation of Archbishop James Ussher as a Prophet," in *Religion and Superstition in Reformation Europe*, ed. Helen Parish and William G. Naphy (Manchester: Manchester University Press, 2002), 119–32.

51. Increase Mather, *The Mystery of Israel's Salvation Explained* (Boston, 1669), 163–64, 98–100. In his church history, Cotton Mather also reports several cases of preternatural guidance, visions, premonitions, and actual prophecy among the founding generation. See *Magnalia*, 1:316, 342, 436, 361, 486, 534–35.

52. *Diary*, 1:86–87. For further accounts of angelic visitations, see 2:263–64 and 2:190.

53. Appendix to Increase Mather, *A Dissertation, Wherein the Strange Doctrine Lately Published in a Sermon, the Tendency of which, Is, to Encourage Unsanctified Persons (while such) to Approach the Holy Table of the Lord, Is Examined and Confuted* (Boston, 1708), 110.

54. Cotton Mather, *A New Offer to the Lovers of Religion and Learning* (Boston: Green, 1714), 2–3, 14. On Mather's spiritualistic hermeneutics in practice, see Hoselton, "Spiritually Discerned," esp. 119–24.

55. *Diary*, 2:329.

56. Ibid., 2:453–54; for the record of another such prayer session in August 1716, see also 2:365–66.

57. Cotton Mather, "VATES. Or, some Remarks upon the spirit of prophecy," unpaginated. Translated from the Latin. Mather quotes from August Hermann Francke, *Programma De Donis Dei Extraordinariis* (*programma* IX), in *Programmata diversis temporibus in Academia Hallensi publice proposita* (Halle, 1714), 208. See also Mather's cautionary advice about extraordinary gifts (with another reference to Francke) in *India Christiana*, 72.

58. Cotton Mather, "VATES," unpaginated.

59. See Douglas L. Winiarski, *Darkness Falls on the Land of Light: Experiencing Religious Awakenings in Eighteenth-Century New England* (Chapel Hill: University of North Carolina Press, 2017), 264–65 and 258.

60. *WJE*, 8:363.

61. Darren M. Pollock, "The Exegetical Basis of Jonathan Edwards' Cessationism," *Jonathan Edwards Studies* 5, no. 2 (2015): 129, quoting *WJE*, 25:283.

62. *WJE*, 25:281.

63. Douglas A. Sweeney, *Edwards the Exegete: Biblical Interpretation and Anglo-Protestant Culture on the Edge of the Enlightenment* (New York: Oxford University Press, 2015), 41.

64. Stephen J. Stein, "American Bibles: Canon, Commentary, and Community," *CH* 64, no. 2 (1995): 169–84, 172.

65. Cotton Mather, *Principles of the Protestant religion maintained*, 24.

PART 4

THE BIBLE AND LIVED RELIGION

12

"AT ANY PRICE GIVE ME THE BOOK OF GOD!"

Devotional Intent and Bible Reading for the Early Evangelicals

BRUCE HINDMARSH

Hans Frei argued famously in 1974 that there was an "eclipse of biblical narrative" in the eighteenth and nineteenth centuries. It is an appropriate and telling image for a period fascinated by astronomy. There was an eclipse. The sun was darkened. Traditional ways of reading the Bible were inhibited, and the Bible no longer *illuminated* the life and events of the present age.

What did Frei mean? He argued that before the rise of historical criticism, Bible reading was strongly realistic, "at once literal and historical, and not only doctrinal or edifying." The smaller stories in the Bible together made up a single historical sequence of events, and the real world was formed by these. The natural environment and human culture were accounted for in a narrative of the temporal world that "covered the span of ages from creation to the final consummation to come." Crucially, this biblical world was "the one and only real world," and so "it must in principle embrace the experience of any present age and reader." The reader was duty bound to fit him or herself into this world by figural interpretation and by mode of life. The events of his or her life were elements in *that* storied world. This realistic biblical narrative, argued Frei, "remained the adequate description of the common and inclusive world until the coming of modernity. As the eighteenth century went on, this mode of interpretation and the outlook it represented broke down with increasing rapidity." Consequently, Frei saw a kind of reversal taking place in the eighteenth century. Instead of trying to fit events and experiences of the present into the real world of Scripture, the attempt was to fit the depicted biblical world into the seemingly *more* real extrabiblical world as we apprehend it.[1] In addition to this reversal of direction, there was a breakdown of figural interpretation. Such interpretation offended against both literary and historical rationality. Figural interpretation was now regarded as the opposite of the literal sense, instead of the literal sense as extended to the whole narrative or unitary canon.

Frei's thesis of an eclipse of biblical narrative harmonizes with the more general account in Charles Taylor of an eclipse (he uses the same word) of transcendental frameworks in this same period. However, he offers an important passing remark in a paragraph about the "falling off in devotion" that came along with this eclipse, saying that moralism would be the dominant mode of religion "until the preaching of Wesley . . . brought something of this life of prayer back to the forefront."[2] This is significant, for this is a path less taken during England's Enlightenment. It also has important metaphysical implications. Indeed, during the period of the so-called eclipse of biblical narrative and of transcendental frameworks, evangelicals such as Wesley, though living in the modern world, approached Scripture with devotional intent and sought to interpret their lives within its narrative, assimilating their experience to the world depicted by the Bible by means of figuration.[3]

Elsewhere I have explored in some detail the way that the early evangelicals responded to the new science, since the evangelical movement arose among the first generation to accept the basic postulates of Isaac Newton.[4] The disenchanted world as described by Newton sharply separated the realm of matter, stripped now of any form principle, from the realm of spirit in a dualism much more stark than any earlier Hellenistic dualism. There was to be no commerce between these two discrete realms in the new science, no ways in which they participated in each other, and so mechanical philosophy removed God summarily from the material world—except to allow him to adjust the orbits of the planets occasionally, something for which Newton still needed a divine agent. For the most part, evangelicals did not reject Newtonianism or the findings of science. Instead, they responded by nesting the world described by Newton back within a transcendent framework, time and again offering up the worship of the mute creation in a paean of "wonder, love, and praise."

But what about Scripture? How should Scripture be read in light of the new scientific metaphysic? For William Whiston and those scientific minds embroiled in the Deist controversy, who were, in Frei's terms, trying to fit Scripture into the narrative of the modern world, treating it as a text like any other, the eclipse was more or less complete. The methodological naturalism of the scientific method necessarily bracketed out the divine authorship of the Bible in a way that those who read with devotional intent did not. The scientific and historical questions were not wrong, but they were incomplete. And the consequences for Bible reading could not be more dramatic. To read with devotional intent as the early evangelicals did was to reenchant the universe and to reanimate the Scriptures. Frei's reversal is itself reversed. The devotional attitude was critical to such reading. For in order to embrace a typological reading of Scripture as something literally true—an account of the real world, as the author intended—one needed to regard the ultimate author as not just human but divine. Absent this transcendental framework and absent this devotional intent, any figuration could only at best be regarded as a "reading backwards."[5]

Devotional Intent Among the Early Evangelicals

To appreciate the hermeneutical and metaphysical significance of the spiritual disposition of the reader, we may begin by examining some of the statements of devotional intent among evangelicals.[6] Three hymns by the Wesleys on the theme *"Before Reading the* SCRIPTURES" were addressed respectively to the Father, Son, and Spirit, and they display an intensive spiritual earnestness about Bible reading by way of invocation. Thus, To the Father,

> While in Thy Word we search for Thee,
>   (We search with trembling Awe)
> Open our Eyes, and let us see
>   The Wonders of thy Law.

To the Son,

> Open the Scriptures now; reveal
>   All which for us Thou art:
> Talk with us, Lord, and let us feel
>   The Kindling in our Heart.

And To the Spirit,

> Come HOLY GHOST, (for mov'd by Thee,
>   Thy Prophets wrote and spoke;)
> Unlock the Truth, Thyself the Key,
>   Unseal the Sacred Book.[7]

The Scriptures invited a trembling awe. One turned the pages with suspended wonder, for here one was in the presence of the divine persons of the Holy Trinity, and one therefore pleaded the agency of Father, Son, and Holy Spirit to enable one to read with understanding. Otherwise one was blind (first stanza) and cold (second stanza), and the meaning of the text locked up tight (third stanza).

Consider four further examples of this devotional intent from this same period. George Whitefield pored over page after page of his Greek New Testament in his rooms at Oxford in the mid-1730s, reading not with scholastic curiosity but with intense spiritual seriousness—reading the Scriptures, as he said, on his knees.[8] Mary Fletcher spoke of the two ways appointed by God to teach the same lesson: "one is the spirit the second the word of God."[9] Or, as John Newton said of the relationship between Scripture and prayer, "The one is the fountain of living water, and the other the bucket with which we are to draw."[10] These were two interpenetrating acts of devotion. "We pray to him who has the keys to open our understanding."[11] Reading the Scriptures would therefore lead Newton often to "turn them into a prayer form."[12] A similar spirit was evident in William Romaine, who urged his readers frequently to mix faith with the reading of scriptural promises: "Meditate on them. Pray to him for increasing faith to mix with them; that he, dwelling in the temple of thy heart, thou mayest have fellowship there with the Father and with the Son."[13] The devotional goal of evangelical Bible reading was thus communion with God. This was the recurring pattern: read, meditate, and pray, that "thou mayest have fellowship." There is tremendous continuity here with the way monastic reading of Scripture has been described in the Middle Ages.[14]

Pietist Antecedents

More immediate antecedents for this devotional attitude to Bible reading may be found in various works by German Pietists in English translation. Anton Böhme (1673–1722) was a Lutheran minister, educated at Halle, who became a key conduit for Pietist devotion in England in the years before the Evangelical Revival. Among his several books and translations that were read by the early evangelicals was a short fifty-four-page essay, *Plain Directions for Reading the Holy Scripture* (1721).

Plain Directions is a good example of a practical Protestant *lectio divina*, an exhortation to read Scripture with the pure spiritual aim of hearing from God personally and being thereby transformed. Böhme emphasized the necessity of bathing one's reading in prayer and meditation, and he included step-by-step examples of specimen meditations and prayers before and after reading. So, for example, before reading, one might pray, "Be graciously pleased to assist me by thy divine Spirit, when I am about reading thy Holy Word. Let him enlighten my Understanding, sanctify my Will, purifie my Affections, guide me into all Truth, remember me of thy Precepts, shed abroad thy Love in my Heart, quicken me by his Presence, and animate me into a ready Performance of all such Duties as thy Word Requireth!"[15] Again, this was all to the end of responding to Scripture in a way that took seriously its divine authorship. Böhme writes several times about a simplicity and singleness of purpose, or what he calls a deeply "Christian intention" in reading Scripture. "A true SIMPLICITY *of Heart*, that is, a sincere and unfeigned Desire to be *made wise unto Salvation, through Faith which is in Christ Jesus*, is the best *Preparative* the Reader can bring to so sacred a Study. If this be attended with an unshaken *Resolution*, to order his whole Life and Conduct according to the *Directions* the Word proposeth, he then cannot fail of obtaining the End, for which the Scripture is given."[16]

Böhme offers several metaphors for such reading. Meditation is the way to suck the divine virtue out of every flower. Again, as one reads, one shakes the boughs that are laden with ripe fruit, so that fruit might drop down into one's hungry soul. He quotes an unnamed church father who says that reading this way is like digging a deep well, searching for the best water down deep. By meditation and prayer—such active digging—in time the believer will find rivers of grace stream down into his heart. In order for the Word to go down thus deep, part of prayerful reading involves self-examination, outward and inward, manners and actions, and also motives and intentions.[17]

For Böhme, even though one does not merit grace, spiritual insight does mature along with growth in holiness: the pure in heart shall see God. There is something here of the patristic doctrine of likeness: like understands like. As the believer grows through the Word of God, and he matures, the Word influencing his actions, so the reverse is also true: "And 'tis then the Works do favour of the Principle whence they flow. If a man doth but faithfully practice what he knows, his Knowledge will certainly increase with his Practice, and his path will shine more and more unto the perfect Day."[18]

With such an attitude, one was prepared to read the whole of Scripture as communicating a unitary divine message. The traditional means by which one's life was assimilated to the world depicted in Scripture as the one and only real world was figuration or typology. This was what an early Enlightenment figure like William Whiston had disallowed. But for the German and English evangelicals, not only did Old Testament types point forward to Christ, but as a reader, one was also represented or figured in the text.

Evangelical Figuration: Salvation History Made Personal

An early evangelical example of this same pattern of figural interpretation may be observed in John Newton's famous hymn "Amazing Grace."[19] The original title of the hymn was "Faith's Review and Expectation," and the first stanzas seem to reflect on a conversion in the past:

> Amazing grace! (how sweet the sound)
>   That sav'd a wretch like me!
> I once was lost, but now am found,
>   Was blind, but now I see.

As the hymn continues, the second stanza seems also to signal a conversion too with its line "The hour I first believed." Then the third stanza becomes a pivot upon which the whole hymn turns, gathering the past up once more into the word "grace" and turning with faith to face the future: "'Tis grace has brought me safe thus far, / And grace will lead me home." The last three stanzas in the original hymn trace the path of the believer through, respectively, the balance of this life ("As long as life endures"), death ("mortal life shall cease"), and the end of the world ("The earth shall soon dissolve").[20]

Although many have pointed out the autobiographical significance of this hymn as a testimony to Newton's sensational conversion as a repentant slave trader, Newton nowhere makes this connection himself. He placed the hymn in the canonical section of the *Olney Hymns* (1779), where hymns were organized according to various passages of Scripture from Genesis to Revelation. It was under the reference 1 Chr 17:16–17, a biblical passage that narrates a key moment in salvation history. This is the account of David responding in amazement to the prophet Nathan's announcement of the Davidic covenant: God's promise to maintain David's line and his kingdom forever. David went before the Lord and said, "Who am I, O Lord God, and what is mine house, that thou hast brought me hitherto?" The first-person language belongs to David first, and only to the singer by figuration or typology. Again, there is a figural movement here from an event in the history of Israel to Christ as antitype, and then to the singer in the present.

The passage that Newton was expounding is one of the high points in biblical theology, and the weight of accumulated Christian covenantal and typological interpretation meant that Newton surely saw in this text the anticipation of Christ as that greater son of David, the one presented as the fulfillment of the divine promise to David in the genealogies of the Gospels. The typology had only to be extended to see in God's grace to David an anticipation of God's grace through Jesus Christ to Newton in his experience, as to the poor lacemakers of his parish in theirs. The title of the hymn and the turning from past to future in stanza 3 suggest the kind of amazed backward and forward looking along the line of salvation history that David was doing in 1 Chronicles, which Newton did persistently in his own devotional life, and which Newton presented for his people as an exemplary pattern. Newton made these typological connections for his people in a sermon on the day the hymn was first sung. He explained the setting in David's life and then "accommodated" the text "to our own use as a proper subject for our meditations on the entrance of a new year."[21] Newton held together the story of David, of Christ, of Newton himself, and of the faithful poor of Olney in an altogether traditional pattern of figuration. In the mouth of the singer, "I" and "me" and "mine" were autobiographical only within the larger context of salvation history.

This pattern of figural reading was altogether characteristic of Newton's preaching and hymn-writing. Another well-known hymn published by Newton in the canonical section of the *Olney Hymns* goes by its first line in modern hymnbooks, "How sweet the name of Jesus sounds." It is a tender encomium to the sacred name of Jesus. The first sentence is actually a question to which the rest of the hymn is an answer:

> How sweet the name of Jesus sounds
>   In a believer's ear?
> It soothes his sorrows, heals his wounds,
>   And drives away his fear.[22]

And the hymn continues in a deeply personal response to the name of Jesus, building momentum as it goes. Thus, the fifth stanza names Jesus ten times, with cascading effect like the change-ringing of English bells:

> Jesus! my Shepherd, Husband, Friend,
>   My Prophet, Priest, and King;
> My Lord, my Life, my Way, my End,
>   Accept the praise I bring.[23]

Again, the surprise to the modern reader might be to find this hymn under the heading SOLOMON'S SONG, indexed to chapter 1, verse 3: "Because of the savour of thy good ointments thy name is as ointment poured forth, therefore do the virgins love thee" (KJV). For this hymn too there is a manuscript sermon notebook in which we can see how Newton made the typological connections for his parishioners: "The soul ranges as it were through the whole of creation to find some worthy similitudes of her Lord.... Let us present consider this in my text. It may lead our thoughts to not only the excellency that is in Christ, but to his suitableness to us, and afford us a glass in which you may see yourselves."[24] Newton was able to employ a directly figural reading of this poem from Israel's Scriptures in a way that the fourteenth-century Franciscan Nicholas of Lyra would have understood as literal-prophetic, and not just literal-historic.[25] There was type and antitype, but this was still a "literal" reading, only extended now over the whole canon of Scripture. No wonder there are profound continuities between Newton's hymn and the affective devotion of earlier writers such as Bernard of Clairvaux in his sermons on this same text, or the devotion to the name of Jesus in the English mystic Richard Rolle, or the exegesis of a Puritan such as Richard Sibbes.[26] It is not that Newton necessarily knew this tradition extensively. But he naturally reproduced its exegesis when he approached the Bible with a similar devotional intent.

Evangelical communities in the eighteenth century were apprenticed to this pattern of figuration not only through individual hymns, but also through the cumulative catechism of singing through a whole *range* of hymns. For example, by taking just one or two stanzas from hymns by Charles Wesley, many of them very well known, one can recover the shape of the whole biblical narrative, sometimes with typological significance, while also noticing how the singer is folded into that narrative by using the biblical language as his or her own:

> *Creation / New Creation*
> Author of every work divine,
> Who dost through both creations shine,
>   The God of nature and of grace!
>
> *Fall*
> Rise, the Woman's Conqu'ring Seed,
> Bruise in Us the Serpent's Head.
> Now display thy saving Pow'r,
> Ruin'd Nature now restore,
>
> *Incarnation*
> Veiled in flesh the Godhead see!
> Hail the incarnate Deity!
> Pleased as man with man to dwell,
> Jesus, our Immanuel.

Cross
He left his Father's throne above—
  So free, so infinite his grace—
Emptied himself of all but love,
  And bled for Adam's helpless race.

Resurrection
Vain the stone, the watch, the seal,
Christ hast burst the gates of hell,
Death in vain forbids him rise,
Christ hath opened Paradise.

Ascension
Jesus the Saviour reigns,
  The God of truth and love;
When he had purged our stains,
  He took his seat above.

Pentecost
Lord, we believe to us and ours
  The apostolic promise given;
We wait the Pentecostal powers,
  The Holy Ghost sent down from heaven.

Christ's Return
Lo! He comes with clouds descending,
  Once for favoured sinners slain.[27]

Even in these short excerpts one gets a vivid sense of the objectivity for Wesley of God's saving work in the sweep of history. And yet this is no dispassionate recounting of history. The singer cannot help but be involved in the story, in personal response, in alleluias of praise, or simply by getting caught up in the rushing syntax, where lines seem to pile up, crashing one after the other like waves on the seashore. The language incorporates the singer into the biblical narrative of God's saving acts in history: *lex orandi, lex credendi*.

Evangelical Figuration: Character Substitution

Many evangelical preachers had a remarkable ability to draw their hearers into the world depicted in the Bible, extending the biblical narrative to encompass the present. Figuration was the key here too not only for seeing Christ in the Old Testament, but also for seeing one's own life in terms of the biblical narrative. George Whitefield's sermon on Saul's conversion in the book of Acts may be taken as an example of this same figural instinct in the pulpit. He preached the sermon in Glasgow on September 12, 1741, and, as happened many times, it was transcribed in shorthand by one of those attending and published immediately after the event as a forty-page tract. On this occasion, Whitefield's rhetorical strategy was clear. The high priest who sent Saul to persecute the Christians in Damascus was equated with unconverted ministers in the present; the followers of "the Way" in the book of Acts were "supposed enthusiasts"; Ananias was an awakened, experienced Christian who knew what to do with Saul; Saul's vision on the Damascus Road was his awakening of conscience; his period of three days' darkness was his evangelical humiliation; his recovery of sight under Ananias's prayers was his New Birth; Paul's companions were "mere hearers"; the believers at Damascus whom he joined were like a Methodist band meeting; and so on. In this way Whitefield brought the scriptural narrative to life in eighteenth-century Glasgow. He presented a lively tableau for his audience, like a scene in a shop window come to life. But then he pressed his point home: "Ah my dear Friends," he implored, "this must be done to you as well as to *Saul*. . . . God must speak to you by Name, God must reach your Heart in particular, ye must be brought to see the Evil of Sin, and to cry out after *Jesus Christ*."[28]

For the laypeople who heard him, this sort of preaching did indeed "speak to them by Name." He hit his mark. Margaret Austin had been abused and abandoned by her husband, left with two children to care for, and yet when she went and heard Whitefield preach on "the Rich man of the Gospel, how he had Laid up treasures on Earth but none in heaven," she knew on the spot, "I was that Person." This was for her a direct, dot-to-dot figuration: "I was that Person." It is testimony to the power of Whitefield's preaching performances that he could leave an utterly destitute single mother convinced that she was a rich young ruler. As she followed the young Methodist preachers around and listened to them preach, she found herself personally addressed in every sermon: *she* was the rich man who went empty away, *she* was the proud Pharisee, *she* was at the foot of the cross watching the soldiers pierce the bleeding side of Christ. "I Saw my Self to be a Lost undone Sinner," she said after one sermon. Again, on another occasion her response was that "the Lord Saw fit to Lett me See my Self."[29] As John Newton said to his parishioners, the text became a mirror. The biblical narrative presented so forcefully by Whitefield reconstructed her own biography. She was assimilated to the biblical world and its account of reality. Instead of the modern world swallowing the Bible, the Bible was swallowing her world. Instead of an eclipse of biblical narrative, there was a new dawn, a light in the darkness. Figuration was the means not only by which the past was seen to climax in Jesus Christ, but also the means by which later events and the present moment itself looped back to find its meaning in Jesus Christ.

This pattern of figural interpretation whereby one saw oneself in the biblical narrative was evident also in hymns where one was substituted in, so to speak, for one of the biblical characters, especially for the characters who encountered Jesus in the Gospels. One of Wesley's hymns on Scripture vividly illustrates this pattern. "These Things were written for our Instruction" invokes Christ to do today what he did in the Gospels, in twenty-one stanzas. So as a reader, one can put oneself in the place of the leper in Matt 8, fall at Christ's feet, and say, "Lord, if you are willing you can make me clean." Or again, as Christ encountered the mute man, so one can cry to Jesus, like him, "Silent, (alas Thou know'st how long) / My voice I cannot raise." But because Jesus is the same today, present to heal, one can add the hopeful expectation, even now: "Thou shalt loose my Tongue," and so on, through all the stanzas.[30] Throughout the hymn, the imaginative encounter with the Christ of the Gospels has all the intensity of the Ignatian Exercises, with its elements of deeply personal invocation, composition of place, and colloquy.[31] And reading thus with devotional intent, time collapses. In an attitude of "trembling awe," one recognizes that the Jesus Christ in the text is the same Jesus Christ alive and present to me this very moment as I am reading.

Evangelical Figuration: Linguistic Substitution

Linguistic figuration is yet a further way that evangelical Bible readers saw themselves in the text of Scripture, and this overlaps with what we have seen already. By this I mean that the writer or reader substitutes verbatim biblical phrases for first-person narrative in a kind of cut-and-paste fashion. The public and private writings of evangelicals were typically woven together this way, like patristic and medieval compositions, as a catena of biblical texts. One placed oneself in the biblical narrative, and one expressed one's own spiritual experience in the language of Canaan.[32] The result is that one's own language glowed under a borrowed sacred light with a kind of spotlight or halo effect. The best illustration of this is again the hymnody of Charles Wesley. As Frank Baker says, "His verse is an enormous sponge filled to saturation with Bible words, Bible similes, Bible metaphors, Bible stories, Bible ideas."[33] So, for example, the last verse of "And Can It Be" is an unbroken chain of biblical allusions:

No condemnation now *I* dread;
Jesus, and all in Him, is *mine*;
Alive in Him, *my* living Head,
And clothed in righteousness divine,
Bold *I* approach th'eternal throne,
And claim the crown, through Christ *my* own.[34]

This reads like a testimony, but notice: "No condemnation now I dread" is the peak statement of Saint Paul in the first verse of Rom 8 that there is therefore now no condemnation for those that are in Christ. "Jesus and all in him is mine" is the climax of Paul's argument in 1 Cor 3:22 that all things are yours in Christ. "Alive in him, my living head" is the new Adam Christology in 1 Cor 15. "And clothed in righteousness divine" alludes to Phil 3:9, where Paul wants to be found in Christ having a righteousness not his own. "Bold I approach th'eternal throne" is the turning point in Heb 10, the declaration that we have confidence to enter the Holy Place through the blood of Jesus. "And claim the crown through Christ my own" is 2 Tim 4:8, where Paul talks of finishing the race and the crown of righteousness to be awarded him by the Lord, and to all who have longed for his appearing. All of these biblical allusions are precise, and most of them pick up on climactic or summary statements in Paul. The entire stanza is built of them, and yet they are pressed into service not as allusions per se, but as words to be sung straight through in a bold confession of first-person devotion (the italicized pronouns are original) and as the climax of a hymn celebrating "love's redeeming work."

The concern was thus less to separate the present horizon from the past to achieve a putative critical objectivity than it was to fuse these horizons seamlessly in the heat of devotion. The early scientific textual criticism of the early Enlightenment critic William Whiston necessarily required a suspension of judgment while one looked at the data of Scripture at right angles, under a microscope, so to speak.[35] Evangelicals were not averse to doing some of this, but this was not the focus of their Bible reading. Their Bible reading was less a two-horizon hermeneutic of the sort described by Hans-Georg Gadamer than it was a one-horizon hermeneutic, within which they might pursue various questions of textual criticism. In this, evangelicals were in harmony with the way the church fathers are often described, approaching Scripture with "reason and faith ... fused together in a single loving intuitive act."[36]

Charles Wesley could easily have "shown his work," so to speak. He could have worked up an exegesis, in context, for each of the passages to which he alludes in a hymn such as "And Can It Be," and then he could have explained rationally, step by step, how this applied to believers deontologically in the present. Instead, though, he grasps the fused meaning immediately, and presents it with a direct devotional intelligence and sensibility. The singer is figured directly in the words of Scripture. When the singer voices the words as her own, "No condemnation now I dread," in the context of the overall salvific message of the hymn, she experiences what the critic Donald Davie describes as an extrapoetic dimension, or a stereoscopic sense of depth that comes of reading, in effect, two texts at once—the text of Saint Paul in Rom 8 and the text of her own testimony.[37] The power of this is incomparably greater than simple instrumental reason.

This pattern of linguistic figuration, pasting the words of Scripture into my own first-person narrative, allowing this to bear the semantic weight of my own story, may be seen in conversion narratives as well. John Pritchard was one of Wesley's lay preachers. As a late adolescent he ran away from home, leaving Ireland without telling his family, only to find himself destitute later in London. He says of himself, "Being visited with a violent fever, I came to myself, and said, 'Father I have sinned against heaven, and in Thy sight, and am no more worthy to be called Thy son,'" quoting Luke 15 and setting his story up as a "prodigal son" narrative.[38] Similarly, the climax of John Cennick's narrative was the moment when joy broke into his soul while in church in Reading, England, in September 1737. In the space of two paragraphs, he pastes at least ten quotations from Scripture. He wrote, "the *Sword of the Lord was dividing asunder my Joints, and Marrow, my Soul and Spirit*," and "*This Joy and Peace in believing*, filled me about three or four Hours," and so on.[39] Women would sometimes assimilate their experience specifically to the experience of women in Scripture. Thus, Ann Martin appropriated the words of the Virgin Mary, saying of herself, "the power of the most highest Overshaw'd me." And Mary Ramsay turned to a different analogue, writing, "With the woman of Samaria, I may say, come see a man that told me all that ever I did."[40] Although this habit could descend into cliché or run to excess, it was more often a powerful means by which ordinary women and men came to see their lives in terms of the biblical narrative.

Evangelical Figuration: Words of Psychological Power

A related pattern of figuration may be observed in the psychological impression made by very short phrases or single sentences of Scripture. These often recurred at high points in the conversion narratives of laypeople. A single locution of Scripture would penetrate the soul and explode like a bunker-busting bomb. In the history of Christianity, many men and women have noted the spiritual efficacy of taking short phrases of Scripture to heart. We can see this in the sentence prayers of John Cassian and Evagrius among the desert fathers; the Jesus prayer of the Sinai tradition, the Philokalia, and the Russian *starets*; the versicles of the Western liturgy, with its repetition of Psalm texts such as "O God make speed to save me"; and so on.[41] William Harmless argues that these monologistic prayers were a powerful mode of biblical meditation that shaped the psyche.[42] For the early evangelicals, similar locutions made a deep psychological impression. We are trained nowadays to read the words of any author within their proper literary and historical context. "A text without a context is a pretext," as the saying goes. And yet a mountain of critical theory would add that any text without a reader has no meaning. It is fascinating that it was so often isolated biblical locutions that carried the real spiritual freight in the eighteenth century. Everything came to a point in this one powerful word, presented with a simplicity that could pierce the soul like an arrow. The discrete biblical text, lifted from the page, was sent to do a special kind of work now in a psychological context.

The young people who boarded at the school run by the Baptist John Collett Ryland in Northampton, England, were evidently trained explicitly to do this. Ryland edited a pamphlet for them from the Puritan Joseph Alleine, *The Voice of God in His Promises*. A copy of the pamphlet is bound with some of the students' own spiritual memoirs and other manuscripts at the Angus Library in Oxford, and it was marked up by them. It was essentially an anthology of scriptural promises, paraphrased in first person, so that the reader might hear the words of the Bible as personal address. For example, "*My son I give unto you in a marriage covenant for ever.* I make him over to you as wisdom, for your illumination; righteousness for your justification; sanctification, for the curing of your corruptions."[43] This was a fill-in-the-blanks primer for hearing God's voice for oneself, today.

The richest archive for observing interior figuration by means of short biblical locutions is in the surviving manuscripts from the Cambuslang Revival in Scotland. The lay convert Janet Jackson commented on the experience explicitly: "When I was kept from My nights rest, some sentences from Scripture would have come unto My Mind with sweetness; and I was frequently made to bless the Lord that such comforting and supporting words to people in trouble are in the Bible."[44] Thus, while spinning at her wheel and in spiritual distress, she notes, "These words came into My Mind with great sweetness & power Thou art a New Creature: upon which I was Made to believe I was no Hypocrite, But a new Creature." (At one point Jackson *was* a little worried when a phrase came to mind and she wasn't quite sure it was in the Bible. But she asked an "experienced acquaintance" and was relieved to find it was in Gal

2:20, or at least it was close.)[45] There are scores of further examples of this phenomenon at Cambuslang. The typical comment was "The word came home with power." At his conversion, George Tassie found "that word came upon my heart with power, 'My Lord, and My God.'"[46] The biblical confession of the disciple Thomas was pasted into George Tassie's narrative, and it reordered the inner world of this Scottish layman near Glasgow in 1741. At Mary Mitchell's conversion, she declared, "That word came unto me with a powerful, ravishing heart overcoming delight . . . as it were a stream of the promises of the new Covenant."[47] In evangelical communities across the North Atlantic this phenomenon recurred, and ministers such as James Robe noted it.

Conclusion

We have observed several patterns of evangelical figural reading of Scripture. Crucially, the early evangelicals approached the text of Scripture not principally with dispassionate scientific intent, but with devotional intent, seeking the meaning of the Bible as the very Word of God. This meant that the Bible was "one book," and figural reading enabled one to read it as such, and to assimilate one's own life to its narrative. Wesley might emend the received *textus receptus* a little in his *Explanatory Notes to the New Testament* to establish a better, more accurate reading, but that was not his highest aim. As Wesley wrote in the preface to his *Sermons on Several Occasions* (1746), he wished to be *homo unius libri*, a man of one book—a restatement of the Reformation *sola Scriptura* principle. Ironically, few evangelicals read more widely than Wesley or did more to promote lay literacy, but still, his statement was more than hyperbole. For Wesley the Bible was principial, the fountain from which all else derived. Wesley's concern in making his *unius libri* declaration was not in the first instance polemical, but spiritual, given the shortness and frailty of life. "I am a creature of a day, passing through life as an arrow through the air. I am . . . hovering over the great gulf, till a few moments hence I am no more seen." The only thing that mattered, comparatively, was to know the way to heaven, and God had condescended to teach the way: "He hath written it down in a book. O give me that book! At any price give me the Book of God!"[48] There was thus a life-and-death urgency about reading Scripture for Wesley, and the first concern was to hear in the rustling of its pages the voice of God speaking to one's own needy condition. Such earnest devotional concern was the force, just below the surface, that drove all evangelical reading in the period.

It made a difference. Evangelicals were reading *with* the grain of the text. And so, far from the biblical narrative being eclipsed by the rise of modernity, it continued to function among them to reorder the lives and experiences of modern women and men. To be sure, evangelicals still lived on the cusp of modernity, and their sense of self and society owed much to the epochal changes of this era. However, their devotion itself did a kind of philosophical work above its intellectual pay grade, as a transcendent perspective on the world was sustained in the age of mechanical philosophy and materialist science. The Pietist and evangelical concern for personal conversion as a transforming work of the Holy Spirit meant that the world itself was seen in a transfiguring light with spiritual senses.[49] As fierce theological battles were fought in the wake of the scientific revolution between the orthodox party in the Church of England and the Deists over the nature of God, the orthodox apologists had gained some victories, but in the process theology had become sterile by losing touch with is sources in doxology.[50] As Leslie Stephen and others have noted, something had been lost. There was a new ethos of skepticism: "The main result of the attack and defence was to lower the general tone of religious feeling." Yet Stephen acknowledges, like Charles Taylor later, that Wesley was something of an exception in this story, saying this torpor only continued "till Wesley . . . forced more serious thoughts upon the age."[51]

Indeed, Wesley and the other evangelicals reinvigorated the ancient pattern of *lex orandi, lex credendi*—that is, that the way of prayer *is* the way of belief. There is coherence to the biblical narrative that is experienced by way of faith and worship. To treat the Scriptures otherwise is not so much wrong as it is a category mistake. In Robert Wilken's beautiful book on patristic theology, *The Spirit of Early Christian Thought*, he includes a chapter on Scripture, in which he quotes one of Augustine's sermons: "For now treat the Scripture as the face of God. Melt in its presence."[52] This is not just the spirit of early Christian thought, though. It is the spirit of Christian devotion in later ages too. In the final stanza of Wesley's hymn "Before Reading the Scriptures," cited earlier, he too writes of seeking the face of God in Scripture, appealing to Moses as a type, and praying, "Before us make Thy Goodness Pass, / Which here by Faith we know." Then, turning to Christ as antitype, he continues: "Let us in Jesus see thy Face, / And die to all below."[53] To see God's face was the highest devotional intent of all.

Finally, let us return to the image of the eclipse: the "eclipse" of biblical narrative. When there is a solar eclipse, it is not of course something observed everywhere universally, but is a local event. So, likewise, it is time to recognize the "eclipse of biblical narrative" in the modern period as something *local*, local to a small number of Western elites preoccupied with certain intellectual problems. Many others would have said, "What eclipse? I still see the noonday brightness of the sun without interruption." As Jonathan Edwards wrote, the

Bible sheds a "light ten thousand times better than [the] light of the sun."[54] Where readers are still willing to read the Bible with sincere devotional intent, the sun shines bright.

Notes

1. Hans W. Frei, *The Eclipse of Biblical Narrative: A Study in Eighteenth and Nineteenth Century Hermeneutics* (New Haven: Yale University Press, 1974), 1, 3–5.

2. Charles Taylor, *A Secular Age* (Cambridge, MA: Harvard University Press, 2007), 227.

3. The personal emphasis on evangelical piety is what led Frei to regard Methodist Bible reading as an insufficient response to the eclipse of biblical narrative. He felt that evangelicals assimilated the Scripture into their own subjective experience: "It is not the lack of an objective savior but the location of the cumulative narrative bond which indicates how loose and tentative the hold of this profound religious movement on a context or world, temporal, eternal, or both, in which one may feel at home" (Frei, *Eclipse*, 153). Reg Ward argued similarly that evangelicals often had "an inability to place the drama of salvation within a larger framework of thought." See W. R. Ward, *Early Evangelicalism: A Global Intellectual History, 1670–1789* (Cambridge: Cambridge University Press, 2006), 132–33. This "partial eclipse," as it were, was not, however, a necessary correlate of evangelical piety, as the example of Jonathan Edwards demonstrates. I explore this in a companion piece. "*Lectio Evangelica*: Figural Interpretation and Early Evangelical Bible Reading," in *The Burden of the Word: Evangelicals and the Bible in Historical Perspective*, ed. Timothy Larsen (Downers Grove, IL: InterVarsity Press Academic, 2021), 32–54.

4. D. Bruce Hindmarsh, *The Spirit of Early Evangelicalism: True Religion in a Modern World* (New York: Oxford University Press, 2018), 102–79.

5. I allude here to the insightful work of Richard B. Hays, especially his *Reading Backwards: Figural Christology and the Fourfold Gospel Witness* (Waco: Baylor University Press, 2014). In discussing the nature of figuration, Hays quotes a private letter from the New Testament critic Markus Bockmuehl: "It seems both a matter of fact and part of the biblical authors' intent that their engagement with the Old Testament is as much a function of the text's own agency in terms of its (divine) *claim and impact on them*, rather than merely their 'use' of it." Hays endorses Bockmuehl's observation here and accordingly rejects the idea that the Gospel writers were merely engaging in fanciful, poetic creativity in handling the Old Testament. Rather, they may well have been "thunderstruck" by "their fresh encounter with Israel's Scripture in light of the story of Jesus" (x–xi).

6. These three paragraphs draw upon Hindmarsh, *Spirit of Early Evangelicalism*, 71–73.

7. John Wesley and Charles Wesley, *Hymns and Sacred Poems* (London, 1740), 41–43.

8. George Whitefield, *A Short Account of God's Dealings with the Reverend Mr. George Whitefield* (London, 1740), 57; and Whitefield, *A Further Account of God's Dealings with the Reverend Mr. George Whitefield* (London, 1747), 9.

9. Quoted in Phyllis Mack and David Wilson, "Mary Fletcher's Bible," in *Dissent and the Bible in Britain, c. 1650–1950*, ed. Scott Mandelbrote and Michael Ledger-Lomas (Oxford: Oxford University Press, 2013), 70.

10. *Works of the Rev. John Newton*, 6 vols. (London, 1808–9), 1:117.

11. Ibid., 6:418.

12. John Newton, MS diary (1751–56), April 29, 1755, Firestone Library, Princeton, NJ.

13. William Romaine, *A Treatise upon the Walk of Faith*, 2 vols. (London, 1771), 1:231.

14. The closest analogue to such intensive devotional attention to Scripture was the centuries-old Benedictine method of sacred reading, formalized by Guigo II in the twelfth century as a

series of steps that lift one from earth to heaven: *lectio, meditatio, oratio,* and *contemplatio*—that is, read, meditate, pray, and have fellowship. The classic study is Jean Leclercq, *The Love of Learning and the Desire for God: A Study of Monastic Culture,* trans. Catharine Misrahi (New York: Fordham University Press, 1982).

15. Anton Wilhelm Boehm [Böhme], *Plain Directions for Reading the Holy Scripture* (London, 1721), 39. He also gives further explicit examples of moving from reading, to a possible meditation, to a possible prayer (lectio, meditatio, oratio), using the example of Gen. 1:1 (pp. 41–45). And then, again, how from prayer one proceeds to self-examination, using questions to probe the heart and link the reading-meditation-prayer to action (pp. 45–50). And, finally, after a further prayer for help, there follow "adspirations" [sic], wherein one aspires to, asks for grace, to apprehend God's truth with a "spiritual will and understanding" (pp. 52–54).

16. Ibid., 29, 28.

17. Ibid., 30–31, 35–36.

18. Ibid., 36–37.

19. I provide a longer reading of this hymn in "'Amazing Grace': The History of a Hymn and a Cultural Icon," in *Sing Them Over Again to Me: Hymns and Hymnbooks in America,* ed. Mark A. Noll and Edith L. Blumhofer (Tuscaloosa: University of Alabama Press, 2006), 3–19.

20. Many modern hymnbooks replace the last three original stanzas with one added by Edwin Othello Excell in 1910 that begins, "When we've been there ten thousand years." The original appeared in the *Olney Hymns* (London, 1779), 53–54.

21. Richard Cecil, *The Life of John Newton,* ed. and augmented by Marylynne Rouse (Fearn, UK: Christian Focus, 2000), 365. Newton used the same language in his *Authentic Narrative* (1764) to "accommodate" the experience of Israel, reflecting back on their wilderness journey, before entering the promised land, to his own similar reflections of God's leading in his life. Cf. Newton, *Works,* 4:260–62.

22. *Olney Hymns,* 72.

23. Ibid., 73.

24. Cecil, *Life of John Newton,* 369.

25. See David Steinmetz, "The Superiority of Pre-Critical Exegesis," *Theology Today* 37 (1980): 30–32.

26. Bernard wrote several sermons on this text, but see esp. sermon 15, "On the Name of Jesus," in *The Works of Bernard of Clairvaux,* vol. 2, *Song of Songs 1,* trans. Kilian Walsh, Cistercian Fathers Series 4 (Kalamazoo, MI: Cistercian, 1981), 105–13. On Richard Rolle and the cult of the Holy Name in England, see Gordon Mursell, *English Spirituality: From Earliest Times to 1700* (London: SPCK, 2001), 191; Richard Sibbes's classic exposition of the Song of Songs is his *Bowels Opened* (1639).

27. For the text of these hymns, the best resource is "Charles Wesley's Published Verse," Center for Studies in the Wesleyan Tradition (directed by Randy Maddox), Duke Divinity School, https://divinity.duke.edu/initiatives/cswt/charles-published-verse (accessed December 27, 2019).

28. George Whitefield, *Saul's Conversion: A Lecture, Preached on . . . September 12th, 1741, in the High-Church-Yard of Glasgow* (Glasgow, 1741), 14.

29. Margaret Austin, MS letter to Charles Wesley, May 19, 1740, John Rylands Library, Manchester.

30. Wesley and Wesley, *Hymns and Sacred Poems* (1740), 71–74.

31. For the Protestant appropriation of the Ignatian and Salesian method of meditation, see Charles Hambrick-Stowe, *The Practice of Piety: Puritan Devotional Disciplines in Seventeenth-Century New England* (Chapel Hill: University of North Carolina Press, 1982), 31–32.

32. Cf. ibid., 73–77. Or, as Mason I. Lowance says of New Englanders, "All literary genres were forms through which the language of Canaan might associate contemporary history with the original biblical dispensation." Lowance, *The Language of Canaan: Metaphor and Symbol in*

New England from the Puritans to the Transcendentalists (Cambridge, MA: Harvard University Press, 1980), 18.

33. Frank Baker, ed., *Representative Verse of Charles Wesley* (New York: Abingdon, 1962), xxv. See also S. T. Kimbrough Jr., "Hymnody of Charles Wesley," in *T&T Clark Companion to Methodism*, ed. Charles Yrigoyen Jr. (New York: T&T Clark, 2010), 45–49.

34. Originally published under the title "Free Grace," in John Wesley and Charles Wesley, *Hymns and Sacred Poems* (London, 1739), 117–19.

35. On biblical criticism in the period, especially in Germany, see Michael C. Legaspi, *The Death of Scripture and the Rise of Biblical Studies* (New York: Oxford University Press, 2010).

36. This is Rowan Williams's description of the patristic tradition as it culminated in Bernard of Clairvaux. Williams, "St. Bernard of Clairvaux," in *Dictionary of Christian Spirituality*, ed. Gordon S. Wakefield (London: SCM Press, 1983), 44–45.

37. Donald Davie, *Purity of Diction in English Verse* (London: Chatto and Windus, 1952), 73.

38. John Telford, ed., *Wesley's Veterans*, 7 vols. (London: Robert Culley, 1912), 6:200.

39. John Cennick, *The Life of Mr. J. Cennick, with an Account of the Trials and Temptations Which He Endured Until It Pleased Our Saviour to Shew Him His Love, and Send Him into His Vineyard*, 2nd ed. (Bristol, 1745), 25–27.

40. I provide these and other examples from the lay Methodist narratives at the John Rylands Library in D. Bruce Hindmarsh, *The Evangelical Conversion Narrative: Spiritual Autobiography in Early Modern England* (Oxford: Oxford University Press, 2005), 149–50.

41. The early evangelicals also picked this up from diverse seventeenth-century writers such as the Anglican Anthony Horneck, *The Happy Ascetick* (London, 1685); the Presbyterian Thomas Gouge, *Christian Directions* (London, 1661); and the Catholic Lorenzo Scupoli, *The Spiritual Combat*, trans. Juan de Castaniza (London, 1710).

42. William Harmless, *Desert Christians: An Introduction to the Literature of Early Monasticism* (Oxford: Oxford University Press, 2004), 392–98.

43. Joseph Alleine, *The Voice of God in His Promises*, ed. John Collett Ryland (London, 1766), 28.

44. William MacCulloch, "Examinations of Persons under Spiritual Concern at Cambuslang, during the Revival in 1741–42," 2 vols., bound MSS, New College, Edinburgh, 1:23.

45. Ibid., 32.

46. Ibid., 146.

47. Ibid., 99.

48. John Wesley, preface, §5, in *Sermons I*, ed. Albert C. Outler, vol. 1 of *The Bicentennial Edition of the Works of John Wesley* (Nashville: Abingdon Press, 1976), 104–5.

49. See, e.g., Hindmarsh, *Spirit of Early Evangelicalism*, 126–27. On the morphology of conversion among Pietists and evangelicals, see Hindmarsh, *Evangelical Conversion Narrative*, 33–60.

50. See further, John Vickers, "Charles Wesley and the Revival of the Doctrine of the Trinity: A Methodist Contribution to Modern Theology," in *Charles Wesley: Life, Literature and Legacy*, ed. Kenneth G. C. Newport and Ted. A. Campbell (Peterborough, UK: Epworth Press, 2007), 288.

51. Leslie Stephen, *History of English Thought in the Eighteenth Century*, 2 vols. (London: Smith, Elder, 1876), 1:273.

52. Robert Louis Wilken, *The Spirit of Early Christian Thought: Seeking the Face of God* (New Haven: Yale University Press, 2008), 50.

53. Wesley and Wesley, *Hymns and Sacred Poems*, 41.

54. Jonathan Edwards, *The Sermons of Jonathan Edwards: A Reader*, ed. Wilson H. Kimnach, Kenneth P. Minkema, and Douglas A. Sweeney (New Haven: Yale University Press, 1999), 109.

13

SPIRIT OF THE WORD

Scripture in the Lives of Evangelical and Moravian Women in the New World, 1730–1830

BENJAMIN M. PIETRENKA AND MARILYN J. WESTERKAMP

Evangelicals and Moravians valued their personal connection with God. The Holy Spirit mentored believers according to the dictates of the Bible, never deviating from the task of revealing the power of the Word. The Savior inspired Moravians' passions so intensely that they often fractured established modes of decorum and institutional structures. Through God, female adherents of the Pietist and evangelical movements nurtured personal appropriations of the Bible's saving truths. Women thus made essential contributions to a transatlantic shift in the spiritual and interpretive authority of the Bible that occurred in the eighteenth century by promoting religious experience as a hermeneutical frame rather than engaging in traditional, learned exegesis. However, the nature of their interpretation always reflected the social and cultural inequalities imposed upon women; gender, race, and class shaped how women experienced, approached, and influenced the religiosity of the eighteenth- and early nineteenth-century world.

Pietists and evangelicals craved the excitement and the movement of the Spirit and the spiritual transformation promised, but they also valued order—ordered systems and ordered behavior as structured through law and custom and delineated in the Bible. White men profited most clearly from the prevailing order. Systems of patriarchal hierarchy and institutional structures supported men as they established their authority to control those around them. In particular, clergymen had worked to understand the exact, true meaning of the Bible's original texts, with training that included the languages of Greek and Hebrew, theological texts from Augustine to Luther and Calvin, and advanced knowledge of philosophy. By denying women and other disfranchised persons these tools, clerical leaders denied them a place at the table of authoritative interpretation. Learning is not necessarily incompatible with experientialism, but for those who embraced and profited from these systems of power, the Spirit sometimes found it difficult to make even an imprint.[1]

Women, on the other hand, were generally limited in their education and influence, their lives characterized by restricted opportunities. Many women in religious communities and congregations had been taught to read within their households, some male clerics introduced their daughters to the world of books and essays, and many exchanged letters and kept diaries. Virtually all were excluded from the formal, classical education provided by the universities. The buttresses of education, institutional authority, and political opportunities were replaced with the skills and constant demands of housewifery, the requirements of hospitality, the intimate exigencies of childbearing, and the never-ending care of children, relatives, friends, neighbors, and the sick. While pain and death touched the lives of everyone, women endured pregnancy, childbirth, the possibilities of stillbirth and sexual assault, and an array of dangers, both physical and psychological, associated with them. While young men trained to be farmers or craftsmen, with those among the more affluent sent to university, young women remained in the household, under the scrutiny of mothers and older women, mastering housekeeping and building connections. Though men and women supposedly sought the same things—grace and conversion—within the structures of public power and church organizations, they ended up with different experiences and expectations. Women seemed more open to grace, embracing the Holy Spirit and realizing power through their experiential piety. From the earliest days of the Great Awakening in the 1730s through the explosion of spiritual enlightenment in the early nineteenth century, women were drawn to God and drew brothers, sons, and husbands after them.

The Bible proved a source of knowledge, understanding, and inspiration for men and women. For believers and the pastors who preached and counseled, the Bible served as a primary tool of order, for the same texts with the same thematics drew a variety of pastors, listeners, and converts together under the same rubrics and hopes. Like most laypersons, women did not arrive at their understanding of what the Bible meant through systematic exegetical study. Women knew and often possessed sophisticated understandings of biblical texts and stories, but do not appear to have turned to them as a method of constructing their theology in the traditional, scholarly fashion. Nor did women express themselves as if the Bible were their first or only source of spiritual knowledge. Instead, women's theology was experimental as they followed the guidance and inspiration of the Spirit. This inspiration, in other words, often liberated women from strict adherence to the text. When recording their speech or actions, women often wrote as if they were expressing the words requested by or channeled through the Spirit. The Bible became an alternative expression of what was in their hearts and minds, a text provided by God that gave clarity to minds and rendered their experiential piety intelligible, even lucid, to themselves. Far from merely seeking information or direction, women found confirmation, even validation of their own interpretations and responses to their experiences. Evangelical and Moravian cultures opened space for women and other disfranchised persons to reach the divinity and take leadership. God moved in remarkable ways.

Personal Relationships and Personal Bibles

In the eighteenth century, women built their lives around relationships, and none was more pivotal than an intense relationship with God. The Pietists and evangelicals who swept through the Atlantic basin worked to establish this special bond, not based on persuading the intellect of its value, but upon heart-centered experiences of God's divine grace. The conversion experience initiated a personal kinship with the divine and empowered believers to appropriate the Word of God "for their own purposes and under their control."[2] Women often turned to the Bible, in its capacity as a divinely inspired spiritual authority, to confirm that their hearts had been genuinely transformed. On her way home from a particularly enlightening worship service at a Reformed Church in Philadelphia in 1741, Margaret Jungmann—a Moravian woman who worked with the mission to Indigenous Americans in New York, Pennsylvania, and Ohio—experienced feelings that "I cannot describe." Matthew 11:28 came into her mind: "Just as you are, you may come to the Lamb, and if only you come, you'll be accepted. Be you so sinful, so full of shame—There's so a thirsting heart ready for you." She believed this verse affirmed the validity of her conversion experience. "Very often did I repeat [these words] to myself. I now presented myself before the dear Savior as sinful and as depraved as I felt myself to be, and I received the forgiveness of my sins from Him."[3] Sarah Osborn, a British-born evangelical in New England, cited a passage from the book of James as a source of assurance and comfort during her initial conversion. "While in the utmost Hurry, anguish, and distress, these words come to me with great power, 'resist the devil and he will flee from you. Draw nigh to God and he will draw nigh to you' [James 4:8]."⁴ Hannah Heaton, another eighteenth-century resident of New England, recorded in her diary that her conversion experience made her feel "as if i could not sleep while the heavens was fild with praises and singing. This night i was brought into the lords prayr. Before i was afraid to say it but now it seemd sweet to call god father. Yea my heart could say every word in it. Ah what sweet peace i felt while my mind was swallowed up in the scripture matthew 5 from 9 to the 14."⁵ For Jungmann, Osborn, Heaton, and other evangelical and Moravian women, the Bible lent authoritative spiritual voice to the feelings of bliss and elation that followed their entry into an intimate relationship with the king of kings.

As with other relationships women formed, however, the establishment and maintenance of their relationship with God were never easy or without difficulties. Like the Puritans before them, evangelical women utilized biblical verses as language to express feelings of utter despair and worthlessness that led to their moment of spiritual transformation. Recalling her youth, Osborn lamented possessing a rebellious worldly disposition and "being averse to the Gospel-Way of Salvation, wrought out by Christ." Believing her former self to be "a Child of Wrath, and Heir of Hell, an Enemy to Him, and his Ways, yea Enmity itself," she could "plainly see the Cause of that Complaint, *Ye will not come to me that ye might have Life* [John 5:40]." Exhibiting her biblical sophistication, Osborn, in this same sentence, made use of a hermeneutical device that became increasingly common among evangelicals and Pietists alike: God transmitting the power of Scripture directly to individual believers. "God convinced me," Osborn wrote, that "He and his Throne would be spotless forever tho' he should cast me off, and condemn me to the hottest Hell," and "*by the Deeds of the Law, no Flesh living should be justified* [Rom 3:20]."⁶ Fanny Newell, an exhorter who traveled with her husband on Methodist circuits in Maine and Vermont in the early nineteenth century, similarly cried out, "Doomed, I am justly—doomed I am justly—O have mercy on a poor hell-deserving sinner!" Then Christ replied to her directly, "Give me thine heart [Prov 23:26]."⁷

Moments of struggle and uncertainty, however, also bred opportunities for self-assertion and allowed women to define their relationship with God more precisely. Emphasizing the Incarnation, Moravians made Jesus Christ the primary object of their "heart religion." They characterized their relationship with him as one between a husband and wife in mystical marriage.⁸ Nikolaus Ludwig von Zinzendorf, the Moravians' spiritual and political leader, often summarized his theology by glossing Isa 54:5, "Your Creator is your husband [*dein Schöpfer ist dein Mann*]."⁹ Adding context to this verse from their own experiences, Moravian women utilized a language of dependence, intimacy, and eroticism to describe their connection with Christ. Upon her acceptance into the Moravian Single Sister's Choir, Benigna Zahm "gave myself anew to the Bridegroom of my soul and made the covenant with Him to become and remain His faithful handmaiden."[10] Moravian women "gave themselves" to Christ many times throughout their lives. When her "dear husband was called home" (i.e., died and went to heaven) in 1792, Catharina Krause "gave myself over to Him anew as the best Husband of my soul for the further guidance and leadership in my state of widowhood; that He might daily stand by me with His grace and help and remain my comforter in all distress."[11] Married in the corporeal world or not, Moravian women always had a husband and provider in Christ.

Evangelical women, like their Moravian colleagues, spoke of their relationship with God in emotional, almost swept language. In verse written to praise and celebrate God "who has done great things for me," Hannah Heaton wrote:

> O glorious Jesus how i long: to get fast hold of thee
> To twine my heart & never part: through a vast eternity
> O love amazing, love indeed: o soul aluring love
> O love of heaven fild with love: o lovely place indeed[12]

However, evangelical women tended to elevate the Holy Spirit as the primary point of contact with the divine. The Spirit guided them to God, convicted the sinful, conveyed the impact of grace, and subsumed their souls through conversion. In a time of doubt during her own conversion process, Fanny Newell took comfort because "the patient, good Spirit of God did not leave me, it followed me crying in my ear, *'this is the way, walk ye in it'* [Isa 30:21]."[13] Jarena Lee, the first authorized preacher in the African Methodist Episcopal Church, cast herself in the role of a naïve and petulant child. "But the Lord led me on: being gracious, he took pity on my ignorance; he heard my wailings, which had entered into the ear of the Lord of Sabaoth." Under the tutelage of the Spirit, Lee "had learned much" and became "able in some degree to comprehend the spiritual meaning of the text, which the ministers took on the Sabbath morning ... which was, 'I perceive thy heart is not right in the sight of God.,' Acts, chap. 8, verse 21." Facilitating her conversion, this text "became the power of God unto salvation to me, because I believed."[14]

Even as they pursued their relationship with the Savior, women lived their lives in close connection with family and friends, calling upon God to guide them and finding reflections of their own awareness in the Bible. Margaret Jungmann remembered family prayers on weekday mornings when "my father each time read us a chapter out of the Bible."[15] Esther Burr, the daughter of Jonathan Edwards, wrote of languor and impatience when her husband was gone, finding no solace among others. She attended sermons the Sunday after he had gone, and was moved by Peter's words, "above all things have fervent Charity among your selves: for Charity shall cover the multitude of sins [1 Pet 4:8]," arousing her awareness that she *"greatly* [fell] short of the Rules, the golden rules that Christ and his apostles gave us."[16] So, too, Zilpha Elaw reflected upon the gift of her sister's presence, noting "as iron sharpeneth iron, so doth the countenance of a man his friend [Prov 27:17]."[17]

Mary Penry, a Welsh-born Moravian in Pennsylvania, progressively interpreted passages from Scripture in her correspondence with family and friends. When asked by her cousin Katherine "whether we shall meet before the Throne of Grace," Mary decisively responded, "I humbly trust we shall," for she found "very Comfortable proofs in your [Katharine's] Letters that you are a *Sincere Believer*. As such I trust we shall be among that number in the Kingdom of Heaven." Still, she admonished her cousin in this regard, paraphrasing Rev 21:5, "against our Knowledge of each other in an After State," for only God could possess true knowledge of individuals in their "after state," meaning after their death. Mary found proof of the logic of her advice in Luke 16:19–31. "The Parable of Dives & Lazarus [seems] to encourage that Hope. It is Plain Dives knew both Abraham and Lazarus yea he even remembered his Brethren in this World and wish'd they might escape the Torments he suffer'd." Heed Abraham's advice, in other words, and learn from "Moses and the Prophets" while there is still time. In any case, she counseled, it was always "best to leave it to our Lord" and let *"Thy Will be Done* [Luke 11:2]."[18] Mary claimed the ability to discern the state of Katherine's soul by reading her letters, and she possessed the confidence to declare as much and provide biblically informed spiritual counsel in epistolary form.

Illness and death frequently strained such close relationships. As the primary caretakers of the family, as well as nurses to neighbors and the sole attendants in the birthing chamber, women experienced intimate relations with those who suffered and the cause of that suffering. Life experience brought them a particular understanding of temporary sickness and physical debility, anxiety in facing childbirth, and the vast, terrifying knowledge of smallpox and measles, including the horrifying treatment of inoculation.[19] Many women were highly knowledgeable and skilled, yet even they could be confused by the unknown and frightened by the prospect of yellow fever. When navigating ailments, from fairly minor injuries to serious, frequently fatal afflictions, the Bible provided memorable prayers, meditations, and a language of explanation. Mary Penry maintained a correspondence with the eminent physician Benjamin Rush, primarily seeking medical advice and reporting treatments she administered to female congregants in the Moravian Single Sisters Choir in Lititz. In these letters, Penry displays a remarkable understanding of and commitment to observational methods, and yet she could not deny the role played by God in these matters. For "if the Lord does not think fitting" to make a patient well again, then "she must be resigned and thankful that her lot is cast where it is [Prov 16:33]."[20]

Jarena Lee suffered five family members' death in six years, including her husband's, leaving her with two infant children. She took some comfort in the promise of God found in Ps 68:5, "I will be the widow's God, and a father to the fatherless." She felt gratified that friends gathered around her and provided financial, emotional, and spiritual support. "Once I was young, but now I am old, yet I have never seen the righteous forsaken, nor his seed begging bread."[21] Sarah, a Moravian missionary in Greenland, "went into a tent where a child lay dead, and spoke to the women that were assembled for the funeral dirge, alledging that text, *Suffer the little children to come unto me* [Matt 19:14; Mark 10:14; Luke 18:16], &c. and telling them that they had no occasion to howl over the child's death, because our Savior loved children very much."[22] Heaton experienced the illness of her son twice. In March 1776, both sons had left in response to their father's treatment, leading a fearful Heaton to ask God to send "that spirit that elijah had and turn the hart of the fathers to the children and the hart of the children to the fathers lest the earth or such families are smitten with a curse [Mal 4:5]." Calvin, one of Heaton's sons, did become sick with pleurisy, but through this illness, his father became more supportive and open to grace. Two years later, Calvin was ill for more than fifty days. Against expectations, he recovered, although when he was well he seemed like "lazarus raised from the grave [John 11]." Nevertheless, following this long suffering, Heaton claimed, "I can say as david it is good for me that I have been afflicted [Ps 119:71]."[23] When Moravian Sarah Grube became "severely ill," "the Savior appeared before my heart, and it seemed to me as though He were standing right in front of me in person and was showing me His hands with the marks of the nails, and said, 'Look, into *these* hands I have inscribed you,' and He assured me that everything He had done and suffered was done for me." Grube knew that Christ himself had spoken to her because she "heard in my heart the words, 'It is finished!' [John 19:30]."[24] The Bible could be both a source of anxiety and a message of comfort, but Christ himself became the primary agent for Moravian women, who then looked to the Bible to confirm it was actually him.

The birthing chamber remained a difficult place for women, for death was ever-present.[25] Heaton's daughter-in-law gave birth in early 1778 and died shortly thereafter. She warned "her nurse not to put off to seek first the kingdom of heaven and the righteousness thereof and all other things shall be added [Matt 6:33]." Several years later, Heaton attended a funeral to mourn a young woman who had died after being in labor for four hours. Heaton appreciated the sermon, built around Ps 49:12, and she continued to call for prayers for the preacher "and all christs ministers that God would make them hunters to hunt zion out of the holes of the rocks where they are hid. O when shall our glorious Solomon ride fourth upon king davids mule. O when shall christs dominion spread from sea to sea and from the river to the ends of the earth [Ps 72:8; I Kgs 1:33; Jer 16:16]."[26] Fanny Newell chronicled her own hazardous confinement, afflicted with a severe fever five days after her son's birth. She wrote of a dream that appeared to offer death and salvation to her, but at the gates of heaven Jesus met her and said, "Fanny ... thou shalt not die, but live and declare the works of the Lord to the children of men [Ps 118:17]."[27] More than any other experience, childbirth set women apart from men. Surviving one pregnancy did not mean long-term health. Rather, one successful delivery simply provided opportunity for another, with risk increasing as births multiplied and a woman aged. Adding to their personal hazard, women would witness births of family, friends, and neighbors. Women were never far from this specter of death.

Female Vocations and the Bible

In their work, these women moved in both the public and private spheres, despite the social constraints placed upon them because of their gender.[28] The Bible operated as a spiritual guide that helped women navigate their traditional roles as wives, mothers, caregivers, congregants, and educators. Sarah Osborn became an amazingly successful and hardworking evangelical mentor. In the 1760s, she hosted various religious groups every night of the week at the school where she taught, including two classes of local children, a young women's society, a class of African American men, a young white men's society, and an evening meeting of heads of families who gathered for "prayer and religious conversations."[29] Moravian women also used the Bible to structure prayer groups and official daily religious meetings for other female choir members. The Single Sister's Choir Diary in Bethlehem, Pennsylvania, in 1776, for example, began by declaring, "We had a blessed entrance into the New Year," and then offered a reflection upon Isa 65:18, "But be ye glad and rejoice for ever in that which I create." On March 25, the "Savior showed himself in a remarkable way to His dear Girls Choir in the morning." Commemorating the acceptance of two new members to the Single Sisters Choir with Brother

Thrane, the sisters celebrated, "the Festival homily over the *Loosung*: And therefore will the Lord wait, that he may be gracious unto you; and therefore will he be exalted, that he may have mercy on you [Isa 30:18]."[30]

The Bible also operated as a crucial instructional device and helpmeet for Moravian women in other capacities. Like their male counterparts, female Moravian believers engaged with the daily *Losung* (biblical watchword), a randomly chosen Bible verse designated in advance by the Moravian Church for every day of the year, and contemplated its significance. Zinzendorf created the *Losungen* to promote congregational unity by having the same passage from Scripture guide everyone's spiritual meditations on any given day.[31] The institution of the *Losung* as an element of lived religion, however, could also highlight the particular circumstances of individual believers. As a local teacher and spiritual guide, the Moravian sister Susel "saw all the sisters in *Classes*," and she "chose for each Class a very beautiful and comforting *Loosung*" as a pedagogical tool.[32] Moravian women ascribed more meaning to some *Losungen* than others. Sister Susel's practice, for example, of choosing especially meaningful *Losungen* to serve her classroom's didactic purposes, beyond the *Losung* officially designated and sanctioned for that day, went far beyond their traditional application.

While female uses of the *Losung* most often appear in the context of favorable, celebratory spiritual circumstances, they could also serve as an implement of admonishment and reprimand. When the single sister Philipina Bömbern stopped attending worship services and abruptly decided to leave Bethlehem and go to Philadelphia because she had "suffered damage to her heart" as a result of a "visit of her mother and bad brother," the other single sisters worried about her potential to "become detrimental to others in the House." Moving swiftly to eradicate this threat to their religious purity and integrity, the single sisters "released [Bömbern] with the text of the day: Every plant, which my heavenly Father hath not planted, shall be rooted up," quoting Matt 15:13.[33] The increasingly diverse uses demonstrate that Moravian women helped the *Losung* transcend its function as a cultural unifier over vast distances. It fell to individuals to determine and narrate how their circumstances infused the text of the *Losung* with meaning. All Moravian women engaged in this personal reflection process and, thus, facilitated the subtle transformation of the *Losung* into a ritual practice meant to guide both their spiritual and corporeal lives.

Women also used the Bible to bolster their personal authority in cultivating relationships with powerful men. In a letter to Benjamin Rush, Mary Penry offered words of consolation after learning that Rush had lost out on an $8,000 court settlement he had recently won in a libel suit against an unsatisfied patient, William Cobbett, who fled the country to get out of paying.[34] "A person who is satisfied with your Medical Skill, with the Talents our Lord has bestowed on you . . . will be very apt to Mortify you," but "let it not pain you my dear Sir it is all for your good." A gloss of John 15:18 authorized her characterization of God's will. Penry told Rush, "all that you suffer is the Natural Consequence of your *not* being of the World—The World sais our Blessed Lord loveth its own, Ye are not of the World &c." She reminded Rush that he was a good person and compared him to biblical figures noted for their devotion and service to Christ. "Pardon me my dear Sir! I do sometimes think you are a *Nicodemus*. He bore a good Character. Joseph of Arimathea the same, they believ'd in Jesus but not openly profess'd—for fear of the Jews [John 3:1–2 & 19:38]." Finally, she encouraged Rush to remain undaunted and to take "Courage (not to lay his Sacred Body in a Tomb, or to purchase Spices to embalm it [as had Joseph of Arimathea]. But to take him into your heart to Live in Him, as he in you.) [John 19:40]."[35] Penry envisioned Rush and his circumstances as biblical leaders, displaying her sophisticated ability to use the Bible, not as a traditional source of theological knowledge, but as an experiential source marking congruence with the will of God. Her method of parsing spiritual meaning and marshaling Bible verses to support her assertions exhibits a powerful sense of self that she filtered through the rhetoric of pious subordination to divine authority as a method of conforming to prevailing gender norms.[36]

The Bible and Countercultural Challenges

In addition to appropriating elements of traditional religious culture for their own purposes, some women moved into roles that were generally off-limits, and they used the Bible to mount direct challenges to prevailing white male clerics, authorities, and institutions. Osborn, for example, was an exceptionally gifted teacher, running a school and a series of classes for a wide range of people, from young white girls to African American men. When some suggested that Osborn should seek the assistance of others in this work since, as a woman, she was not considered fit to lead such classes, her defiance of authority directly engaged her own sense of call. Responding to a criticism that cited Jethro's advice to Moses in the book of Exodus, Osborn spurned the authorities, arguing that she was a servant of God. "I am rather a Servant that Has a Great work assigned Him." She would continue in her tasks until "God in his providence point out a way for it to be better done. . . . Dont think me obstinate then Sir if I dont know How to Let Go these shoals of fish."[37] Similarly, at the age of sixteen, Fanny Newell "arose in obedience to my divine

Master's command, and delivered the message which his Spirit dictated to me." People had gathered at the Methodist meeting to hear the bishop, and, before the bishop could speak, she stood to exhort the people, beginning with Paul's words: "'I speak the truth in Christ, I lie not—my conscience bearing me witness in the Holy Ghost' [Rom 9:1]."[38]

Newell, accompanying her husband on his Methodist circuits, often followed his sermons with extemporaneous prayers. Frequently weak and ill, she nevertheless publicly proclaimed, in defiance of Methodist tradition regarding female speech, that "obedience is better than sacrifice, and to hearken than the fat of rams" [1 Sam 15:22], for the "long suffering mercy of God" teaches us that God is "'not willing that any should perish, but that all should come to repentance' [2 Pet 3:9]." When her husband explicitly asked her to ride with him, she found comfort in Ps 144: "'The Lord teacheth my hands to war and my fingers to fight, so that a bow of steel is broken by my arm.'" On one Sabbath meeting, as she rode along on the circuit, she clearly spoke to people who resisted her authority. "After reasoning a little with flesh and blood, I arose, and spake to the people, and had great liberty in delivering my soul from their blood. Whatever may be said against a female speaking, or praying in public, I care not; for when I feel confident, that the Lord calls me to speak, I dare not refuse."[39] She then worked through a veritable panoply of biblical women, including Deborah and Huldah, to whom "even the elders of Israel went for counsel," Philip's four daughters, and Paul's rule for women "praying or prophesying." She concluded that "'God would pour out his Spirit upon all flesh,' . . . and I see no cause why prophecy in this text does not favor the daughter equally with the son [Acts 2:17]."[40]

Although many evangelical women believed they were called to preach, Christian groups mostly opposed female public speech. Men cited the proscriptions of Paul as well as women's limited intellect and weakness of will. Most white women generally accepted these limitations, contenting themselves with teaching local classes, mentoring children, leading prayers in their households, and guiding young women. The demands of white patriarchy seemed clear and reasonable. African American women, however, stepped forward into preaching. Hearing the Spirit's call, they saw no reason to adhere to the enforced limitations imposed by white patriarchy, even when male privilege was assumed by Black men. Surely, a system that justified the enslavement and restriction of African Americans merited respect from no one. Jarena Lee turned to the lesson of Mary Magdalene.

Richard Allen had told Lee that women could not preach, but she remembered Mary Magdalene. "Did not Mary *first* preach the risen Saviour, and is not the doctrine of the resurrection the very climax of Christianity—hangs not all our hope on this, as argued by St. Paul? Then did not Mary, a woman, preach the gospel? for she preached the resurrection of the crucified Son of God [John 20:11–18].'"[41] Years later, Lee delivered an extemporaneous sermon on Jonah 2:9 when the scheduled preacher lost his spirit. Afterward, Allen stood and confessed to his congregation that he had once denied her the pulpit, but proclaimed that he believed her fit to preach.[42] So, too, Zilpha Elaw recorded that while her husband was hostile to religion, upon learning that she was a preacher, he agreed to go listen to her, though he feared "I would be a laughing-stock." Soon after these events, her husband became ill, and she was troubled since he was still a stranger to "'the Lamb of God who taketh away the sins of the world' [John 1:29]."[43] Elaw was among the few African American preachers who dared to follow a call to preach in Maryland, a slave state. Aware of the risks of enslavement, she came to identify her palpable fear of capture with the temptation of the devil. Speaking as Jesus had, she conquered her fear, declaring, "'get thee behind me Satan, for my Jesus has made me free' [Mark 8:33 and Rom 8:2]."[44] With this confidence, she preached to many who gathered to hear, attracted by her reputation and, undoubtedly, the spectacle.

Zilpha Elaw has been credited with using Scripture to engage in a "politics of origin" that worked to authorize her experiences as a Black woman who believed she had been called to preach. Rather than rejecting the Pauline texts ordinarily used to restrict the ecclesiastical agency of women, Elaw reinterpreted them—especially the accounts of Paul's Damascus Road experience in Acts 9, 22, and 26—in order to "discursively [construct] identities and vocational legitimacy" for herself and other women.[45] She recorded a vision of "a tall figure who came and stood by me. He had long hair, which parted in the front ... and as he stood with open arms and smiled upon me, he disappeared."[46] And she continued: "After this wonderful manifestation of my condescending Saviour, the peace of God which passeth understanding was communicated to my heart; and joy in the Holy Ghost, to a degree, at the last, unutterable by my tongue and indescribably by my pen; it was beyond my comprehension; but, from that happy hour, my soul was set at glorious liberty; and, like the Ethiopic eunuch, I went on my way rejoicing in the blooming prospects of a better inheritance with the saints in light."[47] In comparing herself to the Ethiopian—an official treasurer of the Ethiopian *Candace* (queen) who, according to Acts 8, was baptized by Philip the Evangelist at the behest of the Holy Spirit upon his return to Africa from Jerusalem—Elaw marked herself and the social condition of her African American brethren in antebellum America through the words and persons of Scripture.[48] The Bible became a cultural authority she marshaled to navigate conflicting social pressures and to argue in favor of her liberty as an African American and her legitimacy as a female preacher. As she explained in the dedication of her memoir, "I cannot present you with a more appropriate keepsake ... than the following contour portrait of my regenerated constitution—exhibiting, as did the bride of Solomon, comeliness with blackness [Song 1:5]; and, as did the apostle Paul, riches with poverty, and power in weakness [2 Cor 12:9]."[49]

Rebecca Protten, an African woman converted by Moravians in the eighteenth century, proved to be a gifted and persuasive preacher. Though "well versed in the Holy Scriptures" and possessing a reputation for "research[ing] deeply in the Scriptures," Rebecca believed that "Christ had revealed his word to her, and the visionary force of that inspiration was the only authority she needed."[50] She applied the "radical ethics of the Sermon on the Mount as her guide" in times of personal peril and to the plight of the enslaved peoples to whom she preached in the Caribbean. Though Rebecca's own words have not survived, Moravian missionaries taught potential African converts the messages of "blessed are the meek: for they shall inherit the earth," "salt of the earth," "judge not, lest ye be judged," "Blessed are they which are persecuted," and "Ye are the light of the world" [Matt 5], among others, in their Bible classes. Given her use of the Sermon on the Mount in other contexts, however, it is not unreasonable to imagine that Rebecca also used these passages in her sermons to enslaved Africans as a method of rhetorically subverting the violence and power of the white patriarchy that reigned in the Danish Caribbean and to communicate words of comfort and hope to intensely persecuted people. Colonialist objectives often limited full participation in the Christian religion for non-whites. Protten, like Elaw, however, believed the Bible included them as true people of God. Concerned that her baptism was not valid because there had not been a godfather present, she later "testified that all her *Scrupels* had vanished, because she had found in the Scriptures that the chamberlain baptized by Philip [Acts 8:26–39] also had no godfather." Seemingly a comment upon baptismal sponsors, the text also marks that Protten had found the Ethiopian.[51] The Bible and the Spirit of Christ had the rhetorical power to transform the hopeless condition of Africans living in a world controlled by white Europeans.

The Bible as Experiential Language

Elaw and Protten, like other women in the eighteenth and early nineteenth century, knew the Bible well and could quote and paraphrase with ease. Relevant verses appeared in their minds at times of great significance, whether joyful, emotional, stressful, or painful, and women found the Bible to be a meaningful source of knowledge. Newell, approaching maturity, labored to develop her relationship with God and her community, asking, like "Saul of Tarsus, 'Lord! what wilt thou have me do?' [Acts 9:6]."[52] As she pondered such questions, she found "this holy treasure—the Bible! O what a body of truth—how deep its mines—how rich its treasures. O thou, who alone canst give me true understanding of it, shine forth." Her musings about wisdom and grace demonstrate the importance of biblical texts. These passages begin, "I, Wisdom, dwell with Prudence, and find out knowledge of witty inventions." She followed with a journey through two chapters of Proverbs, verse after verse, but not in biblical order, and finished with "Blessed is the man that heareth me, waiting daily at my gates."[53] In fact, when determining to accept a marriage proposal from a Methodist circuit preacher, she pondered for a month, referring again to Proverbs, asserting, "O God, thou knowest that for thy sake I do this, and not for ease, honor, riches, or pleasure [Prov 3:16]."[54] Newell made this momentous life decision by turning to the Bible, not to systematically search for new and relevant passages that applied to her situation, but for reassurance from passages she already knew and could instantly reference from previous experience.

Evangelical and Pietist women also personally saw themselves and their life experiences in the Bible. In some cases, they identified with active women. Jarena Lee thought of Mary Magdalene as an example for women preaching, while Fanny Newell cited Deborah, Huldah, and Philip's daughters. Two Moravian women thought of Mary Magdalene while pondering their sinfulness and the Savior's forgiveness. One missionary set before her converts "the example of the great sinner Mary Magdalene, and exhorted them to follow it." At the same time, another looked forward to her death, when Jesus "will be pleased to call me, [and] I will kiss the wounds in his hands and feet, yea all his wounds, as Mary Magdalene did."[55] And when the blessed Mary Barbara died, she was praised as "a heart that adhered to our Savior with tender affection, and one who imitated Mary by pondering every thing she heard in a calm and peaceful heart [Luke 2:19]."[56]

Nevertheless, many found themselves not in comparisons with persons in the Bible, but in biblical circumstances that matched their own. Newell suffered illness and fatigue throughout her life, dying at the age of thirty-one. Her diary provides extensive information about her spiritual crises and conversion, but she frequently invoked the language of pain, illness, and cure when charting her relationship with the Spirit. Beginning with a Wesleyan hymn, "How Can a Sinner Lost in Pain, Recover His Forfeited Peace," Newell continues into the Bible's trove: Jesus asking a blind man, "Dost thou believe I am able to do this [Matt 9:28]," telling the father of a possessed son, "If thou canst believe, all things are possible to him that believeth [Mark 9:23]," and reassuring Jairus, "Only believe and [thou] shalt be made whole [Luke 8:50]." Even in the midst of temptation toward despair, she saw herself as "like poor blind Bartimeus of old 'Jesus, thou son of David have mercy on me' [Luke 18:30]." At the finish of her trials, she framed herself as the prodigal son. "The dead is alive, and the lost is found, and it is meet that we should be glad and rejoice [Luke 15:24]."[57]

Heaton's personal engagement also reflected the challenges in her life, especially the illnesses of her sons and their alienation from the family. She feared that their alienation resulted from their father's unjust treatment, and countless times she laments her marriage. She had been warned about marrying an unbeliever, and she felt that the night she married "made way for the curse of god upon me and my family in this world. I Samuel 3–13." Throughout her diary, she described many of her struggles and continued to blame herself: "O how many times has that word been heavy on my mind—o Assyria the rod of my anger the staff in their hand is my indignation [Isa 10:5]."[58]

Conclusion

Women spent their lives balancing the principles of their faith with the constraints placed upon them by society. The Bible operated as a significant resource for their spiritual journeys, but the gendered nature of their life experiences fundamentally shaped how evangelical and Moravian women understood and otherwise engaged with God's Word. Women did listen to sermons, participate in public prayer, and attempt to follow guidance from their pastors. However, they displayed little need for systematic theological exploration or exegetical Bible study. Experiences mattered most, and the Bible operated as a dependable authority that helped women interpret the Spirit's voice and make sense of those experiences.

Even as the fires of evangelical revival receded in the eighteenth century, the Bible, mediated through the Holy Spirit, increasingly functioned as a common language through which women articulated their gendered identities and experiences. As Bibles flew off of antebellum printing presses in record numbers, more women, like Fanny Newell and Jarena Lee, were able to marshal this language of biblicism and the cultural authority it possessed to transcend the new nineteenth-century limitations of gender and race and establish themselves (for a time at least) as public figures who commanded authority on current issues of Christian faith and practice in their own right.[59]

Beyond strict adherence to the text, evangelical and Moravian women empowered themselves and others by allowing the Spirit to speak scriptural truths to them directly. The Spirit guided women, as wives, mothers, household managers, nurses, caregivers, laborers, missionaries, church leaders, and charismatic exhorters, through the gendered and racial quagmire of society and authorized them to construct their own understandings of what the Bible meant. The premium that evangelicals and Moravians placed upon the pursuit and continuous cultivation of a close, personal connection with God ensured that their individual interpretations and applications of Scripture would never deviate from the true meaning of the Word. Sarah Pussimek, an Inuk convert "worker" (*Arbeiterin*) with the Moravian mission in Greenland, articulated this hermeneutical principle most clearly while attending to potential converts among the Kangek people.[60] Having previously received Bible lessons from other Europeans, these Kangek converts "always think, that all must be read out of a book, and when we [the Moravian missionaries] come, they ask directly where our books are." In reply, Sarah explained that "the Holy Ghost was the best schoolmaster; if he rules in the heart, and makes the word of God to become true in one's soul, then a person can also speak without book."[61]

Notes

1. For a wide-ranging discussion of the Holy Spirit among Puritan and evangelical women, see Marilyn J. Westerkamp, *Women and Religion in Early America, 1600–1850: The Puritan and Evangelical Traditions* (New York: Routledge, 1999).

2. Mark A. Noll, *In the Beginning Was the Word: The Bible in American Public Life, 1492–1783* (New York: Oxford University Press, 2015), 202.

3. Margaret Jungmann, *Moravian Women's Memoirs: Their Related Lives, 1750–1820*, trans. Katherine M. Faull (New York: Syracuse University Press, 1997), 50.

4. Catharine Brekus, *Sarah Osborn's World: The Rise of Evangelical Christianity in Early America* (New Haven: Yale University Press, 2013), 67. Also quoted in Noll, *In the Beginning Was the Word*, 193.

5. Hannah Heaton, *The World of Hannah Heaton: The Diary of an Eighteenth-Century New England Farm Woman*, ed. Barbara E. Lacey (DeKalb: Northern Illinois University Press, 2003), 10.

6. Sarah Osborn, *The nature, certainty and evidence of true Christianity.* . . . (Boston: S. Kneeland, 1755), 5.

7. Fanny Newell, *Diary of Fanny Newell, with a Sketch of Her Life and an Introduction* (Boston: Charles H. Peirce, 1848), 79.

8. Craig D. Atwood, "Sleeping in the Arms of Christ: Sanctifying Sexuality in the Eighteenth-Century Moravian Church," *Journal of the History of Sexuality* 8, no. 1 (1997): 25–51.

9. Ibid., 34. Zinzendorf derived his bridal mysticism from several biblical texts, such as Matt 9:15 and 25:1–12, Luke 5:34, John 3:29, Eph 5:23–28, and Rev 18:23. Craig D. Atwood, *Community of the Cross: Moravian Piety in Colonial Bethlehem* (University Park: Penn State University Press,

2004), 91, 91–95. On Moravian bridal mysticism, see Paul Peucker, *A Time of Sifting: Mystical Marriage and the Crisis of Moravian Piety in the Eighteenth Century* (University Park: Penn State University Press, 2015); Peucker, "Blut' auf unsre grünen Bändchen: Die Sichtungszeit in der Herrnhuter Brüdergemeine," *Unitas Fratrum* 49/50 (2002): 41–94.

10. Benigna Zahm, *Moravian Women's Memoirs*, 21. On the Moravian choir system, see Beverly Prior Smaby, *The Transformation of Moravian Bethlehem: From Communal Mission to Family Economy* (Philadelphia: University of Pennsylvania Press, 1988).

11. Catharina Krause, *Moravian Women's Memoirs*, 104.

12. Heaton, *World*, 10, 11.

13. Newell, *Diary*, 52. The Moravians, following Zinzendorf, believed that the Holy Spirit occupied the "mother office" of the Holy Trinity. See Atwood, *Community of the Cross*, 64–70; Atwood, "The Mother of God's People: The Adoration of the Holy Spirit in the Eighteenth-Century Brüdergemeine," *CH* 68, no. 4 (1999): 886–909.

14. Jarena Lee, "The Life and Religious Experience of Jarena Lee," in *Sisters of the Spirit: Three Black Women's Autobiographies of the Nineteenth Century*, ed. William Andrews (Bloomington: Indiana University Press, 1986), 32.

15. Jungmann, *Moravian Women's Memoirs*, 49.

16. Esther Burr, *Journal of Esther Edwards Burr, 1754–1757*, ed. Carol Karlsen and Laurie Crumpacker (New Haven: Yale University Press, 1984), 82.

17. Zilpha Elaw, "Memoirs of the Life, Religious Experience, Ministerial Travels, and Labors of Mrs. Zilpha Elaw," in Andrews, *Sisters of the Spirit*, 71.

18. Mary Penry, "Letter to Meredith Penry, Katherine Penry, and Eliza Powell, July 2, 1795, Lititz, Pennsylvania," in *The Letters of Mary Penry: A Single Woman in Early America*, ed. Scott Paul Gordon (University Park: Penn State University Press, 2018), 106.

19. On women and smallpox inoculations, see Elisabeth Fenn, *Pox Americana: The Great Smallpox Epidemic of 1775–82* (New York: Hill and Wang, 2001).

20. Penry, "Letter to Benjamin Rush, April 21, 1791, Lititz, Pennsylvania," in Gordon, *Letters of Mary Penry*, 78.

21. Lee, "Life and Religious Experience," 41.

22. David Cranz, *The History of Greenland: Containing A Description of the Country, and Its Inhabitants: and Particularly, a Relation of the Mission, carried on for above these Thirty Years by the Unitas Fratrum, at New Herrnhuth and Lichtenfels, in that Country* (London: Brethren's Society for the Furtherance of the Gospel Among the Heathen, 1767), 2:39.

23. Heaton, *World*, 172–73, 245–46.

24. Sarah Grube, *Moravian Women's Memoirs*, 40 (italics in original).

25. See, for example, Judith Walzer Leavitt, *Brought to Bed: Childbearing in America, 1750–1950* (New York: Oxford University Press, 1986); Laurel Thatcher Ulrich, *A Midwife's Tale: The Life of Martha Ballard Based on Her Diary, 1785–1812* (New York: Vintage, 1991).

26. Heaton, *World*, 188, 298.

27. Newell, *Diary*, 174–76; citation 176.

28. Westerkamp, *Women and Religion*; Mary Beth Norton, *Founding Mothers and Fathers: Gendered Power and the Forming of American Society* (New York: Alfred A. Knopf, 1996); Norton, *Liberty's Daughters: The Revolutionary Experience of American Women, 1750–1800* (Boston: Little, Brown, 1980); Linda Kerber, *Women of the Republic: Intellect and Ideology in Revolutionary America* (Chapel Hill: University of North Carolina Press, 1980).

29. Samuel Hopkins, *Memoirs of the life of Mrs. Sarah Osborn* . . . (1799; Catskill, NY, 1814), 81–82.

30. Moravian Single Sisters' Diary, January and March 1776, vol. 3, Moravian Archives Bethlehem (MAB), MAB archive translation, Bethlehem Digital History Project, http://bdhp.moravian.edu/community_records/catalogs_diary/single_sisters/singlesisters1776.html.

31. On the Moravian *Losungen*, see Peter Vogt's chapter in the present volume. Also, Gisela Mettele, *Weltbürgertum oder Gottesreich: Die Herrnhuter Brüdergemeine als globale Gemeinschaft, 1727–1857* (Göttingen: Vandenhoeck & Ruprecht, 2009), 58–59.

32. Moravian Single Sisters' Diary, January 1776, MAB. Benigna von Zinzendorf founded the Bethlehem Female Seminary in Germantown, Pennsylvania in 1742, which functioned mostly as a primary school for girls in the eighteenth century, but later became Moravian College. See Jewel Smith, *Music, Women, and Pianos in Antebellum Bethlehem, Pennsylvania: The Moravian Young Ladies' Seminary* (Bethlehem: Lehigh University Press, 2008).

33. Moravian Single Sisters' Diary, October 1776, MAB.

34. Gordon, *Letters of Mary Penry*, 176n11.

35. Penry, Letter to Benjamin Rush, June 26, 1800, Lititz, Pennsylvania, in Gordon, *Letters of Mary Penry*, 208–9. Parenthetical text appears as in original. Bracketed texts are additions.

36. See Scott Gordon, "Glad Passivity: Mary Penry of Lititz and the Making of Moravian Women," *JMH* 13, no. 1 (2013): 1–26.

37. Jethro called upon Moses to delegate responsibilities to others working under his guidance. Sarah Osborn to Joseph Fish, March 7, 1767, in Mary Beth Norton, "'My Resting Reaping Times': Sarah Osborn's Defense of her 'Unfeminine' Activities, 1767," *Signs* 2 (1976): 528–29.

38. Newell, *Diary*, 112.

39. Ibid., 200, 207–8.

40. Ibid., 207–8. References include: on Deborah, Judg 4–5; on Huldah, 2 Kgs 22:14–20; on Philip's daughters, Acts 21:8–14; on Paul's rule, 1 Cor 11:5. See Catherine Brekus, *Strangers and Pilgrims: Female Preaching in America, 1740–1845* (Chapel Hill: University of North Carolina Press, 1998).

41. Lee, "Life and Religious Experience," 36.

42. Ibid., 44–45. See also, Richard Newman, *Freedom's Prophet: Bishop Richard Allen, the AME Church, and the Black Founding Fathers* (New York: New York University Press, 2008).

43. Elaw, "Memoirs," 83–84.

44. Ibid., 90–99; citation 91. The biblical citation is a splicing together of Mark 8:33 and Rom 8:2.

45. Mitzi Smith, "'Unbossed and Unbought': Zilpha Elaw and Old Elizabeth and a Political Discourse of Origin," *Black Theology* 9, no. 3 (2011): 287–88, 298–301.

46. Elaw, "Memoirs," 56–57. Also cited in Westerkamp, *Women and Religion*, 123.

47. Elaw, "Memoirs," 56–57. Biblical references include Phil 4:7, Acts 8:39, and Col 1:12.

48. Acts 8:26–39. The story of the Ethiopian became foundational for the African American Christian community, with many churches identifying themselves through their Ethiopian roots. See, for example, the Abyssinian Baptist Church in New York City, founded in 1808.

49. Elaw, "Memoirs," 51.

50. August Gottlieb Spangenberg to Nikolas von Zinzendorf, October 25, 1736, R15, Ba10.10, Unity Archives Herrnhut, as cited and reproduced in Jon Sensbach, *Rebecca's Revival: Creating Black Christianity in the Atlantic World* (Cambridge, MA: Harvard University Press, 2005), 66–67.

51. Ibid., 112, 57, 58, 122, 61.

52. Newell, *Diary*, 127–28.

53. Ibid., 137, 128–30. Passages cited include Prov 8:12 and 8:34. Between those two, she cites, in this order, Prov 9:1–6; 8:17; 9:10; 8:13–14; 8:19–21; 8:32; 8:13; 8:11; 8:11.

54. Ibid., 144.

55. Cranz, *History of Greenland*, 2:51, 463.

56. Ibid., 2:221. This Mary is Jesus's mother.

57. Newell, *Diary*, 71, 74, 79, 84. The hymn is Charles Wesley's "How Shall a Lost Sinner in Pain."

58. Heaton, *World*, 172, 96.

59. On "performed biblicism," see Seth Perry, *Bible Culture and Authority in the Early United States* (Princeton: Princeton University Press, 2018), esp. 86–109.

60. On Indigenous "workers" or "national helpers" employed by Moravians and other Protestant groups, see Edward E. Andrews, *Native Apostles: Black and Indian Missionaries in the British Atlantic World* (Cambridge, MA: Harvard University Press, 2013); and Sensbach, *Rebecca's Revival*, 67.

61. Cranz, *History of Greenland*, 2:20.

14

MORAVIANS AND THE BIBLE IN THE ATLANTIC WORLD

The Case of the Daily Watchwords in Bethlehem, PA, 1742–1745

PETER VOGT

When members of the Moravian movement (*Herrnhuter Brüdergemeine*) began establishing themselves in Pennsylvania in the early 1740s, they brought with them from Europe a distinct practice of using the Bible for daily devotion and spiritual guidance, which was known as the *Losungen* or "watchwords." These were collections of short passages from Holy Scripture, as well as lines from hymns, which were arranged in the fashion of a yearly calendar with one or sometimes two readings selected as the watchword for each day. This tradition started in the early days of the Herrnhut settlement, where each evening a Scripture passage or a line from a hymn was announced to be the watchword for the following day and communicated orally within the community. As the movement grew beyond the Herrnhut village, Count Nikolaus Ludwig von Zinzendorf (1700–1760) prepared the first printed edition of daily watchwords for the year 1731. Since then, the Moravian Watchwords, or Daily Texts, have been published without interruption for more than 280 years and include today more than fifty different language editions.[1]

There has been considerable development over the years in how the Moravian watchwords are selected and put together. They have been recognized as a unique feature in the life of the Moravian Church, as well as an important part of Count Zinzendorf's spiritual legacy. They are now increasingly moving into the focus of historical scholarship. Of particular interest is the fact that often the lot was used to determine the selection of the texts, making the Moravian watchwords a prominent example of the Pietist practice of bibliomancy.[2] At the same time, the watchwords are acknowledged as a distinct spiritual tradition with a considerable dissemination and influence beyond the Moravian Church.[3]

Within the larger context of exploring the role of the Bible for eighteenth-century transatlantic evangelicalism, the following discussion will consider the case of the Moravian watchwords in connection with the Moravian expansion to Pennsylvania during the 1740s. Through the watchwords, the Moravians' experience of living and moving within the Atlantic world was intimately tied to their reading of Scripture. The following account of the journey of the first large group of Moravian settlers, who traveled from Germany to Pennsylvania in the spring of 1742, provides a vivid illustration:

> On the 26th of February, Old Style, 1742, in connection with the departure from London [the group] was dedicated as a Sea Congregation of the Lord, the Daily Text being Esther 4:16: "If I perish, I perish," and the word for the daily meditation of the Brethren's Church: "I shall not die, no, no, no, I shall live." They have indeed received passports from the warring nations, but did not dare take them along, but journeyed only under the protection of the Lord. On the first of May, New Style,—the text of the day being Zephania 2:3: "Seek ye the Lord, all ye meek of the earth, which have wrought his judgment: seek righteousness, seek meekness"; "Grant to the souls Thou hast redeemed, O Lord Jesus, Thy comfort"—they were indeed met by a privateer, and because they continued on their regular course, were surveyed by the privateer carefully and from a near position, but it immediately left them without further action.

The report continues to describe the arrival in America:

> They had their first view of America on the 21st of May, New Style, with the Daily Word Psalm 118:17 (compare the Daily Word of Feb. 26 on a preceding page) "I shall not die but live and declare the works of the Lord." . . .
>
> When on the 23rd of May, New Style, they reached land, the word of the Lord in the Daily Texts was Isaiah 65:25: "The wolf and the lamb shall feed together." . . .
>
> They finally reached Pennsylvania on the 4th of June, the Daily Word being Psalm 102:14–15: "Thou shalt arise and have mercy upon Zion: for the time to favor her, yea, the set time, is come. For Thy servants take pleasure in her stones, and favor the dust thereof."[4]

This report by eighteenth-century Moravian writer Georg Neisser documents how the watchwords functioned as daily Scripture readings for the Moravian community, offering to them, as it were, a running divine commentary on the earthly realities that they encountered. The focus of this practice was evidently not so much the desire to interpret Scripture as the question of how Scripture might help them to interpret their world.

At first glance, the idea that individual Bible passages are selected as "watchwords" for every day of the year seems rather straightforward and simple. A closer look at the tradition, however, reveals that the Moravian watchwords as a lived devotional practice in eighteenth-century Pennsylvania involved a set of complex issues. These include (a) the process by which the "watchwords" were chosen, (b) how they were distributed, (c) how they were utilized for worship and devotion, (d) how their message was found to be meaningful and relevant in relation to the believers' life situation, and (e) how subsequently this experience was expressed and communicated within the Moravian community. Written records of Moravian activities in Pennsylvania during the early 1740s, especially the diary of the Bethlehem congregation for the years 1742–45, which has been translated into English, provide ample source material that allows us to explore these complexities in detail. The goal of the following discussion is to show how the case of the Moravian watchwords exemplifies the connection between scriptural hermeneutics, religious practices, and the larger transatlantic setting.

Historical Background

As pointed out above, the beginning of the tradition of the Moravian Daily Texts is bound up with the early history of the Moravian congregation at Herrnhut, which had been founded in 1722 by religious exiles from Moravia on the estate of Count Zinzendorf. After a difficult start, the Herrnhut settlement developed into an intentional Christian community, aspiring to form a God-pleasing congregation according to the model of the apostolic church. Its religious life was shaped by many new religious practices that developed during these early years, including the love feast, the prayer watch, and the use of the watchwords.[5]

Zinzendorf's biographer August Gottlieb Spangenberg informs us that on May 3, 1728, at the end of an evening prayer meeting, Count Zinzendorf offered to the inhabitants of Herrnhut a line from a hymn, short enough to be easily memorized, to take home "as a watch-word for the following day." This incident soon gave rise to the practice that each morning a verse from the Bible or a passage from a hymn was made known in the village through the elders of the congregation, "and since there was found in this custom some similarity to what is called the watchword [*die Losung*] in the military, it was only natural that it would receive the same name and that these texts would be called watchwords [*Losungen*]."[6] Thus, the meaning of the word *Losungen* was initially not derived from the idea of a random selection through the drawing of lots (*losen*) but rather was borrowed from the military concept of a secret password by which members of the same army were able to recognize one another. One of the early reports about Herrnhut emphasized this understanding:

> We seek to get to know each other better every day through the fraternal watchword. . . .
> In the course of each day, as the brethren and the sisters are engaged in their businesses, the watchword of the day is spoken about, so that we all might remain in the same spiritual frame of mind. Thus, since the sayings and citations are always directed at our circumstances, anyone who is not of the same mind with us and does not share the daily struggle will soon be made manifest.[7]

In addition, the daily watchwords also served the purpose of individual spiritual devotion, as each member was asked to meditate on what God might be saying to him or her personally. These early years when the watchwords were given out orally represent the first stage in the development of the watchword tradition.

The beginning of the second stage was marked by the publication of the first printed edition in 1731.[8] Here, the watchword for each day was presented as a combination of a biblical passage and a line from a hymn. This juxtaposition of texts from Scripture and hymnody resulted in a dynamic constellation of divine and human speech, which represented an important part of Zinzendorf's hermeneutics.[9] Furthermore, the preface stated that for the selection of the individual texts the practice of drawing lots was used: "Because we did not know what circumstances we would face on any given day, we left it to providence to select the appropriate word for each day."[10] With this step, the meaning of *Losungen* came to include the aspect of using the lot (*losen*), which was seen as a way to ascertain God's will and thereby lay a claim to a special form of divine authority. Such recourse to the concept of divine providence working through seemingly accidental occurrences was hardly unique. Among eighteenth-century Pietists there was a common practice called *Däumeln* that consisted of randomly placing one's thumb in the Bible and reading the discovered passage as an indication of God's will. Others used sets of cards imprinted with pious poetry, which were often known as *Schatzkästlein*.[11] The innovative part of the Moravian watchwords was that the principle of random selection was incorporated systematically in a steady devotional routine. During Zinzendorf's lifetime, however, the method of drawing lots was not always used. Sometimes the watchwords for a new year were purposely selected by Zinzendorf according to a specific theme from particular sections of the Bible.

It may be noted in passing that besides the *Losungen* there were also other areas in the life of the eighteenth-century Moravian movement where the method of discerning God's will through the drawing of lots was applied.[12] Whenever an important decision had to be made, the lot was usually consulted in order to ascertain Christ's intentions. This happened only after prayerful deliberation, and in addition to the two lots denoting "yes" and "no" there was also an empty lot, which denoted that the question was wrongly posed or required more reflection. The use of the lot expressed the aspiration of the Moravian community to subject itself directly to Christ's rule and to form, as it were, a kind of theocratic commonwealth. Rather than relying entirely on purely rational forms of scriptural exegesis or on subjective forms of prophecy and inspiration, the Moravians considered the lot to be the authoritative medium by which Christ would make his will known among them. Zinzendorf and the Moravians felt strengthened in this belief by numerous reports of episodes that demonstrated the power of God's providential guidance through the lot. Likewise, they showed great interest in all examples of how a given watchword, chosen a long time ago, addressed the situation at hand in amazing ways.[13] There are no indications that Zinzendorf and the Moravians ever saw any conflict between the practice of the lot and the traditional Protestant emphasis on the Bible as the exclusive authority of divine revelation. They probably believed that the watchwords, in combining the principle of scriptural authority with the notion of divine providence working through the medium of the lot, simply increased the actual poignancy and pertinence of God's Word.

The desire to place each day under the guidance and direction of Christ was a crucial factor in the development of the Moravian watchword tradition. Two other factors must be noted. There is, first, the influence of Zinzendorf's conception of Holy Scripture, which surfaces in his description of the watchwords as an "extracted Bible."[14] Zinzendorf did not regard Holy Scripture as a coherent dogmatic system but rather as an erratic collection of texts, containing many statements of divine truth but also numerous instances of insignificant or even erroneous information. For him, the Bible represented something like a dictionary that included for all topics the "most blessed and needful truths," although these were often obscured and overshadowed by flaws and contradictions due to the text's historical and human contingency.[15] Thus, in his interpretation of Holy Scripture, Zinzendorf tended to focus on short passages that he had come to recognize as valid and true. Zinzendorf compiled a large collection of such passages that formed the pool out of which the individual watchwords were drawn. For him, the advantage of using such short passages lay in the fact that they presented all the important biblical truths in a concise and unencumbered fashion.[16]

A second factor that shaped the practical and spiritual significance of the watchwords for the Moravians was the geographical expansion of the Moravian movement.[17] As the Herrnhut congregation evolved into an international network between 1732 and 1750, the printed watchwords increasingly played the role of providing an important spiritual link between the scattered Moravian settlements, outposts, and mission stations. The published edition of 1739 explicitly states that this book was intended for members in forty different locations and undertakings.[18] As historian Gisela Mettele has argued, reading the same watchword on any given day enabled Moravians all over the world to imagine themselves as one large community and thus feel connected to one another despite their geographical dispersion.[19] Moreover, the collective use of the watchwords, as a basis for both personal and communal devotion, ensured some measure of spiritual uniformity within the Moravian community.

During the first years, the appearance and composition of the published watchwords varied greatly.[20] From the beginning, there was a tendency to select the individual watchwords from the books of the Old Testament, usually combined with individual lines from hymns. The watchwords for 1740, which consisted of biblical passages dealing with the figure of Christ, set the pattern for an additional series of readings, which was known as "The Lamb's Texts" or simply "Texts." A third set of daily readings, introduced in 1745, was selected from Jesus's sayings in the Gospels and published under the title "Sayings of the Savior." These collections were printed as small booklets and sent to all Moravian congregations and outposts so that they were available to the community leaders for use in worship and devotions. After Zinzendorf's death, the various editions from 1731 to 1760 were reprinted in a four-volume comprehensive collection, in which the readings for any particular day during this period can easily be found.[21]

The Use of Moravian Watchwords in Pennsylvania

Although a few people connected to the Moravian movement came to Pennsylvania during the 1730s, the first official group of settlers and missionaries arrived in Philadelphia in December of 1740.[22] It is likely that they brought with them copies of the Moravian watchwords for 1740 and 1741. They saw their journey as part of the Moravians' rising missionary outreach across the globe, which had begun with the sending of the first missionaries in 1732 and included by 1740 more than a dozen international locations from Greenland to South Africa. The focus in Pennsylvania was threefold: to establish a permanent settlement, to evangelize among the various groups of German immigrants, and to evangelize the indigenous Indian tribes. The first places where the Moravians established themselves were Nazareth (1740) and Bethlehem (1741), about fifty miles north of Philadelphia. The Bethlehem congregation was formally organized in June of 1742, during Zinzendorf's year-long visit to Pennsylvania (December 19, 1741–January 9, 1743). Bethlehem soon evolved as the center of Moravian activities in Pennsylvania, embodying the Moravian ideal of an intense spiritual life in a community of awakened believers.[23] It was organized after the pattern of Moravian communities in Germany, with a rigid schedule of daily devotions, different membership groups—called "choirs"—according to age, sex, and marital status, as well as a great variety of offices and leadership positions. For the early years, the members of the Bethlehem community even maintained a communal economy.

As in all Moravian places, the events of each day were recorded in a diary, which gives us a detailed view of the developments within the community, its outside contacts, and its religious activities. The original of this diary was kept in Bethlehem, where it has been preserved in the Moravian Archives, yet it was regularly copied and forwarded to Germany so that church leaders were always informed of what was going on.[24] Moreover, portions of the diary were sometimes included in a circular newsletter that was sent from the headquarter to all Moravian places and was usually read aloud to the community during special meetings.[25] A modern English translation of the Bethlehem Diary for the years 1742–45 has been published in two volumes.[26]

The use of the watchwords and their importance for the Moravian Community in Pennsylvania during the 1740s is evident both from the Bethlehem Diary and from other records related to Zinzendorf's Pennsylvania visit. One important instance is found in the published minutes of the so-called Pennsylvania Synods. These synods were ecumenical conferences of representatives of the various German religious groups in Pennsylvania that took place between January and June 1742.[27] They had been initiated by Henry Antes, a settler of Reformed background, in cooperation with Zinzendorf soon after Zinzendorf's arrival and aimed at strengthening the unity of Christian witness among the diverse religious groups. Under Zinzendorf's dominant influence, the character of the gathering gradually changed from being an ecumenical conference to operating as a tight-knit fellowship of believers, based on the model of the Moravian movement in Germany. One sign of this transformation was the introduction of Moravian customs and practices, including the use of the watchwords. The minutes of the third conference begin with a preface that lists the watchwords for several dates of the previous meetings. This preface bears the title "An Extract of the known *Watch Words* which the united Brethren use in all parts of the World for the Year 1742 thereby to keep up their Fellowship in Spirit."[28] Two points are noteworthy: first, the watchwords are described to serve the purpose of preserving the spiritual fellowship within the global Moravian network, and second, the use of the watchwords in the conference minutes seems to bring the conference into a closer association with the Moravians. Subsequently, we find frequent references to the watchwords in the minutes.[29]

Another instance can be found in the 1743 edition of the watchwords, the manuscript of which Zinzendorf completed during his stay in Bethlehem. He included a short preface that emphasized precisely the fact of this exotic location in North America:

> O congregation of the Lamb! Take this book from the hands of your poor members that live among a people more horrid than any other. But your God is the God of Abraham, Isaak, and Jacob, even in the land of the Indians, and His servant Johannes, the wild man, has put to shame many a Laodicean[30] heart. This is a blessed fulfillment of the ancient prophecy in the first watchword of the coming year. . . .
>
> Given in Bethlehem on the Delaware river in North America, on the frontier to the heathen, just before the departure to the various wild nations, in the month of June 1742.[31]

The "wild man" Johannes was a Mohican and one of the first Indian converts.[32] The "prophecy" in the watchword of January 1, 1743, is Deut 30:4, God's promise that he will gather those who have been banished to the most distant lands.[33] These references to the American context, as well as the fact that the manuscript was prepared in Pennsylvania and sent to Germany for printing and distribution within the larger Moravian network, make the 1743 edition a striking example of the global horizon of the Moravian watchwords.

Let us now turn to the Bethlehem Diary and what it says about the role of the watchwords in the religious life of the Moravian community. The published version of the diary, which comes to about 550 pages in print, covers the time from June 1742 to May 1745 and includes the official diary of the congregation plus several sections of other diaries. There are entries for almost all days of this period, in some cases with very detailed descriptions of events, visitors, devotional activities, and important decisions. We find approximately 250 references to the watchwords and other daily readings, which is about one reference for every five days. Sometimes the diary simply states that, for example, the watchword was read during morning devotion or was commented on in the evening service. In other cases, the biblical text is quoted verbatim together with an explanation of why it was significant for this day. There are also passages that provide interesting details about the use of the watchwords, such as information about the arrival of a new book or about their place in the daily devotional routine.

From the beginning, the reading of the watchwords and other biblical texts formed an important part of the spiritual life in Moravian Bethlehem. The following entry in the diary from December 1, 1742, suggests that their significance was closely related to the idea of an extraordinary divine communication: "At today's lovefeast a portion of the watchwords for the coming year was read aloud and note taken of the fact the Saviour plays a special part in the watchwords and in their daily selection—and desires to do so; and therefore the Church should look upon the daily watchwords in no other light than their being a word which the Lord desires to speak to it on that very day."[34] Starting in June of 1742, the daily readings included the readings from the 1742 edition of the watchwords and readings taken from the 1740 edition of the watchwords, which were called "The Lamb's Texts" or simply "Texts." The diary gives ample evidence of how these readings were included in the daily schedule of devotional activities: they were read and spoken on in the morning service and in the evening service, they formed the basis for the service of singing (*Singstunde*), and they were part of special prayer meetings at night. In the weekly and monthly routine, they played a part in preaching services, love feasts, congregational councils, and other congregational gatherings and festivals. They were also used for the observance of birthdays and anniversaries, the appointment of officers, the departure of travelers, and the celebration of baptisms, weddings, and funerals.

It appears that the use of the watchwords and other readings in the schedule of devotional activities was fairly regulated, but could be changed according to needs and circumstances. One source indicates that the daily routine included an exposition of the watchword at the end of the work day, followed by a *Singstunde* on the Lamb's text in the late evening.[35] In July of 1742, it was decided that "the *watchword* of the following day shall always be announced and communicated on the preceding evening. For its purpose would not be carried out if the congregation should not hear the daily watchword until in the evening."[36] Sometimes adjustments were made to accommodate the change of seasons. One example is the entry for October 18, 1744: "The winter arrangements were announced in the congregation council today. Accordingly there will be held: at five o'clock in the morning, following the elder's blessing, a Bible reading; then breakfast; then the service in English; after the midday meal, the address based on the Lamb's text; at dusk the *Gemeinstunde*, in which the watchword is explained; then the evening meal; then the classes and bands; then the *Singstunde*; and finally the hourly intercession."[37] A few months later, the daily schedule was again discussed at a conference and the decision reached to use the Lamb's text during morning devotion, the sayings of the Savior at noon, and the watchwords in the evening.[38]

The idea of a third set of readings was introduced by Zinzendorf in September 1742. For September 7, the diary notes, "in the future one of those discourses of the Saviour which had furnished the watchwords in the year 1736 should daily be selected and discussed in the early service."[39] In other words, the 1736 edition of the watchwords, which was based on the sayings of Jesus, formed the collection of biblical passages from which these texts should be chosen. A printed edition of the "Sayings of Jesus" appeared in 1744.[40] When Bishop Gottlieb August Spangenberg arrived in Bethlehem in the fall of 1744, he most likely brought with him a copy of this book. The entry for December 5, 1744, states that Spangenberg "read to us a two-month portion from the *Sayings of the Savior*, to get a taste of them."[41]

The evidence of the Bethlehem Diary suggests that the spiritual leaders of the Bethlehem congregation frequently spoke on the watchword and other readings in the form of a short exposition or homily, thus interpreting their message for the Moravian congregation on a daily basis. One curious instance, which forms an exception to this rule, is noted in the entry for December 19, 1744: "Because we had no comments to make on the Lamb's text, we held a congregational *Singstunde* based upon it, with a sense of grace."[42] Interestingly, the diary rarely states what the Moravian leaders were saying in their interpretation of these biblical passages. In the case of Zinzendorf, there are some instances where the diary summarizes the content of his remarks, as, for example, on June 25, 1742:

> In the *Singstunde*, Bro. Ludwig spoke very impressively and profoundly about man's state as a sinner and his awareness of being a sinner, basing his remarks on Numbers 24:21, the watchword for today: *Strong is thy dwellingplace, and thou puttest thy nest in a rock.—The five holy wounds of Thine, etc.* This [he said] was something that could neither be imitated nor taken for granted but something regarding which it became immediately apparent under given circumstances whether one possessed it

or not, and it was so to speak the Schiboleth by means of which souls are known.[43]

Other cases are less detailed. For December 20, 1744, the diary records that Spangenberg "delivered the address on the watchword with great grace. Its main content was: he who has been laid hold of by the Saviour cannot leave the Church but must love her and remain united with her."[44] And for December 11, 1743, we find the following entry: "The midday service, based on the text, was blessed to an unusual degree. It dealt with the angels of those who eagerly behold and consider the wonders which the wounds of Jesus produce in the human race, and the fact that they will be present particularly when we maggots shall attach ourselves individually and eternally to his gaping wounds. Its power was felt by the whole congregation."[45]

As the last quote indicates, the use of the watchwords and of other biblical readings sometimes involved the experience of strong emotional effects. The entries in the diary clearly attest to the importance of this emotional side: "Bro. Böhler preached on the text for this day quite edifyingly and with blessing" (July 21, 1743);[46] "Bro. Anton based his remarks on the watchword, 'Jesus Christ is the same today,' and an all-pervading current of grace accompanied his words" (June 22, 1743);[47] Br. Seidel spoke on the watchword with grace and power" (May 30, 1744);[48] "We experienced rich grace today in the services, which dealt with the text and the watchword; blessed and ardent testimony was given to the blood from the wounds [of Christ]" (December 9, 1743).[49] Often it was emphasized that those who spoke did so "with spirit and power,"[50] "with much grace and unction,"[51] "fervently and significantly."[52]

Equally, if not more, important was the emotional response of the congregation, which was frequently noted in the diary: "our hearts were moved,"[53] "a gentle wafting of grace was felt,"[54] the message of the Lamb's text "was a significant topic, most sweet to the heart of a poor sinner."[55] When Spangenberg delivered his first address on the watchword in December of 1744, the diary states that his words "fell full of unction like balsam on the hearts of all of the brethren and sisters."[56] And the entry for February 1, 1744, notes that the explanation of the watchword "aroused such an all-pervading fire of love for our faithful shepherd in the hearts of the brethren and sisters that this could be seen in their eyes."[57]

It is characteristic of Moravian piety that the impact of hearing the watchword is often described in terms of an emotional effect on the heart. One central concept of Zinzendorf's theology was what he called the "religion of the heart," namely the idea that the essence of faith is not intellectual knowledge in the head, but an intuitive awareness of Christ's presence in the heart.[58] The practice of the daily biblical readings, as described in the Bethlehem Diary, reflects this understanding. As we noted above, the diary paid surprisingly little attention to how the watchwords and other readings were interpreted in terms of their conceptual content. Clearly, it was more important that their message was somehow received in the heart, calling forth a sense of awe and elation. A good example is the entry for February 11, 1745: "Today, too, our watchword gave us unusual pleasure, as has generally been the case up to now. Our hearts have laid hold of the word of the Lord, which he gives us by His [!] grace. There it shall remain. In all of our brethren and sisters one encounters hearts filled with humble devotion because of all the grace which the Savior causes to flood through the congregation."[59] Another entry from 1745 suggests that Moravian piety aimed at some sort of correspondence or harmony between the biblical readings and the believers' inner experience: "Our watchword for this day, our Lamb's text, and the state of our hearts were all in tune."[60]

For the Moravians, the focus on emotional experiences was closely tied to the idea of sensing the presence of Christ. Accordingly, some entries in the diary point out how speaking about the watchword or another text was accompanied by a sense of Christ's presence. For December 9, 1743, we read that "the quarter-of-an-hour devotions based on the text at midday and on the watchword in the evening were specially hallowed by the presence of the Lamb and of His Spirit."[61] In another case, the diarist recorded his personal impression: "The lovefeast closed with an exposition of today's watchword, during which the Saviour permitted me to feel His presence in an ineffable manner."[62] Finally, the entry for December 29, 1743, provides a short summary of Böhler's exposition of the Lamb's text in the context of an adult baptism and concludes with the observation, "There was something quite exceptionally powerful, penetrating, lovely, and humbling of our Saviour's majesty discernible among us."[63] While such an effusive description is rather exceptional, these and other entries in the Bethlehem Diary help us to see how members of the Moravian community expected the practice of the watchwords and other daily readings to enable them to feel the nearness of Christ.

Moreover, the Moravians came to interpret and appreciate the significance of a watchword for speaking directly to the circumstances of their lives on that specific day. Sometimes the diary notes that the watchword was seen as "appropriate," as in the case of Ps 118:24 ("This is the day which the Lord hath made; we will rejoice and be glad in it") on June 21, 1742, when the group of Moravian settlers reached Bethlehem.[64] Other entries report how the watchword of the day strikingly matched specific events in the life of the community. Thus we read about Reinhard Ronner, who had been visiting a mission station: "On his return journey on October 29 he experienced personally the confirmation and fulfillment of the watchword for the day, Isaiah 43:2, *When thou passest through the waters, I will be with thee . . . that the stream shall not overflow thee*, etc., when he was obliged to wade through a swollen river."[65] The same biblical passage appears again in the entry of April 20, 1745, which describes the travel experience of Johann Martin Mack and Christian Fröhlich during a visit to the Delaware Indians: "In keeping with the watchword of yesterday, *When you pass through the water, etc. When you walk through the fire you shall not be burned*, etc., they had to run through fire with flames closing over their heads because the woods had caught fire. They went between mountains where not only the old grass but also the dry bushes and the old wood were burning, and they could not escape the fire in any way until the Lord helped them get through it."[66] Another important event, in which the texts from the daily readings were found to speak directly to the experience of the congregation, was the imprisonment of some Moravian missionaries in February of 1745.[67]

In addition to these extraordinary episodes, we find many entries that call attention to the watchword in relation to the circumstances of a person's death, the dedication of a building, the departure for a journey, or the commemoration of an important anniversary.[68] Central for this approach was the assumption that all providential coincidences represented signs of divine government. While it would probably go too far to say the Moravians considered the watchwords and other readings as heavenly prophecies waiting to be fulfilled in their lives, the Bethlehem Diary gives ample evidence that the reading of these texts usually involved the expectation that God was speaking through them to their particular life situation.

Conclusion

The Bethlehem Diary provides a detailed view of how eighteenth-century Moravians in Pennsylvania used passages from the Bible as "watchwords" in their devotional routine. Important aspects of this practice have become clear: (a) short biblical texts were selected for each day of the year, sometimes through the method of drawing lots; (b) annual calendars with these readings were printed and sent to all congregations, outposts, and mission stations, thus forming an important element of connection within the global Moravian network; (c) the readings played an important part in the religious life of the Moravian community in Bethlehem as they were presented and discussed in various ways in the daily and weekly schedule of devotional activities; (d) the diary of the Bethlehem congregation contains numerous references to the watchwords and the other daily readings, especially when they were found to be particularly meaningful and significant in the life of the community; (e) the Bethlehem Diary rarely reported how individual readings were interpreted in terms of their thematic content, but it paid considerable attention to their emotional effects and also to cases of providential agreement with events in the life of the community; (f) experiencing the presence of Christ seems to have been a particularly important part of the watchword-based devotions; and (g) as copies of the Bethlehem Diary were sent to Europe for circulation, members of the larger Moravian community were able to read about, and relate to, the experiences of the Bethlehem congregation, including those that involved the watchwords and the other daily readings.

The transatlantic dimension of this practice is obvious. First of all, it involved the transatlantic circulation of texts. The editions of the watchwords and other collections were prepared and printed in Germany and were sent across the Atlantic to Pennsylvania and other places in the New World. In the case of the 1743 edition, the manuscript was prepared in America and was sent to Germany for printing. Also, copies of the Bethlehem Diary, containing information about the use of the watchwords in Bethlehem, were sent to Germany, where they were used as a resource for circular reports in the Moravian network. The circulation of both watchwords and reports was part of the effort to maintain unity and connection within the global Moravian community.

The awareness of the global scope and connectedness of the Moravian movement played an important role for Moravian identity and piety. Moravians at any given place knew that they were part of a larger community and participants in the endeavor of Christ's global mission. Reading the daily watchwords helped them to feel connected with members in other places and to see that the reach of God's Word was not limited to any particular region. This understanding, as it was expressed in the title page of the 1739 edition of the watchwords with a list of about forty geographic locations, formed the subtext for the use of the daily biblical readings in Moravian Bethlehem. At the same time, the practice of the watchwords was carried out by members of the Bethlehem congregation with an awareness of their specific North American context. As they dealt with the challenge of living on the frontier, advancing mission work, and facing dangerous travels, they looked to the watchwords for support, guidance, and orientation. The steady flow of biblical readings helped them to maintain their sense of spiritual strength and purpose in the midst of a new and foreign country.

As regards scriptural hermeneutics, the Moravian watchword tradition in Pennsylvania presents us with a rather complex story of how biblical readings were believed to express God's message for the members of the community.

The Moravians had no doubt that Christ was speaking to them through the watchwords and other collections of texts. Their basic understanding, as expressed in worship on December 1, 1742, was that the congregation "should look upon the daily watchwords in no other light than their being a word which the Lord desires to speak to it on that very day." From this quote it appears that for the Moravians the watchwords and similar biblical readings represented God's Word in a twofold manner: they expressed the revelation of divine truth in a general sense, and they embodied, by virtue of their selection for a particular day, the quality of an active performance of divine communication. For this performance, the direct and purposeful involvement of Christ was presupposed: "the Saviour plays a special part in the watchwords and in their daily selection."[69] In order to ascertain which readings Christ wanted to be chosen for what day, Zinzendorf and other Moravian leaders usually employed the method of drawing lots. They trusted that the seemingly random results of the lot were guided by God's providential hand, and they also believed that using the lot was the best way to exclude the interference of their own desires and interests.

Members of the Moravian community in Bethlehem who were familiar with the tradition of the watchwords knew that Christ was speaking to them through these readings and were ready to find in them, personally and collectively, a message relevant to their specific life situation. It is important to recognize that this did not happen just once in a while, but in the form of a regular daily discipline, which probably evoked the impression of being in an ongoing conversation with Christ. Certain habits of interpretation and response were part of the process by which Moravians experienced individual readings as meaningful for them. One was the expectation to find connections between the biblical text and external circumstances and events. Another was the Moravians' readiness to feel the power of Christ, as they were willing to let themselves be touched emotionally by the message of the text. A third was their ability to relate the readings from one day to readings of other days in the past and to understand the message of individual texts as part of a larger dynamic development. Finally, the use of the watchwords helped Moravians in Bethlehem to feel connected with the larger Moravian community across the Atlantic.

Altogether, the tradition of daily watchwords in Moravian Bethlehem presents us with the case of a distinct religious practice that involved an intricate way of interpreting Scripture and operated in the context of a global network. In one sense, this practice was uniquely Moravian, yet in another it is also indicative of larger historical trends. It reflects both the firm commitment to the Bible and the transatlantic scope of eighteenth-century Pietism and evangelicalism. It illustrates how Pietists and evangelicals turned to the Bible to make sense of their world, even when they ventured into unknown territories, and how for them the Bible formed a connecting bond between awakened believers in different parts of the world. And finally, it speaks to the focus on Christ and his mission, which fueled the religious activism of the Moravians and other evangelical groups in the transatlantic realm, and shows how they sought to relate the Bible to their faith and actions in profoundly personal and experiential terms, as they expected Christ to communicate to them through individual biblical readings in direct and immediately relevant ways.

Notes

1. Direktion der Brüder-Unität, ed., *Die Losungen der Herrnhuter Brüdergemeine: Geschichte—Entstehung—Verbreitung—Gebrauch* (Basel: Friedrich Reinhardt Verlag, 2003); and William N. Schwarze, "History of the Text Book of the Moravian Church," *Transactions of the Moravian Historical Society* 13, no. 3/4 (1944): 133–62.

2. See Shirley Brückner, "Die Providenz im Zettelkasten: Divinatorische Lospraktiken in der pietistischen Frömmigkeit," in *Geschichtsbewusstsein und Zukunftserwartung in Pietismus und Erweckungsbewegung*, ed. Wolfang Breul and Jan Carsten Schnurr (Göttingen: Vandenhoeck & Ruprecht, 2013), 351–66; Fred van Lieburg, "De Bijbel als orakelboek: Bibliomantie in de protestantse traditie," in *Materieel Christendom: Religie en materiële cultuur in West-Europa*, ed. Arie L. Molendijk (Hilversum: Uitgeverij Verloren, 2003), 81–105; and Arnold Niederer, "Paroles et Textes pour chaque jour: Le tirage au sort de versets bibliques," *Ethnologie Française*, n.s., 17 (1987): 336–41.

3. Peter Zimmerling, *Die Losungen: Eine Erfolgsgeschichte durch die Jahrhunderte* (Göttingen: Vandenhoeck & Ruprecht, 2014); Peter Vogt, "God's Present Voice: The Theology and Hermeneutics of the Moravian Daily Texts (*Herrnhuter Losungen*)," *Communio Viatorum* 50 (2008): 55–73; and Erich Beyreuther, "Die Herrnhuter Losungen und ihre Entstehungsgeschichte," *Unitas Fratrum* 7 (1980): 4–15.

4. Georg Neisser, *A History of the Beginnings of Moravian Work in America*, trans. William N. Schwarze and Samuel H. Gapp (Bethlehem, PA: Moravian Archives, 1955), 53, 54.

5. On the development of Herrnhut, see John R. Weinlick, *Count Zinzendorf: The Story of His Life and Leadership in the Renewed Moravian Church* (Bethlehem, PA: Moravian Church in America, 1989). The most detailed accounts to date are Hanns-Joachim Wollstadt, *Geordnetes Dienen in der christlichen Gemeinde, dargestellt an den Lebensformen der Herrnhuter Brüdergemeine in ihren Anfängen* (Göttingen: Vandenhoeck & Ruprecht, 1966); and Paul Peucker, *Herrnhut 1722–1732: Entstehung und Entwicklung einer philadelphischen Gemeinschaft* (Göttingen: Vandenhoeck & Ruprecht, 2021).

6. August Gottlieb Spangenberg, *Leben des Herrn Nicolaus Ludwig Grafen und Herrn von Zinzendorf und Pottendorf*, 8 vols. (Barby, 1773–75), 474.

7. [Christian David], *Beschreibung und Zuverlässige Nachricht von Herrnhut in der Ober-Lausitz* (Leipzig: Walther, 1753; repr., Hildesheim: Olms, 2000), 69–70.

8. *Ein guter Muth, als das tägliche Wohl-Leben der Creutz-Gemeine Christi zu Herrnshuth, im Jahr 1731* (repr., Stuttgart: Quell Verlag, 1979).

9. On Zinzendorf's hermeneutics, see Arthur J. Freeman, *An Ecumenical Theology of the Heart: The Theology of Count Nicholas Ludwig von Zinzendorf* (Bethlehem, PA: Moravian Church in America, 1998), 124–52. Zinzendorf also made several attempts to prepare new translations of some portions of the Bible. Whether the readings of the watchwords utilized these translations needs further investigation. For introduction, texts, and commentary of

Zinzendorf's translations, see Dietrich Meyer, ed., *Nikolaus Ludwig von Zinzendorf: Bibel und Bibelgebrauch*, vol. 1, *Bibelübersetzung*, Nikolaus Ludwig von Zinzendorf: Werke 7:1 (Göttingen: Vandenhoeck & Ruprecht, 2015).

10. *Ein guter Muth*, preface (n.p.).

11. See Brückner, "Die Providenz im Zettelkasten," 353, 356–57.

12. On the Moravian practice of the lot, see Peter Vogt, "Die Medialität göttlicher Willenskundgebung in der Lospraxis der Herrnhuter Brüdergemeine," in *"Schrift soll leserlich seyn": Der Pietismus und die Medien. Beiträge zum IV. Internationalen Kongress für Pietismusforschung 2013*, ed. Christian Soboth and Pia Schmid (Halle: Harrassowitz, 2016), 465–80; and Elisabeth Sommer, "Gambling with God: The Use of the Lot by the Moravian Brethren in the Eighteenth Century," *Journal of the History of Ideas* 59 (1998): 267–86.

13. See Beyreuther, "Die Herrnhuter Losungen," 13.

14. Quoted in Hans-Christoph Hahn and Hellmut Reichel, eds., *Zinzendorf und die Herrnhuter Brüder: Quellen zur Geschichte der Brüder-Unität* (Hamburg: Wittig, 1977), 244.

15. Quoted in ibid., 192.

16. See Otto Uttendörfer, *Zinzendorfs Gedanken über den Gottesdienst* (Herrnhut: Winter, 1931), 28–29.

17. See Gisela Mettele, "Identities Across Borders: The Moravians as a Global Community," in *Pietism and Community in Europe and North America, 1650–1850*, ed. Jonathan Strom (Leiden: Brill, 2010), 155–77; and Peter Vogt, "'Everywhere at Home': The Eighteenth-Century Moravian Movement as a Transatlantic Religious Community," *JMH* 1 (2006): 7–29.

18. The Good Word of the Lord, 1739, From all the Prophets for His congregations, and servants, at Herrnhut, Herrnhaag, Herrendijk [Holland], Pilgerruh [Denmark], Ebersdorf, Jena, Amsterdam, Rotterdam, London, Oxford, Berlin, Greenland, St. Croix, St. John and St. Thomas [Virgin Islands], Berbice [Guyana], Palestine, Surinam, Savannah in Georgia, among the Moors in Carolina, with the wild Indians in Irene [an island in the Savannah River in Georgia], in Pennsylvania, among the Hottentots [South Africa], in Guinea, in Latvia, Estonia and Lithuania, Russia, on the White Sea, in Lappland, Norway, in Switzerland, [Isle of] Man, Hittland [Scotland], in prison, on pilgrimage to Ceylon, Ethiopia, Persia, on visitation to the missionaries among the heathen, and elsewhere on land and sea. Quoted in *Moravian Daily Texts 2007* (Bethlehem, PA: Moravian Church in North America, 2006), iv–v.

19. Gisela Mettele, *Weltbürgertum oder Gottesreich: Die Herrnhuter Brüdergemeine als globale Gemeinschaft 1727–1857* (Göttingen: Vandenhoeck & Ruprecht, 2009), 58–60.

20. All editions from 1731 to 1761 are listed in Dietrich Meyer, ed., *Bibliographisches Handbuch zur Zinzendorf-Forschung* (Düsseldorf: Blech, 1987), 167–97.

21. *Samlung der Loosungs- und Text-Büchlein der Brüder-Gemeine von 1731 bis 1761*, 4 vols. (Barby, 1762; repr., Hildesheim: Olms, 1987).

22. Neisser, *History of the Beginnings*, 18.

23. On the history of Bethlehem, see Hellmuth Erbe, *Bethlehem, Pa.: Eine kommunistische Herrnhuter Kolonie des 18. Jahrhunderts* (Stuttgart: Deutsches Auslands-Institut, 1929); and Beverly Prior Smaby, *The Transformation of Moravian Bethlehem: From Communal Mission to Family Economy* (Philadelphia: University of Pennsylvania Press, 1988).

24. See Paul Peucker, "The Textual History of the 1742 Bethlehem Diary," *JMH* 18 (2018): 102–12.

25. Carola Wessel, "Connecting Congregations: The Net of Communication Among the Moravians in the Late 18th Century," in *The Distinctiveness of Moravian Culture: Festschrift for Vernon Nelson*, ed. Craig D. Atwood and Peter Vogt (Nazareth, PA: Moravian Historical Society, 2003), 153–72; and Gisela Mettele, "Global Communication Among the Moravian Brethren: The Circulation of Knowledge and its Structures and Logistics," in *Reporting Christian Missions in the Eighteenth Century: Communication, Culture of Knowledge and Regular Publication*

in a Cross-Confessional Perspective, ed. Markus Friedrich and Alexander Schunka (Wiesbaden: Harrassowitz, 2017), 149–67.

26. Kenneth G. Hamilton, ed., *The Bethlehem Diary*, vol. 1, 1742–1744 (Bethlehem, PA: Moravian Archives, 1971); Vernon Nelson, ed., *The Bethlehem Diary*, vol. 2, January 1, 1744–May 31, 1745 (Bethlehem, PA: Moravian Archives, 2001). These volumes are abbreviated as BD.

27. See introduction to Nikolaus Ludwig von Zinzendorf, *Authentische Relation von dem Anlass, Fortgang und Schlusse der am 1. und 2. Januarii Anno 1741/2 in Germantown gehaltenen Versammlung*, bilingual edition, ed. Peter Vogt (Hildesheim: Olms, 1998), vii–lxi.

28. Ibid., 42.
29. Ibid., 67, 94, 108, 109, and 113.
30. Rev 3:14–20.
31. *Samlung*, 1:113.
32. See Neisser, *History of the Beginnings*, 170.
33. *Samlung*, 1:114.
34. BD 1:119.
35. See Erbe, *Bethlehem*, 20.
36. BD 1:38.
37. BD 2:147, cf. BD 1:166–67.
38. BD 2:193, cf. 318.
39. BD 1:82, cf. 84.
40. See Meyer, *Bibliographisches Handbuch*, no. A 417, reprint in *Samlung*, 2:449–94.
41. BD 2:163.
42. BD 2:188.
43. BD 1:18; the term *Schiboleth* refers to Judg 12:5–6. For other examples, see BD 1:45, 111, 124, 126, 132.
44. BD 1:214; according to *Samlung*, 2:188, the watchword was Ps 119:20.
45. BD 1:172; according to *Samlung*, 1:516, the text was 2 Thess 1:7. For other examples of short summaries, see BD 1:181 and 214, and BD 2:63, 235, and 249.
46. BD 1:157.
47. BD 1:151–52.
48. BD 2:80.
49. BD 1:175.
50. BD 2:25.
51. BD 2:76.
52. BD 2:138.
53. BD 2:103.
54. BD 2:196.
55. BD 2:157.
56. BD 1:212.
57. BD 2:29.
58. See Peter Vogt, "'Herzens-Theologie': Menschliche Erfahrung als theologisches Erkenntnisprinzip bei Zinzendorf," in *"Aus Gottes Wort und eigener Erfahrung gezeiget"—Erfahrung, Glauben, Erkennen und Gestalten im Pietismus: Beiträge zum III. Internationalen Kongress für Pietismusforschung 2009*, ed. Christian Soboth and Udo Sträter (Halle: Verlag der Franckeschen Stiftungen, 2012), 41–53; and Vogt, "Headless and Un-Erudite: Anti-Intellectual Tendencies in Zinzendorf's Approach to Education," in *Self, Community, World: Moravian Education in a Transatlantic World*, ed. Heikki Lempa and Paul Peucker (Bethlehem: Lehigh University Press, 2010), 107–26.
59. BD 2:217.
60. BD 2:201.
61. BD 1:174.

62. BD 1:172. According to the editor's introduction, the diarist was probably Peter Böhler.
63. BD 1:181.
64. BD 1:15; see also 1:128.
65. BD 1:104.
66. BD 2:278.
67. See BD II 236–37, cf. 229–30.
68. See BD 1:46, 166, 187, 199, and BD 2:50, 62, 88, 233, 293.
69. BD 1:119.

CONCLUSION

DOUGLAS A. SWEENEY, JAN STIEVERMANN,
AND RYAN P. HOSELTON

As this volume shows, early Pietist and evangelical uses of the Bible proved formative, diverse, and far-reaching, and remain understudied by scholars of the early modern West, not to mention those working on the impact of these movements around the world today. Before the late nineteenth century, most scholarship on Pietism was done primarily by German church historians and focused on mainstream, "churchly" Pietists from the late seventeenth through the mid-eighteenth century. During the 1870s, this scholarship expanded through the work of Heinrich Heppe, Albrecht Ritschl, and their colleagues, who traced the tangled roots of the Pietists' theology in late medieval mysticism and paid more attention to Reformed Pietists in Great Britain and the Netherlands.[1] Since the late twentieth century, research on Pietism has become less theological and more interdisciplinary, international, and diversified, resulting in wide disagreement about the best way to define and periodize their history.[2]

Work on modern evangelicals in the English-speaking world has also been transformed since the nineteenth century, when amateur historians like the best-selling Robert Baird could write massive treatments of *Religion in America* and depict that country's Christians after their own white, mainstream, evangelical image.[3] Research since the 1980s has devoted more attention to people of color and women and has uncovered new connections between Anglophone and other global members of the movement.[4] Yet, as with scholarship on Pietism, work on evangelicals has grown so diverse that it has reached something of a definitional impasse, with many writers questioning the usefulness of terms such as "evangelicalism" in referring to their oftentimes incompatible subjects.[5]

While this volume does not pretend to resolve these historiographical challenges, we hope it illustrates the promising possibilities of approaching these movements through international and even global interpretative frameworks. And we hope that it demonstrates the fruitfulness of concentrating on specific topics and trajectories, rather than continuing debates over definitions and demarcations in the abstract. The focused studies on the Bible in Pietism and evangelicalism in this book provide fresh insights into the lives and times of eighteenth-century men and women in the North Atlantic world, whose religious networks, practices, and cultures made a lasting imprint on later generations.

The basic interpretive paradigms and biblical practices of early Pietists and evangelicals examined in this volume continued well into the nineteenth century and beyond. Though transformed by new times, awakened Protestants carried the quest for true supernatural religion by the Word into their scholarship, revivalism, experiential piety and devotion, print and reading cultures, missions, apocalyptic curiosities, benevolent activism, and lay voluntarism. Many of the early evangelical and Pietist commentaries were reprinted and read throughout the nineteenth century. In America, for instance, the works of Adam Clarke and Philip Doddridge enjoyed enormous popularity, as did Johann Albrecht Bengel's commentaries or the annotated Halle Bibles in German-speaking lands. Also, contacts and collaborations between British and American evangelicals and German (neo-)Pietists continued after the Napoleonic Wars in the context of mass migrations and new awakening movements.[6] The Evangelical Alliance (1846) was the culmination of decades of such networking and today has branches all around the globe. Seeking to propagate the Word, British and American Bible and tract societies worked closely (and exchanged translations) with sister organizations in Germany and the Netherlands, as they flooded their respective societies with millions of cheap Bibles, parabiblical works, and Scripture-based devotional writings for lay readers.[7] An amazingly popular title was *Elias der Tishbiter* (*Elisha the Tishbite*) (1828–33) by the Rhenisch-Prussian Pietist Friedrich Wilhelm Krummacher, who "novelized" biblical figures and stories to appeal to broader audiences. *Elisha the Tishbite* had numerous British and American editions.

Exchanges also intensified in the area of academic theology and exegesis, especially as German universities attracted numerous American students, many of them evangelicals. Historians have tended to view the emergence of "German higher criticism" as the teleological end point of the Enlightenment's encounter with the Bible, overlooking more conciliatory forms like the sophisticated but apologetically and devotionally oriented biblical criticism of nineteenth-century evangelicals and neo-Pietists. For example, Andover's Moses Stuart, often dubbed "the father of biblical Science in America," and Edward Robinson, the pioneer of biblical archaeology in the United States, were both deeply influenced by the Halle Pietist exegete and theologian August Tholuck—as were numerous other students from the United States and Britain. Several of Tholuck's exegetical and theological works appeared in American editions.[8] New England theologians more generally were attracted to Tholuck's Pietist version of *Vermittlungstheologie* (mediating theology), which sought to reconcile an openness to modern culture, knowledge, and *Wissenschaftlichkeit* with a biblicist, doctrinally conservative, and conversion-oriented faith.[9] There was also a great deal of continuity between the eighteenth-century evangelical-Pietist model and the great exegetes of the Princeton school, such as Albert Barnes and Joseph Addison Alexander. Such genealogies could be even further extended into the twentieth century. We hope this volume reveals the importance of the history of the Bible among these champions of "true Christianity" and plays a small part in inspiring further exploration of their influential exegetical traditions and legacies.

Notes

1. Heinrich Heppe, *Geschichte des Pietismus und der Mystik in der reformierten Kirche, namentlich der Niederlande* (Leiden: Brill, 1879); Albrecht Ritschl, *Geschichte des Pietismus* (Bonn: Marcus, 1880–86).

2. See esp. *GdP*, *PuN*, and Wolfgang Breul and Thomas Hahn-Bruckart, eds., *Pietismus Handbuch* (Tübingen: Mohr Siebeck, 2021).

3. Robert Baird, *Religion in America: Or an Account of the Origin, Relation to the State, and Present Condition of the Evangelical Churches in the United States; with Notices of the Unevangelical Denominations* (New York: Harper and Brothers, 1844), which went through many editions in several languages.

4. See esp. Mark A. Noll, David W. Bebbington, and George A. Rawlyk, eds., *Evangelicalism: Comparative Studies of Popular Protestantism in North America, the British Isles, and Beyond, 1700–1990* (New York: Oxford University Press, 1994); Brian Stanley, *The Global Diffusion of Evangelicalism: The Age of Billy Graham and John Stott* (Downers Grove, IL: IVP Academic, 2013); and Mark A. Noll, David W. Bebbington, and George M. Marsden, eds., *Evangelicals: Who They Have Been, Are Now, and Could Be* (Grand Rapids, MI: Eerdmans, 2019).

5. See, for example, Donald W. Dayton and Robert K. Johnston, eds., *The Variety of American Evangelicalism* (Knoxville: University of Tennessee Press, 1991).

6. See Andrew Kloes, *The German Awakening: Protestant Renewal After the Enlightenment, 1815–1848* (New York: Oxford University Press, 2019); Jan Stievermann, "Jonathan Edwards, American Evangelicalism, and the Prussian *Erweckungsbewegung*, ca. 1815-1850," in *Edwards, Germany, and Transatlantic Contexts*, ed. Rhys Bezzant (Göttingen: Vandenhoeck & Ruprecht, 2021), 169-90.

7. Thomas Hahn-Bruckart, "Die deutschsprachige Publizistik der American Tract Society bis zur Mitte des 19. Jahrhunderts," in *"Schrift soll leserlich seyn": Der Pietismus und die Medien; Beiträge zum IV. Internationalen Kongress für Pietismusforschung 2013*, ed. Christian Soboth et al. (Halle: Verlag der Franckeschen Stiftungen, 2016), 193–207.

8. See August Tholuck, *A Commentary on the Gospel of Saint John* (New York, 1842); Tholuck, *Exposition of St. Paul's Epistle to the Romans* . . . (Philadelphia, 1844); Tholuck, *A Translation and Commentary of the Book of Psalms for the Use of the Ministry and Laity of the Christian Church* (Philadelphia, 1858).

9. See Annette Aubert, "Transatlantic Nineteenth-Century Protestantism: Academic Religious Networks," in *Zwischen Aufklärung und Moderne: Erweckungsbewegungen als historiographische Herausforderung*, ed. Thomas A. Kuhn and Veronika Albrecht-Birkner (Münster: Lit Verlag, 2017), 103–18.

CONTRIBUTORS

Ruth Albrecht is Professor of Church History at Universität Hamburg and has authored and edited numerous studies on Pietism and gender, including *Johanna Eleonora Petersen: Theologische Schriftstellerin des frühen Pietismus* and *Begeisterte Mägde: Träume, Visionen und Offenbarungen von Frauen des frühen Pietismus.*

Robert E. Brown is Professor of Religion at James Madison University, where he teaches courses on American Religious History. He is the author of *Jonathan Edwards and the Bible* and the editor of the ninth volume of Cotton Mather's *Biblia Americana: The Pauline Epistles.* He has published widely on colonial American religion, including chapters in three Oxford University Press Handbooks: *The Bible in America, Jonathan Edwards,* and *Early Evangelicalism.*

Crawford Gribben is Professor of Early Modern British history at Queen's University Belfast, and is the author of a number of studies on the literary cultures of puritanism and evangelicalism, including *God's Irishmen: Theological Debates in Cromwellian Ireland, John Owen and English Puritanism: Experiences of Defeat,* and *An Introduction to John Owen.* He also serves as coeditor of the Palgrave Macmillan series Christianities in the Trans-Atlantic World, 1550–1800 and the Edinburgh University Press series Scottish Religious Cultures.

Michael A. G. Haykin is Chair and Professor of Church History at The Southern Baptist Theological Seminary, and the director of the Andrew Fuller Center for Baptist Studies, which operates under the aegis of Southern Seminary. He also serves on the core faculty of Heritage College and Seminary, Cambridge, Ontario, and is the director of the research center Newton House in Oxford, England. He has written extensively in the area of Christianity in late antiquity and British Dissent in the long eighteenth century.

Bruce Hindmarsh is the James M. Houston Professor of Spiritual Theology and Professor of the History of Christianity at Regent College, Vancouver, and the author of *The Spirit of Early Evangelicalism: True Religion in a Modern World.*

CONTRIBUTORS

Ryan P. Hoselton is Instructor and postdoctoral Research Associate (*Wissenschaftlicher Mitarbeiter*) in the Faculty of Theology and the American Studies program at Ruprecht-Karls-Universität Heidelberg. He has written various studies on eighteenth-century transatlantic evangelicalism, and he serves on the editorial team for the *Biblia Americana* project (10 vols.).

Kenneth P. Minkema is the Editor of *The Works of Jonathan Edwards* and Director of the Jonathan Edwards Center, Yale University, and a Research Faculty member at Yale Divinity School. Recent publications include *Classics of Western Spirituality: Jonathan Edwards, Spiritual Writings*, coedited with Kyle C. Strobel and Adriaan C. Neele; *William Bradford's "Of Plimoth Plantation": The 400th-Anniversary Edition*, coedited with Francis J. Bremer and Jeremy D. Bangs; and *A Cotton Mather Reader*, coedited with Reiner Smolinski.

Adriaan C. Neele is Professor of Historical Theology and Director of the Doctoral Program at Puritan Reformed Theological Seminary. His most recent publications include *Before Jonathan Edwards: Sources of New England Theology*, and *Petrus van Mastricht (1630–1706): Text, Context, and Interpretation*.

Benjamin M. Pietrenka is a postdoctoral scholar and lecturer at the Heidelberg Center for American Studies at Ruprecht-Karls-Universität Heidelberg. In addition to working on the *Biblia Americana* project, he will soon complete his first book manuscript, entitled "Religion on the Margins: Embodied Moravian Pieties and Transatlantic Provinces of the Self," which examines the early modern history of Moravian religious identity formation through the lens of believers and missionaries operating in the Atlantic world. His research and teaching interests include the entangled histories of America in the colonial and early national periods, religion, gender, race, German culture, and Indigenous peoples.

Isabel Rivers is Professor of Eighteenth-Century English Literature and Culture at Queen Mary University of London, with interests in the relations between literature, religion, philosophy, and the history of the book in the long eighteenth century. Recent publications include *Vanity Fair and the Celestial City: Dissenting, Methodist, and Evangelical Literary Culture in England, 1720–1800*; "*The Pilgrim's Progress* in the Evangelical Revival," in *The Oxford Handbook of John Bunyan*, edited by Michael Davies and W. R. Owens; and "Inward Religion and Its Dangers in the Evangelical Revival," in *Heart Religion: Evangelical Piety in England and Ireland, 1690–1850*, edited by John Coffey.

Douglas H. Shantz is Professor Emeritus of Classics and Religion at the University of Calgary, Canada. He has published books, articles, chapters, and reviews on the radical Reformation and on early modern German Pietism. He is the author of *An Introduction to German Pietism* and editor of *A Companion to German Pietism, 1660–1800*.

Jan Stievermann is Professor of the History of Christianity in the United States at Heidelberg University. He is the Executive Editor of the *Biblia Americana* project and Director of the Jonathan Edwards Center Germany. He edited the critical edition of vol. 5 of *Cotton Mather's Biblia Americana: Proverbs—Jeremiah* and is currently editing vol. 10, *Hebrews–Revelation*. Among other publications, he is the author of *Prophecy, Piety, and the Problem of Historicity: Interpreting the Hebrew Scriptures in Cotton Mather's "Biblia Americana,"* and coeditor of *Cotton Mather and Biblia Americana—America's First Bible Commentary*, *A Peculiar Mixture: German-Language Cultures and Identities in Eighteenth-Century North America*, and *The Oxford Handbook of Jonathan Edwards*.

Douglas A. Sweeney is Dean and Professor of Divinity at Beeson Divinity School, Samford University. He has published widely on the history of Christian thought, American religious history, and the work of Jonathan Edwards. Recent publications include *Edwards the Exegete: Biblical Interpretation and Anglo-Protestant Culture on the Edge of the Enlightenment* and *The Oxford Handbook of Jonathan Edwards* (coeditor).

Peter Vogt is Director of Theological Education in the German Moravian Church and Co-Pastor of the Herrnhut congregation. Academic interests include Zinzendorf's theology, the history and practices of the Moravian Church, and eighteenth-century Pietism. He has published numerous articles on Zinzendorf and the Moravians and edited eight books, including *Zwischen Bekehrungseifer und Philosemitismus*, a source collection documenting the relationship of Pietist groups to Jews and Judaism; *Von Goethe bis Grass*, an anthology of literary texts with allusions to the Moravians; and *Our Moravian Treasures*, a manual for theological education in the worldwide Moravian Church.

Marilyn J. Westerkamp is Professor of History, University of California, Santa Cruz. She is the author of *Triumph of the Laity: Scots-Irish Piety and the Great Awakening, 1625–1760*, *Women and Religion in Early America, 1600–1850: The Puritan and Evangelical Traditions*, and *The Passion of Anne Hutchinson: An Extraordinary Woman, the Puritan Patriarchs, and the World They Made and Lost*.

SCRIPTURE INDEX

OLD TESTAMENT
Genesis
   1:1, 240n15
   11, 115
   30, 66
   30:14, 65
Exodus
   32:15, 30
Leviticus
   27, 187
Numbers
   14:21, 117
   24:21, 270
Deuteronomy
   23:3, 190
   25, 188
   29:11, 42
   30:4, 268
Joshua
   10, 8, 183
   10:12, 197n7, 197n9
   10:12–13, 198n13
   10:12–14, 198n12, 198n15
   10:13, 197n6, 198n14, 198n17
Judges
   4–5, 259n40
   11, 8, 186
   11:30–40, 198n21
   11:39, 198n21
   11:40, 198n19
   12:5–6, 278n43
   15:4–5, 64, 71n43
Ruth
   1, 188
   3:11, 189
   4:17, 189
1 Samuel
   3–13, 256
   15:22, 252
   16:12, 174
   26, 99

2 Samuel
   1, 99
1 Kings
   1:33, 249
2 Kings
   22:14–20, 259n40
1 Chronicles
   11:39, 190, 198n26
   17:16–17, 228
   29, 205
Nehemiah
   3:5, 68n15
Esther
   4:14, 192
   4:16, 262
   7:8, 191
   9:10, 192
Psalms
   27, 70n30
   45, 170, 172
   45:10, 156
   49:12, 249
   68:5, 248
   72:8, 249
   77:12, 121
   102:14–15, 262
   118:17, 249, 262
   118:24, 272
   119, 19
   119:20, 278n44
   119:71, 248
   144, 252
Proverbs
   3:16, 255
   8:8, 63
   8:11, 259n53
   8:12, 259n53
   8:13, 259n53
   8:13–14, 259n53
   8:17, 259n53
   8:19–21, 259n53

Proverbs (*continued*)
  8:32, 259n53
  8:34, 259n53
  9:1–6, 259n53
  9:10, 259n53
  16:33, 248
  23:26, 245
  27:17, 247
Song of Solomon (or Song of Songs)
  1:15, 254
  1:9, 167
  2:1, 168, 179n16
  2:15, 59, 64, 71n43
  2:16, 66
  4:13–16, 66
  4:16, 66
  5:10, 8, 168–74, 176, 178n16, 179n20
  5:10–16, 175
  5:13, 180n40
  5:16, 168
  6:10, 113, 167
  7:7–8, 66
  7:13, 66, 72n55, 72n57
  8:2, 66
Isaiah
  1:18, 171, 174, 181n46
  10:5, 256
  30:18, 250
  30:21, 246
  32:3–4, 115
  35:1, 114
  43:2, 273
  53, 118
  53:2, 178n16
  53:3, 174
  54:5, 245
  56:7, 62
  58:1, 124
  60:3, 114
  60:9, 114
  62:4–5, 72n58
  63:1–2, 174
  65:18, 249
  65:25, 262
Jeremiah
  16:16, 249
  23:6, 118
Ezekiel
  31:3–5, 212
  31:7, 212
  31:9, 212
Daniel
  2:45, 214
  12:4, 211, 213
  12:9, 213

Hosea
  3:4–5, 112
  5:15, 117
Joel
  2:28, 8, 113, 200, 204, 207–8, 210
Jonah
  2:9, 253
Habakkuk
  2:15, 124
Zephaniah
  2:3, 262
Malachi
  4:5, 248

NEW TESTAMENT
Matthew
  4, 135
  4:4, 29
  4:23, 145n10
  4:25, 145n11
  5, 152, 254
  5:6, 156
  5:8, 156
  5:9, 153
  5:19, 95
  6:33, 249
  8, 233
  8:11, 152
  9:15, 257n9
  9:28, 256
  9:37, 153
  11:5, 142, 145n, 147n34
  12, 145n12
  12:13, 135
  12:41, 145n16
  12:50, 146n22, 147n32
  13:58, 147n32
  15:13, 250
  16:15, 146n17
  16:17, 147n35
  19:14, 248
  22, 101
  22:21, 99
  24:24, 29
  25:1–12, 257n9
  28:19–20, 111
Mark
  1:44, 147n32
  5, 147n32
  5:16–17, 146n17
  6:6, 147n32, 147n33
  8:31–33, 152
  8:33, 253, 259n44
  9:23, 256
  9:39, 95

SCRIPTURE INDEX 291

10:14, 248
10:15, 157
11:31, 95
12, 99, 101
12:38–40, 95

Luke
1:70, 83
2:19, 255
3:23, 147n32
4:38–39, 146n17
4:41, 147n32
5:34, 257n9
6:20–26, 152
8:28, 146n17
8:50, 256
9:3, 145n13
10:2, 95, 153
10:26–27, 124
11:2, 247
11:33, 147n32
13:11, 143
15, 235
15:24, 256
16:19–31, 247
18:16, 248
18:30, 256

John
1:29, 253
1:41–42, 147n36
3:1–2, 251
3:2, 135, 145n11
3:3, 141
3:10–11, 147n35
3:29, 257
5:40, 245
8:47, 156
10:37, 146n17
11, 248
11:57, 95
12:38, 121
14, 132
15:18, 251
16:12–15, 137
16:13, 144n2
16:23, 62
17:3, 62
19:30, 248
19:40, 251
20:11–18, 253

Acts of the Apostles
2, 115, 208
2:16–18, 205
2:17, 204, 207, 252
5, 105n10
5:29, 99, 101

6, 153
8, 253
8:21, 246
8:26–39, 254, 259n48
8:39, 259
9, 253
9:6, 255
15:2, 95
21:8–14, 259n40
22, 253
26, 253
26:18, 114

Romans
3:20, 245
6:23, 124
8, 234–35
8:2, 253, 259n44
9:1, 252
11, 112
11:10, 143, 147n36
11:25, 113
12, 156
12:7–9, 153
13, 93, 101–4, 105n10, 13,
13:1–7, 105n11
15:25–28, 153
16:1–2;12, 153

1 Corinthians
3:22, 234
11:5, 259
12, 218n26
13:8, 146n24, 207
15, 234
15:3, 153
16:1–2, 146n18
16:3, 153
16:15, 153

2 Corinthians
2:2, 122
3:6, 85
3:8, 85
4:6, 63
8:18–22, 153
12:9, 254

Galatians
2:20, 236
3:28, 162n3
4, 166
4:22, 178n13

Ephesians
2:20, 157
3:19, 157
4:15, 164n44
4:23, 156
5:23–28, 257

Ephesians (*continued*)
  5:30, 157
  6:15, 189
Philippians
  2:25, 152–53
  2:29, 153
  2:30, 153
  3:9, 234
  4:2, 153
  4:7, 259
Colossians
  1:12, 259n47
2 Thessalonians
  1:7, 278n45
1 Timothy
  2:5, 62
  3, 153
  3:8–10, 153
  5:9–10, 153
2 Timothy
  2:8, 63
  4:8, 234
Hebrews
  1:1–2, 83
  1:14, 83
  2:6, 62
  6:10, 153
  9:27, 140, 146n27
  10, 234
  12:2–3, 146n17
James
  3:1–2, 153
1 Peter
  2:9, 142, 147n36
  2:22, 169
  4:8, 247
  4:11, 153
2 Peter
  1:4, 142

  1:20–21, 83
  1:21, 80
  2, 99, 101, 105n10, 105n13, 107n44
  2:13, 105n12
  3:9, 252
  3:18, 206
1 John
  1:7, 121
  4:10, 121
  4:12, 147n28
  5:7, 84
Revelation
  1:5, 169
  1:8, 158–59
  1:11, 159
  2, 30
  2:16, 218n29
  3, 30
  3:4, 174
  3:10, 29
  3:14–20, 278n30
  4, 174
  6:2, 114, 174
  7:9, 174
  11, 204
  11:15, 114
  14:6, 210, 213
  17, 112
  18, 112
  18:23, 257n9
  19, 112
  19:13, 174
  20, 204
  21:5, 247
  22:2–5, 152
  22:6, 160
  22:13, 160
  22:19, 160

GENERAL INDEX

Africa/African, 5–6, 27, 62–63, 65, 67, 109–10, 115, 119, 124, 253–54, 267, 277n18
African American, 249, 251–54, 259n48
African Methodist Episcopal Church, 246
a-millennialist/a-millennialism. *See* eschatology
Anglican, 3–4, 61, 92–93, 95, 98, 100, 103–4, 109, 135–36, 171–72
  See also Church of England
apocalypse, 3, 5, 8, 10, 114, 195, 204–5, 207–9, 212
Arminian, 3, 36, 188
Arndt, Johann, 2, 19, 30, 201
Arnold, Gottfried, 30, 155–57
Augustine of Hippo (Augustine), 18, 30, 134, 243, 238

Baptist(s), 4, 8, 36–37, 41, 80, 87, 92, 99, 116, 120, 124, 131, 142, 166–81, 236, 259n48
Baxter, Richard, 6, 91–98
Bengel, Johann Albrecht, 5, 24–28, 31–32, 46–47, 281
Berleburg Bible, 18, 25, 30, 64, 203, 208, 211
Bible
  devotional reading of, 32, 40, 62, 74, 168, 196, 202, 224–26, 229–30, 233, 237–39, 261–74, 282
  figural reading of, 9, 19, 143, 159, 170, 193, 207, 216, 223–38
  preaching of, 1, 7, 9, 24, 28, 45, 58, 62–64, 78, 95, 111, 116, 122–24, 142, 167, 182, 229, 231, 243, 252–54
  printing of, 19, 21, 23, 26, 47, 77–78, 111, 117–18, 256
  translation of, 5, 7, 17–19, 21–32, 44, 46, 58–59, 61–62, 64–67, 73, 77–83, 110–11, 117–18, 120, 155, 161, 166, 171, 281
"Biblia Americana," 4, 66, 93, 97–100, 135, 139, 142, 183–84, 186, 189–92, 202–3, 206, 213–14, 217
  See also Mather, Cotton
Biblia Pentapla, 25–26, 30, 32, 65
biblical criticism, 56, 84–86, 282
  See also historical-critical method
biblicism, 2, 4, 6, 12n12, 73–76, 86, 152, 168, 179n17, 181n58, 196, 201, 256, 260n59, 282

Böhme, Anton Wilhelm, 5, 110, 113, 117–18, 201–2, 206, 226–27
  and *Plain Directions for the Reading the Holy Bible*, 202, 226
Böhme, Jacob, 30, 157, 159, 201
Brainerd, David, 5, 111, 114, 121–22

Caribbean, 2, 70n31, 110, 122–23, 254
Calvin, John, 55, 57, 92, 132, 143, 167, 243, 248
  See also Calvinism/Calvinist/Calvinistic
Calvinism/Calvinist/Calvinistic, 3, 6, 37, 63, 75, 86, 92, 120, 166, 173, 188
  See also Calvin, John
Canstein, Carl Hildebrand Freiherr von, 22–23
  See also Canstein Bible Society in Halle
Canstein Bible Society in Halle, 20, 22–23, 28, 117
  See also Halle, Canstein, Carl Hildebrand Freiherr von
Carey, William, 120
Catholicism, 86, 109, 111–12, 125, 193
  See also Roman Catholic
cessationism, 205, 207
Christocentric, 4, 7, 118, 120–21, 185
Church of England, 3, 36–39, 41, 43, 45–47, 48, 91–93, 109, 238
  See also Anglican
Cocceian exegesis, 57–58, 63–64, 67
  See also Cocceius, Johannes
Cocceius, Johannes, 5, 56–58, 64–66, 186
  See also Cocceian exegesis
collegia pietatis, 17–18, 32, 151
Congregationalism/Congregationalist(s), 3–4, 36, 38, 46, 131, 171
Cotton, John, 170
Council of Trent, 18

Danish/Denmark, 25, 110, 123, 254, 277n18
Die Marburger Bibel. See Marburg Bible
dispensationalism, 159–60, 208, 210
Dissent/Dissenter(s), 3, 36–38, 43, 47, 49, 61, 93, 96, 99–100, 107n52, 171–72, 205, 208, 211, 214
  See also Nonconformity/Nonconformist(s)

Doddridge, Philip, 5–6, 43–49, 281
Drusius, Johannes, 56–57, 65–67
Dutch, 5–6, 26, 55–72, 109–10, 117, 122, 168, 172, 186
　Great Awakening of, 61 (see also Great Awakening)
　See also Netherlands
Dutch Bible. See *Statenbijbel/Statenvertaling*
Dutton, Anne, 5, 8, 168, 172, 174–76

early evangelicalism, 1, 4, 32, 74, 86, 92, 138, 182, 195, 201
　and relationship with Pietism, 2–4, 200–201, 275, 281
　See also evangelicalism
Ebersdorf Bible, 28
Edwards, Jonathan, 4, 5, 8, 41, 45, 64–66, 75, 131, 176, 182, 195, 200–203, 205, 207, 215–16, 238–39, 247
　and John Owen, 87
　and missions 111, 114–15, 120–22, 202
　eschatology of, 207–8, 216
　exegesis of, 66, 115, 117, 182–86, 188, 190–91, 193, 194–97, 203
　on miracles, 133–34, 136–43
　sources used by, 45, 65, 75, 87, 187
　writings of: "Blank Bible," 45, 64, 183–85; "Controversies," 140; "Notes on Scripture," 66, 183, 185, 187; "Notes on the Apocalypse," 143, 183, 207, 216; "Miscellanies," 136–37, 140
Elaw, Zilpha, 247, 253–54
Enlightenment, 18, 31–32, 56, 76, 131, 183
enslavement/enslaved, 9–10, 62, 115, 120, 122–24, 252–54
eschatology, 28–29, 113, 205, 217
　millennialist view of, 7, 150, 204–5, 207–8, 213
　a-millennialist view of, 195, 204
　postmillennialist view of, 28, 205, 207, 216
　premillennialist view of, 197, 205, 208
evangelicalism, 1, 3–5, 8–10, 47, 67, 75, 174, 262
　and Puritanism, 9, 67, 76
　and Enlightenment, 3–4, 6, 32, 76, 112, 133, 138
　defining features of, 2–4, 76
　See also early evangelicalism

Francke, August Hermann, 5, 20, 22, 32, 62, 110, 114, 117–18, 161, 200, 202
　and the *Luther Bible*, 21 (see also Luther, Martin)
　on Bible reading, 21–22, 202–3
　on eschatology, 207–8
　on revelation, 210–11

Frankfurt, Germany, 66, 148–52, 208
Frelinghuysen, Theodorus Jacobus, 5, 58, 63
Fresenius, Johann Philipp, 118, 122
Fuller, Andrew, 5, 8, 87, 166

gender, 9, 149, 155–56, 161–62, 242, 249, 251, 256–57
Geneva Bible, 74, 77–79
German Lutheranism, 17, 27
German New Testament, 23, 26
German Pietism, 5, 17–24, 32, 62–67, 200, 203, 211, 226
　and engagement with British evangelicalism, 200–201
　See also Halle, Pietism, Pietist movement
Gill, John, 8, 75, 168, 172–76
Glüsing, Johann Otto, 25–26, 32
Gockinga, Hyleke, 61
Great Awakening, 2, 132, 205, 207, 215, 243
Gregory of Nyssa, 169
Gründler, Johann Ernst, 113, 118–19, 121

Halle, 5, 17, 20–23, 45, 66, 110, 154, 226
　Pietism of, 41, 114, 117–19, 201–3, 206–7, 211, 214, 216, 281–82 (see also German Pietism)
　See also Canstein Bible Society in Halle
Harris, Howell, 174–75
Haug, Johann Friedrich, 18, 25, 30
Heaton, Hannah, 5, 245–46
Hellenbroek, Abraham, 63–64, 66
Herrnhut, Germany, 2, 121, 261, 263–64, 266
historical-critical method, 183, 187, 201–2, 223–25
　See also biblical criticism
history of redemption, 5, 7–8, 57–58, 64, 111–16, 124, 146n16, 186, 196, 203–4
Holy Spirit, 19, 22–23, 111–14, 142, 203, 238, 243–44, 246, 253, 255–57
　and missions 113–14, 121
　gifts of, 140, 152, 204, 206–7, 214–15
　illumination of the, 7, 17, 19–23, 29, 32, 120, 152, 201, 206, 209, 211–12, 215–16, 227, 236, 238
　role in Bible reading, 6, 10, 19, 74, 76, 79, 80, 85, 87, 117–18, 148, 150, 155, 200, 202–4, 206, 209, 215, 225–27, 242, 244
　See also pneumatology/pneumatological
Horche (or Horch), Heinrich, 5, 18, 28
　and Marburg Bible, 28–30

Junckherrot, Johann Jakob, 24
Junius, Robert, 62

Kabbalah, 3, 151, 195, 203
Kayser, Johann (Timotheus Philadelphus), 24
King James Bible, 44
  translation of, 77, 79–81

Lee, Jarena, 246, 248, 252–53, 255–56
Leusden, Johannes, 56
lex orandi, lex crendidi, 231, 238
Locke, John, 6, 102–4, 132–33, 135
Losungen. *See* watchwords
Luther Bible. See Luther, Martin
Luther, Martin, 18–19, 28, 132, 143, 148, 243
  and the *Luther Bible*, 21–25, 27–28, 152, 157, 161
  on Luther's translation, 19, 21, 24–27, 155

Marburg Bible (*Die Marburger Bibel*), 18, 28–30, 64, 203, 211
Mather, Cotton, 4, 5, 6, 58, 87, 98, 110, 131, 182, 195–97, 200 (*see also* "Biblia Americana")
  and the Pietists, 202–3, 214
  biography of, 97–98
  exegesis of 66, 99, 102–3, 134, 183–86, 186–88, 188–91, 191–94, 205–6, 211–13
  on eschatology, 205
  on miracles, 133–38, 140–43
  on politics and biblical commentary, 100, 102–4
  on the Holy Spirit, 113, 131, 201
Mather, Increase, 87, 97, 212
Methodism. *See* Methodist
Methodist, 3–4, 31, 36, 43, 45, 49, 173
  See also Wesley, John
Middle Colonies, 63–65, 111
millennialist/millennialism. *See* eschatology
Moravians, 21, 63, 110, 122, 242, 245–56, 261–79
  and casting of lots, 264–65, 273, 275
  See also *Unitas Fratrum*

Nadere Reformatie (Dutch Further Reformation); 2, 6, 55, 58, 62–65, 67, 109
  See also Protestant Reformation, Dutch
Native American, 3, 5, 109–11, 114–15, 119, 121–24, 127n39
New England, 3, 6, 41, 64–65, 67, 92, 97–99, 109–10, 114, 131, 133, 182, 190, 203–4, 244, 282
Newell, Fanny, 245–46, 249, 251–52, 255–56
new birth, 3–4, 10, 86, 111, 121, 123, 134, 141–42, 160, 196, 202, 213, 232
Newton, Isaac. *See* Newtonian/ Newtonianism
Newton, John, 5, 37, 41, 226, 228, 229–30, 232
Newtonian/Newtonianism, 135, 224

Nonconformity/Nonconformist(s), 6, 41, 47, 91–108, 167
  See also Dissent/Dissenter(s)

Occom, Samson, 5, 111, 116, 123–24
Osborn, Sarah, 244–45, 249, 251
Origen, 26, 167, 169, 170, 172, 176
  and Origenist tradition of interpretation, 171–73, 176
Owen, John, 6, 41, 47, 73–90, 171, 175, 184, 194

parousia, 204, 208, 210, 213
Pennsylvania, 9, 110, 116, 151, 244, 247, 249, 261–63, 266–68, 273–74
Perkins, Williams 170
Petersen, Johann William, 200, 203, 208, 210, 213, 216
Petersen, Johanna Eleonora, 5, 7, 150, 157–61, 200, 208, 210, 213
Pietism, 25, 63, 93, 149, 161, 183, 196, 200, 280
  and reliance on the Spirit, 8, 17, 201 (*see also* Holy Spirit)
  and the Bible, 4–5, 31–32, 200, 275–76, 281
  diversity of, 1–3
  movement of, 7, 149, 154, 182, 207–8
  radical form of, 18, 24, 28, 30, 64, 150, 161–62, 203, 208, 211, 215–16
  women of, 149–50, 154
  See also Halle, German Pietism
pneumatology/pneumatological, 3, 201, 205
  See also Holy Spirit
Poole, Matthew, 58, 61, 65–67, 98, 187
postmillennialist/postmillennialism. *See* eschatology
premillennialist/premillennialism. *See* eschatology
Presbyterianism/Presbyterian(s), 3–4, 38, 43, 80, 92, 100, 110, 214, 241n41
Protestant International, 3, 111
Protestant Reformation, 3, 18, 30, 110, 112–16, 148–50, 157, 159, 194, 204, 237
  and post–Reformation period, 2, 55, 154
  (see also *Nadere Reformatie* [Dutch Further Reformation])
Protten, Rebecca, 5, 254–55
Puritans, 2, 6, 8, 67, 76, 78, 81, 97–98, 131, 132, 168, 204, 245
  See also Puritanism
Puritanism, 6, 62, 67, 76, 212
  See also Puritans

Quakers, 25, 81–82, 84, 99, 131, 206
Quedlinburg, 154–57, 209

Rambach, Friedrich Eberhard, 6, 45
redemptive history. *See* history of redemption
Reitz, Johann Henrich, 18, 24, 26, 28
Roman Catholic, 61, 112, 132, 138, 140, 157
  See also Catholicism

Scharschmidt, Anna Catharina, 7, 150, 154–57, 161
  and *Useful Excerpts of Joh. Angeli Silesii's "The Cherubinic Wanderer"*, 154–55
Schütz, Johann Jakob, 7, 149, 150–54, 161
  and *Rules of Christian Life*, 150–53
Scotland/Scottish 3, 65, 110–11, 194, 236–37, 277n18
sensus literalis, 202–3
Sibbes, Richard, 170–71, 176
singstunde, 269–70
slave/slavery. *See* enslaved/enslavement
Society for Promoting Christian Knowledge (SPCK), 37, 39–40, 109–10, 118
Society for the Propagation of the Gospel in Foreign Parts (SPG), 103, 109
Society in Scotland for Propagating Christian Knowledge (SSPCK), 110–11, 114, 116
Spangenberg, Gottlieb August, 28, 115, 121–22, 263, 270–71
Spener, Phillipp Jakob, 5, 18–20, 22, 32, 112, 117, 148–51, 202, 207–8, 210–11
  on rules for study of God's Word, 19–20
  Pia Desideria by, 2, 18, 117, 148, 207
  Spiritual Priesthood by, 148–50

Statenbijbel/Statenvertaling (Dutch Bible), 55–56, 58–60, 64–67
Stennett I, Joseph, 8, 168, 171
Synod of Dort, 58–59, 64

Tranquebar, India, 110, 113, 117–18, 206
Trommius, Abraham, 60
typology, 57–58, 138, 185, 190–97, 203, 225–30

Unitas Fratrum, 2, 115
  See also Moravians

Vertrecht, Jacob, 62
Vitringa Sr., Campegius, 56–58, 66
Voetius, Gisbertus, 57, 109
  exegesis of, 58, 63–64, 67

Wales/Welsh, 3, 89n16, 173–75, 247
watchwords, 9, 23, 28, 157, 250, 262–75
Wesley, Charles, 5, 45, 230, 233–35
Wesley, John, 3, 31, 38, 43, 75
Whitefield, George, 3, 5, 74, 111, 174, 215, 226

Ziegenbalg, Bartholomäus, 5, 110, 113, 118, 120–21, 206
Ziegenhagen, Friedrich Michael, 110
Zinzendorf, Nikolaus Ludwig von, 1, 23, 116, 245–46, 261
  and *Bibelfest*, 1, 24
  translation philosophy of, 24–25

www.ingramcontent.com/pod-product-compliance
Lightning Source LLC
Chambersburg PA
CBHW022038290426
44109CB00014B/895